Praise for

THE

NAZI
HUNTERS

"A history that reads like an adventure story."

—*The Florida Times-Union*

"The last former Nazis are dying out, and so, too, are those whose life's work was to hunt them down. Nagorski tells their stories evenhandedly, uncovering a fascinating cast of characters from all over the world and placing their efforts in a broader perspective."

—*Foreign Affairs*

"A comprehensive treatment of the dogged men and women whose heroic efforts restored a measure of justice to millions of murdered souls."

—*The Weekly Standard*

"Vivid and detailed . . . a tribute to, and a record of, a unique handful of people who devoted their lives to justice."

—*Overseas Press Club*

"[Nagorski] provides fascinating insight into those who continued to pursue war criminals after the spotlight had faded."

—*Library Journal*

"Far more intriguing than any Hollywood production. . . . [Nagorski] has a discerning eye and a gift for the revealing anecdote."

—*City Journal*

"In a world that is, alas, awash in crimes against humanity, we have an urgent need to address these complex and controversial questions."

—*The Jerusalem Post*

"An extremely valuable, highly readable book."

—*Arizona Jewish Post*

"*The Nazi Hunters* comes at a significant point, at the juncture between living memory and the historical record.... [Nagorski's] account is highly objective and balanced.... It's a narrative that will hold you, even if you've followed this story over the decades."

—*The Dallas Morning News*

"A detailed look at the grim work of tracking Nazis over the decades since World War II.... Absorbing."

—*Kirkus Reviews*

"An admirably accessible and intimate narrative.... [Nagorski] reveals the differences in tactics, politics and personalities that have led to feuds among the Nazi hunters themselves.... For all their rivalries and failings, the Nazi hunters are saluted by Nagorski for their accomplishments: not just in helping to prosecute the most egregious of the perpetrators, but also in etching the details of Nazi crimes—beyond doubt or dispute—in the historical record."

—*The Forward*

"An important work—a well-written and revealing book about the darkest acts of World War II."

—Alan Furst, author of *The Spies of Warsaw* and *Kingdom of Shadows*

"The world failed the victims not only during the Holocaust but afterward, as perpetrators were allowed to go on with their lives. A few determined Nazi hunters tried to bring justice. This is their story. It must be read."

—Alan M. Dershowitz, author of *Abraham: The World's First (but Certainly Not Last) Jewish Lawyer*

"Andrew Nagorski spins a gripping, historically urgent narrative. *The Nazi Hunters* is really about the present: are we willing to do the consuming and often thankless work of holding criminals from the Balkans to the Middle East and Africa accountable for unspeakable acts? This could not be a more timely reminder of the world's moral responsibility toward perpetrators of war crimes."

—Kati Marton, author of *The Great Escape* and *Enemies of the People*

"A fascinating collective portrait of a variety of Nazi hunters. Some, Simon Wiesenthal and the Klarsfelds, are well known. But the most fascinating aspect of the book is Nagorski's portrayal of less-well-known figures: the Polish judge Jan Sehn, who first investigated the Nazi death camps; the German prosecutor Fritz Bauer, who instigated both the capture of Eichmann and the Frankfurt Auschwitz trial; and William Denson, who convicted hundreds of the most notorious concentration camp guards."

—Christopher Browning, author of *Ordinary Men* and *The Origins of the Final Solution*

"A war continued after World War II to bring its mass murderers to justice. Andrew Nagorski tells the story of the dogged search for the killers that was made by some, as well as the accommodations made by others to let this sordid chapter of history remain buried. Meticulously researched, superbly written, *The Nazi Hunters* is fascinating—disturbing, to be sure—but fascinating."

—Douglas Waller, author of *Disciples* and *Wild Bill Donovan*

"A definitive and invaluable contribution to the historical record. Integrating the diffuse strands of a great decades-long drama before a vanishing window of history has closed, the author has crafted the fascinating and emotionally galvanizing narrative of the hunt for notorious Nazi fugitives ranging from Adolf Eichmann and Josef Mengele to the SS officers and concentration camp commandants who fled from the ashes of Germany's defeat in World War II. Not only an investigative and intelligence page-turner, *The Nazi Hunters* tells the story of an epic and global quest for justice rather than revenge."

—Gordon M. Goldstein, Adjunct Senior Fellow, Council on Foreign Relations, and author of *Lessons in Disaster: McGeorge Bundy and the Path to War in Vietnam*

ALSO BY **ANDREW NAGORSKI**

Hitlerland

The Greatest Battle

Last Stop Vienna

The Birth of Freedom

Reluctant Farewell

THE

NAZI HUNTERS

ANDREW NAGORSKI

SIMON & SCHUSTER PAPERBACKS

New York   London   Toronto   Sydney   New Delhi

For Alex, Adam, Sonia and Eva,
And, as always, for Krysia

Simon & Schuster Paperbacks
An Imprint of Simon & Schuster, Inc.
1230 Avenue of the Americas
New York, NY 10020

First Simon & Schuster trade paperback edition May 2017

SIMON & SCHUSTER PAPERBACKS and colophon are
registered trademarks of Simon & Schuster, Inc.

Illustration credits are listed on page 373.

For information about special discounts for bulk purchases,
please contact Simon & Schuster Special Sales at
1-866-506-1949 or business@simonandschuster.com.

The Simon & Schuster Speakers Bureau can bring authors
to your live event. For more information or to book an
event, contact the Simon & Schuster Speakers Bureau at
1-866-248-3049 or visit our website at www.simonspeakers.com.

Interior design by Joy O'Meara

Manufactured in the United States of America

10 9 8 7 6 5 4 3 2

The Library of Congress has cataloged the hardcover edition as follows:

Nagorski, Andrew, author.
    The Nazi hunters / Andrew Nagorski. — First Simon & Schuster
hardcover edition.
        pages   cm
    Includes bibliographical references and index.
    1. Nazi hunters—History.   2. World War, 1939–1945—Atrocities.
3. War criminals—Germany—History.   4. Fugitives from justice—
Germany—History.   5. Holocaust, Jewish (1939–1945).   I. Title.
    D803.N34   2016
    940.53'18—dc23
2015027334

ISBN 978-1-4767-7187-8

Contents

Contents

Cast of Characters

THE HUNTERS:

Fritz Bauer (1903–1968): A German judge and prosecutor from a secular Jewish family, Bauer spent most of the Nazi era in exile in Denmark and Sweden. Returning to Germany after the war, he provided the Israelis with the key tip that led to the capture of Adolf Eichmann. In the 1960s, he orchestrated the Frankfurt Auschwitz trial.

William Denson (1913–1998): The U.S. Army chief prosecutor at the Dachau trials after the war, which focused on the personnel who ran the death machinery in Dachau, Mauthausen, Buchenwald, and Flossenbürg. He prosecuted 177 people, winning guilty verdicts for all of them. In the end, ninety-seven of them were hanged. But there was controversy about his handling of some of those cases.

Rafi Eitan (1926–): The Mossad agent who was in charge of the commando unit that kidnapped Adolf Eichmann near his home in Buenos Aires on May 11, 1960.

Benjamin Ferencz (1920–): At age twenty-seven, Ferencz was the chief prosecutor in what the Associated Press called the "biggest murder trial in history": the Nuremberg trial of the commanders of the Einsatzgruppen, the special squads that conducted mass killings of Jews, Gypsies, and other civilian "enemies" on the Eastern Front before the killings were shifted to the gas chambers of the camps. All twenty-two defendants were convicted, and thirteen were sentenced to death. Several of the sentences were later reduced, and only four were hanged.

Tuvia Friedman (1922–2011): A Polish Jewish survivor of the Holocaust, Friedman first served in the security forces of the postwar Polish communist regime, seeking revenge against captured Germans and anyone else accused of helping the former occupiers. He then set up the Documentation Center in Vienna, collecting evidence to help convict SS officers and others guilty of war crimes. In 1952, he closed his center down and moved to Israel, where he continued to insist he was on the trail of Eichmann and other war criminals.

Isser Harel (1912–2003): The Mossad chief who succeeded in arranging the kidnapping of Eichmann in Buenos Aires in 1960 and his transport to Israel on a special El Al flight, which led to Eichmann's trial and execution in Jerusalem.

Elizabeth Holtzman (1941–): When she became a member of Congress in 1973, the Brooklyn Democrat quickly began looking into charges that many alleged war criminals were living peacefully in the United States. As a member of the House immigration subcommittee and later its chair, she successfully pushed for the creation of the Justice Department's Office of Special Investigations (OSI) in 1979. OSI led the effort to find, denaturalize, and deport Nazi war criminals.

Beate Klarsfeld (1939–): A risk taker par excellence, she was the more flamboyant half of the Nazi hunting German-French couple. Her father served in the Wehrmacht and she knew very little about the Third Reich's legacy until she moved to Paris to work as an au pair and met her future husband, Serge Klarsfeld. In 1968, she famously slapped West German Chancellor Kurt Georg Kiesinger, who had been a member of the Nazi Party. Along with Serge, she also tracked and confronted SS men guilty of deporting Jews and other crimes in occupied France.

Serge Klarsfeld (1935–): Born into a family of Jews in Romania who then moved to France, he had a strong personal motive to document, publicize, and pursue top Nazis who had been responsible for the deportations and deaths of Jews in France: his father died in Auschwitz. Meticulously gathering incriminating evidence, he publicized the Nazis' records—and, like his wife, Beate, was not afraid to confront the wartime Nazis directly, ignoring the risks.

Eli Rosenbaum (1955–): He first joined the Justice Department's Office of Special Investigations as an intern, and from 1995 to 2010 was its longest-serving director. While serving as general counsel of the World Jewish Congress in 1986, he led the campaign against former U.N. Secretary-General Kurt Waldheim during his campaign for the Austrian presidency. That led to his bitter clash with the man he had once idolized: Simon Wiesenthal.

Allan Ryan (1945–): From 1980 to 1983, he served as the director of the Justice Department's Office of Special Investigations, leading the new unit in its early battles to identify and strip Nazi war criminals of their U.S. citizenship.

Jan Sehn (1909–1965): A Polish investigating judge who grew up in a family of German descent, he produced the first detailed account of the history and operation of Auschwitz. He handled the interrogation of Rudolf Höss, the camp's longest serving commandant, and convinced him to write his memoirs before he was hanged in 1947. He also helped his German counterpart Fritz Bauer by providing testimony for the Frankfurt Auschwitz trial in the 1960s.

Simon Wiesenthal (1908–2005): Born in a small town in Galicia, he survived Mauthausen and other ordeals and became the most famous Nazi hunter, operating out of his Documentation Center in Vienna. While widely credited with tracking down several prominent war criminals, Wiesenthal was sometimes attacked for allegedly embellishing his role and accomplishments, particularly in the hunt for Eichmann. He also clashed with the World Jewish Congress during the Kurt Waldheim controversy.

Efraim Zuroff (1948–): The founder and director of the Simon Wiesenthal Center's office in Jerusalem, Zuroff was born in Brooklyn but settled in Israel in 1970. Frequently referred to as the last Nazi hunter, he has mounted highly publicized, controversial campaigns to locate and prosecute surviving concentration camp guards.

THE HUNTED:

Klaus Barbie (1913–1991): Known as "the Butcher of Lyon," the former Gestapo chief in that French city was responsible for thousands of deaths and personally tortured countless victims. His most prominent victims: Jean Moulin, the hero of the French Resistance, and the forty-four Jewish children who were given shelter in the tiny village of Izieu—and perished in Auschwitz. The Klarsfelds tracked him to Bolivia, waging a long campaign to get him to stand trial in France. Given a life sentence in 1987, he died in prison four years later.

Martin Bormann (1900–1945): Hitler's personal secretary and head of the Nazi Party Chancellery, he had disappeared from Hitler's bunker in Berlin after his boss committed suicide on April 30, 1945. While there were reports that he had been killed or committed suicide almost immediately, there were also persistent rumors that he had escaped from the German capital—and even tales of sightings and shootouts in South America and Denmark. In 1972 his purported remains were found at a Berlin construction site, and DNA evidence in 1998 confirmed his identity. The conclusion was that he died on May 2, 1945.

Hermine Braunsteiner (1919–1999): A former guard in the Majdanek and Ravensbrück concentration camps, she was called "Kobyła"—the Polish word for mare—because of her habit of viciously kicking women prisoners. In 1964, Simon Wiesenthal discovered that she had married an American after the war and was living in Queens, New York. He tipped off *The New York Times*, which ran a story that triggered a lengthy legal battle to strip her of her citizenship. Sent to West Germany, she was given a life sentence in 1981, and released for health reasons in 1996. She died in a nursing home three years later.

Herbert Cukurs (1900–1965): A famed Latvian aviator before World War II, he became known during the German occupation as "the Hangman of Riga," and was responsible for the killing of about thirty thousand Jews. After the war, he settled in São Paulo, Brazil, where he still flew his own plane and operated a marina. Lured to Montevideo, Uruguay, on February 23, 1965, he was killed by a Mossad hit squad. This was the only known assassination by the Israeli agency of a fugitive war criminal.

John Demjanjuk (1920–2012): From the 1970s until his death in 2012, he was at the center of one of the most complex legal battles of the postwar era, which played out in the United States, Israel, and Germany. The retired autoworker from Cleveland had served as a death camp guard—but initially he was mistaken for "Ivan the Terrible," a particularly notorious guard in Treblinka. In 2011, a German court found him guilty for serving as a guard in Sobibor, and he died less than a year later. His case set a new precedent for how the German courts could handle the prosecution of the dwindling number of alleged war criminals who were still alive.

Adolf Eichmann (1906–1962): One of the chief architects of the Holocaust who organized the mass deportations of Jews to Auschwitz and other concentration camps, he was kidnapped by Mossad agents in Buenos Aires on May 11, 1960. Tried and condemned to death in Jerusalem, he was hanged on May 31, 1962. Everything about his case generated headlines and controversy, including an impassioned debate about "the banality of evil."

Aribert Heim (1914–1992): Nicknamed "Dr. Death" because of his gruesome, murderous record while he served as a doctor in Mauthausen, he vanished after the war, prompting highly publicized searches for him up until a few years ago—and fanciful tales that he had been spotted in Latin America or assassinated in California. In fact, as *The New York Times* and the German TV station ZDF reported in 2009, he had found refuge in Cairo, converted to Islam, and taken the name Tarek Hussein Farid. He died there in 1992.

Rudolf Höss (1900–1947): The longest serving commandant of Auschwitz. He was captured by the British in 1946, testified as a witness in Nuremberg, and then was sent to Poland to stand trial. Jan Sehn, the Polish investigating judge, convinced him to write his autobiography before he was hanged. His descriptions of how he kept making "improvements" in the machinery of death provide some of the most chilling testimony in the vast literature of the Holocaust.

Ilse Koch (1906–1967): The widow of Buchenwald's first commandant, she was dubbed "the Bitch of Buchenwald" during her trial by the U.S. Army in Dachau that featured lurid testimony about her sexual taunting of prisoners before they were beaten and killed. Combined with stories about lamp shades allegedly made of the skin of those prisoners, her case was probably the most sensational postwar trial. She was sentenced to life in prison, but General Lucius D. Clay reduced her term to four years. A German court gave her another life sentence in 1951, and she committed suicide in prison in 1967.

Kurt Lischka (1909–1989), Herbert Hagen (1913–1999), and Ernst Heinrichsohn (1920–1994): Serge and Beate Klarsfeld targeted these three former SS officers because of their role in deporting Jews from France during the war. All three had been living peacefully in West Germany before the Nazi hunters mounted their campaign to confront them—and, in Lischka's case, even attempted to kidnap him—in the 1970s. On February 11, 1980, a court in Cologne found them guilty of complicity in the deportation of fifty thousand Jews from France to their deaths, and they received sentences ranging from six to twelve years in prison.

Josef Mengele (1911–1979): The Auschwitz SS doctor known as "the Angel of Death" was particularly infamous because of his medical experiments on twins and other camp inmates, along with his role in the selection of arriving prisoners for the gas chambers. The search for Mengele, who had fled to South America, lasted long after his death. He drowned while swimming off a beach in Brazil in 1979, but his family members kept this secret until his remains were discovered in 1985.

Erich Priebke (1913–2013): This former SS captain had organized the execution of 335 men and boys, including seventy-five Jews, in the Ardeatine Caves near Rome on March 24, 1944, in retaliation for the killing of thirty-three German soldiers earlier. Until 1994, he lived a comfortable life in the Argentine resort city of San Carlos de Bariloche. But then an ABC News team caught up with him, and correspondent Sam Donaldson grilled him for a few minutes on the street. The result: Argentina extradited him to Italy in 1995, and he was sentenced to life in prison in 1998. He was kept under house arrest due to his age and died there in 2013.

Otto Remer (1912–1997): The key player in the aftermath of the July 20, 1944, botched assassination of Hitler, Major Remer was the commander of the Guards Battalion Grossdeutschland in Berlin. Initially prepared to carry out the orders of the plotters, he changed course when he learned Hitler had survived and started arresting the plotters. In 1951, he was the leader of a West German far-right party when he branded the plotters as traitors. Fritz Bauer successfully prosecuted him for defamation in 1952, aiming to prove that the plotters were the true patriots. He was given a three-month sentence and his party was banned, prompting him to flee to Egypt. He returned to West Germany in the 1980s, benefiting from an amnesty, and resumed his right-wing agitation. Facing new charges of inciting hatred and racism, he moved to Spain in 1994, where he died three years later.

Arthur Rudolph (1906–1996): Part of the team of German rocket scientists who were brought to the United States after World War II, he developed the Saturn V rocket, which sent the first astronauts to the moon. But Eli Rosenbaum of the Justice Department's Office of Special Investigations pressured him to give up his U.S. citizenship and leave the country in 1984 based on evidence that he had worked thousands of prisoners to death while producing V-2 rockets during the war. He died in Hamburg.

Kurt Waldheim (1918–2007): When the former United Nations secretary-general emerged as the leading candidate in the 1986 Austrian presidential election, new evidence indicated he had hidden a significant chapter of his wartime record—his service in the Balkans on the staff of General Alexander Löhr, who was tried and hanged later in Yugoslavia as a war criminal. The World Jewish Congress mounted an intensive campaign against Waldheim, but he still won the election. Simon Wiesenthal blamed the WJC for the anti-Semitic backlash that ensued, putting the rifts between the Nazi hunters on full display.

THE
NAZI
HUNTERS

Introduction

One of the most famous German films right after the end of World War II was called *Die Mörder sind unter uns*—"The Murderers Are Among Us." Susanne Wallner, a concentration camp survivor played by Hildegard Knef, returns to her devastated apartment in the ruins of Berlin. She finds Hans Mertens, a former German army surgeon already living there, succumbing to alcoholism and despair. The surgeon runs into his former captain, now a prosperous businessman, who had ordered the Christmas Eve massacre of one hundred civilians in a Polish village in 1942. Haunted by such memories, Mertens decides to kill the captain on the first postwar Christmas Eve.

At the last moment, Wallner convinces Mertens that such an act of vigilante justice would be a mistake. "We cannot pass sentence," she tells him. The surgeon understands. "That's right, Susanne," he replies as the film ends. "But we must bring charges. Demand atonement on behalf of millions of innocent murder victims."

The film was a spectacular success, attracting huge audiences. But its message was fundamentally misleading. It was left to the Allies, not to the German people, to arrange the early war crimes trials. The victors soon largely abandoned such efforts, focusing instead on the emerging Cold War. As for most Germans, they were far more eager to forget their recent past than to contemplate atonement.

Among the chief perpetrators who were not immediately arrested or who were caught and not initially recognized by their Allied captors, there was certainly no talk of atonement either. There was only the impulse to flee. In Adolf Hitler's case, it was by committing suicide in his bunker along with Eva Braun, whom he had just married. After poisoning their six children, Joseph Goebbels, his propaganda chief, and his wife, Magda, followed suit. In the 1976 bestselling novel *The Valhalla Exchange*, the fictional Goebbels explains why he chose that course. "I have no intention of spending the rest of my life running around the world like some eternal refugee," he declares.

But most of his colleagues and other Nazis guilty of war crimes had no intention of following Hitler's example. Many of the lower ranking perpetrators did not even feel compelled to hide: they quickly blended in with the millions who were seeking to rebuild their lives in a new Europe. Others, who felt more at risk, found ways to flee the continent. For a long time, it looked like many of the people in both categories had succeeded in eluding responsibility for their crimes, often with the support of loyal family members and networks of *Kameraden*—Nazi Party comrades.

This book focuses on the relatively small band of men and women— both those serving in official positions and those operating independently— who worked to reverse their initial successes, not letting the world forget their crimes. These pursuers demonstrated tremendous determination and courage as they kept up their fight even when the governments representing the victors and the rest of the world grew increasingly indifferent to the fates of the Nazi war criminals. In the process, they also explored the nature of evil and raised profoundly troubling questions about human behavior.

Those who have attempted to bring the murderers to justice have been loosely labeled as Nazi hunters—but they have not been anything like a group with a common strategy or basic agreement on tactics. They often have been at odds with each other, prone to recriminations, jealousies, and outright rivalries, even as they pursued roughly the same goals. In some cases, this undoubtedly weakened their effectiveness.

But even if everyone involved in the pursuit of Nazi criminals had put aside their personal differences, the results would not have been significantly different. And by any absolute measure, those results can't justify the claim that justice was done. "Anyone who seeks a balance between the crimes that were committed and the punishment will be ultimately frustrated," said David Marwell, a historian who has worked for the Justice Department's Office of Special Investigations, the United States Holocaust Memorial Museum, and the Berlin Document Center, and served as the director of the Museum of Jewish Heritage in New York. As for the original pledge of the victors to prosecute all of those responsible for war crimes, he curtly added: "It's too difficult."

Too difficult to succeed on a grand scale, yes, but the efforts by those who refused to give up on the notion of holding at least some Nazi war criminals to account developed into an ongoing postwar saga unlike any other in the history of mankind.

At the end of past wars, the victors often killed or enslaved the vanquished, plundering their lands and exacting speedy retribution. Summary executions, not trials or any other legal proceedings aimed at weighing the evidence to determine guilt or innocence, were the norm. Revenge was the motive, pure and simple.

Many of the Nazi hunters were also initially motivated by revenge, particularly those coming out of the camps or those victors who helped liberate them and saw the stunning evidence of the horrors that the fleeing Nazis left behind: the dead and the dying, the crematoriums, the "medical" facilities that served as torture chambers. As a result, some Nazis and their collaborators were at the receiving end of immediate retribution at the end of the war.

But from the first Nuremberg trials to the hunt for war criminals in Europe, Latin America, the United States, and the Middle East that has sporadically continued to this day, the Nazi hunters have focused most of their efforts on initiating legal proceedings against their prey— demonstrating that even the most obviously guilty should have their day in court. It was no accident that Simon Wiesenthal, the most famous Nazi hunter, titled his memoirs *Justice Not Vengeance.*

Even when justice was so obviously falling short, with the guilty often getting away with the mildest punishments or in many cases not facing any sanctions at all, the other goal that began to emerge was education by example. Why pursue an aging camp guard during his final days? Why not let the perpetrators quietly fade away? Many U.S. officials were more than happy to do so, especially as their attention was diverted to a new enemy—the Soviet Union. But the individual Nazi hunters were not about to let go, arguing that each case offered valuable lessons.

The point of the lessons: to demonstrate that the horrendous crimes of World War II and the Holocaust cannot and should not be forgotten, and that those who instigated or carried out those crimes—or others who may carry out similar crimes in the future—are never beyond the law, at least in principle.

In 1960 when a Mossad team kidnapped Adolf Eichmann in Argentina and flew him to Israel for trial, I was thirteen years old. I have no recollection of how much I was aware of what had happened, whether I was paying attention to the media coverage at all, but something had clearly sunk in. I know that because of a vivid memory from the following summer when Eichmann was already on trial in Jerusalem.

During a family visit to San Francisco, I was sitting in a luncheonette with my father. At one point, I started examining the face of an old man sitting at the other end of the counter. I leaned over to my father, pointed him out and whispered: "I think that may be Hitler." My father grinned and let me down gently. Of course I had no idea then that, while working on this book half a century later, I would interview Gabriel Bach, the last surviving prosecutor in the Eichmann trial, and the two Mossad agents who led the team that seized him.

Eichmann's kidnapping, trial, and hanging marked the beginning of a growing awareness that many Nazi criminals had gone unpunished, and signaled a gradual revival in interest in their crimes. It also soon spawned an outpouring of books and movies about Nazi hunters, often based more on myths than realities. I avidly read those books and watched those movies, fascinated by the characters—both the heroes and the villains—as much as by the nonstop action.

There was much more than the great chase that captured the popular imagination. Especially for the postwar generation, the larger questions about the nature of the people who were objects of that chase, and even about their family and neighbors, were just as riveting. To this day, there are no easy answers to the question why so many millions of Germans and Austrians, along with collaborators in most of the lands they conquered, could have willingly enlisted in a movement dedicated to mass murder.

During my stints as *Newsweek*'s bureau chief in Bonn, Berlin, Warsaw, and Moscow during the 1980s and 1990s, I often found myself examining the legacy of the war and the Holocaust. Whenever I lapsed into thinking I would encounter no more surprises, only variations of similar stories, I was brought up short by some startling new revelation.

In late 1994, I was preparing my report for a cover story *Newsweek* had scheduled to mark the fiftieth anniversary of the liberation of Auschwitz on January 27, 1995. I had interviewed numerous survivors from many countries in Europe. Each time I was uneasy asking them to relive the horrors of those years, and I always told them to feel free to stop at any point if they felt the process was too painful. In most cases, though, the stories poured out of them; once they started, they just kept going and no further prompting was necessary. No matter how many such stories I heard, I was always mesmerized—and at times truly stunned.

After interviewing a Dutch Jewish survivor whose story was particularly moving, I automatically apologized for making him go through it in such detail, saying that of course he must have told his family and friends about his odyssey many times. "I never told anyone," he replied. Seeing my expression of disbelief, he added: "No one ever asked." He had carried his burden all alone for fifty years.

Three years later another encounter offered a glimpse of those who carry a very different kind of burden. I interviewed Niklas Frank, the son of Hans Frank, who had served as Hitler's governor general of Poland during the occupation, presiding over an empire of death. A journalist and author who described himself as a typical European liberal, Niklas cared deeply about democratic values. He took a special interest in Poland, particularly during the 1980s when the independent trade union Solidarity was leading the human rights struggle that ultimately toppled that country's communist regime.

Born in 1939, Niklas was only seven when he saw his father for the last time in Nuremberg, shortly before he was hanged as a war criminal. Along with his mother, he was led into the prison. His father pretended that nothing was amiss. "Well, Nikki, soon we'll all be together again for Christmas," he said. The young boy left "seething mad," he recalled, because he knew his father was about to be hanged. "My father lied to everyone, even his own son," he said. Later in life he thought about what he wished his father had said instead: "Dear Nikki, I'll be executed because I did terrible things. Don't lead the kind of life I led."

Then came another line I will always remember. Describing his father as "a monster," he declared: "I'm against the death penalty, but I believe my father's execution was totally justified."

In all my years as a foreign correspondent, I had never heard anyone speak that way about a father. That sentiment led Niklas to one more conclusion. He pointed out that Frank is a common name and most people he meets don't know that he is the son of a major war criminal unless he tells them. Nonetheless, he knows the truth and cannot put it out of his mind. "There isn't a day when I don't think about my father and especially everything that the Germans did," he said. "The world will never forget this. Whenever I go abroad and say that I'm German, people think 'Auschwitz.' And I think that's absolutely just."

I told Niklas that I felt lucky that I did not have to live with his sense of inherited guilt, since, as it happened, my father fought on the losing side when Germany invaded Poland in 1939. I knew that rationally the happenstance of birth is no reason to feel morally superior or inferior. Niklas knew that, too. But I fully understood why his one wish in life was to have a father he didn't have to be ashamed of.

Niklas's attitude was hardly typical for family members of Nazi war criminals. But to my mind his raw, brutal honesty exemplified what is best in Germans today—the willingness of many of them to confront, on a daily basis, their country's past. It took a long time for that to happen, though, and much of that would never have happened at all if it were not for the Nazi hunters and their arduous, often lonely struggles, not just in Germany and Austria, but all over the world.

That struggle is now coming to an end. Most of the Nazi hunters, along with the hunted, will soon only exist in our collective memories, where myth and reality are likely to become even more intertwined than they are today. Which is why their stories can and should be told now.

CHAPTER ONE

The Hangman's Handiwork

"My husband was a military man all his life. He was entitled to a soldier's death. He asked for that. I tried to get that for him. Just that. That he should die with some honor."

The widow of a hanged German general speaking to an American judge at Nuremberg, from the 2001 Broadway production of *Judgment at Nuremberg* written by Abby Mann

On October 16, 1946, ten of the twelve top Nazis whom the International Military Tribunal had condemned to death by hanging were sent to the gallows, which had been hastily constructed in the Nuremberg prison gym where American security guards had played a basketball game only three days earlier.

Martin Bormann, Adolf Hitler's right-hand man, who had escaped from his bunker in Berlin during the final days of the war and then seemingly vanished, was the only one of the twelve convicted and sentenced in absentia.

As the highest ranking Nazi in Nuremberg, Hermann Göring—who had served Hitler in a variety of functions, including president of the Reichstag and commander in chief of the air force, and aspired to succeed *der Führer*—was due to be hanged first. The court's verdict spelled out his unambiguous role: "There is nothing to be said in mitigation. For Göring was often, indeed almost always, the moving force, second only to his leader. He was the leading war aggressor, both as political and military leader; he was the director of the slave labor program and the creator of the oppressive program against the Jews and other races at home and abroad. All of these crimes he has frankly admitted."

But Göring eluded the hangman by biting into a cyanide pill shortly before the executions were to begin. Two weeks earlier he had returned to his cell after the verdicts were read, "his face pale and frozen, his eyes popping," according to G. M. Gilbert, the prison psychiatrist who was there to meet the condemned men. "His hands were trembling in spite of his attempt to appear nonchalant," Gilbert reported. "His eyes were moist and he was panting, fighting back an emotional breakdown."

What particularly incensed Göring and some of the others was the planned method of execution. Corporal Harold Burson, a twenty-four-year-old from Memphis who was given the assignment to report on the trial and write the daily scripts for the Armed Forces Network, recalled: "The one thing that Göring wanted to protect above everything else was his military honor. He made the statement more than once that they could take him out and shoot him, give him a soldier's death, and he would have no problem with that. His problem was that he thought that hanging was the worst thing they could do to a soldier."

Fritz Sauckel, who had overseen the slave labor apparatus, shared those sentiments. "Death by hanging—that, at least, I did not deserve," he protested. "The death part—all right—but *that*—That I did not deserve."

Field Marshal Wilhelm Keitel and his deputy General Alfred Jodl pleaded to be spared the noose. Instead, they asked for a firing squad, which would offer them, in Keitel's words, "a death which is granted to a soldier in all armies of the world should he incur the supreme penalty." Admiral Erich Raeder had been sentenced to life imprisonment, but he requested the Allied Control Council "to commute this sentence to death by shooting, by way of mercy." Emily Göring reportedly later claimed that her husband only planned to use the cyanide capsule if "his application to be shot was refused."

That left ten men to face the hangman, U.S. Army Master Sergeant John C. Woods. Herman Obermayer, a young Jewish GI who had worked with Woods at the end of the war, providing him with basic materials such as wood and rope for scaffolds for earlier hangings, recalled that the beefy thirty-five-year-old Kansan "defied all the rules, didn't shine his shoes and didn't get shaved."

There was nothing accidental about the way Woods looked. "His dress was always sloppy," Obermayer added. "His dirty pants were always unpressed, his jacket looked as though he slept in it for weeks, his M/Sgt. stripes were attached to his sleeve by a single stitch of yellow thread at each corner, and his crumpled hat was always worn at an improper angle."

The only American hangman in the European theater, Woods claimed to have dispatched 347 people during his fifteen-year career up to that point; his earlier victims in Europe had included several American servicemen convicted of murder and rape, along with Germans accused of killing downed Allied pilots and other wartime offenses. This "alcoholic, ex-bum" with "crooked yellow teeth, foul breath, and dirty neck," as Obermayer put it, knew he could flaunt his slovenly appearance since his superiors needed his services.

And no more so than at Nuremberg, where suddenly Woods was "one of the most important men in the world," Obermayer noted, and yet betrayed no nervousness as he carried out his assignment.

Three wooden scaffolds, each painted black, were set up in the gym. The idea was to use two of them alternately, keeping the third in reserve if anything went wrong with the mechanism of the first two. Each scaffold had thirteen steps, and ropes were suspended from the crossbeams supported on two posts. A new rope was provided for each hanging. As Kingsbury Smith, the pool reporter at the scene, wrote: "When the trap was sprung, the victim dropped from sight in the interior of the scaffolding. The bottom of it was boarded up with wood on three sides and shielded by a dark canvas curtain on the fourth, so that no one saw the death struggles of the men dangling with broken necks."

At 1:11 a.m., Joachim von Ribbentrop, Hitler's foreign minister, was the first to arrive in the gym. The original plan was for the guards to escort the prisoners from their cells without manacles, but, following Göring's suicide, the rules had changed. Ribbentrop's hands were bound as he entered, and then the manacles were replaced with a leather strap.

After mounting the scaffold, "the former diplomatic wizard of Nazidom," as Smith archly put it, proclaimed to the assembled witnesses: "God protect Germany." Allowed to make an additional short statement, the man who had played a critical role in launching Germany's attacks on country after country concluded: "My last wish is that Germany realize its entity and an understanding be reached between the East and West. I wish peace to the world."

Woods then placed the black hood over his head, adjusted the rope, and pulled the lever that opened the trap, sending Ribbentrop to his death.

Two minutes later, Field Marshal Keitel entered the gym. Smith duly noted that he "was the first military leader to be executed under the new concept of international law—the principle that professional soldiers cannot escape punishment for waging aggressive wars and permitting crimes against humanity with the claim they were dutifully carrying out orders of superiors."

Keitel maintained his military bearing to the last. Looking down from the scaffold before the noose was put around his neck, he spoke loudly and clearly, betraying no signs of nervousness. "I call on God Almighty to have mercy on the German people," he declared. "More than two million German soldiers went to their death for the fatherland before me. I follow now my sons—all for Germany."

While both Ribbentrop and Keitel were still hanging from their ropes, there was a pause in the proceedings. An American general representing the Allied Control Commission allowed the thirty or so people in the gym to smoke—and almost everyone immediately lit up.

An American and a Russian doctor, equipped with stethoscopes, ducked behind the curtains to confirm their deaths. When they emerged, Woods went back up the steps of the first scaffold, pulled out a knife that was strapped to his side, and cut the rope. Ribbentrop's body, his head still covered by the black hood, was then carried on a stretcher to a corner of the gym that was blocked off with a black canvas curtain. This procedure would be followed for each of the bodies.

The break over, an American colonel issued the command: "Cigarettes out, please, gentlemen."

At 1:36, it was the turn of Ernst Kaltenbrunner, the Austrian SS leader who had succeeded the assassinated Reinhard Heydrich as the chief of the Reich Security Main Office (RSHA), the agency that oversaw mass murder, the concentration camps, and all manner of persecution. Among the people who reported to him: Adolf Eichmann, who had been in charge of RSHA's Department of Jewish Affairs, responsible for implementing the Final Solution, and Rudolf Höss, the commandant of Auschwitz.

Unlike Kaltenbrunner, whom American troops had tracked to his hideout in the Austrian Alps at the end of the war, Eichmann's whereabouts were still unknown. Höss, who had been captured by the British in northern Germany, testified at the Nuremberg trial, but he would face a different hangman's noose later.

Yet from the scaffold Kaltenbrunner still insisted, as he had to the American psychiatrist Gilbert earlier, that somehow he knew nothing about the crimes he was accused of. "I have loved my German people and my fatherland with a warm heart. I have done my duty by the laws of my people and I am sorry my people were led this time by men who were not soldiers and that crimes were committed of which I had no knowledge."

As Woods produced the black hood to put over his head, Kaltenbrunner added: "Germany, good luck."

Alfred Rosenberg, one of the earliest members of the Nazi Party, who served as the de facto high priest of its deadly racist "cultural" creed, was the most speedily dispatched. Asked if he had any final words, he did not respond. Although a self-professed atheist, he was accompanied by a Protestant chaplain who prayed at his side as Woods pulled the lever.

After another short break, Hans Frank, Hitler's gauleiter or governor general of occupied Poland, was ushered in. Unlike the others, he had told Gilbert, after his death sentence was announced: "I deserved it and I expected it." During his imprisonment, he had converted to Roman Catholicism. As he entered the gym, he was the only one of the ten who had a smile on his face. He betrayed his nervousness by swallowing frequently, but, as Smith reported, he "gave the appearance of being relieved at the prospect of atoning for his evil deeds."

Frank's last words seemed to confirm that: "I am thankful for the kind treatment during my captivity and I ask God to accept me with mercy."

Next, all that Wilhelm Frick, Hitler's minister of interior, had to say was "Long live eternal Germany."

At 2:12, Smith noted, the "ugly, dwarfish little man" Julius Streicher, the editor and publisher of the venomous Nazi party newspaper *Der Stürmer*, walked to the gallows, his face visibly twitching. Asked to identify himself, he shouted: "Heil Hitler!"

Allowing for a rare reference to his own emotions, Smith confessed: "The shriek sent a shiver down my back."

As Streicher was pushed up the final steps on the top of the gallows to position him for Woods, he glared at the witnesses and screamed: "Purim Fest, 1946." The reference was to the Jewish holiday that commemorates the execution of Haman, who, according to the Old Testament, was planning to kill all Jews in the Persian Empire.

Asked formally for his last words, Streicher shouted: "The Bolsheviks will hang you one day."

While Woods was placing the black hood over his head, Streicher could be heard saying "Adele, my dear wife."

But the drama was far from over. The trapdoor opened with a bang, with Streicher kicking as he went down. As the rope snapped taut, it swung wildly and the witnesses could hear him groaning. Woods came down from the platform and disappeared behind the black curtain that concealed the dying man. Abruptly the groans ceased and the rope stopped moving. Smith and the other witnesses were convinced that Woods had grabbed Streicher and pulled down hard, strangling him.

Had something gone wrong—or was this no accident? Lieutenant Stanley Tilles, who was charged with coordinating the Nuremberg and earlier hangings of war criminals, later claimed that Woods had deliberately placed the coils of Streicher's noose off-center so that his neck would not be broken during his fall; instead, he would strangle. "Everyone in the chamber had watched Streicher's performance and none of it was lost on Woods. I knew Woods hated Germans . . . and I watched his face become florid and his jaws clench," he wrote, adding that Woods's intent was clear. "I saw a small smile cross his lips as he pulled the hangman's handle."

The procession of the unrepentant continued—and so did the apparent mishaps. Sauckel, the man who had overseen the vast Nazi universe of slave labor, screamed defiantly: "I am dying innocent. The sentence is wrong. God protect Germany and make Germany great again. Long live Germany! God protect my family." He, too, groaned loudly after dropping through the trapdoor.

Wearing his Wehrmacht uniform with its coat collar half turned up, Alfred Jodl only offered up the last words: "My greetings to you, my Germany."

The last of the ten was Arthur Seyss-Inquart, who had helped install Nazi rule in his native Austria and later presided over occupied Holland. After limping to the gallows on his clubfoot, he, like Ribbentrop, presented himself as a man of peace. "I hope that this execution is the last act of the tragedy of the Second World War and that the lesson taken from the world war will be that peace and understanding should exist between peoples," he said. "I believe in Germany."

At 2:45, he dropped to his death.

Woods calculated that the total time from the first to the tenth hanging was 103 minutes. "That's quick work," he declared later.

While the bodies of the last two condemned men were still dangling from their ropes, guards brought out an eleventh body on a stretcher. It was covered by a U.S. Army blanket, but two large bare feet protruded from it and one arm in a black silk pajama sleeve was hanging down on the side.

An Army colonel ordered the blanket removed to avoid any doubt about whose body was joining the others. Hermann Göring's face was "still contorted with the pain of his last agonizing moments and his final gesture of defiance," Smith reported. "They covered him up quickly and this Nazi warlord, who like a character out of the Borgias, had wallowed in blood and beauty, passed behind a canvas curtain into the black pages of history."

In an interview with *Stars and Stripes* after the hangings, Woods maintained that the operation had gone off precisely as he had planned it:

"I hanged these ten Nazis in Nuremberg and I am proud of it; I did a good job. Everything went A1. I have . . . never been to an execution which went better. I am only sorry that that fellow Göring escaped me; I'd have been at my best for him. No, I wasn't nervous. I haven't got any nerves. You can't afford nerves in my job. But this Nuremberg job was just what I wanted. I wanted this job so terribly that I stayed here a bit longer, though I could have gone home earlier."

But in the aftermath of the hangings, Woods's claims were fiercely disputed. Smith's pool report left no doubt that something had gone wrong with Streicher's execution, and probably also with Sauckel's. A report in *The Star* of London claimed that the drop had been too short and the condemned men were not properly tied, which meant they hit their heads as they plunged through the trapdoor and "died of slow strangulation." In his memoirs, General Telford Taylor, who helped prepare the International Military Tribunal's case against the top Nazis and then became the chief prosecutor in the subsequent twelve Nuremberg trials, pointed out that the photographs of the bodies laid out in the gym seemed to confirm such suspicions. Some of the faces appeared to be bloodied.

This prompted speculation that Woods had bungled some parts of the job. Albert Pierrepoint, the British Army's highly experienced hangman, did not want to criticize his American counterpart directly, but he did refer to newspaper reports of "indications of clumsiness . . . arising from the unalterable five-foot drop and the, to me, old-fashioned four-coiled cowboy knot." In his account of the Nuremberg trial, German historian Werner Maser asserted that Jodl took eighteen minutes to die, and Keitel "as much as twenty-four minutes."

Those claims did not tally with Smith's pool report, and some of the subsequent accounts of the hangings may have deliberately exaggerated or sensationalized what went wrong. Still, the hangings were hardly the smooth operation that Woods insisted he had carried out. He tried to deflect the criticism prompted by the photographs by saying that sometimes victims bit their tongues during hangings, which would account for the blood on their faces.

The debate about Woods's performance only underscores the issue that several of the condemned men raised in the first place: why was hanging chosen over the firing squad? Woods was genuinely convinced about the virtues of his trade. Obermayer, the young GI who had known Woods when he carried out earlier executions, recalled "a more-or-less drunken moment" when one soldier asked the hangman whether he would like to die at the end of a rope or by some other means. "You know, I think it's a damn good way to die; as a matter of fact, I'll probably die that way myself."

"Aw, for Christ's sake, be serious, that's nothing to kid about," another soldier interjected.

Woods wasn't laughing. "I'm damn serious," he said. "It's clean and it's painless, and it's traditional." He added: "It's traditional with hangmen to hang themselves when they get old."

Obermayer was not persuaded about the putative advantages of hanging over other forms of execution. "Hanging is a special kind of humiliating experience," he said, looking back at those encounters with Woods. "Why so humiliating? Because when you die, all your sphincters lose their elasticity. You become a shitty mess." In his view, it was hardly surprising that the top Nazi officials at Nuremberg pleaded so desperately for the firing squad instead.

Nonetheless, Obermayer was convinced that Woods was sincere in his belief that he was carrying out a job that needed to be done with maximum efficiency and decency. Pierrepoint, his British counterpart, whose father and uncle had plied the same trade, made a similar claim at the end of his career: "I operated, on behalf of the State, what I am convinced was the most humane and dignified method of meting out death to a delinquent," he wrote. Among Pierrepoint's victims during his tour in

Germany were the "Beasts of Belsen," including the former commandant of Bergen-Belsen Josef Kramer and the infamously sadistic guard Irma Grese, who was only twenty-one when she went to the gallows.

Unlike Woods, Pierrepoint lived to an old age, and eventually turned against the death penalty. "Capital punishment, in my view, achieved nothing except revenge," he concluded.

Obermayer, who had returned to the United States before the hangings at Nuremberg, remained convinced that Woods approached all of his assignments, including his most famous one, with professional detachment. It was "just another job for him," he wrote. "I'm sure his approach to it was much more like that of the union workman who stands on the slaughtering block in a Kansas City packing house than that of the proud French fanatic who guillotined Marie Antoinette in the Place de la Concorde."

But in the aftermath of the war and the Holocaust, it was hardly surprising that the notions of revenge and justice were often intermingled, whatever the motives of the executioners themselves.

As for Woods, he was proved wrong in his prediction about how he would die. In 1950, he accidentally electrocuted himself while repairing a power line in the Marshall Islands.

CHAPTER TWO

"An Eye for an Eye"

"If this Jewish business is ever avenged on earth, then have mercy on us Germans."

Major Wilhelm Trapp, the commander of Reserve
Police Battalion 101, one of the most notorious
German killing squads in occupied Poland

It wasn't just "this Jewish business" that prompted cries for revenge as the Allied armies made their final push into Germany, although the maniacal, methodical implementation of the Final Solution against an entire race of people was in a category of its own. Every country that had been overrun by Hitler's troops—its citizens terrorized and murdered, many of its cities and towns reduced to rubble—had ample motivation to seek payback. In particular, the Nazis' treatment of *Untermenschen*, the Slavic "subhumans" to the east who were to be enslaved and worked or starved to death, triggered the fury of the Soviet Union's Red Army.

Hitler's policies of mass murder in the newly conquered territories and brutal treatment of Soviet POWs, which ensured that most Red Army troops quickly became convinced that capture meant near certain death, constituted a generous gift to Stalin's propaganda efforts to whip up hatred of the invaders.

In August 1942, Ilya Ehrenburg, a war correspondent for the Red Army newspaper *Krasnaya Zvezda*, penned his most famous lines: "Now we know. The Germans are not human. Now the word 'German' has become the most terrible swear word. Let us not speak. Let us not be indignant. Let us kill. If you do not kill the German he will kill you. . . . If you have killed one German, kill another. There is nothing jollier than German corpses."

Before the term "Nazi hunters" first surfaced, there was hunting for Nazis—or more accurately, hunting for Germans. There was little time or inclination to draw distinctions between the rank-and-file troops and civilians and their military and political leaders. The motive was simple: victory and vengeance. But as Hitler's armies encountered growing resistance and their ultimate defeat looked more and more likely, the Allied leaders began grappling with the issue of how far to push the doctrine of retribution, how many should pay the ultimate price for their country's crimes.

When the foreign ministers of the Big Three powers met in Moscow in October 1943, they agreed to jointly try major German war criminals while others who were responsible for more geographically circumscribed atrocities would be "sent back to the countries in which their abominable deeds were done." Although this Moscow Declaration set the stage for future trials, Secretary of State Cordell Hull left no doubt that he saw any judicial proceeding for the top political leaders as a mere formality. "If I had my way, I would take Hitler and Mussolini and Tojo and their arch-accomplices and bring them before a drumhead court-martial," he declared to the delight of his Soviet hosts. "And at sunrise on the following day there would occur an historic incident!"

At the Tehran conference six weeks later, Joseph Stalin charged that Winston Churchill, who had drafted the key language of the Moscow Declaration, was too soft on the Germans. As an alternative, he proposed the kind of solution that he so freely applied in his own country. "At least fifty thousand—and perhaps a hundred thousand—of the German command staff must be physically liquidated," he declared. "I propose a salute to the swiftest possible justice for all Germany's war criminals—justice before a firing squad! I drink to our unity in killing them as quickly as we capture them. All of them!"

Churchill immediately expressed his outrage. "I will not be party to any butchery in cold blood," he said. He went on to distinguish between the war criminals who "must pay" and those who had simply fought for their country. He added that he would rather be shot himself "than sully my country's honor by such infamy." President Franklin D. Roosevelt tried to defuse the tense moment by making a lame joke. Perhaps, he proposed, the two leaders could arrive at a reasonable compromise on the number of Germans to be shot—"say, forty-nine thousand, five hundred."

But by the time of the Yalta summit in February 1945, the positions of Churchill and Stalin on what to do with Nazi war criminals had undergone a seemingly startling evolution. Guy Liddell, head of counterespionage at MI5, had kept wartime diaries that were only declassified in 2012. According to his entries, Churchill backed a plan put forward by some of his officials that "certain people should be bumped off" while others would be imprisoned without resorting to Nuremberg trials. What was meant by "certain people" was the top Nazi leadership. Summing up the reasoning behind this recommendation, Liddell wrote: "This would be a much clearer proposition and would not bring the law into disrepute."

As Liddell's diary makes clear, this created an odd realignment of the Big Three. "Winston had put this forward at Yalta but Roosevelt felt that the Americans would want a trial," he wrote a few months after the summit. "Joe supported Roosevelt on the perfectly frank grounds that Russians like public trials for propaganda purposes. It seems to me that we are just being dragged down to the level of the travesties of justice that have been taking place in the USSR for the past 20 yrs."

In other words, Stalin saw Roosevelt's push for trials as just another opportunity to replicate the Soviet show trials of the 1930s, which was exactly what Churchill wanted to avoid—even at the price of authorizing summary executions of top Nazis without any judicial process. Although the Americans would prevail, setting the stage for Nuremberg, the seeds of doubt about those proceedings had already been planted.

• • •

In the final stage of the war, much of the Red Army gave full vent to their fury. They had fought for nearly four years on their own soil, enduring staggering losses and watching the devastation wrought by the German invaders. Then, as they mounted their drive for Berlin, their enemy refused to surrender to the inevitable. German troops died in record numbers—more than 450,000 in January 1945 alone, the month when the Soviet Union launched its largest offensive of the war. This was more than the United States lost during the entire war on all fronts.

That was no accident. The Nazi leaders had stepped up the terror against their own people to force obedience to Hitler's order to resist till the end. New "Flying Courts Martial of the Führer" traveled to threatened areas to order summary executions of soldiers who were suspected of desertion or undermined morale, effectively allowing them to shoot almost anyone. This was an eerie echo of Stalin's orders to carry out frenzied executions of his own officers and men during the German offensive against his country, ostensibly for the same reasons. Although undermanned and completely outgunned, German units kept inflicting heavy casualties on the attackers.

All of which ensured an orgy of violence—endorsed by the top Soviet leadership. In his orders to the First Belorussian Front just before the January 1945 offensive in Poland and then Germany, Marshal Georgy Zhukov declared: "Woe to the land of the murderers. We will get our terrible revenge for everything."

Even before they reached the German heartland, the Red Army troops had acquired a reputation for raping women—in Hungary, Romania, and then Silesia, where often little distinction was made between German and Polish women who were trapped in the historically disputed borderland of their two countries. Once the Soviet offensive reached deeper into German territory, horrifying tales of rape emerged from almost every city and village taken by Red Army troops. Vasily Grossman, the Russian novelist and war correspondent, wrote: "Terrible things are happening to German women. A cultivated German man explains with expressive gestures and broken Russian words that his wife has been raped by ten men that day."

Of course such accounts did not appear in Grossman's officially sanctioned dispatches. In some cases, superior officers did stop the rampages and a degree of order was gradually restored a few months after the German surrender on May 8, but far from completely. Rough estimates put the number of German women raped by Soviet forces in the final period of the war and in the months afterward at 1.9 million; there was also a huge surge of suicides by women who had been raped, often multiple times.

As late as November 6 and 7, 1945, the anniversary of the Bolshevik Revolution, Hermann Matzkowski, a German communist who was appointed as the mayor of a district of Königsberg by the new Soviet authorities, noted that the occupiers appeared to have been given official sanction for additional retribution. "Men were beaten, most women were raped, including my seventy-one-year-old mother, who died by Christmas," he wrote. The only well-fed Germans in the town, he added, "are women who have become pregnant by Russian soldiers."

Soviet soldiers were not the only ones who raped German women. According to a British woman who was married to a German in a village in the Black Forest, French Moroccan troops "came at night and surrounded every house in the village and raped every female between 12 and 80." American troops were also responsible for rapes, but nothing like on the scale that was happening in the territory conquered by the Red Army. Unlike what was taking place further east, these were usually individual instances of rape, and at least in some cases punishment was meted out to the rapists. John C. Woods, the U.S. Army hangman, executed American murderers and rapists before he performed his much more famous duties at Nuremberg.

Retribution also came in the form of the mass expulsion of ethnic Germans from the parts of the Reich that would be allocated to Poland, Czechoslovakia, and the Soviet Union (Königsberg, to be renamed Kaliningrad) according to the newly redrawn map of the region, as established by the victors. Millions of Germans had already begun their chaotic flight from those territories as the Red Army advanced. Some had followed Hitler's armies east only six years earlier, participating in the brutal measures against the local population that would now come back to haunt them.

According to the Potsdam agreement signed by Stalin, the new U.S. President Harry Truman, and the new British Prime Minister Clement Attlee on August 1, 1945, the population transfers after the war were to take place "in a humane and orderly fashion." But the reality of the situation stood in stark contrast to such reassuring rhetoric. Aside from dying from hunger and exhaustion on their desperate treks west, the expellees were often attacked by their former subjects—including forced laborers and concentration camp prisoners who had managed to survive the death marches and executions by their Nazi overlords right up until the last days of the war. And even those who had endured less were eager for revenge.

A Czech member of a militia unit recalled the fate of one victim. "In one town, civilians dragged a German into the middle of a crossroads and set alight to him. . . . I could do nothing, because if I had said something, I should have been attacked in my turn." A Red Army soldier finally shot the German to finish him off. The total of expelled ethnic Germans from East-Central Europe in the late 1940s is usually put at 12 million, with estimates of the death toll varying widely. In the 1950s, the West German government claimed that more than one million had died; more recent estimates put the number at about 500,000. Whatever the exact numbers, there was little agonizing about the fate of those Germans among the victors in the East. They were making good on Marshal Zhukov's promise of "terrible revenge."

On April 29, 1945, the U.S. Army's 42nd Infantry Division, known as the Rainbow Division because it was initially composed of National Guard units from twenty-six states and Washington, D.C., entered Dachau and liberated the approximately 32,000 survivors in the main camp. Although not technically an extermination camp and its one gas chamber had never been used, the main camp and a network of subcamps had worked, tortured, and starved thousands of prisoners to death. Designed as the first full-fledged concentration camp of the Nazi era, it was used mostly for those categorized as political prisoners, although the proportion of Jewish inmates increased during the war years.

The American troops were confronted by scenes of horror they had never imagined possible. In his official report, Brigadier General Henning Linden, the assistant division commander, described what the first glimpse of Dachau was like:

"Along the railroad running along the northern edge of the Camp, I found a train of some 30–50 cars, some passenger, some flatcars, some boxcars all littered with dead prisoners—20–30 to a car. Some bodies were on the ground alongside the train, itself. As far as I could see, most showed signs of beatings, starvation, shooting, or all three."

In a letter to his parents, Lieutenant William J. Cowling, Linden's aide, described what he saw in more graphic language: "The cars were loaded with dead bodies. Most of them naked and all of them skin and bones. Honest their legs and arms were only a couple of inches around and they had no buttocks at all. Many of the bodies had bullet holes in the back of their heads. It made us sick at our stomach and so mad we could do nothing but clench our fists. I couldn't even talk."

Linden was met by an SS officer carrying a white flag, along with a Swiss Red Cross representative. As they explained that they were there to surrender the camp and its SS guards, the Americans heard shots from inside the camp. Linden dispatched Cowling to investigate. Riding on the front of a jeep carrying American reporters, he entered through the gate and came upon a cement square that looked deserted.

"Then suddenly people (few would call them that) came from all directions," Cowling continued in his letter home. "They were dirty, starved skeletons with torn tattered clothes and they screamed and hollered and cried. They ran up and grabbed us. Myself and the newspaper people and kissed our hands, our feet and all of them tried to touch us. They grabbed us and tossed us into the air screaming at the top of their lungs."

Linden and more Americans arrived at the scene, and more tragedy struck. When the prisoners surged forward to embrace them, some ran into the electrified barbed wire and were immediately killed.

As the Americans worked their way through the camp, examining more gruesome piles of naked bodies, and the starved and in many cases typhus-ridden survivors, some SS guards eagerly surrendered but a few opened fire at prisoners who were trying to break through the fence—and some even appeared to challenge the U.S. troops as they entered. In those cases, retaliation was swift.

"The SS tried to train their machine guns on us," Lieutenant Colonel Walter J. Fellenz reported, "but we quickly killed them each time a new man attempted to fire the guns. We killed all seventeen SS."

Other soldiers reported watching prisoners chasing down guards—and feeling no inclination to intervene. Corporal Robert W. Flora recalled that the guards they captured were the lucky ones: "The ones that we didn't kill or capture were hunted down by the freed inmates and beaten to death. I saw one inmate just stomping on an SS Trooper's face. There wasn't much left of it."

Flora told the incensed prisoner that he had "a lot of hate in his heart." The prisoner understood and nodded.

"I don't blame you," Flora concluded.

Another liberator, Lieutenant George A. Jackson, came upon a group of about two hundred prisoners who had formed a circle around a German soldier who had been trying to escape. The German was wearing a full field pack and carrying a gun, but there was little he could do as two skeletal prisoners tried to catch him. "There was complete silence," Jackson noted. "It seemed as if there was a ritual taking place, and in a real sense it was."

Finally, one of the prisoners, who Jackson estimated could not have weighed more than seventy pounds, grabbed him by his coattails. The other pursuer seized his rifle and began to hit him on the head. "At that point, I realized that if I intervened, which could have been one of my duties, it would have become a very disturbing event," Jackson recalled. Instead, he turned and walked away, leaving the area for about fifteen minutes. "When I came back, his head had been battered away," he noted.

The crowd of prisoners had disappeared; nothing but the corpse was left as evidence of the drama that had just played itself out there.

As for Lieutenant Cowling, his role in liberating Dachau led him to reflect on how he had routinely taken German prisoners up to that point—and how he would change his behavior in the future. "I will never take another German prisoner armed or unarmed," he vowed in his letter to his parents two days after that searing experience. "How can they expect to do what they have done and simply say I quit and go scot free. They are not fit to live."

As the Red Army advanced, Tuvia Friedman, a young Jew in the central Polish city of Radom, made plans not only to escape the camp where he worked as a slave laborer but also to avenge the loss of most of his family in the Holocaust. "More and more, I found myself thinking of vengeance, of the day when we Jews would pay the Nazis back, an eye for an eye," he recalled.

With German troops preparing to evacuate, Friedman and two fellow prisoners escaped through a sewer that led from a factory. Snaking their way through the muck, they emerged into the woods on the other side of the barbed wire of the camp. They washed in a stream and struck out on their own. Friedman later recalled their sense of exhilaration: "We were afraid, but we were free."

Various Polish partisan units were already operating in the area, fighting not just the Germans but also among themselves. At stake was the future of Poland after the German occupation ended. The largest and most effective resistance movement in occupied Europe was the Polish Home Army (AK), which was also resolutely anticommunist and reported to the Polish government-in-exile in London. The much smaller People's Guard (GL) was organized by the communists, serving as the spearhead for the Soviet planned takeover of the country.

Friedman, who was using the name Tadek Jasinski to disguise his Jewish identity not just from Germans but also from anti-Semitic locals, eagerly signed up with a militia unit organized by a Lieutenant Adamski of the communist partisans. Their assignment, as Friedman noted, was "to put an end to the anarchistic activities" of the Home Army and "to ferret out and arrest Germans, Poles and Ukrainians who had engaged in wartime activity that was 'detrimental to the best interests of Poland and the Polish people.'"

"With burning enthusiasm, I embarked on the last chore," Friedman reported. "Working with several militiamen who had been placed under my command, feeling my gun securely in my holster, I arrested one known war criminal after another."

Friedman and his comrades certainly tracked down some genuine war criminals. They found a Ukrainian foreman named Shronski, for instance, "who had beaten more Jews than he could remember," and who in turn had led them to another Ukrainian who was later hanged. But the definition of what constituted "the best interests of Poland" also often meant arresting anyone who did not welcome the prospect of Soviet domination once the war ended, including some of the bravest Polish resistance fighters during the German occupation.

Even as its army continued to do battle with the retreating German forces, the Kremlin arrested sixteen Home Army leaders in Warsaw and flew them to Moscow's infamous Lubyanka prison. Tortured by the "liberators" of Poland, they were subjected to a show trial in June, shortly after the war in Europe was officially over. Their reward for fighting the Nazis for six years: imprisonment for "diversionary activities against the Soviet state."

Such distinctions mattered little to Friedman. He had felt the sting of Polish anti-Semitism on more than one occasion and had thrown in his lot with those who saw the Red Army purely as liberators.

But it wasn't the ideology of Poland's soon-to-be new masters that attracted Friedman. His real priority was to inflict payback against the Germans—and the communists simply gave him the opportunity to do so.

Assigned to Danzig, Friedman and five friends from Radom journeyed to the Baltic port city, watching German troops making their way west, trying to get out while they still could. "Some were pitiful sights, unable to walk, their bandaged heads crimson-stained," Friedman wrote.

"Try as we might we felt no pity, no sympathy. The butchers had run amok; they were responsible for the consequences."

Much of the city was alight, with Red Army and Polish police units dynamiting buildings that were close to collapsing. "It was like being in Rome at the time of Nero's famous conflagration," Friedman added.

The new arrivals were exuberant at the sudden reversal of fortunes. "We felt like men from another planet, whose arrival had sent the inhabitants of earth fleeing in terror." They swooped into apartments that Germans had evacuated in such haste that their clothing and personal possessions, including German money, were left scattered on the floor. In one dwelling, they came across porcelain vases—"probably Dresden," Friedman pointed out—and treated them like soccer balls, leaving only smashed pieces behind.

In a more disciplined manner, they then continued on their self-proclaimed mission of finding "the Nazis who had murdered and butchered, to seek some degree of vengeance and bring them to justice." Reporting to the Ministry of State Security, the eager recruits were told to help round up all remaining German men between the ages of fifteen and sixty. "Let us find the Nazi scum and cleanse the city," their new superior officer told them.

In his memoirs, Friedman had recalled his older sister Bella's reaction to the first deportations of Jews from Radom—specifically, that "they go like sheep to the slaughter." It was a refrain that would haunt discussions of the Holocaust for a long time. But in noting his own satisfaction at the terror he inspired in Danzig as he interrogated and imprisoned Germans there, Friedman used the same freighted analogy: "Now, the tables had turned, and thanks to my smart Polish uniform, I could order these once proud members of the master race about like so many frightened sheep."

He admitted that he was "quite merciless" with the prisoners he interrogated, beating them to extract confessions. "My heart was filled with hate. I hated them in defeat as I had hated them in their brutal moments of victory."

Writing long after the war, he declared: "Today, looking back, I am somewhat ashamed, but one must remember that that was the Spring of 1945, the Germans were still fighting to the bitter end on two fronts against the Allied forces as well as the Russian forces, and I had still not heard one word about whether any one member of my family had survived the Nazi camps." He and others were still also discovering more evidence of the horrors committed by the Germans, such as a room filled with naked bodies displaying the telltale signs of systematic torture. But he also claimed to have experienced the first pangs of unease about his growing reputation as "the unmerciful one."

Then word came that Bella had survived Auschwitz, prompting Friedman to turn in his uniform and head back to Radom. There, both of them decided to leave Poland, which they felt was an increasingly alien country. Anti-Semitic violence was still all too commonplace, and no other immediate family members had returned from the camps. Their original plan was to go to Palestine, joining the stream of Jewish survivors who were helped by Brichah ("flight" in Hebrew), the underground organization whose mission was to organize illegal escape routes from Europe for them. This was the postwar exodus that set the stage for the creation of the state of Israel.

But Friedman's journey was soon interrupted, and he ended up for several years in Austria instead. There he could pursue his passion for hunting Nazis. He was determined to keep settling scores—although abandoning the brutal, indiscriminate methods championed by Poland's new communist masters.

Seeing the big tank with an American flag waving from its turret rolling into the Mauthausen concentration camp near the Austrian city of Linz on May 5, 1945, the emaciated prisoner in his striped uniform was eager to touch the white star on its side. But he couldn't summon the strength to walk the final few yards to reach it. His knees buckled and he collapsed face first. As an American soldier lifted him up, the prisoner managed to point to the tank and touch the star—before he fainted.

When he came to in the barracks where he found himself lying alone in his bunk, Simon Wiesenthal knew he was a free man. Many of the SS guards had fled the night before, there was only one person to a bunk, the dead bodies that had been there in the morning were now gone, and the smell of DDT filled the air. Most importantly, the Americans brought in big soup kettles. "This was *real* soup, and it tasted delicious," Wiesenthal recalled.

It also made him and many of the other prisoners violently ill since they could not digest such rich fare. But in the days ahead, which Wiesenthal remembered as a period of "pleasant apathy" after the daily struggles in the camp to stay alive, a steady diet of more soup, vegetables, and meat, along with pills administered by American doctors in white coats, brought him back to the land of the living. For many others—Wiesenthal puts the figure at three thousand—it was too late. They died of exhaustion or starvation after their liberation.

Wiesenthal was no stranger to violence and tragedy even before World War II and the Holocaust. On December 31, 1908, he was born in Buczacz, a small town in eastern Galicia that was at the time part of the Austro-Hungarian Empire; after World War I it belonged to Poland, and today it is a part of Ukraine. Its population was heavily Jewish, but the entire region was a mix of nationalities and languages, which meant that Wiesenthal grew up hearing German, Yiddish, Polish, Russian, and Ukrainian.

The region was soon engulfed by the violence of World War I, the Bolshevik Revolution, and the ensuing civil wars there pitting Russians, Poles, and Ukrainians against each other. Wiesenthal's father, a successful commodities dealer, died early in the war fighting for the Austrian army. Wiesenthal's mother took her two sons to Vienna afterward, but returned to Buczacz once the Russians had retreated in 1917. When Simon was twelve, a marauding Ukrainian cavalryman slashed his thigh, leaving him with a scar for life. When Simon was still a teenager, his younger brother Hillel died from a spinal injury caused by a fall.

Wiesenthal studied architecture in Prague, but returned home to marry his high school sweetheart, Cyla Müller, and set up an office that designed residential buildings. During his student days and back in Buczacz he had many Jewish and non-Jewish friends, and he never gravitated to radical left-wing politics as many young people at the time did. The one political idea that intrigued him related to a different cause than the ones they espoused. "As a young person, I was a Zionist," he reminded me and other interviewers frequently.

The Holocaust was no abstraction for him, any more than it was for Friedman and other survivors. He and his family lived through the first part of the war in Lwów, or Lviv as the city is now known, which was first taken over by Soviet forces as a result of the Molotov-Ribbentrop Pact that divided Poland between Germany and the Soviet Union, and then was swiftly overrun by the German army during Hitler's 1941 invasion of the Soviet Union.

The Wiesenthals were at first confined to a ghetto in the city, then held in a nearby concentration camp, and next assigned to the Ostbahn (Eastern Railroad) Repair Works. There, Simon painted Nazi insignia on captured Soviet locomotives, and worked as a sign painter. All of which was merely an interlude in a procession of concentration camp experiences, escapes, and adventures that would lead to Mauthausen as the war was ending. He managed to arrange for Cyla's escape, which allowed her to go into hiding in Warsaw under an assumed Polish Catholic name. But fate was not so kind to his mother.

In 1942, Wiesenthal warned his mother that another deportation was likely and that she should be ready to hand over a gold watch that she still possessed to avoid getting caught up in it. When a Ukrainian policeman showed up at her door, she did as instructed. But, as he painfully recalled: "A half hour later, another Ukrainian policeman came and she had nothing left to give him, so he took her away. She had a weak heart. My one hope is that she died in the train, and she didn't have to undress and walk to the gas chamber."

Wiesenthal recounted numerous stories about his own seemingly miraculous escapes from death. During a roundup of Jews on July 6, 1941, for instance, he claimed to have been in a row of people lined up against the wall by Ukrainian auxiliary troops who, while taking swigs of vodka, started shooting people in the neck. As the executioners were getting closer to him and he stared blankly at the wall in front of him, he suddenly heard church bells—and a Ukrainian shouting "Enough! Evening Mass!"

Much later when Wiesenthal became a global celebrity and he was increasingly embroiled in disputes with other Nazi hunters, the accuracy of such stories was often questioned. Even Tom Segev, the author of a largely sympathetic biography of him, suggests caution in accepting his version of events. "As a man with literary aspirations, Wiesenthal tended to indulge in flights of imagination and more than once preferred to revel in historical drama rather than sticking to pure fact, as if he did not believe in the power of the true story to make enough of an impression on his audience," he wrote.

But there is no doubt about the harrowing nature of Wiesenthal's ordeal during the Holocaust, and that he only narrowly eluded death in any number of situations. There is also no doubt that, like Friedman and countless other survivors, as Wiesenthal put it, "I did have a strong desire for revenge." Friedman, who would soon meet Wiesenthal in Austria and initially cooperate with him in some of their efforts to track Nazi perpetrators, more than confirmed that. "He emerged from the camp at the war's end, an embittered, ruthless, vengeful pursuer of Nazi criminals," Friedman wrote.

But Wiesenthal's first experiences after liberation did not spur him to the kind of brutality that Friedman admitted to. He was still far too weak to even consider assaulting anyone, and he was in no position to take such actions even if he had wanted to. And, by all indications, he moved beyond the simple desire for vengeance relatively quickly.

Nonetheless, like Friedman, he was astounded by the instant role reversals at the end of the war—and how this transformed his former tormentors. When he had recovered enough in Mauthausen to move about, he was attacked by a Polish camp trusty, a former prisoner with special privileges, who beat him for no apparent reason. Wiesenthal decided to report the incident to the Americans. As he waited to file his complaint, he watched American soldiers interrogating SS men. When one particularly brutal guard was brought into the room, Wiesenthal instinctively turned his head, hoping to avoid his notice.

"The sight of this man had always brought cold sweat to the back of my neck," he recalled. But then he saw what was happening, and he couldn't believe his eyes. Escorted in by a Jewish prisoner, "the SS man was trembling, just as we had trembled before him." The man who had inspired so much fear now was "a contemptible, frightened coward . . . the supermen became cowards the moment they were no longer protected by their guns."

Wiesenthal quickly came to a decision. He walked into the war crimes office in Mauthausen and offered his services to a lieutenant there. The American looked at him skeptically, pointing out that he had no relevant experience.

"And, incidentally, how much do you weigh?" he asked.

Wiesenthal said he weighed fifty-six kilos (123 pounds). That triggered a laugh from the lieutenant. "Wiesenthal, go and take it easy for a while, and come to see me when you *really* weigh fifty-six kilos."

Ten days later Wiesenthal was back. He'd put on some weight, but still far from enough, and he had tried to disguise his pale complexion by rubbing red paper on his cheeks.

Evidently impressed by his enthusiasm, the lieutenant assigned him to a Captain Tarracusio, and soon Wiesenthal was on his way with him to arrest an SS guard named Schmidt. He had to walk up to the second floor of his house to get him. If Schmidt had resisted, the former prisoner would have been in no position to do anything because he was trembling from the exertion of mounting the stairs. He may also have been trembling because of his nervousness about what would happen. But Schmidt was trembling, too, and, after Wiesenthal sat down and caught his breath, the SS man held his arm as he helped him down the stairs.

When they reached the jeep where Captain Tarracusio was waiting, the SS guard cried and pleaded for mercy, arguing that he was both a little fish and had helped many prisoners.

"Yes, you helped the prisoners," Wiesenthal replied. "I've often seen you. You helped them on their way to the crematorium."

As Wiesenthal told it, this was the beginning to his work as a Nazi hunter. He would never move to Israel, although his daughter, son-in-law, and grandchildren now live there. For him, Israel was the road not taken. But his personal journey involved working with—and, at times, crossing swords with—those in Israel who later sought to bring one of the chief architects of the Holocaust to justice: Adolf Eichmann.

Both Wiesenthal and Friedman claimed that they almost immediately embarked on the hunt for the man who organized the mass deportations of Jews to Auschwitz and other concentration camps. But in the earliest postwar period, the main news concerned those who were already captured or were easier to capture, and their subsequent trials. Nazi hunting—and punishment for the Nazis—was still primarily the job of the victors.

CHAPTER THREE

Common Design

"We're a very obedient people. It's our greatest strength and our greatest weakness. It enables us to build an economic miracle while the British are on strike, and it enables us to follow a man like Hitler into a great big mass grave."

The fictional German magazine publisher Hans Hoffmann in Frederick Forsyth's 1972 bestselling novel *The Odessa File*

In the aftermath of Germany's defeat, most of Hitler's former subjects were eager to disassociate themselves from the mass murders and atrocities committed in their name. Soldiers of the victorious armies and survivors of the camps routinely encountered Germans who assured them that they had opposed the Nazis all along—not actively, but in their hearts. Many also claimed they had helped Jews and other victims of the Nazi regime. "If all the Jews had been saved that I was told about in those months there would have been more Jews alive at the end of the war than there were when it began," Wiesenthal dryly noted.

While many Germans were initially dismissive of Nuremberg and other trials as "victors' justice," there were also those who found something almost comforting in the notion that the masterminds of Germany's undoing would be summarily punished. Saul Padover, an Austrian-born historian and political scientist who served in the U.S. Army from Normandy through the advance into Germany, took copious notes on German attitudes. Meeting a young woman who had been a leader of the Bund Deutscher Mädel, the League of German Girls, which was the counterpart of the Hitlerjugend or Hitler Youth for German teenage boys, he recorded in his notebook the conversation with her.

Asked about her role in the league, she "lied," as Padover wrote, that she was "forced" to be one of its leaders. What did she think should be done with the top Nazis? "For me, you can hang them all," she replied.

The young woman was hardly alone in her willingness to see some of the Nazi bigwigs pay with their lives, which at the same time helped her distance herself from what had happened. Like many Germans, she maintained that she had not even known about most of the horrors of the Third Reich.

Peter Heidenberger, who had spent the final period of the war with a German parachute division in Italy and then a brief period as a POW, arrived in the town of Dachau shortly after the concentration camp there had been liberated. He was looking for his fiancée, who had fled from their hometown of Dresden after it was bombed on February 13, making her way to friends there. "You know, Dachau is a very nice town; they have a castle there," he declared, summoning his memories decades later. Walking up the hill to the castle, he was questioned by an American sentry whether he knew what had happened in the camp below. "I told him I hadn't been there, didn't know anything [other than] it was a prison camp," he said. "He didn't believe me."

But soon Heidenberger found himself learning much more—more than enough to share the sentiments of the young woman from the League of German Girls. "They should have all been put up against the wall and we would have had more justice," he said, recalling his initial reaction to what he heard.

Heidenberger's views would change over time because of his exposure to the other set of trials that was taking place parallel to those in Nuremberg. Dachau was the setting for the U.S. Army prosecution of the people who implemented the policies of the top Nazi officials, including those who were hanged at Nuremberg. These were the on-the-ground perpetrators, the SS officers and others who ran not just Dachau but also other concentration camps. The Americans were looking for a stringer—a freelance journalist—who could report on the Dachau trials for Radio Munich, a new station the victors had set up. A local official recommended Heidenberger as a well-educated German with no Nazi background.

The young German had to learn what a stringer was and he had zero reporting experience, but he readily agreed. "The nice thing was that we got fantastic food in the camp," he noted. He would soon prove to be a valuable reporter for a growing number of outlets, including the German News Agency and Reuters. While much less known than the main Nuremberg trial, the Dachau proceedings provided remarkable details about what the Third Reich meant in practice.

Those were the kind of details that Truman had in mind when long after his presidency he spelled out the original purpose of all the trials: "to make it impossible for anyone ever to say in times to come, 'Oh, it never happened—just a lot of propaganda—a pack of lies.'" In other words, the postwar trials were meant not just to punish the guilty; they also were critical to establishing the historical record.

Unlike many of his contemporaries, William Denson had not served on the battlefields of Europe. The Alabama native—whose great-grandfather fought in the Civil War on the side of the Confederacy, whose grandfather was a state Supreme Court justice who had risked ostracism by defending black Alabamans, and whose father was a respected local lawyer and politician—graduated from Harvard Law School and went on to teach law at West Point. But in early 1945, he was tapped for duty as one of the judge advocate generals, or JAGs, in Germany. At thirty-two, Denson found himself—minus his wife, who had no intention of joining him in a devastated country—preparing to prosecute cases in an occupied land he was encountering for the first time.

Stationed with other JAG staffers in Freising, a short distance from Dachau, he was initially skeptical about the horrifying reports coming from camp survivors. "I thought here were some people who had been mistreated in the concentration camps and they were seeking revenge, and that they were really doing a job drawing on fantasy rather than reality," he explained decades later. But he was soon convinced by the consistency of the testimony he was gathering. Since the witnesses "related substantially the same things, then I knew the events had occurred, because these witnesses did not have a chance to get together ahead of time and fabricate their stories."

Any lingering doubts were swept away by the grisly accounts provided by the liberators of Dachau and other camps. At the same time, those accounts rekindled the debate about whether those responsible for mass murder and torture deserved anything more than summary execution. When General George S. Patton rushed to see Ohrdruf, a subcamp of Buchenwald that was a nightmarish spectacle of death worthy of a Hieronymus Bosch painting, he screamed from his jeep: "See what these sons of bitches did? See what these bastards did? I don't want you to take a prisoner!"

But Denson and his colleagues in the JAG office were convinced that trials were absolutely necessary—both to punish the guilty and to lay out the gruesome facts for everyone to know, then and in the future. Hearing the details of what U.S. troops had seen at Dachau and the stream of other testimonies, "I finally reached a point where I was ready to believe most anything," Denson declared. And he was more than ready when he was told to start moving on the cases against the perpetrators as quickly as possible. The argument about summary executions vs. trials was over.

Denson's main interrogator was Paul Guth. Born into a Jewish family in Vienna, Guth was sent to school in England; afterward, he went to the United States and was promptly picked for intelligence training in Camp Ritchie, Maryland, the training ground that had a large contingent of Jewish refugees from Germany and Austria. After graduating first in his class, Guth received further training in England and then ended up in Freising. He would prove to be one of the Army's most effective interrogators.

But when Guth went to address the prisoners who were held in the camp barracks that had until recently housed their victims, he hardly made an intimidating impression—quite the opposite. The SS men had expected they would be executed; instead, Guth read out forty names of those who were slated to go on trial before an American military tribunal. He also told them they were free to choose their defense lawyers, the tab would be picked up by their captors, and they could not be compelled to testify if they did not want to. As Joshua Greene, Denson's biographer, wrote: "The Germans could hardly believe their ears."

When the trial opened on November 13, 1945, the courtroom was packed. The International Military Tribunal would only begin its deliberations in Nuremberg a week later, so the room was heavy with top brass like General Walter Bedell Smith, Eisenhower's chief of staff, and Senator Claude Pepper of Florida. Many journalists were in the room as well, including luminaries like Walter Lippmann and Marguerite Higgins. But Lippmann and Higgins did not even stay the whole first morning, and by the end of the week almost all their colleagues had followed them to Nuremberg, which was the big draw and would generate the major headlines. Soon, the only reporters who could be counted on to cover all the Dachau proceedings were Heidenberger and a *Stars and Stripes* correspondent.

Just as the forty accused were startled by the way they were put on trial, the spectators were taken aback by Denson as he made his presentation as the chief prosecutor. "The German spectators, unfamiliar with American legal practice, were awed by the trial lawyer theatrics," Heidenberger recalled. Denson approached the bench and started off his statements by declaring in his Southern accent, "May it please the court . . ." It wasn't just the accent that captivated Denson's audience. "He had a very pleasant way that was very effective presenting his case," Heidenberger added.

The young German reporter was even more impressed when he walked into Denson's office for the first time—and gratified that the American immediately accepted him as a full-fledged member of the journalistic community. "You know the American custom of having your feet on the desk," he mused decades later. "He had his feet on his desk and he treated me like a newspaper guy."

But Denson's soothing demeanor masked an iron determination to win convictions against all the defendants. Unlike the Nuremberg defendants, those on trial at Dachau were not the architects of the policies; they could not be charged with plotting crimes against humanity. Instead, Denson set out to prove that the personnel who operated the concentration camp knew exactly what its purpose was, and that it was enough to prove that they were part of the "common design"—or "community of intention"—to commit those criminal acts. It was not necessary to prove what specific crimes had been committed by each of the accused.

In his opening statement, the lanky Alabaman spelled out the framework of his case:

> May it please the court, we expect the evidence to show that during the time alleged a scheme of extermination was in process here at Dachau. We expect the evidence to show that the victims of this planned extermination were civilians and prisoners of war, individuals unwilling to submit themselves to the yoke of Nazism. We expect to show that these people were subjected to experiments like guinea pigs, starved to death, and at the same time worked as hard as their physical bodies permitted; that the conditions under which these people were housed were such that disease and death were inevitable . . . and that each one of these accused constituted a cog in this machine of extermination.

The defense attorneys argued strenuously against this "cog in the machine" accusation, but to no avail. Later, such a sweeping approach would be rejected, and most trials would focus on the particular deeds allegedly committed by individual defendants.

Unlike in Nuremberg where almost all the evidence produced by the prosecution was in the form of incriminating documents that the Germans had produced themselves, the Dachau trial relied on a steady procession of witnesses who provided Denson with chilling testimony about the workings of this machinery of extermination, including the last transport of Jews from Dachau. As Ali Kuci, an Albanian prisoner, testified, 2,400 Jews were ordered into the train wagons on April 21; on April 29 when U.S. troops liberated the camp, those were the wagons that were overflowing with dead bodies. Kuci and other prisoners dubbed the train, which never left the station, as the "Morgue Express." Only six hundred of the prisoners survived, he added. The SS guards had not allowed anyone to approach it as the others inside starved to death.

Denson also relied on confessions obtained from some of the defendants by Guth and other interrogators, leading to allegations that they had used coercive methods. Guth strenuously denied such charges, but the speed and outcome of the Dachau trial would prompt lingering questions about how carefully legal procedures were observed. As Denson summed up his case, he declared: "I wish to emphasize that these forty men are not charged with killing. The offense is in a common design to kill, to beat, to torture and starve." In other words, it was the "common design" that was critical to the case against them, rather than individual acts of murder.

He also dismissed all pleas from the defendants that they were merely following orders, castigating them for "failing to refuse to do what was obviously wrong." He added: "The answer that 'I was ordered to do it' has no part in this case." This helped establish a principle that would be followed in subsequent trials. Wrapping up his case, Denson declared: "These accused will have turned back the hands of the clock of civilization at least a thousand years if this court in any manner condones the conduct that has been presented to it."

The conditions of the German masters-turned-prisoners had sometimes created the misleading impression that they were benefiting from the benevolence of the victors. Lord Russell of Liverpool, who served as the deputy judge advocate for the British Army of the Rhine, visited Dachau in this period and was startled by what he saw of the German prisoners. "Each one of these lived in comfort in a light airy cell, had electric lighting, and in winter central heating, a bed, a table, a chair, and books. Well fed and sleek they looked, and on their faces was a look of slight astonishment. They must indeed have wondered where they were."

But on December 13, 1945, when the military tribunal announced its verdicts, any such misperception was banished. It found all forty men guilty, and thirty-six were sentenced to death. Of the thirty-six who were sentenced to death, twenty-three were hanged on May 28–29, 1946.

On his visit to the camp, Lord Russell emerged from one of its buildings and noticed something that struck him as particularly odd: "Nailed to a pole on the crematorium roof, a little rustic nesting box for wild birds, placed there by some schizophrenic SS man."

This prompted his final reflection on what he had just observed. "Then and then only was it possible to understand why the nation which gave the world Goethe and Beethoven, Schiller and Schubert, gave it also Auschwitz and Belsen, Ravensbrück and Dachau," he wrote.

Unlike many of the other members of the Army's legal team, Denson did not return to the United States when the first Dachau trial ended. He remained in charge of the prosecution teams in the subsequent trials that continued through 1947. Although those trials focused on the death machinery in such camps as Buchenwald, Flossenbürg, and Mauthausen, they also took place within the confines of the Dachau camp compound. Denson personally prosecuted a record 177 cases against concentration camp guards, officers, and doctors, winning guilty verdicts in all of them. In the end, ninety-seven of them were hanged.

As he prepared to fly home in October 1947 to return to civilian life, *The New York Times* lauded his record: "Colonel Denson has been outstanding for his intensive work on the prosecution staff of the War Crimes Commission at Dachau. Frequently taking one major case during the daytime and working far into the night on the preparation of another, he had become over a period of two years a symbol of justice among the SS men and women administrators in Adolf Hitler's concentration camps."

But the strain of that pace—and of the unremittingly gruesome facts that he had to reconstruct on a daily basis—took its toll on Denson. His weight had dropped from 160 to less than 120 pounds. "They said I looked more like an exhibit out of the concentration camp than anybody I put on the stand," he recalled later. In January 1947, he collapsed and spent two weeks in bed. Nonetheless, it seemed as if each new case made him more determined to carry on.

Denson's wife, Robina, who had stayed in the United States, filed for divorce. According to his biographer, she had thought "that she was gaining a social partner from an aristocratic family, not a legal missionary who would run off to prosecute Nazis."

Heidenberger, who had become increasingly friendly with Denson and the other Americans at Dachau, claims this was not the only catalyst for his wife's decision. "Hell, what ruined his marriage were all those German fräuleins," he said. "Americans had it all, they had the nylons and got the women. We were a bit *schockiert* about the honorable German fräuleins. Bill told me about the parties he went to in Munich. It must have been very wild." Robina Denson found out about such escapades, Heidenberger maintained, prompting her to end what was already a largely defunct and childless marriage.

Soon, Denson found himself particularly attracted to a young German woman who was also in a loveless marriage. A genuine countess, Huschi, as she was called by her friends, had fled her family's Silesian estate on a horse-drawn cart with her six-month-old daughter before the Red Army arrived, and then survived the bombing of Dresden. At the end of the war, she was in a Bavarian village, and greeted the first American tank to show up there with the announcement, delivered in perfect English: "We surrender this village to you!" Hearing such stories, Denson was charmed and intrigued. But it wasn't until much later, when he discovered that Huschi had also divorced and moved to the United States, that they reconnected—and married on December 31, 1949. By all accounts, it was a happy marriage in every way.

Later in life, Denson looked back at his time in Germany as "the highlight of my career." But it wasn't without controversy. After the Dachau camp trial, he found himself prosecuting cases that triggered both the most sensational headlines and the most heated debate. This was particularly true of the trial of the Buchenwald defendants in the spring of 1947.

The record of that camp, Denson told the tribunal, was "a chapter of infamy and sadism unparalleled in recorded history." And no case was as lurid as the one against Ilse Koch, the widow of Buchenwald's first commandant. Even before the trial started, Heidenberger recalled, some of those eager to testify spread "the wildest stories about her as a sex monster." Under questioning from Denson, former inmates testified that she had delighted in provoking the prisoners with her sexuality—and then had them beaten or killed.

Digging ditches for cables one day, ex-prisoner Kurt Froboess recalled looking up to see Koch. "She was wearing a short skirt, standing with her legs straddled over the ditch without any underwear," he said. Then she demanded to know what the prisoners were looking at and beat them with her riding crop, he added.

Others testified that she possessed lamp shades, a knife sheath, and book covers made of human skin. "It was common knowledge also that tattooed prisoners were sent to the hospital from work details where Ilse Koch had passed by and seen them," said Kurte Sitte, who had been a Buchenwald prisoner during the entire war. "These prisoners were killed in the hospital and the tattooing stripped off."

Heidenberger, who covered all these testimonies, has no doubt that Koch was guilty of systematic brutality, but was also the subject of unconfirmed rumors. Her reputation as an "oversexed" sadist preceded her trial, and she was particularly hated by the inmates because of the way she flaunted her sexuality and power. When she showed up to testify in her case, the fact that she was obviously pregnant—even though she had been imprisoned since her capture—only added to the inflamed passions in the court. This prompted a scramble among the journalists to find the right nickname for her. According to Heidenberger, a *Stars and Stripes* reporter rushed into the press room to announce: "I've got it. We call her the Bitch of Buchenwald."

The name stuck and she became the she-devil of the trials. It didn't help her cause that the prosecution also brought in the shrunken head of a Polish prisoner who had reportedly escaped from the camp, and then was captured and executed. According to one of the witnesses, it had been displayed to visitors by the camp authorities. Although the prosecution pointed out that there was no demonstrated connection to Koch, it was admitted as evidence.

Soloman Surowitz, one of the American lawyers on Denson's team in the Buchenwald case, became convinced that the uproar over Koch was undermining the whole notion of due process—and he resigned from the case. "I can't stand it," he told Denson. "I don't believe our own witnesses—it's all hearsay."

The two men parted without acrimony, and Denson remained convinced that he had to present the evidence he had, which was strong enough to convict her with or without confirmation of some of the most sensational claims. Koch was sentenced to life imprisonment, but her case would take several more twists and turns as the atmosphere around the war crimes trials began to shift. And, back in the United States later, Denson would find himself on the defensive about Koch, particularly when the stories about lamp shades made of human skin looked increasingly questionable.

Heidenberger admitted his misgivings about his own role in playing up some of the unverified stories in his articles, contributing to the sensationalized atmosphere around the trial. But he has no doubt that Koch and the other defendants in the Buchenwald case fully merited their guilty verdicts. And despite their flaws, those trials convinced him that he was wrong in his initial belief that the major perpetrators should have faced summary execution instead of a judicial process. "In spite of the legal issues raised by the war crimes trials, they furnished the best and most reliable evidence of what actually happened during the Holocaust," he concluded.

In 1952, Heidenberger immigrated to the United States with his wife and two sons. As one of the first German reporters in Washington after the war, he found himself attending Truman's press conferences in the White House. But he had already studied law in Germany and soon enrolled in George Washington University Law School. After graduating, he launched his legal career in Washington, sometimes representing victims who were seeking reparations from the German government and later as an advisor to the German government on Holocaust cases. Among his early colleagues and mentors was his old friend William Denson.

CHAPTER FOUR

The Penguin Rule

"His voice was excellently modulated, his hands well-shaped and carefully groomed, and he moved gracefully and self-confidently. The only blemish in the perfection of his personality was that he had killed ninety thousand people."

Judge Michael Musmanno, describing defendant Otto Ohlendorf
during the trial of the commanders of the Einsatzgruppen,
the special execution squads deployed on the Eastern Front

Wearing a sailor cap, a short-sleeve blue shirt, and navy pants held up by black suspenders, Benjamin Ferencz sat on a lounge chair outside a modest one-bedroom bungalow in Delray Beach, Florida, looking like a typical retiree when I visited him there in early 2013.

But there was nothing typical about this ninety-three-year-old who stood just barely five feet tall when he got up to flex his biceps, showing off the results of his daily workouts at the gym. Or, more significantly, when he recounted his memories of going from Harvard Law School, where he was a scholarship student from New York's rough neighborhood aptly known as Hell's Kitchen, to getting off his landing craft at Omaha Beach, finding himself in water that came up to his waist while for most others it came up to their knees.

And, especially, when he described how, through a combination of luck and persistence, he ended up, at age twenty-seven, in Nuremberg as the chief prosecutor in what the Associated Press called, without any hyperbole, "the biggest murder trial in history." Yet, even more than the Dachau trials, it was a trial that was so overshadowed by the International Military Tribunal's headline-grabbing proceedings against the major Nazi leaders that it usually gets at most passing mention in the history books.

Born in Transylvania into a Hungarian Jewish family that came to the United States when he was an infant, Ferencz was always a scrapper, driven by his passions and not intimidated by any challenge. Living in the basement of one of the apartment buildings in Hell's Kitchen, where his father worked as a janitor, he was initially rejected by the public school both because, at six, he looked too small and because he spoke only Yiddish. But after attending various schools in other parts of the city, he was singled out as one of the "gifted boys," became the first person in his family to go to college, and then went on to get his law degree at Harvard, never having to pay tuition.

When Corporal Ferencz was transferred from the infantry to the Judge Advocate Section of General Patton's Third Army at the end of 1944, he was thrilled, particularly when he was told that he would be part of a new war crimes team. As U.S. troops were fighting their way into Germany, there were numerous reports of Allied fliers who had parachuted into German territory and then were murdered by local residents. Ferencz was assigned the task of investigating such cases and carrying out arrests as needed. "The only authority I had was the .45 caliber gun around my waist and the fact that the U.S. Army was swarming all over town," he noted. "Under such circumstances, Germans are very obedient and I do not recall ever encountering resistance."

Despite his size, Ferencz brought with him more than his share of New York–style chutzpah. Later, when General Patton's headquarters was located on the outskirts of Munich, he was on latrine duty on the day Marlene Dietrich showed up for a performance for the troops. As the junior member of the team, he was told to make sure that she was not disturbed in her room as she took a bath first. "After waiting a reasonable time—to be sure that she was at least in the tub—and eager to do my duty, I simply walked into the room where she sat calmly immersed only in her splendor," he recalled. He must have been rattled a bit by his own audacity, since, while retreating, he said: "Oh, pardon me, Sir."

Dietrich was merely amused when he apologized, laughing particularly at his use of "Sir." When she learned he was a Harvard-trained lawyer, she invited him to join her for lunch with the officers. Since Ferencz was an enlisted man, he suggested that she explain that he was an old friend from Europe, which she happily did. As a result, he went from latrine duty to sitting opposite the superstar at lunch. Before she was ushered out by Patton, she gave Ferencz her calling card.

As he investigated more of the downed flier cases, Ferencz was intent on doing his job—but he wasn't vindictive in the process. On occasion, he even had ambivalent feelings about the results of his actions. Investigating the beating and bludgeoning of a downed pilot after a bombing raid near Frankfurt, he questioned a young woman who had joined the mob attacking the pilot. She admitted her participation but, in tears, explained that her two children had been killed in the bombing. Sensing a degree of remorse, Ferencz only put her under house arrest. "The truth is, I felt sorry for her," he recalled. But he had no such feelings for a fireman who had reportedly struck the fatal blow and then boasted that he was covered with American blood.

Months later, Ferencz went to see the war crimes trial where both of them were among the defendants. The fireman was sentenced to death. When the young woman was sentenced to two years, she fainted. Ferencz asked a medic who came to check on her whether she was all right. The medic assured him that she was, but also threw in the information that she was pregnant; the father was one of the U.S. soldiers guarding her. "Strange things happen in times of war," Ferencz noted.

But the young investigator's mood changed drastically when he was assigned to enter just liberated concentration camps and gather any evidence that could be used against those who had been in charge of these charnel houses. Initially, what he saw in camp after camp—the bodies strewn everywhere, the skeletal survivors—prompted near disbelief. "My mind would not accept what my eyes saw," he wrote later. "I had peered into Hell." At Buchenwald, he collected two shrunken heads of prisoners that had been kept by SS officers on display. They would be entered into evidence by Denson in the subsequent trial.

Ferencz felt a mounting fury, which translated into a burning desire to take swift action or, at times, no action at all when he witnessed the victims turning against their tormentors. Arriving at the Ebensee camp, he ordered a group of passing civilians to collect and bury the bodies. When some enraged inmates captured an SS officer, possibly the camp commandant, while he was trying to flee, Ferencz saw them beat the man and then tie him to one of the metal trays used for sliding bodies into the crematorium; they slid him back and forth over the flames until he was roasted alive. "I watched it happen and did nothing," Ferencz recalled. "I was not inclined to try."

At Mauthausen, he found piles of human bones at the bottom of a quarry, the remains of slave laborers who had been thrown off a cliff once they no longer were capable of working. Driving to nearby Linz, he picked an apartment to appropriate from a Nazi family, ordering them out so that he and his men could stay there. Before returning to Mauthausen the next morning, he emptied the dressers and closets in the apartment of clothing, taking it all to the camp to give to the nearly naked prisoners. That evening, a young woman who had lived in the apartment returned and asked if she could retrieve some of her clothing. "Help yourself," Ferencz said. When she saw the empty closets, she started shouting that her clothing had been stolen.

"I was in no mood to be called a thief by any German," Ferencz recalled. While she was still screaming, he pulled her by the wrist downstairs, explaining that he would take her to the camp so that she could personally tell the ex-prisoners to return her clothes. Terrified at that prospect, she shouted even louder for him to let her go. Ferencz agreed—but only after she bowed to his demand that she say that the clothing was a gift, not stolen by anyone. He had transformed his anger into a harsh lesson about who the truly aggrieved parties were.

• • •

After a brief stint back in the United States provided him the opportunity to get married, Ferencz returned to Germany to join General Taylor's team that was working on the war crimes trials in Nuremberg. The first and most famous of those trials, conducted by the International Military Tribunal, had culminated in the sentencing of the top Nazi luminaries like Göring, Ribbentrop, and Keitel on October 1, 1946, but a dozen more Nuremberg trials would follow, run as U.S. military tribunals. One of them was triggered by a chance discovery in Berlin that changed Ferencz's life.

Upon his return to Germany with his new wife, Ferencz was dispatched to Berlin to set up a branch of war crimes investigators there. In the spring of 1947, one of his best researchers rushed into his office to let him know about a major discovery. While rummaging through a Foreign Ministry annex near Tempelhof Airport, he had found a remarkable set of secret reports sent to the Gestapo. They provided full details, filed on a daily basis, on the mass shootings and first experimental gassings of Jews, Gypsies, and other civilian "enemies" on the Eastern front by Einsatzgruppen—the special execution squads assigned that task before the killings were shifted to the gas chambers of the camps.

On a small adding machine, Ferencz started tallying up the number of victims mentioned in these laconic reports of shootings. "When I passed the figure of one million, I stopped adding," he recalled. "That was quite enough for me." Ferencz rushed back to Nuremberg to tell Taylor of these findings, urging him to put this evidence to good use in another trial. This chance discovery provided precise information on which unit—and which commanders—were responsible for the wholesale killing of Jews, Gypsies, and others as German troops attacked the Soviet Union in 1941.

Taylor's initial reaction was cooler—and more calculated—than Ferencz had expected. The general explained that the Pentagon was unlikely to appropriate more funds and personnel for trials beyond the ones already planned for. Besides, the public didn't seem particularly eager to see more trials. Ferencz wouldn't let go, arguing that if no one else would take the case on, he would do so personally, on top of his other duties.

"Okay, you've got it," Taylor assented, making him the chief prosecutor. He was only twenty-seven at the time.

Ferencz moved back to Nuremberg to prepare his case. The challenge was how to handle the huge body of evidence against approximately three thousand members of the Einsatzgruppen who had methodically murdered civilians on the Eastern Front. Ferencz explained that he chose the most senior and best-educated SS officers to put on trial since it was impossible to do more than that. For starters, the Nuremberg courtroom had only twenty-four seats in the defendants' dock. Noting that "justice is always imperfect," Ferencz admitted this was only "a small sampling of major defendants." Of the original twenty-four he decided to prosecute, one committed suicide before the trial and another collapsed during the reading of the indictment. That left twenty-two.

The trial ran from September 29, 1947, to February 12, 1948, but Ferencz presented the prosecution's case in a mere two days. "I suppose that the Guinness Book of World Records might have noted it as the fastest prosecution in a trial of such magnitude," he wrote later. He was convinced that the documents provided more damning evidence than any witnesses could. "I didn't call any witnesses, for a good reason," he explained. "I may not have had any experience, but I was a damn good criminal law student at the Harvard Law School. And I know that some of the worst testimony you can get is eyewitness testimony.... I had the reports, and I could prove the validity of the reports, although they challenged them, of course."

In his opening statement, Ferencz charged the defendants with "the deliberate slaughter of more than a million innocent and defenseless men, women, and children ... dictated, not by military necessity, but by that supreme perversion of thought, the Nazi theory of the master race." Then he broke down the big number to show exactly how this was possible. The evidence showed that the four Einsatzgruppen, each composed of five hundred to eight hundred men, "averaged some 1,350 murders per day during a 2-year-period; 1,350 human beings slaughtered on the average day, 7 days a week for more than 100 weeks."

Ferencz used a new term to describe the crimes of the defendants:

genocide. It was coined by a Polish Jewish refugee lawyer, Raphael Lemkin, who—as early as 1933—had tried to warn the world that Hitler was deadly serious about his threat to exterminate an entire race. Ferencz met Lemkin—"the somewhat lost and bedraggled fellow with the wild and pained look in his eyes," as he put it—in the halls of the Nuremberg courthouse, where he was fervently lobbying to win recognition of genocide as a new category of international crime.

"Like the Ancient Mariner of Coleridge's poem, he collared anyone he could to tell them the story of how his family had been destroyed by the Germans," Ferencz recalled. "Jews were killed just because they were Jews." He would then end with pleas to back his efforts to recognize genocide as a special crime. Ferencz deliberately included the term in his opening statement as a result of Lemkin's intense appeals, defining it as "the extermination of whole categories of human beings."

The young prosecutor concluded his initial presentation with a line that would resonate among those seeking a measure of justice for such monumental crimes for decades to come; in fact, it would be quoted fifty years later by the head of the new United Nations special tribunals for crimes in Yugoslavia and Rwanda. "If these men be immune, then law has lost its meaning, and man must live in fear," Ferencz declared. After he wrapped up the prosecution case on the second day, the remaining months of the trial were devoted to the testimony of the defendants.

Michael Musmanno, the presiding judge from Pennsylvania, was soon persuaded that Ferencz "had not been engaging in figures of speech but in numerals of cast iron reality." And he described the diminutive prosecutor as "David taking Goliath's measure" as he demolished the defendants' attempts to shift the blame for their killing sprees to anyone but themselves, or maintained that they had tried to be as "humane" as possible as they carried out their murderous tasks.

Musmanno was accompanied by two other judges who helped him handle the trial, but, as Ferencz noted, he completely dominated the proceedings. The son of Italian immigrants, Musmanno had defended famed anarchists Nicola Sacco and Bartolomeo Vanzetti in the 1920s, and he regularly displayed a flair for drama. He launched a crusade against drunk driving as a criminal court judge in the mid-1930s, ordering twenty-five men serving time for alcohol-related offenses to attend a funeral of a miner killed by a drunken driver. He also warned that anyone questioning the existence of Santa Claus—people who contributed to the heartbreak of children, as he put it—would be held in contempt of court. "If the law recognizes John Doe it will certainly recognize Santa Claus," he declared.

Ferencz wasn't sure what to make of this flamboyant figure at first. He was annoyed by the fact that Musmanno kept overruling his objections to the defense's presentation of evidence that he characterized as "remote hearsay, obviously falsified documents, or biased witnesses that should have been excluded." The judge then told Ferencz and his team outright what they had suspected: he was going to keep accepting anything the defense submitted "up to and including the sex life of a penguin." This gave birth to the term "the Penguin Rule."

But Ferencz also noted that Musmanno was fascinated by the testimony of defendants like Otto Ohlendorf, the father of five who had studied both law and economics, boasted a doctorate in jurisprudence, and had commanded Einsatzgruppe D, probably the most notorious killing squad. The young prosecutor had included Ohlendorf precisely because he was one of the best-educated mass murderers in history.

Turning to address Ohlendorf directly, Musmanno chose his words carefully. "The soldier who goes into battle knows that he must kill, but he understands that it is a question of battle with an equally armed enemy. But you were going out to shoot down defenseless people. Now, didn't the question of the morality of that order enter your mind? Let us suppose that the order had been—and I don't mean any offense in this question—suppose the order had been that you kill your sister. Would you not have instinctively morally appraised that order as to whether it was right or wrong—morally, not politically or militarily—but as a matter of humanity, conscience, and justice?"

Ohlendorf looked shaken; he opened and clenched his fist and his eyes shot around the courtroom. As Musmanno recalled later, "He was aware that a man who would kill his own sister made of himself something less than human." All he could do was to try to avoid answering the question. "I am not in a position, your Honor, to isolate this occurrence from the others," he replied.

But to the prosecution, Ohlendorf not only still insisted that he had no right to question his orders but tried to portray the executions he conducted as self-defense, since, as Ferencz summed up his argument later, "Germany was threatened by Communism, Jews were known to be bearers of Bolshevism, and Gypsies could not be trusted."

Such reasoning certainly did little to help Ohlendorf's case—or those of other defendants. All the more so because they had been in a position to know better, something that was not lost on Musmanno. "It is to be doubted that one could find at a casual reading table in a public library as many educated persons as were gathered in the defendants' dock of the Einsatzgruppen trial in Nuremberg," he wrote later.

General Taylor, who stepped in to make the closing statement for the prosecution, emphasized that the defendants were the leaders of "the trigger men in this gigantic program of slaughter," and that the record clearly demonstrated "the crimes of genocide and the other war crimes and crimes against humanity charged in the indictment." Significantly, it was now not just Ferencz but also Taylor, who was overseeing all the subsequent Nuremberg trials, employing the new term of genocide, coined by Lemkin.

As a judge back in Pennsylvannia, Musmanno had never sentenced anyone to death. A devout Catholic, he was troubled enough about the prospect of handing down such verdicts to retreat to a nearby monastery for several days. Ferencz had not explicitly asked for death sentences; as he explained later, he was not against the death penalty but "I could never figure out a sentence that would fit the crime."

When the judge emerged to pronounce judgment, Ferencz was startled by what he heard. "Musmanno was much more severe than what I expected," the prosecutor recalled. "Each time he said 'Death by hanging' it was like a hammer blow that shocked my brain." The judge issued thirteen such verdicts, and sentenced the remaining defendants to prison terms ranging from ten years to life.

Ferencz finally understood why Musmanno had insisted on "the Penguin Rule." He had wanted "to give the accused every possible right," as Ferencz put it. "He was confident that he would not be deceived by spurious submissions, and that in the end, the court would have the last word." When it did so, "I suddenly developed a much greater respect and affection for Judge Michael Musmanno," he concluded.

Much later, as happened with the Dachau verdicts, the charges would be reviewed and the sentences reduced in several cases. Looking back as a ninety-three-year-old, Ferencz offered the final figures: "I had three thousand Einsatzgruppen members who every day went out and shot as many Jews as they could and Gypsies as well. I tried twenty-two, I convicted twenty-two, thirteen were sentenced to death, four of them were actually executed, the rest of them got out after a few years." Then, he added somberly: "The other three thousand—nothing ever happened to them. Every day they had committed mass murder."

While Ferencz was proud of his record, he was also frustrated by some of his experiences in Nuremberg—particularly the attitudes of the accused and their accomplices. He avoided talking to any of the men he prosecuted outside of the courtroom, except in a single case—that of Ohlendorf. Ferencz exchanged a few words with him after he was sentenced to death. "The Jews in America will suffer for this," the condemned man, who would be among the four who were hanged, told him. Ferencz added: "He died convinced that he was right and I was wrong."

Few Germans expressed themselves quite so bluntly to the victors, but contrition was extremely rare. "I never had a German come up to me and say I'm sorry all the time I was in Germany," Ferencz pointed out. "That was my biggest disappointment: nobody, including my mass murderers, ever said I'm sorry. That was the mentality."

"Where is justice?" he continued. "It was only symbolic, it's only a beginning, that's all you can do."

Corporal Harold Burson, the twenty-four-year-old combat engineer who covered the International Military Tribunal's proceedings in Nuremberg against the top Nazi leaders for the Armed Forces Network, was exasperated by the constant claims of Germans he met that they had neither supported the Nazis nor knew what they had done. "You never knew anybody who was a Nazi or who knew what the concentration camps were," he sardonically recalled. Or, as Richard Sonnenfeldt, a German Jew who had escaped his homeland, served in the U.S. Army, and then took the job of chief interpreter at Nuremberg, put it: "In postwar Germany, it was interesting how so many Nazis had disappeared along with the Jews!"

Such efforts by Germans trying to justify themselves to the victors were so widespread that the playwright and screenwriter Abby Mann ridiculed them when he wrote his play *Judgment at Nuremberg*. "There are no Nazis in Germany," his fictional American prosecutor vents privately to the judge before the trial begins. "Didn't you know that, Judge? The Eskimos invaded Germany and took over. That's how all those terrible things happened. It wasn't the fault of the Germans. It was those damn Eskimos!"

Burson was convinced the Nuremberg trials were critically important precisely because the German people needed to see the record of the Third Reich illustrated in all of its gruesome details. "I felt they had to have this indelibly imposed on them so that they would never forget it," he said. The key players in the trial saw their task even more broadly. In his opening speech at the International Military Tribunal, Sir Hartley Shawcross, the British chief prosecutor, vowed that the proceedings "will provide a contemporary touchstone and an authoritative and impartial record to which future historians may turn for truth and future politicians for warning."

Burson's daily radio scripts reflected his sense of awe that he was witnessing such an epochal event. "The spectators in the court knew today that they were conscious participants in the shaping of modern history," he wrote at the start of the proceedings. The judges from the four victorious powers—the United States, Britain, France, and the Soviet Union—"filed in to begin the world's first attempt to establish international law as an actual law among nations."

Among his fellow GIs at Nuremberg, Burson regularly encountered mutterings that there was no need for trials since summary executions of the top Nazis would have been quicker and easier. In his scripts, Burson countered that view, quoting the reasoning of Supreme Court Justice Robert H. Jackson, the chief U.S. prosecutor in that lead trial: "We must never forget that the record on which we judge these defendants today is the record on which history will judge us tomorrow." Or, as Burson put it in his script: "We do not desire to employ the Nazi way . . . 'to take 'em out and shoot 'em' . . . for our system is not lynch law. We will dispense punishment as the evidence demands."

Looking back nearly seven decades later, Burson—who would go on to become the cofounder of the giant global public relations firm Burson-Marsteller—admitted: "In my scripts there's a tinge of naïveté that I might not have brought to it today," especially when it came to his faith that the newly formed United Nations would prevent such crimes in the future. But he remained convinced that Jackson, who shaped so much of the Nuremberg strategy, was sincere in his determination "to give them as fair a trial as could be done where the winner tries the loser"—and to set new international standards of justice.

Among more seasoned reporters, including notables like William Shirer, Walter Lippmann, and John Dos Passos, there was initially considerable skepticism—"that this is a show, that it's not going to last very long, most of them will get hung anyway," as Burson put it. And back in the United States, the courtroom dramas sparked not just skepticism but often outright opposition, flowing from both sides of the political divide.

Milton Mayer wrote in his column for *The Progressive* that "vengeance will not raise the tortured dead," and that the evidence from the liberated concentration camps "would not under ordinary American judicial practice be held sufficient for conviction in a capital crime." In *The Nation*, critic James Agee even suggested that the film clips from Dachau's liberation were propagandistic exaggerations. Speaking after the International Military Tribunal announced its verdicts but before the hangings, Republican Senator Robert A. Taft declared: "About this whole judgment there is the spirit of vengeance, and vengeance is seldom justice." The hangings of the eleven condemned men, he added, "will be a blot on the American record which we shall long regret." (As noted earlier, ten were hanged in the end because Göring committed suicide.)

Even some of those who saw the trials as an important first step toward establishing new international norms of justice admitted to doubts about their value. "Punishing the German war criminals created the feeling that in international life as well as in civil society, crime should not be allowed to pay," Raphael Lemkin, the Polish lawyer who had coined the word "genocide," declared. "But the purely juridical consequences of the trials were wholly insufficient." His persistent lobbying efforts would result in the U.N. General Assembly's adoption of the Convention on the Prevention and Punishment of the Crime of Genocide in 1948.

Many members of the legal teams in Nuremberg had found little time to ponder the deeper significance of the trials. "The historical value of the Nuremberg trials was hardly perceived by those who were involved in the process," Ferencz maintained. "Many of us were very young, enjoying the euphoria of victory, and the excitement of new adventures." Even during the trials, there could be festive touches nearby. Herman Obermayer, the Frankfurt-based young Jewish GI who had worked earlier with hangman John Woods, visited the main trial for a day, observing Göring and the other defendants. That same evening he watched a performance of the Radio City Rockettes, who were there to entertain the troops.

Yet for those involved in the proceedings for any length of time, it was hard to miss the significance and symbolism, even if the long-range implications were far from clear. Gerald Schwab, who along with the rest of his Jewish family had fled Germany and moved to the United States in 1940, had donned a U.S. Army uniform and served as a machine gunner in the Italian campaign before his superiors assigned him as an interpreter for captured Germans. As soon as he was discharged, he signed up for a similar civilian job in Nuremberg. "I thought it was wonderful: you realized you were participating in historical events," he recalled.

Schwab did not usually reveal anything about his German Jewish background to the defendants, feeling that they had enough to contemplate already. But when he found himself in the same room as Field

Marshal Albert Kesselring, who was waiting to testify, the veteran commander asked him where he had learned his German. Schwab explained his origins and his family's last-minute escape. "This must be a great satisfaction for you to be here," Kesselring noted. Schwab replied: "You're right, Field Marshal."

Among Germans the most common complaint was that the trials were no more than victors' justice. "No, they were not," Ferencz emphatically shot back. "If we wanted victors' justice, we would have gone out and murdered about half a million Germans." Revenge was not the motive, he continued; instead, the object was "to show how horrible it was, in order to deter others from doing the same."

In his opening statement to the International Military Tribunal, Justice Jackson had pointed out the real accomplishment of the trials: "That four great nations, flushed with victory and stung with injury, stay the hands of vengeance and voluntarily submit their captive enemies to the judgment of the law is one of the most significant tributes that Power has paid to Reason." Given the scale of the vengeance inflicted before the trials, particularly by the Red Army, Jackson's declaration could be dismissed as overly self-congratulatory. But that would be a mistake. It was precisely because "the hands of vengeance" were so powerful, and could have become even more deadly, that Jackson was largely right.

So, too, were other members of the legal teams who argued that the trials, however imperfect, were both necessary and successful. "Never have the archives of a belligerent nation been so completely exposed as were those of Nazi Germany at the Nuremberg trial," wrote Whitney R. Harris, who led the case against Ernst Kaltenbrunner, the highest level Nazi security official in the dock. "The result is a documentation unprecedented in history as to any major war." According to General Lucius D. Clay, the military governor of Germany in the immediate aftermath of its defeat, "The trials completed the destruction of Nazism in Germany."

In the ensuing decades, Ferencz came to believe that the trials, no matter how symbolic in terms of punishing only a fraction of those responsible for the Third Reich's crimes, contributed to "a gradual awakening of the human conscience." Perhaps. But there was an even more compelling argument for holding the trials, which was implicit in the actions of all those committed to making them work. It was spelled out by Robert Kempner, a German Jewish lawyer who had escaped to the United States and then returned as part of Jackson's prosecution team. "Without them all these people would have died for no reason and no one was responsible and it will happen again," he noted.

In fact, the Dachau and Nuremberg trials were far from the concluding chapter in the efforts to bring Nazis to justice. It would prove necessary to track down and prosecute—or, at least, expose—other Nazis for years and decades to come. And to continue educating a public, both in Germany and elsewhere, that was increasingly eager to turn its attention elsewhere.

And the trials had far from answered all the questions that the Nazi era had raised. Most significantly, the biggest questions of all were still left dangling. Judge Musmanno summed up what they were in his reflections on his Nuremberg experience:

"The great problem which I personally faced in the Einsatzgruppen trial was not in reaching a decision on the guilt or innocence of the defendants. That question began to resolve itself as the trial neared its end. What troubled me as a human being was the question as to how and why such well-schooled men should have strayed so far and so completely from the teaching of their childhood which embraced reverence for the biblical virtues of honesty, charity, and cleanliness of spirit. Did they completely forget those teachings? Were they no longer aware of moral values?"

Those were questions that would be asked again and again.

CHAPTER FIVE

My Brother's Keeper

"A German will think he has died a good German if he waits at a curb at a red light, and then crosses on a green one though he knows perfectly well that a truck, against the law that it may be, is bearing down upon him to crush him to death."

American journalist William Shirer, quoting a German
woman exasperated by her countrymen's willingness to
follow Hitler, in a diary entry on January 25, 1940

Many of those who initially saw it as their mission to bring Nazis to justice were not Jewish—most prominently, Nuremberg chief prosecutors Robert H. Jackson and Telford Taylor, Judge Michael Musmanno in the Einsatzgruppen case, and Dachau chief prosecutor William Denson. It was not surprising, though, that other members of the legal teams in both Nuremberg and Dachau, like Benjamin Ferencz, were Jewish, or that Holocaust survivors like Simon Wiesenthal and Tuvia Friedman were eager to help the victors in any way they could in rounding up the perpetrators and developing the cases against them. Their motives hardly required any explanation.

But Jan Sehn was in a different category altogether, about as original a Nazi hunter as could be imagined. He was someone who, to this day, is largely unknown to the outside world and even to his fellow Polish countrymen. In the Institute for National Remembrance in Warsaw and the Holocaust Museum Archives in Washington, there are countless testimonies from concentration camps survivors that are signed by him as the investigating judge. He also wrote the first detailed account of the history, organization, medical experiments, and gas chambers of Auschwitz, the camp whose name has become synonymous with the Holocaust.

Sehn orchestrated the trial of Rudolf Höss (not be confused with Hitler aide Rudolf Hess, who was given a life sentence in Nuremberg), the camp's commandant, who mounted the scaffold on the "death block" of Auschwitz on April 16, 1947. He was deliberately hanged in the exact place where so many of his victims had died earlier. Most significantly, Sehn coaxed Höss into writing his personal story before his execution, producing a volume that to this day provides what is arguably the most chilling glimpse into the mind of a mass murderer in human history. Yet that memoir, too, is often overlooked in the flood of volumes about the crimes of the Third Reich, its impact mostly forgotten.

Perhaps the reason Sehn and his legacy have received so little attention is the fact that he did not record anything personal: no diary, memoirs, or even articles that offered a self-portrait of any sort. His writings were strictly reports and transcripts based on the testimony and other evidence that he gathered as a member of the High Commission for the Investigation of Hitlerite Crimes in Poland, the Polish Military Commission Investigating German War Crimes—and, of course, as the investigating judge in the Höss trial and subsequent trial of other Auschwitz personnel, including SS officers. He also handled the case against Amon Göth, the sadistic commandant of the Płaszów concentration camp in Kraków who was featured in Steven Spielberg's film *Schindler's List.* Perhaps if Sehn had not died in 1965 at the age of fifty-six, he would have told more of his story.

But perhaps not. There was a strong reason why Sehn kept the focus on his work rather than on his personal journey. He was convinced he had something to hide, and he hid it from even his closest colleagues until the end of his life.

It was no secret that the Sehn family was of German descent, although its exact origins remain obscure. In a region of constantly shifting borders and empires, there was nothing unusual about that. When Jan Sehn was born in 1909 in Tuszów, a Galician village that is now in southeastern Poland but then was part of the Austro-Hungarian Empire, the household languages were both German and Polish. Arthur Sehn, a grandnephew of Jan who was born half a century later and has tried to track down the family history, believes the Sehns are descendants of German settlers who were wooed to Galicia in the late eighteenth century by Holy Roman Emperor Joseph II, the ruler over the Hapsburg territory that absorbed much of southern Poland. The successive partitions of Poland by Russia, Prussia, and Austria-Hungary wiped the country off the map for more than a century.

After World War I, Poland reemerged as an independent state. Most of the Sehn family remained in the southeastern rural region, continuing to make a decent living out of farming. But Jan left for Kraków to study law at the Jagiellonian University from 1929 to 1933, which launched him on his legal career. In 1937, he started working in the investigation branch of the Kraków court. As former colleagues recalled, he immediately demonstrated his "passion for criminal science." But the German invasion of Poland that marked the outbreak of World War II two years later meant that he had to put everything on hold.

Sehn stayed in Kraków during the war and found a job working as the "secretary" of an association of restaurants. There is no evidence he was involved with the underground Polish resistance movements or collaborated in any way with the German authorities; he was simply trying to survive the six long years of German occupation. But the other members of his family, who had continued to farm in southeastern Poland, had a very different experience.

Living in a village called Bobrowa, also in southeastern Poland, Jan's brother Józef made a fateful decision early during the occupation. One of the first actions of the German overlords was to encourage *Volksdeutsche*—Poles of German descent—to register as ethnic Germans. His grandson Arthur, the family historian, discovered the records that show that Józef promptly registered his whole family: his wife, three sons, and father. By siding with the victors, Józef almost certainly calculated that he was opting to protect himself and his family. Soon, as a *Volksdeutsche*, he was appointed mayor of his village.

When it was evident that Germany was losing the war and its army was in retreat, Józef vanished from the village. Even his three sons did not know what happened to him then. "The children were not allowed to know," recalls one of them, who is also named Józef. Two of the boys were sent to Kraków, staying with their uncle Jan and his wife for several months. Their father, as they would only learn years later, had fled to northwestern Poland, changed his name, and worked as a forester in an isolated community—"as far from civilization as possible," as Arthur Sehn puts it—until his death in 1958. He was even buried under his assumed name. For the rest of his life, he had feared that Poland's new rulers would punish him as a collaborator.

Although Józef and Jan Sehn had taken different paths in life at an early age, Jan clearly knew about his brother's role during the occupation. His willingness to take in two of his sons near the end of the war indicated as much. They also had a sister who appears to have had indirect contacts with her fugitive brother, and she probably kept Jan updated about him.

Jan and his wife were childless, but that didn't make them easy surrogate parents. "He was very stern," his nephew Józef recalls. When Jan was informed by his wife about some alleged misbehavior, he didn't hesitate to administer old-fashioned punishment—with his belt. But he also helped his nephew get a temporary job in one of Kraków's restaurants and provided him shelter when he and his brother needed it most.

Even before the war was completely over, Jan began his quest for incriminating evidence against the Germans. Maria Kozłowska, a younger neighbor of his in Kraków who later worked at the Institute of Forensic Research, which he headed from 1949 until his death, recalls that in Wrocław—or Breslau, as the city was called before it was incorporated into Poland— "he looked for documents among the smoldering ruins. He traveled all over Poland looking for evidence."

Kozłowska and others who later worked with Sehn always assumed that it was his passion for law and justice that spurred him to gather the evidence of Nazi crimes with such determination and persistence, constructing the cases that would send many of the perpetrators to the gallows. He was fully dedicated to helping the new Poland recover from the devastation of the occupation and the loss of roughly six million people, representing a staggering 18 percent of its prewar population; of those who perished, about three million were Polish Jews, nearly 90 percent of the total of that group.

All of those were good reasons why he was so dedicated to his mission, but not the full explanation. While Sehn's colleagues knew that his family had distant German roots—the last name itself was a clear indication of that—they had no reason to consider this to be a motivating factor. The ancestry of many Poles was similarly mixed, which made his family situation look like nothing unusual—so long as the recent family history went unnoticed. Kozłowska knew he had a sister in Wrocław, but didn't know anything about the brother who had disappeared. She certainly did not know about his personal odyssey during the occupation and after Germany's defeat.

That was no accident. Arthur, the family historian, is reluctant to make any definitive statement about his great-uncle's motives, but he suspects that the secret he kept about his brother's side of the family—which surely would have been known to the new communist rulers of Poland—was also a factor in his passionate quest for justice. "Maybe he was extra eager to be on the right side and point the finger," he says. "It might be perceived as somewhat opportunistic, but maybe his motives were clear and pure."

Whatever his motives, Jan Sehn soon produced dramatic results.

Rudolf Höss served as the commandant of Auschwitz from the time he oversaw its creation in 1940 until late 1943. A former army barracks located near the town of Oświęcim, or Auschwitz in German, the main camp received its first transport of 728 Poles in June 1940. These were

Polish political prisoners, usually affiliated with resistance movements. In most cases, they were Catholics, since the deportation of Jews had not yet begun.

As former political prisoner Zygmunt Gaudasiński pointed out, "The camp was created to destroy the most valuable part of Polish society, and the Germans partly succeeded in this." Some prisoners, like Gaudasiński's father, were shot; torture was commonplace, and the early mortality rate was very high. For the early prisoners who did not quickly perish, their chances for survival began to improve once they latched on to jobs—in the kitchens, warehouses, and other places—that offered them shelter on a daily basis. Of the 150,000 Polish political prisoners who were sent to Auschwitz, about 75,000 died there.

After Germany invaded the Soviet Union in June 1941, Soviet POWs were dispatched to Auschwitz. SS chief Heinrich Himmler envisaged the influx of a huge number of POWs and drew up plans for the camp's expansion by building a second large complex at Birkenau, two miles away. The first POWs were put to work constructing the new facilities in conditions that horrified even the hardened Polish political prisoners. "They were treated worse than any other prisoners," said Mieczysław Zawadzki, who served as a nurse in a sick bay for POWs. Fed only turnips and tiny rations of bread, they collapsed from hunger, exposure, and beatings. "The hunger was so bad that they cut off the buttocks from the corpses in the morgue and ate the flesh," Zawadzki recalled. "Later, we locked the morgue so they couldn't get in."

With most Soviet POWs dying quickly and no subsequent influx, Himmler instructed Höss to prepare the camp to play a major role in the Final Solution for European Jews. Coordinated by Adolf Eichmann, transports of Jews from all over Europe transformed Auschwitz-Birkenau into the most international of the camps. And while it continued to be both a complex of labor camps and a death camp, it soon became the largest single death factory of the Holocaust, with Birkenau's gas chambers and crematoriums working to full capacity. More than one million victims, about 90 percent of whom were Jews, perished there.

In late 1943, Höss was reassigned to the Concentration Camp Inspectorate, which meant stepping down as commandant of Auschwitz. But soon he was sent back to Auschwitz to prepare for the arrival of more than 400,000 Hungarian Jews in the summer of 1944. He was so successful in carrying out this operation against the largest national group of Jews dispatched to Auschwitz (most Polish Jews had been killed in other death camps before Auschwitz-Birkenau became fully operational) that his superiors and colleagues dubbed the operation *Aktion Höss.*

In April 1945 when the Red Army fought its way into Berlin and Hitler committed suicide, Höss would write later, he and his wife, Hedwig, thought about following in their leader's footsteps. "With the Führer gone, our world had gone," he lamented. "Was there any point in going on living?" He had obtained poison, but then claimed that they decided against this course for the sake of their five children. Instead, they traveled to northern Germany, separating there to avoid detection. Taking the name and papers of Franz Lang, a junior seaman who had died, Höss reported to the Naval Intelligence School on the island of Sylt.

When British forces captured the school, they moved the staff to an improvised camp north of Hamburg. As they singled out the senior officers who were then dispatched to prison, the victors paid little attention to the man they believed was Franz Lang. Höss was soon released, and started working on a farm in the village of Gottrupel near the Danish border. For eight months he lived in a barn there, working diligently and arousing no suspicion among the locals. Since Hedwig and the children were living in St. Michaelisdonn, about seventy miles away, he was able to maintain sporadic indirect contact with them.

That proved to be Höss's undoing. In March 1946, Lieutenant Hanns Alexander, a German Jew who escaped to London before the war and then served in the British Army as a war crimes investigator, had picked up the family's trail and was convinced that they knew where the former commandant was hiding. Local British forces had been monitoring the family already, and they had seen a letter from Höss to his wife, prompting them to bring her to a local prison. Alexander grilled Hedwig about her husband, but she refused to tell him anything. Keeping the mother in custody, he went to see the children. They, too, refused to say where their father was hiding, even when the frustrated Alexander threatened to kill their mother if one of them didn't volunteer the information.

Alexander had enlisted in the British Army as soon as the war broke out, eager to help in the fight against the country of his birth. As a Nazi hunter representing his new country after the fighting was over, he was not about to give up so easily. He decided to take Klaus, the twelve-year-old son, who was the most visibly shaken by Alexander's threats, back to the same prison where his mother was being held, keeping them in separate cells.

At first, Hedwig remained defiant, claiming that her husband had died. But Alexander played a final card to break her. As a train was driven near the prison so that she would clearly hear it, he told her that Klaus was about to be loaded aboard and sent to Siberia—and she would never see him again. Within a few minutes, Hedwig gave up her husband's location and the name he was using. Alexander then led the raiding party that captured him in the barn late in the evening of March 11. If there were any doubts about Höss's true identity, his wedding ring banished them. After Alexander threatened to cut off his finger if he did not give up the ring, the former commandant handed it over. The inscription read "Rudolf" and "Hedwig."

Alexander, like so many of the early Nazi hunters, wasn't quite ready to let the system of military justice take over. He deliberately stepped away from his men, telling them that he would be back in ten minutes and needed Höss in the car "undamaged" at that point. The soldiers knew they had the green light for some payback, which they quickly delivered, pummeling him with ax handles. By the time it was over, Höss was stripped of his pajamas and beaten. Wrapped in a blanket without any shoes or socks, he was loaded into a truck and transported back to town. There, he was made to wait while Alexander and his men celebrated their success in a bar. As a final indignity, Alexander took off Höss's blanket and ordered him to walk naked across the square, which was still covered with snow, to the prison.

After his initial interrogations by the British, the Allies decided that Höss should be sent south to Nuremberg, where the main trial had been under way for four months. Leon Goldensohn, a U.S. Army psychiatrist who was among those who was allowed to question the new arrival in early April, was struck by what he saw when he entered his isolation cell. "He sat with both feet in a tub of cold water, his hands clasped in his lap, rubbing them together," he noted. "He said he had frostbite for two weeks and that soaking his feet in the cold water relieved the aching."

This somewhat pathetic forty-six-year-old man was suddenly finding himself much in demand as the trial of the more senior Nazi officials continued. Even in a facility that now housed some of the greatest criminals of all time, the former commandant of Auschwitz attracted special attention, particularly among those charged with examining the mental state of Hitler's executioners.

Whitney Harris, a member of the American prosecution team, elicited Höss's confession without any difficulty. According to Harris, Höss was "quiet, unprepossessing and fully co-operative." Right at the start of that confession, he dropped a bombshell, estimating "that at least 2,500,000 victims were executed and exterminated there [at Auschwitz] by gassing, and burning, and at least another half million succumbed to starvation and disease, making a total dead of about 3,000,000."

Höss later told Goldensohn that Eichmann had reported those figures to Himmler, but they could be "too high." In fact, those numbers would prove to be inflated, although of course the real totals of Auschwitz's victims—now generally believed to be between 1.1 million and 1.3 million—were horrific enough. In any case, when Höss testified before the International Military Tribunal, repeating the numbers he had provided in his confession to Harris, he stunned everyone in attendance, even the top Nazis in the dock. Hans Frank, Hitler's former governor general of occupied Poland, told the American psychiatrist G.M. Gilbert: "That was the low point of the entire trial—to hear a man say out of his own mouth that he had exterminated 2½ million in cold blood. That is something that people will talk about for a thousand years."

But it was the way Höss spoke—describing how he methodically carried out his orders to expand Auschwitz into a highly efficient extermination camp—that also chilled his listeners. There was no doubt that he knew what those orders meant. In his confession, he declared: "The 'final solution' of the Jewish question meant the complete extermination of all Jews in Europe."

He recounted how he tested the newly constructed gas chambers: "It took from three to fifteen minutes to kill the people in the death chamber depending on climatic conditions. We knew when the people were dead because their screaming stopped." And he talked with apparent pride about the "improvements" he oversaw at Auschwitz, the four gas chambers that could hold two thousand people each, as opposed to the earlier gas chambers at Treblinka that could only hold two hundred people at a time.

"Another improvement" over Treblinka, where most victims knew what awaited them, he noted, was the lengths to which "at Auschwitz we endeavored to fool the victims into thinking that they were to go through a delousing process." But he admitted that there was only so much they could do to prevent word from getting out about the purpose of the camp, pointing out that "the foul and nauseating stench from the continuous burning of bodies permeated the entire area and all of the people living in the surrounding communities knew that exterminations were going on at Auschwitz."

Höss was not facing legal judgment in Nuremberg, since the Americans had decided to bring him in as a witness rather than a defendant at that late date, thinking he would help provide evidence against the top Nazis. In what General Taylor, the chief prosecutor, called "an extraordinary decision," the defense lawyer for Ernst Kaltenbrunner, the chief of the Reich Security Main Office, decided to put Höss on the stand to testify for his client. The lawyer wanted him to confirm that Kaltenbrunner, despite having overall responsibility for the entire apparatus of terror and mass murder, had never visited Auschwitz. Höss obliged on that score and some other seemingly minor particulars. But the overall impact of his testimony only helped seal the fate of Kaltenbrunner and the others who received death sentences.

Whitney Harris concluded that, because of his role at Auschwitz,

Höss became "the greatest killer of history." He also appeared to have experienced no emotion as he took on his assignments. "Devoid of moral principle, he reacted to the order to slaughter human beings as he would have to an order to fell trees," Harris added.

The two U.S. Army psychiatrists, who talked separately with Höss in Nuremberg trying to figure out his personality, came to similar conclusions. In their first session, G. M. Gilbert was immediately struck by his "quiet, apathetic, matter-of-fact tone of voice." When the psychiatrist tried to press him about how it was possible to kill so many people, the former commandant responded in purely technical terms: "That wasn't so hard—it would not have been hard to exterminate even greater numbers." He then went on to explain the math of killing ten thousand people a day. "The killing itself took the least time," he added. "You could dispose of 2,000 head in a half hour, but it was the burning that took all the time."

Gilbert tried again to press him on the larger question of why he didn't express any reservations or feel any qualms when Himmler informed him that Hitler had ordered the Final Solution. "I had nothing to say; I could only say '*Jawohl*,'" he responded. Couldn't he have refused the order? "No, from our entire training the thought of refusing an order just didn't enter one's head," Höss continued. He claimed anyone who did so would have been hanged. It also didn't occur to him that he could be held responsible for the consequences of what he was doing. "You see, in Germany it was understood that if something went wrong, then the man who gave the orders was responsible." Gilbert tried again by asking about the human element. Höss cut him off: "That didn't enter into it."

To Leon Goldensohn, he offered a similar explanation, although its wording was even more striking: "I thought I was doing the right thing. I was obeying orders, and now, of course, I see that it was unnecessary and wrong. But I don't know what you mean by being upset about these things because I didn't personally murder anybody. *I was just the director of the extermination program in Auschwitz* [my italics]. It was Hitler who ordered it through Himmler and it was Eichmann who gave me the order regarding the transports."

Höss signaled his understanding that the psychiatrists were trying to categorize him. "I suppose you want to know in this way if my thoughts and habits are normal," he told Gilbert on another occasion. He then provided his own answer: "I am entirely normal. Even while I was doing this extermination work, I led a normal family life, and so on."

Their conversations took on an increasingly surreal character. When Gilbert asked him about his sex life with his wife, he responded: "Well, it was normal—but after my wife found out about what I was doing, we rarely had desire for intercourse."

The notion that perhaps he was doing something wrong only occurred to him, he told Gilbert, after Germany's defeat. "But nobody had ever said these things before; at least we never heard of it." The next step in Höss's journey would be back to Poland; the Americans had decided to fly him to Warsaw and hand him over to the authorities there for trial. The former commandant recognized that this would be his final journey, but nothing appeared to shake his lethargic demeanor.

Gilbert's conclusion at the end of his sessions with the prisoner: "There is too much apathy to leave any suggestion of remorse and even the prospect of hanging does not unduly distress him. One gets the general impression of a man who is intellectually normal but with the schizoid apathy, insensitivity and lack of empathy that could be hardly more extreme in a frank psychotic."

Jan Sehn, who had helped prepare some of the testimonies of Auschwitz survivors that were used by the prosecution team in Nuremberg, had also continued to lay the groundwork for the trial of Höss and other Auschwitz personnel in Poland. By the time he was able to interrogate the former commandant at length in Kraków, he had accumulated a wealth of damning testimony. But he was more eager than ever to elicit everything he could from the country's most famous prisoner.

Sehn was a stern taskmaster, as his nephews and co-workers quickly discovered. Later in his career when he served as the head of the Institute of Forensic Research, situated in an elegant nineteenth-century villa that he had procured for it, he was a stickler for details. He checked that his employees arrived promptly at eight in the morning, and reprimanded anyone who failed to do so. But he also was quick to help any staffer in need. Zofia Chłobowska recalled arriving late one morning because her son had been hospitalized. When she explained what had happened, Sehn insisted that she use the institute's car and driver every morning to visit her son as long as he was being treated.

The dapper, handsome jurist, who also taught law at the Jagiellonian University, was usually referred to as "the professor" by his staff. But if that signaled respect tinged with a bit of distance, he easily mingled with both the Kraków elite and his subordinates. A chain-smoker, he was almost always holding a lit cigarette in a jade or wooden holder as he received visitors, and often reached into his office closet for a choice bottle of vodka to treat them with a shot. When employees like the institute's pharmacologist Maria Paszkowska pulled out a bottle of homebrew, he happily participated in the office tastings. Much of the homebrew was produced right in the institute, using strawberries, cherries, plums, or whatever else was in season.

When Sehn began his interrogations of Höss in November 1946, he treated him with unfailing courtesy. His goal was to gather every possible bit of information about Auschwitz's operations—and about Höss's personal history. Like the American psychiatrists, he wanted to understand the personality of the man who had been responsible for the biggest killing factory in history. He had the former commandant brought from prison to his office in the mornings, and the interrogations would end by noon.

Sehn reported with satisfaction that Höss "testified willingly and provided exhaustive answers to all the questions of the investigator." If Höss had any doubts about agreeing to Sehn's request that he also start writing down everything he could remember, they quickly evaporated. Guided by the judge's questions, he wrote extensively in the afternoons, often after a lunch provided by Sehn at his own expense. When there were breaks of a few days between their sessions, Sehn reported, "he wrote also of his own initiative when he noticed that something touched on at the margin of the interrogation was of interest to the interrogator."

As his rendezvous with the hangman neared, Höss asked Sehn to deliver his wedding ring—the same ring that had betrayed his identity to the British search party at the end of the war—to his wife after his death; his interrogator agreed. "I must admit that I had never expected such decent and considerate treatment as I received in Polish custody," the former commandant declared. He also more than welcomed the writing assignments Sehn gave him. "Such employment spared me hours of useless and enervating self-pity," he wrote. He saw the writing as "absorbing and satisfying," producing every evening "the satisfactory feeling that not only had I put another day behind me, but also I had done a useful job of work."

That "useful job of work" would eventually form the basis of Höss's autobiography, which was first published in Polish in 1951, four years after he was hanged.

"In the following pages I want to try and tell the story of my inner-most being," Höss wrote at the start of his memoirs, which would later be published in German, English, and other languages. He described a lonely childhood on the outskirts of Baden-Baden among isolated farmhouses near the woods. "My sole confidant was my pony, and I was certain he understood me," he recalled. He had no desire to spend time with his sisters, and, while he claimed that his parents treated each other with "loving respect," they never displayed any signs of affection.

He was forbidden to go into the woods alone, he wrote, "since when I was younger some travelling gypsies had found me playing by myself and had taken me away with them." According to his account, a peasant who knew the family encountered the Gypsies on the road and, recognizing the boy, delivered him back to his home.

It doesn't take a psychologist to recognize that this bit of family lore, whether true or not, inculcated the notion that there were dangerous strangers out there with evil intentions. The other part of his upbringing involved his father's plans for him to become a priest. A devout Catholic and a former soldier in German East Africa, the father was a salesman who was frequently away from home, but later the family moved to Mannheim and he traveled much less. Spending more time with his son, he insisted on a strong religious upbringing and told him about the good work of missionaries in Africa. That produced the desired effect upon the boy. "I was determined that I myself should one day be a missionary in the gloomy jungles of darkest Africa," he recalled. "I was taught that my highest duty was to help those in need."

Then there was the predictable moment of disillusionment with religion, which Höss recounts as if it can explain his whole subsequent path in life. When he was thirteen, he "unintentionally" threw one of his classmates down the stairs of his school, and the boy broke his ankle in the fall. Höss rationalized that hundreds of pupils must have fallen down those steps before, and it was only his bad luck that his classmate was hurt. Besides, he immediately went to confession and "made a clean breast of the incident." The confessor was a friend of his father, and told him about his son's misdeed when he was a guest at his house that same evening. The next day Höss's father punished him for not telling him what he had done.

The younger Höss was shocked by his confessor's "undreamed of betrayal," pointing out that it is a basic tenet of Catholicism that priests are never supposed to reveal what they are told in the confessional. "My faith in the sacred priesthood had been destroyed," he wrote. His father died a year later, and when World War I broke out he longed to join in the fighting despite his young age. He enlisted secretly at age sixteen, and was soon deployed to Turkey and then Iraq. In his first battle with British and Indian troops, he admitted that he was "seized with a terror" as he saw his fellow soldiers cut down by bullets, and he could not do anything. But as the Indian soldiers moved closer, he overcame his fear and shot one of them. "My first dead man!" he wrote, with the exclamation mark signaling his pride. He noted that he never felt the same degree of fear in the face of death again.

If this were not the story of a future mass murderer, there would be nothing all that remarkable about it. Which is precisely the point. Höss presents himself as an ordinary teenager who had to grow up fast because he was plunged into a war where he was wounded twice. His wounds also put him in a situation where he would have to let down his guard, overcoming his instinct since early childhood to shun "all demonstrations of affection." A nurse who was taking care of him had at first made him uneasy with her "tender caresses," but then something changed. "Under her guidance stage by stage until its final consummation," he experienced "a wonderful and undreamed of experience . . . at last I too fell under the magic spell of love."

Höss confessed that he never would have been able "to summon enough courage" to start the affair and that it had a major impact on his thinking. "In all its tenderness and charm, it was to affect me through the rest of my life," he wrote. "I could never again speak flippantly of such matters; sexual intercourse without real affection became unthinkable for me. Thus I was saved from casual flirtations and brothels."

As in so much of Höss's account, he simply ignored anything that contradicted the portrait he was painting of himself. In Auschwitz, he began to pay special attention to an Austrian prisoner, Eleanor Hodys, a non-Jewish seamstress who had been caught forging a Nazi document. When she was working in his villa, he startled her by kissing her on the lips, causing her to lock herself in the bathroom. Soon she was locked up in a cell in the interrogation block. Careful to avoid detection by his own guards, Höss started visiting her in secret; she resisted him again at first, but then gave in. She became pregnant, and was moved to a dark, tiny cell in the basement, where she was kept naked and given minimal food. When she was finally released, she was six months pregnant and, at the commandant's behest, sent to a doctor who performed an abortion.

Not a word about this sordid episode appears in Höss's memoirs, of course. Looking back at his life as he awaited execution, he clung to the notion that his coming-of-age story demonstrated that he was a man of principle—and, yes, a bit of an old-fashioned romantic. He proudly pointed out that he had commanded men in their thirties when he was only eighteen at the end of World War I, and he was awarded the Iron Cross, First Class. "I had reached my manhood, both physically and mentally, long before my years," he proclaimed.

His mother had died while he was fighting, and he promptly quarreled with his remaining relatives, including the uncle who had become his guardian and still wanted him to become a priest. Renouncing whatever inheritance he had from his parents, Höss was "full of rage" when he left his relatives and decided to join one of the Freikorps (Free Corps) units—as the paramilitary bands of former soldiers claiming to defend the defeated country's honor were called—in the Baltic states. "I would battle my way through the world alone," he wrote. His new comrades were, like him, "misfits in civilian life," as he put it. He also joined the Nazi Party in 1922, pointing out that he was "in firm agreement" with its goals.

He was ready to do anything to administer the Freikorps version of justice. "Treachery was punished with death, and there were many traitors to be punished," he noted. Despite the general lawlessness of that period when countless political murders went unpunished, the authorities convicted Höss for his role in one such killing in 1923, sentencing him to ten years hard labor. Höss was unrepentant, "completely convinced that this traitor deserved to be put to death."

He wrote with evident self-pity that "serving a sentence in a Prussian prison in those days was no rest-cure." He complained about the strict rules and punishment for any violation of them. Even after running Auschwitz and serving in other Nazi camps, it never occurred to him that those conditions were infinitely better than anything his prisoners had to endure.

The other notable aspect of his account is his indignation—and sense of moral superiority—when it came to his fellow prisoners. He claimed that he overheard a prisoner describe how he had killed a pregnant woman and servant girl with an axe, and then silenced four screaming children by bashing their heads against the wall. "This appalling crime made me long to fly at his throat," Höss insisted, presenting himself as a humanitarian at heart. As for the general prison population, "their souls lacked ballast," he maintained. He was equally contemptuous of his jailers "whose delight in the power they wielded increased in proportion to the lowness of their mentality."

Still nurturing that combination of self-pity and sense of moral superiority, Höss was released from prison in 1928 as part of a general amnesty. The Nazis would soon capitalize on the economic desperation of most Germans in the aftermath of Wall Street's collapse in 1929. A year after Hitler took power in 1933, Höss joined the SS troops assigned to the newly created Dachau concentration camp for political prisoners and started training other young men for duty there. He had thought about turning to farming earlier, he wrote, but then decided that he wanted to remain in the military. "I gave no thought to the reference to concentration camps," he claimed. "To me it was just a question of being an active soldier again, of resuming my military career . . . the soldier's life held me in thrall."

That SS soldier's life—even in the earliest version of a Nazi concentration camp—included ever-new heights of brutality. There were no battles to fight with armed enemies; instead, the task was to terrorize and, in many cases, kill helpless prisoners. Höss repeatedly insisted in his writings for Sehn that he was more sensitive than other SS guards. When he attended his first flogging of a prisoner, the man's screams made him feel "hot and cold all over." While other SS men viewed such infliction of pain "as an excellent spectacle, a kind of peasant merry-making," he declared: "I was certainly not one of these."

But he also warned of the dangers of "showing too much kindness and goodwill towards the prisoners" who were capable of deviously outsmarting their jailers. By 1938, he was promoted to the job of adjutant at Sachsenhausen, another concentration camp. Soon, he was marching almost every day with his execution squad, giving them the order to fire once the prisoner was positioned by the post, and he would then administer the coup de grâce. He claimed the victims were "saboteurs" or war resisters who were undermining Hitler's efforts. Whether the prisoners were communists, socialists, Jehovah's Witnesses, Jews, or homosexuals, they all were considered internal enemies.

Höss had no problem with that. He claimed he was "not suited for this kind of service," which meant that he had to work doubly hard not "to reveal my weakness." What weakness? "I never grew indifferent to human suffering." But, he insisted, Hitler's early successes demonstrated that "the means and the ends" of the Nazis were right. In late 1939, he was promoted to commandant of Sachsenhausen. The following year, he was given his assignment in Auschwitz.

Jan Sehn argued that his famous prisoner was not completely disingenuous when he wrote about his lack of enthusiasm for carrying out some of his tasks—or at least that he did not share the enthusiasms of his most openly sadistic subordinates. "The ideal commandants of concentration camps in the National Socialist sense were not the personally brutal, licentious and depraved creatures of the SS, but Höss and people like him," he pointed out. In other words, they were technocrats fueled by their ambition to rise in the ranks by fulfilling their assignments, rather than primarily motivated by a burning desire to torture and murder their charges. But if torture and mass murder were part of their job, so be it.

In his writings for Sehn about his years at Auschwitz, Höss was far more expansive than in his testimony and conversations in Nuremberg. He was tasked with organizing the new camp out of the existing buildings and adding the whole new Birkenau complex, and he claimed that his original intention was to break with the precedent set by other camps, providing "better treatment" of the prisoners to get more work out of them by "both housing and feeding them better."

By his reckoning, however, his good intentions were "dashed to pieces against the human inadequacy and sheer stupidity of most of the officers and men posted to me." In other words, the brutality of his subordinates could not be contained—and, of course, it wasn't his fault. As a result, he sought refuge in his obsessive dedication to his job. "I was determined that nothing should get me down," he wrote. "My pride would not allow it. I lived only for my work."

He paid a price for giving up his original intention of running a more efficient, less gratuitously violent camp, he insisted. "I became a different person in Auschwitz. . . . All human emotions were forced into the background." The pressures of his superiors, coupled with the "passive resistance" of his subordinates to carry out his wishes, led him to drink heavily, he wrote. Hedwig, his wife, tried to arrange parties with friends to lighten his mood, but they failed to do so. "Even people who hardly knew me felt sorry for me," he added, once again indulging in the self-pity that permeates so much of his account.

When Himmler issued the order in 1941 to set up the gas chambers that would enable mass exterminations, Höss did not hesitate to begin implementing it. "It was certainly an extraordinary and monstrous order," he wrote. "Nevertheless the extraordinary reasons behind the extermination programme seemed to me right." It was just another order to be obeyed, he continued, signaling that he only recognized it was monstrous as he faced execution. "I did not reflect on it at the time. . . . I lacked the necessary breadth of view."

He personally observed the gassing of Soviet POWs, who were used to test the effectiveness of Zyklon B, the gas designed for the mass killings. "During the first experience of gassing people, I did not fully realize what was happening, perhaps because I was too impressed by the whole procedure," he wrote. When a group of nine hundred POWs was gassed, he heard the desperate prisoners throwing themselves against the doors. When he viewed their bodies after the chamber was aired out, he added, "It made me feel uncomfortable and I shuddered, although I had imagined that death by gassing would be worse than it was." He added that the gassings "set his mind at rest," since he could see that it would be possible to carry out the mass extermination of the Jews next.

Soon, the camp's machinery of death was working full-time and Höss was there to check on it regularly. While many of the doomed fell for the deception that they were going to the showers, others realized what was happening. The commandant noticed that mothers who did so "nevertheless found the courage to joke with their children to encourage them, despite the mortal terror visible in their own eyes." One woman on the way to the gas chamber walked up to Höss and pointed to her four children, whispering to him: "How can you bring yourself to kill such beautiful, darling children? Have you no heart at all?" Another mother tried to throw her children out of the gas chamber as the door was closing. "At least let my precious children live," she pleaded—of course, to no avail.

Höss claimed that he and the other guards were affected by "such shattering scenes" and that they were tormented by "secret doubts." But that was all the more reason to suppress them. "Everyone watched me," he noted, which meant he could not afford to show any hesitation or mercy. He also claimed he never hated Jews since "the emotion of hatred is foreign to my nature." Nonetheless, he conceded: "It is true that I looked upon them as the enemies of our people."

For all his talk of hidden doubts, his pride in the efficiency of the killing machinery he constructed is evident in his write-ups for Sehn. He even pointed out with regret that the selection process still left many sick prisoners alive who "cluttered up the camp," and that his bosses should have followed his advice and kept a smaller, healthier workforce—in other words, sent even more Jews and others to their deaths.

While Höss nonchalantly wrote that he never could complain of boredom at Auschwitz, he insisted that he was "no longer happy" once the mass exterminations began. The reason he provided reveals more about his character than anything else in his memoirs. Everyone in Auschwitz believed he lived "a wonderful life," he noted, and it was true that his wife had "a paradise of flowers" in their garden, his children were pampered, and they were all able to indulge their love of animals, keeping tortoises, cats, and lizards, visiting the stables and the kennels where the camp dogs were held. Even the prisoners who worked for them were eager to do them favors, he boasted, with no apparent recognition why that was the case. But, he added, "Today I deeply regret that I did not devote more time to my children. I always felt I had to be on duty all the time."

Höss penned those lines right after his descriptions of the heart-wrenching pleas of mothers trying to save or at least calm their children as they were driven into the gas chambers. He clearly saw no connection between them. As Sehn wrote in his introduction to the Polish edition of his memoirs, "All of his depictions of mass murder" appear to be written "by a totally disinterested observer."

To Sehn and others earlier at Nuremberg, Höss formally said he took responsibility for his actions and understood why he would have to pay with his life for them, yet he kept shifting the real blame on Hitler and Himmler, who issued the orders. At the same time, he proudly explained that even as the war was ending, "My heart clung to the Führer and his ideals, for those must not perish."

Primo Levi, the Italian Jewish writer and Auschwitz survivor, provided an introduction to a later edition of Höss's autobiography. "It's filled with evil, and this evil is narrated with a disturbing bureaucratic obtuseness," he wrote. The author comes across as "a coarse, stupid, arrogant, long-winded scoundrel, who sometimes blatantly lies," he added. But Levi also called the volume "one of the most instructive books ever published." It demonstrates how a man who in other circumstances would probably have been "some sort of drab functionary, committed to discipline and dedicated to order" evolved "into one of the greatest criminals in history."

The book shows, he continued, "how readily evil can replace good, besieging it and finally submerging it—yet allowing it to persist in tiny grotesque islets: an orderly family life, love of nature, Victorian morality." Nonetheless, Levi acknowledged that Höss's account was largely truthful, including his insistence that he was no sadist who enjoyed inflicting pain. In that sense, he was "a man who was not a monster and who never became one even at the height of his career in Auschwitz."

Those were themes that would come up again in the other most famous case of another architect of the Holocaust, Adolf Eichmann. Were the chief perpetrators monsters or seemingly ordinary human beings? In many ways, Höss provided more ammunition than Eichmann would at a later time for those espousing the second view. It was an interpretation that would later become known as "the banality of evil" thesis.

As noted earlier, Höss, while providing evidence in both Nuremberg and Kraków, misled his interrogators about the number of Auschwitz's victims. His initial estimate that the tally was two and a half to three million was buttressed by some of the testimonies of the camp's surviving members of the *Sonderkommando*—the male Jewish prisoners who were formed into squads to herd the new arrivals to the gas chambers. Most members of those special units were subsequently killed as well, but a few survived. Two of them testified right after the war that over four million people had been gassed at Auschwitz. That became the official figure put forward by the Soviet and Polish authorities, and the book Sehn wrote about the camp stuck with that number. In fact, the Polish communist government did not budge on that point right up until its downfall in 1989, despite mounting evidence that it was considerably inflated.

Among those who either are Holocaust deniers or at least believe that the overall number of victims is vastly exaggerated, Sehn and his writings are often targeted, with some calling him "a Soviet dupe." But while both the Soviet and Polish commissions that first investigated Auschwitz were undoubtedly predisposed to accept the most damning testimonies, the notion that the original numbers were a product of deliberate falsification is not justified by the evidence.

Since it was both Höss and some survivors who provided the early higher numbers, it is hardly surprising that they were taken seriously. Pointing out that SS officers burned about 90 percent of the camp's records before abandoning the camp, Piotr Cywiński, the current director of the Auschwitz-Birkenau State Museum, noted that it took a considerable amount of time before accurate estimates could be pieced together. "I wouldn't assume bad will on the part of the war commissions," he said. "At a certain point, the Soviet commission went with the notion 'the more the better.'" And once that became the official line in the Stalin era, "you would have had to be a crazy person to try to contradict statements from the Politburo."

Franciszek Piper, a Polish historian in the Auschwitz-Birkenau State Museum during both the communist and post-communist eras, painstakingly calculated the first much lower estimate of the number of the camp's victims: between 1.1 million and 1.5 million. He was finally able to publish a book with his findings in 1992, after the fall of communism. Although he knew the official figures were wrong long before they were officially changed, he noted that the authorities probably feared taking any step that could appear "to minimize the crime of genocide in general and the crimes perpetrated in Auschwitz in particular." Besides, he added, "anyone who would try to reduce the estimates in those times would be attacked as a defender of murderers."

In reality, the four million figure roughly corresponds to the total number of Jews who perished in *all* the death camps and ghettos after more than a million had been killed by the Einsatzgruppen, the special execution squads on the Eastern Front. This was largely coincidental. But it underscores the fact that the revised figures for Auschwitz have not changed the estimate of the overall number of Holocaust victims.

As for Sehn, he was hardly an ideologue of the new regime. In fact, even after he became the director of the Institute of Forensic Research in 1949, he did not join the Communist Party, which would normally be expected of anyone in such a position. Instead, he joined the Alliance of Democrats (Stronnictwo Demokratyczne), which he referred to as "the illegitimate child" of the communists—in other words, a small party the regime tolerated to provide a facade of pluralism. Interestingly, this would be one of the two small parties that broke with the communists in 1989, ending their rule by throwing their weight in parliament behind Solidarity.

To be sure, that was long after Sehn's death, but his instinct was clearly to maintain good relations with the new rulers while also keeping them at arm's length where he could. During his tenure as director of the Institute of Forensic Research from 1949 to his death in 1965, he managed to avoid the formation of a Communist Party organization there; almost all similar institutions had such an in-house unit. "During his tenure, there was never any political pressure," former co-worker Zofia Chłobowska maintains.

At the same time, he nurtured a close friendship with Józef Cyrankiewicz, a prewar Polish Socialist Party leader and an Auschwitz survivor who later served as prime minister in communist Poland. Without such connections, he probably would never have been given the responsibility of handling the Auschwitz investigation and trial, or allowed to travel abroad. As was typical of those times, he always had a "bodyguard" when he traveled out of the country, particularly to Germany where he delivered evidence for other trials. Although he received anonymous death threats as he kept up his pursuit of Nazi criminals, the bodyguard's real purpose was to make sure he did not have any unauthorized contacts with foreigners.

Sehn was never vindictive when he interrogated Höss and his accomplices. "He was humane in dealing with the perpetrators because he
knew what fate awaited them," Chłobowska pointed out. He also knew
that the prisoners were more responsive when they were treated well,
making them more forthcoming about their monstrous deeds. He was
convinced that his job was to elicit the fullest possible testimony from the
former commandant, which would provide the most damning evidence
against him. Under his skillful direction, Höss unleashed a cascade of
words that did exactly that.

At least subconsciously, Sehn may have begun his war crimes investigations because he wanted to demonstrate how different he was from his
brother, who, as a self-proclaimed *Volksdeutsche*, had worked as a village
mayor under the German occupiers. But his determination to convict the
perpetrators and gather testimony from their victims was sustained well
beyond any point where that might have been the decisive factor.

Sehn was always especially solicitous in his dealings with the camp
survivors who provided him with their gruesome accounts—and on at
least one occasion Sehn took a political risk to help them. His former
colleague Kozłowska recalled his gathering of testimony from Polish
women survivors of medical experiments at the Ravensbrück concentration camp. "They were often devastated psychologically, and he was
able to convince them that it was still worth living," she said. In the early
communist era, he also managed the unusual feat of convincing the authorities to permit a group of about a dozen of those survivors to travel
to Sweden for recuperation.

In those days, ordinary citizens usually had no chance to travel outside the Soviet bloc since the authorities feared they would not return.
And, in fact, only two or three members of the group of Ravensbrück survivors returned, which could have been enough to doom Sehn. Thanks
to his friendship with Prime Minister Cyrankiewicz, he weathered that
crisis.

Another Ravensbrück survivor, limping on battered legs from beatings she had received at the camp, periodically showed up in the institute's offices "to scream out how she was wronged," Kozłowska recalled,

adding that "of course she was tremendously wronged." Sehn made sure his staffers treated her well. They provided her with pencil and paper and a place to sit, and she would write furiously for hours. The result was usually illegible but she would leave calmed down, at least for a couple of weeks.

In his efforts to convict the perpetrators, Sehn never forgot who had really suffered—and was never taken in by Höss's pathetic attempts to portray himself as someone to be pitied. The former commandant was someone who needed to be studied thoroughly, allowing him to present his whole self-incriminating story—and someone who needed to pay the ultimate price. That was how Sehn saw his mission.

CHAPTER SIX

See Less Evil

"In our view, punishment of war criminals is more a matter of discouraging future generations than of meting out retribution of every guilty individual. Moreover, in view of future political developments in Germany . . . we are convinced that it is now necessary to dispose of the past as soon as possible."

A secret telegram sent from the Commonwealth Relations Office
in London to Commonwealth members Canada, Australia, New
Zealand, South Africa, India, Pakistan, and Ceylon on July 13, 1948

The war had not even ended when some of the victors began questioning whether hunting and prosecuting Nazi war criminals made sense. The judges and prosecutors at Nuremberg, along with the war crimes investigators and Holocaust survivors like Simon Wiesenthal and Tuvia Friedman, believed passionately in transforming the rhetoric of their leaders about seeking justice into reality. But others were already looking ahead to the postwar world and what they saw as the inevitable confrontation with a new totalitarian enemy—the Soviet Union.

In the spring of 1945, Saul Padover, the Austrian-born historian and political scientist who was serving in the U.S. Army as it moved deeper into German territory, wrote detailed notes of his conversations with local Germans and, occasionally, the Americans who were put in charge of their cities and towns. Part of his assignment was to gauge popular attitudes and also spur the process of identifying and removing Nazis from prominent positions. Padover met with an unnamed lieutenant colonel whom he identified as the MG (military governor) of an industrial city in the Rhineland, and recorded the senior officer's skepticism about those efforts. The notes are rough, but their import is clear:

> Not our concern to discover what Germans think. Find democrats? Can't find democrats even in U.S. I don't care who runs this country, & who lives here, so long as don't bother MG. More worried Russian threat than German problem. Only U.S. strong enough fight Russia; England is a laugh. Committee in this city supposed screen Nazis; not my business. I really don't have anything vs. Nazis unless they work against me. This list Nazi lawyers you gave me, maybe valid, maybe not, but member Nazi party not necessarily bad.

General George Patton was no less caustic about his superiors' efforts to punish or at least remove Nazis from a broad range of positions in postwar Germany. While he was serving as the military governor of Bavaria in 1945, he wrote to his wife: "What we are doing is to utterly destroy the only semi-modern state in Europe so that Russia can swallow the whole."

Even some German Jews who had fled their homeland in the 1930s were coolly pragmatic about the challenges they faced when they returned to a vanquished Germany as newly minted Americans. Peter Sichel was twelve in 1935, when his parents shipped him out of Berlin to a British school. He recalls his mother's warning when Hitler's regime enacted the Nuremberg racial laws that year: "All the Jews are going to be killed"—and how most of their friends thought she was crazy for saying so. In 1938, his parents managed to flee Germany as well. By 1941, Sichel had arrived in the United States and six months later, after Pearl Harbor, he volunteered for the Army.

During the war, Sichel served in the OSS, the Office of Strategic Services, which was the precursor to the CIA. He recruited German POWs for spy missions, and, when the war ended, the young captain was the last head of the 7th Army OSS detachment located in Heidelberg. But like the lieutenant colonel Padover encountered, he was dismissive of the efforts to identify and punish all but the highest-level members of Hitler's regime. "Our mission was to find high Nazi officials, members of the security service and high SS officials," he said. His heart was hardly in that task. "Don't ask who we caught, what we caught," he added with a shrug.

At a conference in London a year earlier, he had told his superiors that they had no need to be worried about resistance from hard-core Nazis once the war was won. "It's not like the first World War," he explained. "There's absolutely no doubt about the terrible things they've done. They're going to be in hiding, but they're not going to be trying to make life difficult for us." He added that while his former countrymen were highly effective when fighting as a group, "the Germans do not lend themselves to individual fighting." He was proven right. The fears that *Werwolf* forces—those trained for a guerrilla struggle against the Allies— would prove to be a formidable opponent quickly evaporated.

Soon after Germany's defeat, Sichel was transferred to Berlin where he continued his clandestine activities for the OSS—and then for the CIA once the new agency replaced the dissolved OSS. A Berlin operation was set up that reported back to the main CIA station in West Germany, and Sichel rose to chief of that Berlin base by 1950. The priority of his team, he pointed out, was getting intelligence on the Russians, protecting German scientists and technicians so they did not get snatched by them and dispatched to the Soviet Union. They also helped arrange to get the scientists, regardless of what they had done for the Nazis, to West Germany, from where some of them were sent to the United States. "There were not many people fighting the last war," he noted.

As for the war criminals, he added: "It's a horrible thing to say but I really didn't care much. It was always my philosophy that the criminals ought to be shot and then we should forget about the whole thing. Everyone who was really bad should be gotten rid of, and [as for] everyone else who was weak, let's look forward and not look back." As far as he was concerned, the initial round of trials in Nuremberg and elsewhere had pretty much taken care of the problem.

That was a far cry from the initial assumption of Germany's new masters. On May 10, 1945, President Truman signed a declaration outlining an ambitious "denazification" process for a defeated Germany. "All members of the Nazi Party who have been more than nominal participants in its activities, all active supporters of Nazism or militarism and all other persons hostile to Allied purposes will be removed and excluded from public office and from positions of importance in quasi-public and private enterprises," it declared. It then defined the categories of offenders who would be banned under those terms, using language that was sweeping enough to encompass a very broad array of the Third Reich's adherents.

All four occupying powers—the United States, Britain, France, and the Soviet Union—in principle agreed that denazification was essential. Germans seeking positions of almost any kind had to fill out the soon-to-be infamous *Fragebogen*, questionnaires with 131 queries about everything from their physical characteristics to their past political affiliations, and denazification panels were to then rule on who was disqualified from public and private jobs. The German writer Ernst von Salomon would later publish *Der Fragebogen*, a book that consisted of his lengthy, mocking answers to each of the questions about his activities during the Nazi era.

But the challenge the victors faced in determining how to deal with a people who had largely marched to the beat of the Nazi drummers was both serious and daunting. Eight and a half million Germans had belonged to the Nazi Party, and their full membership records had survived the war thanks to a paper mill manager in Munich who had deliberately ignored instructions to pulp them. Millions more were involved in Nazi-affiliated organizations. If everyone who had in some way served the Third Reich were excluded from public and private positions, there would be few people left. Noel Annan, a senior intelligence officer in the British zone, aptly described what even the most fervent proponents of denazification instinctively knew: "Democracy in Germany could not be born unless it was delivered with the forceps of de-Nazification; but it was also important not to crush the infant."

As Germans dutifully filled out the *Fragebogen*, the occupiers could hardly keep up with the mounting paperwork. The Americans were particularly ambitious at first, ordering everyone over eighteen to fill out the questionnaires and seeking to do as thorough a review as possible. They did get through nearly 1.6 million questionnaires by the end of 1946, leading to the dismissal of 374,000 Nazis from their jobs. But the backlog of cases was in the millions and there was no way for U.S. personnel to handle it all. As General Lucius Clay, the military governor of the American zone, put it: "We couldn't have tried [all of] them in a hundred years." He concluded that denazification had to "to be done by the Germans."

This fit in with his desire to encourage Germans who were considered relatively untainted by the Nazi era to gradually take responsibility for local affairs. The *Spruchkammern*, the local denazification tribunals in the American zone, were not technically courts, but they did have prosecutors and defendants—and they were charged with determining who were the "major offenders," "offenders," "lesser offenders," "followers," or "persons exonerated."

The process was riddled with problems from the start. Many former Nazis claimed to be *Muss-Nazis*, compelled to take party membership but in reality harboring anti-Nazi views. As the victors never tired of joking, Hitler clearly never had any followers. While some tribunal members tried to carry out their mandate, others were only too happy to clear former Nazis on the basis of highly dubious testimony. Germans soon popularized a term for the widespread whitewashing of reputations: *Persilschein*, a certificate named after the laundry detergent Persil. Nonetheless, there was initial support for the process among Germans: in 1946, 57 percent of those polled in the American zone approved of it. But confidence in its fairness kept dropping. By 1949, only 17 percent approved. In some cases, tribunal buildings and the vehicles and homes of their members were vandalized.

Clay later conceded that both the questionnaires and the tribunals were largely a failure. "But I don't know what else you could have done," he declared, making a legitimate point. In a society that had been so dominated by Hitler and his movement, no one had a recipe for success when it came to denazification. Nonetheless, Clay also argued that the Germans who handled denazification, for all their evident shortcomings, did succeed in exposing many Nazis and excluding them from leadership positions. "They may not have cleaned their own houses thoroughly, but they at least removed the major dirt," he wrote.

All of the occupying powers were quick to make exceptions to the rules, as in the case of the rocket scientists that the Russians and the Americans were particularly intent on pursuing. The British and the French found ways to quickly undo decisions that backfired. In June 1946, 179 executives and employees of the Volkswagen factory in the British zone were dismissed. But the factory was producing vehicles mainly for the British; by February 1947, 138 of that number were back at work. The French had initially fired three quarters of the teachers in their zone. But they reconsidered when the school year was to begin in September, inviting them all back to their classrooms.

The Soviet authorities repeatedly accused the Western powers of collaborating with former Nazis and allowing them to occupy a large number of key posts. Once the occupation officially ended in 1949 and East and West Germany were formed, the Kremlin continued to portray West Germany as a Nazi haven. While there is no doubt that many former Nazis emerged unscathed from the denazification process in the Western zones of occupation and quickly embedded themselves in comfortable positions in the new democratic state, the Soviet record was far from exemplary either.

To be sure, the Red Army had inflicted brutal retribution during its final push to Berlin, and the last surviving German POWs imprisoned in the Soviet Union were not released until 1956. And in 1949, new East German courts handled many cases in true Stalinist fashion, condemning defendants with breathtaking speed: during a mere two and a half months, they convicted 3,224 former Nazi officials in proceedings that took an average of twenty minutes each.

But just like the Western powers, the new Soviet masters were faced with the practical question of how to fill a huge number of positions in their zone and then the new East German state. And just like the Western powers, they were ready to overlook past affiliations when it suited their purposes—in some cases, even more so. Former Nazi Party members found it easy to switch their allegiance to the newly formed Sozialistische Einheitspartei Deutschlands (SED), as the German Communist Party was called. Already in 1946, 30 percent of the members in local SED groups were former Nazis. As General Clay caustically noted, "joining the SED erased the 'Nazism' of the joiner."

German historian Henry Leide, who combed through massive volumes of East German files to produce a detailed study of that country's record in dealing with the Nazi past, pointed out that such statistics were no anomaly. "Along with the many innocent people who were convicted, almost all the seriously accused Nazi criminals were released and they could (wrongly) claim that they had repented for their crimes," he wrote.

Repentance and redemption, in the form of embracing the communist cause, offered a fast track to careers in all parts of East Germany's new society—universities, medicine, politics, the security services, among others. The real enemies, as far as the Soviet zone's new masters were concerned, were those Germans who were suspected of anticommunism in any form. They were considered far more dangerous than former Nazis.

In June 1948, the Kremlin launched its blockade of West Berlin, cutting off all road, railroad, and canal routes to the city from Western-controlled parts of Germany. Its goal was to isolate and effectively swallow this Western enclave in the middle of the Soviet zone, driving out the Americans, the British, and the French. The Western Allies responded by mounting the massive Berlin Airlift, with a continual stream of cargo planes making 270,000 flights to deliver more than two million tons of essential supplies until the Soviet Union lifted the blockade on May 12, 1949. It was a spectacular show of resolve that saved West Berlin and accelerated the momentum toward the formal creation of two German states right afterward. The Cold War had started in earnest.

It was no accident that 1948 was also the year when Western governments were visibly losing interest in the further prosecution of war criminals and began the process of reducing the sentences of those who had already been convicted. The secret telegram that the Commonwealth Relations Office sent around the world on July 13, 1948, offered very specific instructions on how "to dispose of the past as soon as possible." While urging the conclusion of any cases awaiting trial by August 31 of that year, it added that "no fresh trials should be started" after that date. "This would particularly affect cases of alleged war criminals, not now in custody, who might subsequently come into our hands," it concluded.

The atmosphere was changing in Washington, too. The critics of the war crimes trials had received additional ammunition when lawyers for many of those convicted argued for commutation of sentences. In the case of the Waffen SS troops who were convicted for carrying out the Malmedy massacre of American POWs, there were charges that incriminating statements had been obtained through a variety of ruses and threats of violence. No such accusations were made in the broad range of cases handled at Dachau by William Denson, but the prosecutor—who had already returned to the United States—would also soon find his record under new intense scrutiny.

The U.S. Army set up five review boards to examine the sentences to date and then provide recommendations to General Clay. In theory, this was merely a routine measure to ensure that justice was served, but the political atmosphere of the times certainly encouraged the notion that leniency would be a positive signal. By accepting many of the recommendations for leniency of the review boards that examined all the Dachau trials, Clay acted in the spirit of the times—although he vehemently rebuffed accusations that he had in any way gone soft on war criminals.

The Dachau trials had led to convictions of 1,416 of the 1,672 defendants. "I set aside 69 convictions, commuted 119 sentences, and reduced 138, leaving 1090 sentences," Clay pointed out. Citing doubts about the reliability of the testimony of some concentration camp survivors in the trials, he commuted 127 of the 426 death sentences to life imprisonment. But it was Clay's decision to reduce the life sentence of the most notorious Dachau defendant—Ilse Koch, "the Bitch of Buchenwald"—to four years that stunned Denson, who was back in Washington, and generated an immediate backlash in the capital.

Clay later explained that Koch was "a sordid, disreputable character" who had earned "the bitter hatred" of the prisoners who testified against her by "flaunting her sex," but that the evidence did not convince him that she was "a major participant in the crimes of Buchenwald." The stories that she had lamp shades made of the human skin of prisoners, he added, were discredited when it became apparent that they were made of goatskin.

Denson called Clay's action a "mockery of the administration of justice." The Koch case generated new headlines and triggered an investigation by a Senate subcommittee headed by Homer Ferguson of Michigan. At the hearing, Denson stood by his original portrayal of Koch as an exceptionally sadistic tormentor of countless prisoners. He explained that the allegations that she had picked out prisoners to be skinned and then used that material for lamp shades, while generating the most lurid news reports, were not central to his case. "I did not feel that this skin business was of so much importance," he declared. "The gravamen of her action was in beating prisoners and causing them to be beaten so that they died. That was the real basis for that sentence, I am sure."

Asked if Koch was less culpable than the other Buchenwald defendants, Denson responded by alluding to her role as the wife of the camp's first commandant, which meant that she had no official duties. "I think she was more culpable. This was gratuitous on her part," he said. "There was no reason for her exercising the authority she exercised . . . the people I talked to felt the only reason she was sentenced to life imprisonment instead of death was because she was pregnant." Denson also argued that Clay's decision would draw criticism in Germany, despite the growing calls there for an end to punitive measures by the Allies. "Decent German people are also shocked by the reduction of sentence," he declared.

Among the subcommittee members, there was no sympathy for Koch, even if some of them raised questions about the handling of the Dachau trials. "From what I know so far about the case, the woman should have her neck broken," Arkansas Senator John McClellan declared. The sub-committee concluded that there was no justification for the reduction of Koch's sentence. Echoing Denson, Senator Ferguson wrote in his final report: "Every act committed by Ilse Koch as shown by the evidence was that of a volunteer. Such voluntary action, contrary to every decent human instinct, deserves utter contempt and denies mitigation."

Stung by the sharp criticism of his decision to reduce Koch's sentence, Clay suggested that he may have reached a different conclusion if he had seen more of the evidence against Koch. He pointed out that the Senate subcommittee "which unanimously criticized this action heard witnesses who gave testimony not contained in the record before me."

Denson would be vindicated in another way as well. Chancellor Konrad Adenauer, the first leader of the newly created West German government, quickly backed efforts to introduce some form of amnesty for many of those who had faced prosecution. "In view of the confused times behind us, a general tabula rasa is called for," he declared in one of his first cabinet meetings. But after Koch had served her four years as mandated by Clay, a West German court convicted her for incitement of murder and physical mistreatment of German prisoners, sentencing her to life imprisonment—exactly the sentence that Denson had won when he had prosecuted her. As he had predicted, the Germans were no happier about her going free than the Americans were.

Peter Heidenberger, the young German reporter who had covered the Dachau trials, later interviewed Koch in her new prison. He confessed to feeling almost sorry for the then dumpy-looking woman who had once been seen as an erotic monster of mythic proportions. For all her former putative allure, she came across as "a small town secretary, a little bit oversexed, but somebody you wouldn't want to associate with," he declared. Discussing her case decades later, he pointed out that she, too, fit the definition of "the banality of evil," throwing in the term that would only be coined long after Koch's conviction.

In 1963, largely forgotten by everyone else, Koch received a visit in prison from her teenage son, Uwe, who had just learned about his mother—the woman who had been pregnant with him when she first stood trial in Dachau. Uwe began visiting her periodically. In 1967, he arrived at the prison only to learn that Koch had hanged herself. His mother had left a note for him. "I cannot do otherwise," she wrote. "Death is for me a liberation."

While popular sentiment was clearly behind Denson in the Koch case, there was far less consensus about the Dachau trials in general. Denson had won conviction after conviction by demonstrating that the defendants played a role in the "common design" of the concentration camps, which meant that they were part of the "community of intention" to commit criminal acts. Critics charged that this categorization was too broad, and that other aspects of the Dachau trials fell far short of providing due process.

Among the harshest critics was none other than Benjamin Ferencz, the young Nuremberg prosecutor who won convictions against twenty-two top leaders of the Einsatzgruppen. The Dachau trials were "utterly contemptible," he declared. "There was nothing resembling the rule of law. More like court-martials. . . . It was not my idea of a judicial process. I mean, I was a young, idealistic Harvard law graduate."

Denson staunchly defended the Dachau trials right up to his death in 1998, arguing that they were as fair as they could be under the circumstances—and absolutely necessary. While insisting he took no special pride in the convictions he won and the death penalties that were carried out, he told a class at Drew University in 1991: "There is something, however, that does create a sense of pride in my heart. When a survivor comes up to me and says, 'We thank you for what you've done for us.'"

Ferencz and Denson had much in common: they were both young men when they prosecuted what would prove to be historic cases against those who had implemented the most draconian decisions of Hitler's regime. They believed in the notion that those who murdered and tortured at will had to pay the price for their actions. This was both to set a precedent for future generations and for the sake of their victims who deserved nothing less, as Denson indicated—and Ferencz certainly agreed.

But Ferencz has always insisted his Nuremberg trial, far more than the Dachau trials or any subsequent efforts to bring Nazis to justice, achieved those aims. The men he convicted, he argues, were "majors and colonels who shot thousands of people every day, thousands of children," he points out. There was no need to talk about "common design" since there was well-documented evidence of how they carried out those mass killings. And these weren't just the trigger men, but the commanders of the units full of trigger men. As far as he was concerned, this set the bar as high as it could go.

Ferencz had a strong case, but his attitude also betrays a trait that would become increasingly visible among the relatively small group of people who would become known as Nazi hunters: their tendency to see their own efforts as always the most important, and to question—and often denigrate—the performance and, at times, the motives of others in the same field.

Ironically, though, several of the Einsatzgruppen leaders benefited from more leniency than the "lesser Nazis," as General Clay called them, who were tried in Dachau. Despite growing pressure to drastically reduce many sentences, Clay stood firm in early 1949 when he reviewed the cases of Ferencz's twenty-two Einsatzgruppen commanders, reaffirming all thirteen death sentences. But then John J. McCloy, a Wall Street lawyer who had served as assistant secretary of war, replaced Clay and took the title of U.S. High Commissioner. In 1950, he set up an Advisory Board of Clemency to review the sentences in the Einsatzgruppen case and other trials. With Adenauer and others pressing for the commutation of all death sentences, both the advisory board and then McCloy moved to accommodate them—if not fully, at least to a large extent.

In early 1951, McCloy accepted almost all the recommendations of the advisory board and even made further reductions in the terms of some of those in prison, while commuting more death sentences than it had suggested. In the end, he only upheld four of the thirteen death sentences in Ferencz's Einsatzgruppen case. With the major power rivalry intensifying, the priority was to line up West Germany as an ally in the struggle against communism. McCloy believed he had nonetheless defended the principle that some crimes were too big to allow for mercy by holding fast on the four men from Ferencz's trial. They were hanged on June 7, 1951.

Telford Taylor, Ferencz's boss who had made the closing argument in the Einsatzgruppen case, branded McCloy's actions "the embodiment of political expediency." Ferencz, who had never specifically asked for the death penalty, was more understanding, pointing out that McCloy's training as a business lawyer never included condemning men to die. "To sign a paper saying, hang them, I knew he had difficulty with that," he said. But he added that "if punishment was imposed for good reason, it should not be reduced without good reason. In most cases there was no good reason that I was aware of."

In a letter to Ferencz in 1980, McCloy hinted at second thoughts about his decision. "If I had all the facts I now have, I might have reached a more just result," he wrote. By 1958, all the remaining Einsatzgruppen leaders who were convicted at Nuremberg were out of prison, including those who had been initially sentenced to death. They, like so many of their former partners in mass murder, lived out the rest of their lives as free men.

After "the biggest murder trial in history," Ferencz had no desire to continue prosecuting war criminals. He turned his attention elsewhere— namely, to seeking material assistance for the survivors. With the help of both Clay and then McCloy, who provided initial loans to set his plans in motion, Ferencz named himself director general of the Jewish Restitution Successor Organization "to impress the Germans with a title," he recalled. He hired staff and sent them to real estate registries around the country with instructions to claim any property transferred after 1933 or that listed a Jewish name. Next he helped set up the United Restitution Organization with offices in nineteen countries, and involved himself in complex negotiations with Adenauer's new government, other countries, and numerous victims, not only Jews. Ferencz stayed with his family in Germany until 1956 to continue this work, and all four of his children were born in Nuremberg.

While Ferencz stresses that it took a long time for many Germans to shed their anti-Semitism and acknowledge their victims, he was impressed by the willingness of the new German authorities to begin what would be an unprecedented effort to compensate them. "It never happened in history that a country paid its victims individually—inspired by Adenauer who said terrible crimes were committed in the name of the German people," he pointed out.

But it was his role as the chief prosecutor in the Nuremberg Einsatzgruppen trial that fueled the passion that has continued to consume him into his tenth decade. At every opportunity he has argued that conflicts must be resolved through "law not war," and urged support for the International Criminal Court. On August 25, 2011, Ferencz delivered the closing argument in the Court's first trial in The Hague, the case against Thomas Lubanga Dyilo, a Congolese rebel leader accused of recruiting child soldiers. Ferencz was ninety-one when he spoke on that occasion, invoking the lessons of Nuremberg. In July 2012, Dyilo was found guilty and sentenced to fourteen years in prison.

Today, Ferencz is dismissive of the value of pursuing some of the cases against aging, relatively minor Nazi camp guards and officials. "Forget it," he said. "For Christ's sake, I'd throw those small fish back into the pond."

Most Nazi hunters who followed Ferencz took a different view, rejecting his notion that only Nuremberg-level defendants merited prosecution. That would effectively provide immunity to the vast majority of mass murderers. Ferencz argued that he still wants to ensure that big fish from any era are held to account, providing an example for the whole world to see—even if, in the case of the Nazis, he continued to insist that his fish were almost the only really big ones.

A big part of the motivation for holding the war crimes trials was exactly that: to provide examples of justice at work for the whole world to see. By presenting the record of the Third Reich, aggression by aggression, mass murder by mass murder, atrocity by atrocity, the trials were critical to establishing exactly what had happened—and establishing the principle that the perpetrators bore direct responsibility for those crimes, whatever they understood their orders to be. To make sure that the evidence reached a broad audience, the Allies represented at Nuremberg set up a film unit that was supposed to lead to the joint production of a documentary about the International Military Tribunal proceedings against the major defendants.

Not surprisingly, the American and Soviet representatives could not agree on a common approach, and those two victors decided to make separate documentaries. But more startling was the fate of their respective efforts: the Soviets produced a film that they distributed relatively quickly, while the American filmmakers were immediately caught up in fierce internal battles about what kind of documentary they should make—and, ultimately, were blocked from showing the result of their labors in the United States. After it was shown in Germany in the late 1940s, the American film, which was called *Nuremberg: Its Lesson for Today*, was largely forgotten.

The reason for the film's consignment to seeming oblivion: it was not completed until 1948, the year when Washington's political priorities had shifted dramatically. "The Cold War was the major factor, because we were investing in rebuilding Germany," said film producer Sandra Schulberg. "It became really inconvenient to rub people's noses in the story of the Nuremberg trial and the Nazi atrocities when you were trying to bring Germany back into the European community."

Schulberg was born in 1950 but has a direct personal connection to the documentary. Her father was Stuart Schulberg, the film's writer and director, who had joined the Marines after Pearl Harbor and was assigned to the OSS film unit, headed by the famed director John Ford. His brother Budd Schulberg, already a successful novelist and later the writer of the Academy Award–winning script for *On the Waterfront,* had enlisted in the Navy and was also assigned to the OSS film unit. Both of them ended up racing around Germany and its former occupied territories searching for incriminating Nazi footage right after the war.

The Nazis had sought to destroy much of that celluloid evidence, and the Schulbergs found themselves ordering the Third Reich's former enforcers to help them collect what was left. In the northern Bavarian town of Bayreuth, Stuart and his small team commanded resentful SS prisoners to prepare a large stash of film footage for transport. Two GIs stood guard with their guns pointed at them as they loaded the heavy crates. "They still had their black uniforms on, and their cocky little overseas hats," Stuart recalled. "The Aryan SS-ers were suffering—we could see that. Whenever they got orders from us, their lips curled a little. It reminded me of the tigers and lions who perform in the circus ring, obeying in a sullen, whipped, mad way."

Such footage proved extremely valuable to the prosecutors at the Nuremberg International Military Tribunal, allowing them to strengthen their case by showing dramatic images. The OSS produced *The Nazi Plan*, a history of the National Socialist movement, and *Nazi Concentration Camps*, using film shot by U.S. and British troops as they liberated the camps. When screened at the trial, the latter film, in particular, stunned even the defendants.

After he was discharged in late 1945 and returned to the United States, Budd Schulberg declined an offer to write the script for the American film about the trial itself, suggesting Stuart instead. Pare Lorentz, known as "FDR's moviemaker," was the head of the War Department's Film, Theater and Music section and in that capacity took charge of the Nuremberg project. Taking up Budd's suggestion, he asked Stuart to write the script, and fought a battle to prevent General Clay's military government from taking the film over; back in Washington, the War Department and the State Department also entered the fray. By 1947, Lorentz was so frustrated by the infighting, along with funding and other problems, that he resigned from the War Department.

Stuart labored on, producing several drafts of the proposed script for review, enduring often angry critiques from those who wanted to put their own mark on it. But in the end, his version won out. The film was organized around the four counts leveled at the defendants: conspiracy, crimes against peace, war crimes, and crimes against humanity. In straightforward but compelling terms, it laid out the Third Reich's record in each of those areas, weaving in footage from the trial itself. Chief U.S. Prosecutor Robert Jackson had authorized the filming of portions of the trial.

In mid-1947 as the Americans finally began work on their film, they learned that the Soviets had completed their version, which of course focused on the Red Army's role in defeating Germany, largely ignoring the contribution of the Western Allies. This led to embarrassing headlines in the U.S. media. "Claim Internal U.S. Army Snarl Let Reds Beat Yanks on Nuremberg Film," *Variety* proclaimed on June 11.

While some senior U.S. officers in Germany were still hoping to delay or even derail the documentary, the Soviet film may have spurred its completion and release. The American film premiered before a German audience in Stuttgart on November 21, 1948, and it was shown throughout West Germany in 1949. Stuart reported that the critical reception was "unexpectedly good," and it played to packed houses. "Audiences sat through the picture in stunned silence and then filed out, wordless and disturbed," he wrote. He quoted an information official of the U.S. military government as saying: "This film tells the Germans more about Nazism in 80 minutes than we've been able to tell them in three years."

Even before that success in Germany, Supreme Court Justice Jackson, who had returned from Nuremberg, and others were pushing for its release in the United States as well. The New York Bar Association had requested a screening of the film, but Washington refused to authorize it. The only film they could obtain, it turned out, was the Soviet version. Infuriated by that news, Jackson wrote to Secretary of the Army Kenneth Royall on October 21, 1948, making a passionate appeal for the distribution of the film back home. He reported that he had already written to Harrison Tweed, the president of the New York Bar Association, who had called him up afterward to ask if he could read his angry letter to the group "if he cut out the profanity." Jackson's response: "I told him he could read it if he would not cut out the profanity."

Jackson's fundamental argument was that the film served multiple purposes: helping Germans understand why they needed democracy; counteracting the Soviet propaganda film that gave "the impression that they conquered and then conducted the trials pretty much single-handed"; and furthering the goals of both Roosevelt and Truman by presenting an accurate version of the historical record that explained why the war had to be fought in the first place and the perpetrators brought to justice. "I cannot see why we should not reap for the United States whatever advantage it has," he concluded.

Royall was unmoved by any of those arguments. "In this country no general release is under consideration," he wrote back to Jackson. "It is my opinion that the theme is contrary to present policies and aims of the government; therefore, it is felt that the picture at this time can be of no significant value to the Army and Nation as a whole."

Many Army officers had objected to the trials of German officers in the first place, but it was the dawn of the Cold War that was the decisive factor. Americans were now supposed to view the West Germans as allies, and the film was seen as undermining that effort. William Gordon, public relations director for Universal Pictures, who saw the film, argued against any general distribution, particularly objecting to the footage of the camps and other atrocities as "too gruesome to stomach—and I mean that literally."

This act of censorship did not go unnoticed. Writing in the *New York Daily Mirror* on March 6, 1949, in a column titled "The Hall of Shame," Walter Winchell mocked the rationale that the film could spur anti-German feeling in the United States. "Could there be any wilder idiocy?" he wrote. "Those whose duty it was to eradicate Nazism are now endeavoring to eradicate evidence of its brutality—thus making themselves accessories to Nazi crimes."

Pare Lorentz, who initially had been in charge of the film project before he quit and returned to civilian life, had even offered to buy the documentary from the Army so that he could distribute it to movie theaters himself. That, too, was a nonstarter. A *Washington Post* story on September 19, 1949, mentioned suggestions "that there are those in authority in the United States who feel that Americans are so simple that they can hate only one enemy at a time. 'Forget the Nazis,' they advise, 'and concentrate on the Reds.'" William Shirer, the famed journalist who would later write *The Rise and Fall of the Third Reich*, had been to a special screening of the film for critics and writers. He denounced the Army's efforts to block the film's distribution as a "scandal."

But nothing could change the Army's and the government's mind. The film was never released to the general public in the United States. Despite his disappointment, Stuart Schulberg continued to produce new films on denazification and reeducation for the U.S. military government in Germany, and then served as the chief of the Marshall Plan Motion Picture Section in Paris from 1950 to 1952, working on films designed to foster reconciliation between France and Germany.

In 2004, a quarter century after Stuart Schulberg's death, his daughter Sandra presented a retrospective of the Marshall Plan films at the Berlin Film Festival. The series was preceded, at the behest of festival director Dieter Kosslick, by a screening of the German version of her father's Nuremberg film, which she had never seen. She was immensely impressed.

When she returned to the United States, Sandra viewed the American version, and realized that the filmmakers had substituted narration in lieu of using the courtroom recordings of the English-language speakers. That prompted her to embark with filmmaker and sound editor Josh Waletzky on an ambitious effort to restore the film using the courtroom sound so that audiences could hear all the major trial participants speaking in their own languages: German, English, Russian, and French. They asked actor Liev Schreiber to record Stuart's original English narration. The newly restored film was released in American theaters for the first time in the fall of 2010. By 2014, Schulberg had produced a high-definition Blu-ray version as well.

At long last, Americans had access to her father's work. In the post Cold War world, no one was left to object.

CHAPTER SEVEN

"Like-Minded Fools"

"Nothing belongs to the past. Everything is still part of the present and could become part of the future again."

Fritz Bauer, the attorney general of Braunschweig and then Hesse,
explaining his relentless push to make his countrymen acknowledge
the crimes committed in their name during the Third Reich

The Americans who had been deeply involved in the war crimes trials and their aftermath were not alone in recognizing the rapid loss of interest in prosecuting Nazis or in exposing what they had done during their twelve-year reign of terror. The freelance Nazi hunters, who had been motivated by the horrors they had personally experienced and witnessed as Holocaust survivors, also found themselves wavering in their resolve in the face of the growing indifference or even hostility to keeping their cause alive. They, too, had to decide whether they should devote their energies to new personal and political agendas. As demonstrated by the dawn of the Cold War in the late 1940s and the outbreak of the Korean War in 1950, the 1950s would prove to be a very different decade from the one that preceded it, with very different issues dominating the headlines.

After he was liberated in Mauthausen on May 5, 1945, Wiesenthal remained in the nearby Austrian city of Linz, working for the OSS. That organization's top officer there provided him with the support he needed in the form of a pass that attested to the fact that he was doing "confidential investigative work" for the OSS, and requesting that he should be allowed to "move freely in American-occupied Austria." When the OSS closed its Linz office at the end of 1945, he switched over to the U.S. Army's Counter Intelligence Corps (CIC). His job remained the same: helping the Americans identify and capture Nazis. In many cases, though, the victors had little interest in keeping them locked up and released detainees almost immediately.

Wiesenthal joined CIC officers in making arrests and gathering evidence for trials. He also began working intensively with displaced persons, mostly Holocaust survivors, who were scattered all over the region. He recognized early on that they could provide valuable testimony against the perpetrators. As he helped them with everything from obtaining medical care to filling out U.S. visa applications and, most importantly, tracking missing relatives, he developed a broad network of sources. He sent around questionnaires to get their personal stories, all of which could provide new leads as well as a starting point for assessing their background.

Never afraid of controversy, Wiesenthal insisted that those seeking positions in Jewish organizations involved in the resettlement of displaced persons in the American zone produce two witnesses to offer testimony that they had not been collaborators in the camps—specifically, that they had not been *Kapos*, SS-appointed supervisors of fellow prisoners. He freely admitted that "this made me many enemies" among fellow survivors. It wasn't the first time and certainly wouldn't be the last. While countless displaced persons were grateful for his help, he was quickly embroiled in the inevitable feuds between the various refugee groups, often pitting former victims against each other in the scramble to survive and build new lives.

At the newly created Jewish Committee in Linz, Wiesenthal and others made up lists of survivors, exchanging copies with those who drifted in carrying their own lists as they looked for family members and friends.

But he did not expect to find the one person he was most concerned with on any of those growing lists: his wife, Cyla. He had lost contact with her after she had gone to Warsaw to live under an assumed Polish Catholic name. He later heard that during the 1944 Warsaw Uprising German troops had used flamethrowers to destroy the building on Topiel Street where she had been staying with the wife of a Polish poet. "I didn't believe in miracles. I knew that all my people were dead," he recalled. "I had no hope that my wife was alive."

Yet, miraculously indeed, Cyla had escaped just before her street was leveled. Rounded up with other survivors of the uprising, she was sent as a forced laborer to a machine gun factory in the Rhineland. There, she was liberated by the British. She, too, had heard that her spouse was dead. A mutual friend in Kraków, whom Simon had been writing to, was able to give her the startling good news that her husband was alive and waiting for her. In December 1945, the couple was reunited after Simon arranged for an Auschwitz survivor who was going back to Poland to escort her to Linz. The following September Cyla gave birth to a daughter, Paulinka, their first and only child.

Wiesenthal was intent on building a new life for himself in other ways as well. As much as he had admired the Americans who liberated him from Mauthausen and then offered him the opportunity to hunt Nazis, he found it difficult to accept the rapidly evolving new situation and attitudes. A CIC colleague told him bluntly: "You'll see how quickly things change. The Germans are needed against the Russians. Good Germans alone are too few."

Wiesenthal was stunned by the eagerness of former Nazis to serve the occupation forces—and how effectively they sold themselves as experts in the West's new battle with the Soviet Union. "The Americans in particular had an incredible talent for being taken in by tall, blond, blue-eyed Germans, simply because they looked exactly like American officers in the cinema," he recalled. The victors were also susceptible to the pleas for the release of local Nazis by their "best secret weapon—the *Fräuleins*," he added. "A young American was naturally more interested in a pretty, complaisant girl than in one of 'those SS men,' whom everyone wanted to forget like a bad dream."

But Wiesenthal had no intention of forgetting them or their crimes. In 1946, he published his first book, *KZ Mauthausen*, a collection of his black-and-white drawings based on his concentration camp experiences. By the following year, he was running the newly created Historical Documentation Center in Linz, where he collected every bit of evidence he could get about Nazi criminals, mainly from displaced persons, the survivors who were still adrift in the postwar chaos. Wiesenthal had convinced Avraham Silberschein, a former teacher in his Galician hometown of Buczacz, to fund the center when they met at a Zionist Congress in Basel in 1946. He only provided backing for a shoestring budget, but the irrepressible Wiesenthal was off and running.

There were plenty of people who did not appreciate his efforts, especially in a postwar Austria that was trying to portray itself as the first victim of the Third Reich rather than an enthusiastic supporter. In reality, Austrians had assumed a disproportionate percentage of top Nazi positions in the machinery of terror, especially when it came to running the concentration camps. "Austrians accounted for only 8 percent of the population of the Third Reich, yet Nazis from Austria were responsible for half of the murders of Jews committed under Hitler," Wiesenthal wrote. As a result, they had a lot to lose if Nazi hunting continued in earnest. Wiesenthal's activities and calls for the uprooting of "all of the wild growths on Nazism" in Austria produced a predictable backlash in the form of threatening letters, and he obtained a permit to carry a pistol in 1948.

This was also the period when the Brichah organization was smuggling Jews from Europe to Palestine, and Wiesenthal cooperated with its operatives in Austria. As someone who believed he would follow the same route soon, he supported those efforts to get Jews to what would soon become Israel. But he always opposed the Brichah operatives who advocated violent reprisals against those responsible for Nazi crimes.

Ironically, the Jewish escape routes from Europe, many of which traversed Austria and ended up at Italian ports so that the refugees could board ships there, often overlapped with the "ratlines" of Nazi fugitives to South America. In many cases, the Nazis were helped by ostensibly humanitarian groups organized by the Catholic Church; Austrian Bishop Alois Hudel was well known for his pro-Nazi sentiments and assisted numerous war criminals on their journeys. Wiesenthal demanded an accounting from the Vatican until the end of his life, including the opening of its archives, but he was also careful to point out that the Catholic Church helped save many Jews.

"It seems to me probable that the Church was divided: into priests and members of the religious orders who had recognized Hitler as the Antichrist and therefore practiced Christian charity, and those who viewed the Nazis as a power of order in the struggle against the decline of morality and Bolshevism," he wrote. "The former probably helped the Jews during the war, and the latter hid the Nazis when it was over."

As he foraged for evidence that he hoped would lead to the capture and conviction of more Nazi criminals in Austria, Wiesenthal was often frustrated by what he saw as the naïveté of many of the new U.S. troops on duty, but he was even more irritated by the attitudes of the British occupation forces. Crossing into the British zone to gather evidence against a war criminal, he was questioned by a sergeant who "didn't seem to care" about his hunt for Nazis. "What do you think about the illegal transports to Palestine by way of Italy?" the sergeant immediately asked. As Wiesenthal concluded, the British were much more concerned about stopping the flow of refugees to Palestine "than about Nazi criminals in their zone."

With all sides seemingly losing interest in the pursuit of perpetrators still on the loose, Wiesenthal was giving increasing thought to moving to Israel, which had come into existence as an independent state in 1948. Cyla was a proponent of such a move from the very beginning, according to Paulinka. "In 1949, my parents were ready to go to Israel," their daughter said. Simon made his first visit there that year, believing that this would become their new home.

Along with Simon's cooperation with the Brichah, he had provided at least indirect support to the Zionist movement in other ways as well. In 1947, he published his second book, which focused on Palestinian leader Haj Amin el-Husseini, who had been the British-appointed grand mufti of Jerusalem. In 1936, the mufti stirred up riots against Jewish settlers, which led to his dismissal from his post and exile from Palestine. But from abroad he continued to urge Muslims to rise up against Jews, and he urged support for Nazi Germany. He met with Hitler in November 1941, telling the German leader: "The Arabs were Germany's natural friends because they had the same enemies as had Germany, namely . . . the Jews." Hitler replied by pledging German backing for the Arab cause.

According to Wiesenthal's account, the Palestinian had also visited Auschwitz and Majdanek with Eichmann to learn about the machinery of the Final Solution. As Wiesenthal's biographer Tom Segev points out, "there is no reliable evidence for its [this story's] veracity," and Wiesenthal failed in his efforts to get the book published in English. But his interest in the mufti's activities remained undiminished, and he passed along anything else he picked up to Silberschein, his funder, who he believed was then relaying the information to Israel.

On his first visit to Israel in 1949, Wiesenthal brought more documents about the contacts between Arabs and the Nazis. He also reported that it was on this visit that Boris Guriel, an Israeli Foreign Ministry official, urged him to stay in Europe, since the new state's intelligence service needed him there. Segev refers to Wiesenthal "as a recruit in Israel's secret services" in that period, and he was provided with an Israeli travel document that helped him obtain an Austrian residency permit. He also was outfitted with press credentials as a correspondent for a couple of Israeli publications.

But Wiesenthal's relationship with the nascent Israeli intelligence services was hardly clear-cut. He provided reports on anti-Semitism and political developments in Austria, maintaining contacts with Israeli diplomats there. But, according to Segev, they saw him as "a partner," which implies that he was something less than a full-fledged intelligence agent. By 1952, the Israelis had decided not to renew his travel documents; they also rebuffed his appeals that he be paid by the consulate for continuing to supply information or that they take him on as an employee. While he protested loudly enough to get his travel documents renewed until the end of 1953, he was on his own after that.

Wiesenthal could have become an Israeli citizen simply by moving to Israel, but at that point he wanted both Israeli citizenship and to remain in Austria. While failing in that effort, he managed to obtain Austrian citizenship. Despite Cyla's eagerness to move to Israel, he had changed his mind. Although it did not look that way at the time, this would prove to be the critical decision that enabled him to gain growing international recognition in the decades to come.

Tuvia Friedman, who had exacted revenge on Germans in Danzig at the end of the war when he served in the new Polish communist security forces there, had ended up in Vienna, where he took charge of another small Documentation Center. In those and other ways, his initial experiences and activities were similar to Wiesenthal's in Linz. He and his colleagues collected testimony and documents from the Jews who were arriving in Vienna from Eastern and Central Europe, offering them as evidence in the trials of SS and other security officers. "Our office kept the Austrian police busy arresting dozens of suspects," he boasted.

On one occasion, a Romanian Jewish student from the University of Vienna came to him with a pack of letters he had discovered in a drawer in his rented room in an Austrian woman's house. They were from SS Lieutenant Walter Mattner, who had served in the Ukraine shortly after Germany attacked the Soviet Union in June 1941. The student had read the letters, he told Friedman, and thrown up. They were missives addressed to his wife in Vienna, who was pregnant at the time. They described the systematic shooting of Jews, matter-of-factly mentioning that the number of victims in Kiev was 30,000 and in Mogilev 17,000. He also wrote about the public hangings of Communist Party officials that local civilians were forced to watch. "Here in Russia I can appreciate what it means to be a Nazi," he added.

Friedman took the letters to an Austrian police inspector, who was visibly shaken by them. He called in several colleagues to read them as well. "I understood the shame that these men felt," Friedman noted.

The police tracked down Mattner a couple of days later in a small town in Upper Austria, and brought him back to Vienna. The inspector who had first read the letters invited Friedman to witness his interrogation of the prisoner. When Mattner quickly admitted that he had written the letters, the inspector angrily shot back: "God damn you! How could you write to your pregnant wife that you were shooting children in Russia, without mercy?"

Mattner tried to excuse himself. "I—I wanted to look important to her," he said. According to Friedman, that earned him a slap from the inspector, who pointed out that his letters were explicit about his involvement in mass murder. When Mattner started claiming that he shot above the heads of prisoners, the inspector slapped him again. "Why did you shoot Jews with such pleasure in Russia?" he demanded.

Mattner kept trying to defend himself, saying he had been "the best friend of Jews" in Vienna and shopped at Jewish stores until 1938, the year of the Anschluss that incorporated Austria into the Third Reich. Whatever happened afterward, he insisted, was not his fault. "It was Hitler's propaganda, it poisoned people, and all that wild power in our hands," he said.

Watching with mounting anger, Friedman abruptly left, fearful that he might throw himself at the prisoner. Mattner was tried and hanged.

During the immediate postwar period when the Allied occupation troops were looking on, Austrian courts did handle more cases than generally realized: 28,148 people were tried, and 13,607 of those were convicted. But, as Friedman, Wiesenthal, and others were discovering, the rapidly changing political environment in the early days of the Cold War meant that the enthusiasm for such trials was rapidly diminishing and many of those convicted were quickly released. In Austria, a country that was clinging to its alibi that it was Hitler's first victim, many Nazis were not only eluding prison but also returning to their old jobs.

"The situation grew embarrassing," Friedman recalled. "It seemed that half of the Austrian policemen had carried out Nazi-ordered pro-grams against Jewish communities, especially in Poland. I began to feel resistance against my Documentation Center, and against me." Police officials like the ones who had cooperated with him earlier were sidelined.

Exasperated, Friedman went to discuss the situation with his chief contact at the CIC headquarters in Vienna. "This is Austria, Friedman," the Jewish U.S. Army major told him bluntly. "The Russians want to lower their Iron Curtain over it, and we don't want it to happen. And these people are playing us both against the middle. They're not stupid, you know. And they simply don't want their courts filled with Nazi war crimes trials."

The strategy appeared to work, with the Allied occupation forces—including the Soviet contingent—withdrawing from Austria in 1955, allowing that country to become independent and neutral. From 1956 to 2007, not coincidentally, Austria held a mere thirty-five trials of Nazis accused of crimes.

Like Wiesenthal, Friedman also worked with the Brichah as it funneled Jews to Palestine. In 1947, a year before Israel's founding, he had a revealing exchange with a leader of the Haganah, the Jewish paramilitary organization whose members often accompanied the refugees as they were smuggled to Palestine. The official applauded Friedman's efforts to bring Nazis to justice but cautioned him to remember the first priority: the establishment of a Jewish state. "Put your whole heart into this task, Tadek," he told him. "The Nazis can wait. We can no longer wait for a Jewish homeland."

Friedman claimed he provided support for Haganah squads that seized trucks transporting weapons destined for Arab countries—and then diverted them to Jewish units in Palestine. In 1949, the year after the founding of the Jewish state, a new Israeli agent showed up in Vienna who took over local intelligence activities. Friedman was given to understand that his services in that arena were no longer needed. "An odd feeling developed in Vienna at that time," he noted. "There were the Israelis; and there were the other Jews. I was, technically, a Polish subject."

He continued working in his Documentation Center, but, like Wiesenthal's office in Linz, it was struggling to keep afloat. By the early 1950s, the flow of Jewish refugees into Austria had slowed significantly, and funding was drying up. Even more discouraging was the rapidly declining interest in its work. "My files were bulging with documents, with sworn affidavits," Friedman recalled. "But nobody clamored to get at them and use them to prosecute Nazis. The Germans did not want them; the Austrians did not want them; nor did the Western Allies nor the Russians."

By 1952, the Vienna Documentation Center closed its doors, and Friedman sent off his files to Yad Vashem in Jerusalem, the new Israeli institution for documenting and commemorating the Holocaust. Friedman decided to follow his files, moving to Israel that same year. He vowed to continue his efforts to track Nazis from there, but he recognized he also had to make a new life for himself in his new country.

In recalling that era, Friedman noted that he had withheld one file from his shipment of his former center's documents to Jerusalem. "That was the file on Adolf Eichmann," he declared.

During his time in Vienna, Friedman had met and corresponded frequently with Wiesenthal in Linz. "We agreed to help each other, exchanging information, and co-operating in every way possible," Friedman maintained. This willingness of two self-proclaimed Nazi hunters to cooperate was genuine at the beginning. Friedman had worked for the Polish communists at the end of the war in Danzig while Wiesenthal had worked for the Americans in Austria. This made them somewhat suspicious of each other, but they were both committed to the same cause of tracking Nazi criminals. It was only later that this common goal became a source of barely concealed rivalry.

According to Friedman, they were both preoccupied early on with the search for Eichmann, the mastermind of the logistics of the Final Solution who had disappeared at the end of the war. Wiesenthal claimed he was told about Eichmann and his role by Asher Ben-Natan, an Austrian-born Jew who had fled to Palestine in 1938, joined the Haganah, and, after the war, ran the Brichah operation in his former homeland using the name Arthur Pier. Meeting in Vienna on July 20, 1945, Wiesenthal recounted, "Arthur" gave him a list of war criminals drawn up by the Jewish Agency's political department; it included Eichmann's name and the affiliations "high official of Gestapo H.Q., Department for Jewish Affairs, member of the NSDAP [National Socialist Party]."

According to both his first and second autobiographies, Wiesenthal then got another tip from an unlikely source: his landlady on Landstrasse 40, a couple of houses away from the OSS office in Linz. One evening when he was studying his lists of war criminals, she came in to make his bed and looked over his shoulder. "Eichmann," she said. "That must have been the SS General Eichmann who was in command of the Jews. Did you know that his parents live here, in this street, just a few houses along at number 32?"

Eichmann only had the rank of lieutenant colonel, despite his critical role in the Holocaust, but the landlady was right about where he had lived. Wiesenthal reported that, acting on this tip, two Americans from the OSS office visited the Eichmann house two days later and talked to his father, who insisted he hadn't heard anything from his son since the end of the war.

This was the beginning of what Wiesenthal described as his increasingly obsessive search for Eichmann, which led to the questioning of a woman named Veronika Liebl in the spa town of Altaussee. She admitted she had been married to Eichmann, but claimed they were divorced in Prague in March 1945 and she had had no contact with him since then. As Wiesenthal pursued the case further, he reported that he became known as "Eichmann Wiesenthal" around Linz, and he was "swamped with information." A key goal was to find a photo of Eichmann, who had made a point of keeping his distance from cameras when he was orchestrating mass murder. Wiesenthal reported that one of his colleagues managed to get a 1934 photo of him from a former girlfriend in Linz, which was added to the warrant for Eichmann's arrest.

Later, when Wiesenthal's critics and rivals began attacking him for what they claimed was his vastly inflated account of his role in the hunt for Eichmann, they tried to dissect and dismiss almost every part of his increasingly complex narrative of events. In some cases, they even questioned whether he had begun his search for Eichmann right after the war as he always insisted.

Friedman, who had arrived in Austria from Poland in 1946, reported that "Arthur"—Asher Ben-Natan—was also the first person to tell him about Eichmann, describing him as "the greatest murderer of them all." When the new arrival admitted he hadn't heard of him, he added, the Brichah leader instructed him: "Friedman, you must find Eichmann. I will say it to you again: *You must find Eichmann.*"

There is no doubt that both Wiesenthal and Friedman took an interest in Eichmann's whereabouts very soon after the war, whatever the exact timing. Robert Kempner, a German-born Jewish member of the U.S. prosecution team at Nuremberg, wrote in his memoirs that Wiesenthal came to him there and asked: "Do you have material against a certain Adolf Eichmann? Will he be charged by you?"

In 1947, according to Wiesenthal's account, an American friend informed him that Veronika Liebl, who was also known as Vera, had requested that the district court declare her alleged ex-husband dead "in the interest of the children." A purported witness had sworn under oath that he saw Eichmann killed during the fighting in Prague on April 30, 1945, just as the war was ending. Wiesenthal discovered that the witness was married to Liebl's sister, information that he passed along to an American intelligence officer, who in turn let the district court know about this suspicious circumstance. As a result, the court turned down Liebl's appeal to have Eichmann declared dead. "This unspectacular move was probably my most important contribution to the Eichmann case," Wiesenthal wrote.

His critics later questioned whether a death declaration would have changed anything—or deterred the Israelis from hunting Eichmann. But given the general decline in interest in pursuing war criminals, everything that kept the issue alive—and the perpetrators alive in the minds of potential pursuers—could have played a crucial role. According to Friedman, three Israelis arrived in Austria in 1950 to search for Eichmann. At the time, they believed he was still hiding in Austria after successfully eluding identification when he was detained by Allied troops in a series of temporary camps at the end of the war.

But 1950 was the year when Eichmann made his way to Genoa under the name Ricardo Klement, and from there sailed to Argentina. Friedman indicated that the Israelis did not search for him for long. In that same year, "Arthur permitted the hunt for Eichmann to come to an end," he declared.

Only he and Wiesenthal refused to accept that the hunt was over, Friedman insisted. They continued to exchange whatever stories were circulating about Eichmann. "The truth was that no one knew anything," he wrote. "And with each passing day, there was less and less interest in Eichmann, and in Nazis." After Friedman moved to Israel in 1952, he came back for a visit to Austria before the year was out. There, he met again with Wiesenthal, who told him to "keep reminding the Israelis about Eichmann . . . make them do something."

As Friedman recalled, Wiesenthal offered a final thought when they shook hands as he was embarking on his return journey to Israel in January 1953: "Think of it," Wiesenthal told him. "When Eichmann is caught, he will be tried by a Jewish court in a Jewish state. History, and our people's honor, Tadek—both are at stake."

For Wiesenthal, the most significant near break in the Eichmann case came in that same year, 1953. According to his account, he met an elderly Austrian baron who shared his passion for stamp collecting. The baron's name, which he only revealed later, was Heinrich Mast, a former counterespionage officer. Wiesenthal described his views as "Catholic-monarchist," which meant he was "always skeptical of the Nazis." After hearing about Wiesenthal's work, he pulled out a letter from someone he described as a former army comrade who was in Buenos Aires, serving as an instructor for President Juan Perón's regime. He pointed to the last paragraph in the letter. Wiesenthal stated he "gasped" when he read it: "Imagine whom else I saw—and even had to talk to twice: this awful swine Eichmann who commanded the Jews. He lives near Buenos Aires and works for a water company."

The baron asked rhetorically: "How do you like that? Some of the worst criminals got away."

Wiesenthal was excited but recognized that he could not pursue this lead on his own. Given the influence of Nazis in Peron's Argentina, Eichmann could feel safe there, he realized. "As an adversary, I was now too lightweight for him," he added. According to Wiesenthal, he consulted with Arie Eschel, the Israeli consul in Vienna, who suggested he put all the information he had collected about Eichmann, including what he had learned from the baron, in a report to the World Jewish Congress (WJC) in New York. He followed those instructions and sent one copy to WJC President Nahum Goldmann and another to the Israeli consulate in Vienna.

Wiesenthal reported that he received no response from Israel. After two months, he did get a letter from Rabbi Abraham Kalmanowitz of the WJC, acknowledging receipt of his information and asking for Eichmann's address in Buenos Aires. When Wiesenthal replied that he would need funds to send someone to Argentina to try to get it, Kalmanowitz turned him down, adding that the FBI had informed Goldmann that Eichmann was in Damascus, which effectively put him out of reach, since Syria would not extradite him.

It was 1954 by then, and, like Friedman who had left two years earlier, Wiesenthal concluded that there simply was not enough interest in his efforts to track down Nazis. "American Jews at that time probably had other worries," he wrote. "The Israelis no longer had any interest in Eichmann; they had to fight for their lives against [Egyptian leader Gamal Abdel] Nasser. The Americans were no longer interested in Eichmann because of the Cold War against the Soviet Union." He felt that "along with a few other like-minded fools, I was quite alone." On another occasion, he pointed out that the "post-war phase of Nazi hunting was over."

Nonetheless, Wiesenthal stuck by his decision to remain in Austria. Later, he would explain that he did so because he recognized that he had to be in Europe to continue his work as a Nazi hunter. But 1954 was also the year when he was compelled to close the Linz Documentation Center, just as Friedman had done with his center two years earlier. He, too, packed up the center's archives and shipped them off to Yad Vashem in Jerusalem. It was a clear signal that he had concluded that his records would now be primarily of use for historians instead of prosecutors. But, as Friedman had done, he kept his Eichmann file. "I honestly don't know why, because in truth I had given up," he declared. Wiesenthal remained in Linz, working for Jewish relief organizations, writing articles for the local press, and finding other ways to keep busy and support his family.

Later, after Eichmann was abducted in Buenos Aires in 1960, Wiesenthal's account about his meeting with the baron and the lack of follow-up would be hotly disputed. After all, it suggested that the Israelis had missed a chance to track down Eichmann much earlier. Isser Harel, the Mossad chief who would ultimately oversee the capture of Eichmann, was infuriated by this version of events, which Wiesenthal first publicized in his initial volume of memoirs, which was published in 1967. If Wiesenthal's story was accurate, this reflected badly on him.

Eichmann's capture would be Israel's most spectacular foray into the Nazi hunting field. But it would also set the stage for a lifelong battle between Wiesenthal and Harel.

In Germany itself, of course, the appetite for pursuing Nazis, whether to bar them from particular jobs or to prosecute them, had largely disappeared by the early 1950s. By the middle of the decade, Western Allies were holding fewer than two hundred war criminals; the rest had benefited from the successive amnesties. Chancellor Adenauer declared in 1952: "I think we now need to finish with this sniffing out of Nazis." It would seem unlikely, therefore, that a new Nazi hunter would emerge in, of all places, a Germany that desperately wanted to take their new leader at his word.

But that's exactly what happened. A hunter emerged who was nothing like Wiesenthal or Friedman, who were both more flamboyant and operated usually on their own. Fritz Bauer was much more like Jan Sehn, the Polish investigating judge who had constructed the cases against Auschwitz commandant Rudolf Höss and other concentration camp personnel.

The two men had very different histories: Bauer was raised as a secular German Jew and he survived most of the Nazi era in exile; Sehn was brought up in a Catholic family with German roots, and his brother had registered as a *Volksdeutscher*—an ethnic German—during the occupation. But those differences were less important than their similarities. Both Bauer and Sehn were chain-smoking judges and prosecutors with a low-key style, who focused on meticulously laying the groundwork for victories in the courtroom. At a time when cooperation across the Iron Curtain was a rarity, they proved it could happen, working together to collect evidence for trials.

Most significantly, both viewed their mission as one of not only punishing the perpetrators but also setting out the historical record—providing the foundations for educating current and future generations. In Germany, the land of the perpetrators, much more so than in Poland, this was both an urgent task and a challenge of staggering proportions.

Bauer was more of a public figure in Germany than Sehn was in Poland. He generated headlines as early as 1952 by prosecuting a landmark case against a former Nazi general. His aim was to demonstrate that resistance to Hitler was a noble act, not treason. In the 1960s, he orchestrated Germany's own Auschwitz trial, which began the process of shaking the country out of its willful amnesia about the Holocaust and other crimes of that era. He became a familiar participant in televised discussions about how the country should deal with its Nazi past. But he operated completely behind the scenes when he played a pivotal role in the Eichmann saga in the late 1950s.

All of which should have won him widespread recognition. Yet Bauer never received his country's highest award for distinguished service, and after his death in 1968 at age sixty-four, he was largely forgotten. Outside Germany, he was never well known in the first place. It's only in the past few years that Germans have begun to rediscover Bauer—and, as so often happens in the case of Nazi hunters, this process has been accompanied by heated controversies. But it's a process that was long overdue.

As Irmtrud Wojak, the author of the first major biography of Bauer, a well-researched tome that was published in 2009, pointed out: "At a time when people hardly wanted to hear about this past anymore and the word 'closure' was mentioned increasingly frequently" he was the person who admonished them at every turn that the recent past could not be dismissed so easily. Wojak argued that he "contributed significantly to the fact that Germany has developed into a state based on the rule of law."

Bauer's persistence in reminding his countrymen of the crimes committed in their name won him far more enemies than it did admirers, along with many more threats than Sehn ever had to deal with in Poland. Anonymous callers would shout: "Jewish pig, die!" And a typical letter writer asked: "Have you in your blind fury not understood that most of the German people are sick and tired of the so-called Nazi criminal trials?" But he was very popular with students, particularly those studying law.

Ilona Ziok, whose powerful documentary about Bauer premiered at the 2010 Berlin Film Festival and put him back in the public spotlight, emphasized how lonely a battle he waged throughout his life. Titled *Death by Installments*, the documentary portrayed him as "the historical figure," in Ziok's words, that she is convinced he was. Her film also made clear how isolated he often felt. "Essentially, Bauer had nothing but enemies," it pointed out.

The resurrection of Bauer as a historical figure has accelerated since that first biography and documentary. Ronen Steinke, an editor at the *Süddeutsche Zeitung*, published a shorter, breezier biography of Bauer in 2013. It included some touchier subjects that the earlier book and film had omitted, prompting charges that he was sensationalizing Bauer's story. When the Jewish Museum of Frankfurt opened a Fritz Bauer exhibition in April 2014 that drew heavily on Steinke's version of events, Wojak and Ziok were particularly incensed. The controversies soon spilled into print, triggering a broader debate within the intellectual community.

The arguments begin with the question of Bauer's Jewish roots and how much emphasis should be put on that part of his identity. His family in Stuttgart was so secular, Ziok said, that "for the Jews, he wasn't a Jew; for Hitler he was a Jew." Or, as Bauer characterized it, he was a Jew according to the Nuremberg laws that enshrined Nazi racial policy—but in no other way. According to the Jewish Museum's exhibit, "Fritz Bauer's family was representative of the Jewish middle class in the German empire" and in his childhood home "Jewish festivals were celebrated for as long as one of the grandmothers was living in the household." But the signs also pointed out: "The family saw itself as secular. Assimilation was associated with the promise of social recognition and equality."

Bauer's father, a World War I veteran, was a staunch German nationalist—and Fritz's upbringing was typical for the times, which made him understand why so many of his generation responded so obediently to orders. Speaking to students in 1962, he recalled that "there were many people who were brought up like me . . . in an authoritarian way. You sit obediently at the table, and you shut up when dad speaks, you don't have the right to say anything . . . we all know this type of father. I myself sometimes have nightmares when I think of when I had the cheek on a Sunday afternoon to move my left arm instead of obediently keeping it under the table."

"The authoritarian education in Germany was really the foundation of German ethics," he continued. "The law is the law and an order is an order—that is the alpha and omega of German efficiency." But if that appeared to place him squarely in the German cultural tradition, he added that his parents did add a caveat that could easily be interpreted as the product of their Jewish values, no matter how nonobservant they were. "You must always know yourself what is right," they told him.

Bauer did not dwell on his personal experiences with anti-Semitism while he was growing up, but he could hardly avoid the topic altogether since he spent part of his university years in Munich just as the Nazis were on the rise there. In talking to students, he recalled seeing "the rowdy crowds of Nazis" and their bright red posters proclaiming: "Jews not allowed entry here." When Foreign Minister Walther Rathenau, the most prominent Jewish member of the government, was assassinated in 1922, he added, "We were deeply shaken, and we had the impression that the Weimar democracy, on which our heart was set . . . was endangered."

Two years earlier, while still in high school, Bauer joined the Social Democratic Party and remained a fiercely engaged partisan his entire life.

The Frankfurt exhibition called him "a Jewish Social Democrat," which Ziok and Wojak feel made it sound like both terms had equal weight. In fact, most of Bauer's early troubles with the Nazis stemmed from his political views, particularly his defense of the Weimar Republic in the face of attacks from both the far right and the far left. He firmly believed in a left-leaning social order that adhered to democratic principles.

Appointed the youngest judge in Stuttgart in 1930, Bauer was particularly interested in making the law more favorable for young criminal offenders, providing them with the chance for rehabilitation. A year later, *NS-Kurier*, the local Nazi newspaper, ran a story under the headline: "A Jewish District Judge is abusing his office for party purposes." The story demanded to know if the Justice Ministry was "defending the behavior of the Jew Bauer?" No doubt that Bauer's primary sin, in the eyes of the Nazis, was his Social Democratic politics, but they were happy to seize on his Jewish identity to make their point.

In this case, they failed—but not completely. Bauer decided to sue the paper for defamation. The court ultimately ruled in his favor, but it was not an unambiguous triumph. The *NS-Kurier* proclaimed: "The expression 'Jewish district judge' is defamatory."

Hitler came to power in late January 1933; by late March, Bauer, along with Kurt Schumacher and other prominent Social Democrats, were dispatched to Heuberg, the first Nazi concentration camp in Württemberg. There was no doubt that he was targeted because of his party affiliation. He was released in November of that same year, and both the Steinke biography and the Frankfurt exhibit declare that this happened only after he and several other prisoners signed a loyalty oath to the new regime. "We unconditionally support the fatherland in the German fight for honor and peace," it declared. Schumacher, who would become the postwar leader of the Social Democrats, refused to sign it and was held in a string of concentration camps until he was freed by the British at the end of the war. Bauer always expressed his admiration for Schumacher's "incredible belief and courage."

At the Frankfurt exhibit, there was a copy of a newspaper that printed the loyalty oath, listing the released prisoners who signed it. The second name listed was "Fritz Hauer." The organizers of the exhibit wrote that off as a typo, and pointed out that there was no other prominent prisoner with a name so close to Bauer's. They also maintained that other records leave no doubt that Bauer signed. But in her lengthier biography, Wojak made no mention of the loyalty oath, and Ziok also ignored it in her documentary. Both maintained they omitted it because there was no definitive proof that Bauer signed it.

"If he signed it, he did it for his family," Ziok added. "He did everything to get his family out." Despite her irritation at what she believed to be the excessive focus on Bauer's identity as a Jew, she conceded that he had to know that the anti-Semitic policies of the Nazis meant that he and his family could be soon persecuted precisely for that reason, even if his initial incarceration was for political reasons.

If the dispute about the loyalty oath seems relatively minor, the controversy about another aspect of Bauer's life—his sexual orientation—was much more heated. In 1936, he fled to Denmark, where his sister and her husband had already settled two years earlier. At first, he saw the country as a liberal paradise. "The Danes enjoy their country's good fortune with a non-brooding, matter-of-factness that always amazes foreigners," he wrote.

But according to Steinke's biography and the Frankfurt exhibit, the police in this seemingly liberal country regularly shadowed him and brought him in for questioning about his alleged contacts with gay men. In 1933, Denmark had been the first country in Europe to decriminalize consensual sex between men, but gay prostitution was still outlawed. A police report exhibited in Frankfurt claimed he admitted to having had two sexual encounters but denied paying for sex.

Wojak suggested that the publicizing of questionable police reports appeared to be aimed at besmirching Bauer's reputation. "It is playing to prejudices against homosexuals that still exist," she said. Ziok is convinced that Bauer was "asexual—I don't think he had sexual contacts with anyone." But then she added, "Even if he was [gay], that's his business." Both of them avoided this topic in their portrayals of Bauer.

Monika Boll, the Frankfurt exhibition's curator, defended the decision to include this part of Bauer's story in the exhibit. "It's not a matter of seeking to out him," she insisted as she walked me around the exhibit on opening day. "You'd think that in Denmark he was politically safe. But there, suddenly, he was prosecuted again in a way that touched his personal life. That's an aspect that must be acknowledged historically. That's the only legitimate reason to make these files public. They don't discredit Fritz Bauer; they discredit the authorities who made these observations."

Ironically, the infighting among those who have given Bauer's history new prominence often obscured the fact that all the parties basically agree on his major accomplishments. This was more of a split between those who feel that he should be presented in only a positive light and those who feel that the airing of such controversies about his personal life in no way detracts from his stature.

When German forces invaded and occupied Denmark in 1940, Bauer was once again at risk. With the help of Danish Social Democrats, he spent much of his time in hiding. In 1943, he married Anna Marie Petersen in the Danish Lutheran Church, which by all accounts was a move designed to give him protection. That same year, Hitler ordered the deportations of Jews from Denmark, but the Danish resistance responded by organizing a legendary rescue effort that allowed about seven thousand Jews to escape to Sweden. Bauer, his sister and brother-in-law, and their parents were among them.

In Sweden, Bauer was the editor of *Sozialistische Tribüne*, the émigré publication for German Social Democrats. One of his younger coeditors was the future West German Chancellor Willy Brandt, who impressed Bauer with his ability of make friends in international circles. Bauer described him as "smart like an American."

When the war ended, Bauer and his family decided to return to Denmark. In his farewell speech to a gathering of anti-Nazi activists on May 9, 1945, right after Germany's surrender, he spelled out his attitude about the future of his homeland:

> Germany is a *tabula rasa* . . . a new and better Germany can and must be
> built from the foundations up. . . . We recognize Germany's obligation

to pay the price for the war crimes committed in its name. . . . The war criminals and criminals . . . who brought Nazism to power and started a war, the criminals of Buchenwald, Belsen and Majdanek should be punished with all severity. . . . No one of us demands pity for the German people. We know that Germans will have to work to gain respect and sympathy for years and decades to come.

He also published a book in Sweden that year with the prescient title: *Die Kriegsverbrecher vor Gericht* (The War Criminals in Court). In 1947, he wrote an article entitled "The Murderers Among Us"—which would serve two decades later as the title of Wiesenthal's first memoirs. Bauer's choice was almost certainly inspired by the first postwar German film dealing with the unmasking of a war criminal, which bore a title with almost identical wording: "The Murderers Are Among Us."

Bauer wanted to contribute to the work of rebuilding respect for Germany from the very beginning. From Denmark, he wrote to his friend Schumacher that he had appealed to the Americans to allow him to travel back to Stuttgart, filling out the numerous forms they requested, but he did not receive permission. He conceded he could not be sure of the reason, but he voiced the suspicion that "they [the Americans] don't want any Jews" returning to take jobs in the public sector. While Brandt and other colleagues were able to return to Germany soon after the war ended, Bauer only followed in 1949. His first job was in Braunschweig, where he was the director for district courts and then district attorney general. This would be the setting for his first confrontation with those who had eagerly served the Third Reich.

The case that established Bauer's reputation as the chief legal challenger of the Nazis did not involve accusations of war crimes or crimes against humanity. There was nothing so grandiose about it. Nonetheless, it centered on a critical question for postwar Germany: how to view those German officers and civilians who attempted to assassinate Hitler on July 20, 1944.

Colonel Claus von Stauffenberg had placed a briefcase with a bomb under the conference table where Hitler was going over war plans with his senior officers at his Wolf's Lair headquarters in East Prussia. Because one of the officers happened to push the briefcase behind the leg of the table, Hitler survived the explosion. Were the conspirators heroes or traitors?

As anyone who watched the 2008 movie *Valkyrie* starring Tom Cruise knows, the key player in the drama that followed was Major Otto Remer, the commander of the Guards Battalion Grossdeutschland in Berlin. He had been wounded eight times during combat, and Hitler had awarded him the Knight's Cross with Oak Leaves. There was no question about his loyalty. But during the confusion in the immediate aftermath of the explosion at Wolf's Lair, the conspirators in Berlin attempted to take command in Berlin. They told Remer that Hitler was dead and instructed him to arrest Propaganda Minister Goebbels.

When Remer showed up at the minister's office with twenty men to do so, Goebbels informed him that the Führer was very much alive—and that he would prove it. Picking up the phone, he got Hitler on the line, who promptly ordered Remer to arrest the plotters. They were subsequently hunted down and executed or forced to commit suicide. Remer was promoted to major general before the war ended.

In postwar West Germany, Remer helped launch a far-right party, the Socialistische Reichspartei, and mobilized supporters with vitriolic tirades against the country's newly elected leaders. As his party began to make a mark in regional elections in 1951, Remer attracted national attention. *Der Spiegel*, the weekly newsmagazine, characterized him in terms that echoed early descriptions of Hitler. He was "39 years old, slim, with an emaciated face and the flaring eyes of the fanatic," the magazine reported.

Remer charged that Germany's new democratic leaders were "recipients of orders from foreign powers." As infuriating as such statements were to the politicians, they were not enough to trigger legal retaliation. But Remer took a step too far during an election rally in Braunschweig on May 3, 1951. He not only defended his actions during the July 20 aborted coup but added a similar accusation about the plotters. "Those conspirators were to a great degree traitors to their country and were paid by foreign powers," he declared.

For Bauer, this was an opportunity to take a stand that, in many ways, embodied his approach to the question of how to address Germany's recent past. He was not interested in trying to punish Remer for his role in rounding up the plotters who had nearly engineered the assassination of Hitler. By prosecuting a defamation case against Remer based on his characterization of the plotters as traitors, Bauer had a larger goal in mind. He wanted to educate the German public about what constituted patriotic behavior during Hitler's rule.

The trial opened on March 7, 1952, attracting sixty German and foreign journalists. In the Braunschweig courtroom, Bauer offered an impassioned summation with one clear philosophical and political message: "Didn't everyone who recognized the injustice of the war have the right to resist and prevent an unjust war?" In fact, he added, "An unjust state like the Third Reich cannot be the object of treason." There was no evidence to support Remer's claim that foreign countries had paid the conspirators, but the most important point that Bauer drove home was that these men were acting out of love of their country, which had been betrayed by a monstrous regime.

Privately, Bauer viewed the military conspirators' motives as not quite as noble as he portrayed them in the courtroom. In a letter he had written in March 1945, he noted: "The anti-Nazi sentiment [of the July 20 plotters] arose not from ethical or political anti-Nazism, but from the fact that Hitler was losing the war." Their object in assassinating Hitler was "to move away from the idea of unconditional surrender," he added, and to allow Germany to emerge from the war as an independent country.

Still, his summation in the Braunschweig trial was a genuine cri de coeur. "It's the task of the prosecutors and the judges of the democratic legal state to rehabilitate the heroes of the 20th of July without conditions or limitations because of the facts that we know today and because of the eternal principles of law," he asserted. He added a personal note about his high school days in Stuttgart, where one of his fellow students was Claus von Stauffenberg. His former schoolmate and the others involved in the conspiracy "saw it as their task to protect the legacy of Schiller," he argued, invoking the country's beloved poet, playwright, and philosopher. In other words, the conspirators were moved by a deep sense of loyalty to Germany's history and culture; they were true patriots.

Judge Joachim Heppe, who had served as an officer in Stalingrad and was then a prisoner of war in Russia, declared that he was "deeply moved" by the moral issues Bauer had raised. In fact, Bauer was so focused on making his argument demonstrating the morality of the plotters' actions that he forgot to ask for a specific sentence for Remer. The court found him guilty of defamation and sentenced him to three months imprisonment—a sentence that he never served because he fled to Egypt and then returned in time to benefit from another amnesty.

For Bauer, though, the trial was a huge victory. The court had agreed with him that the Third Reich was a regime that did not honor the rule of law; therefore, those who had resisted were morally justified in doing so. The resisters, the court declared in its judgment that echoed Bauer's sentiments, "worked for the removal of Hitler, and thereby of the regime he led, entirely from ardent love of the *Vaterland* [fatherland] and selfless awareness of responsibility to their *Volk* [people] extending to unhesitating self-sacrifice. Not with the intent of damaging the *Reich* or the military power of the *Reich*, but only to help both."

A poll taken before the trial showed that 38 percent of Germans approved of the actions of the German resistance; by the end of 1952, the year of the trial, 58 percent of Germans expressed their approval. Bauer had not only moved the needle significantly, he had also started a debate that would continue for decades.

Such trials, Bauer believed, were critical to making Germans understand what had happened during the nightmare years and what constituted decent—and indecent—behavior. The punishment meted out was far less important than the lessons learned. But he was under no illusion that the battle to educate the public about individual responsibility and morality was over. Despite the positive shift in attitudes after the Remer trial, he knew that many of his countrymen were still unrepentant about the Nazi era and even willing to protect war criminals. Which made it all that more important to continue pursuing them whenever possible.

That was why when, in 1957, Bauer received a tantalizing tip from a blind half Jewish German émigré in Argentina about the whereabouts of Eichmann, he, too, decided to act according to his own conscience. Rather than passing on this information through normal German channels, he relayed the tip to the Israelis. By so doing, he triggered a chain of events that culminated in a trial that would mesmerize not only Israel and Germany but the entire world.

CHAPTER EIGHT

"Un Momentito, Señor"

> *"It was well known that there was at least one strong Jewish under-*
> *ground unit that had been working ceaselessly since the end of the*
> *war in all parts of the world, tracking down Nazi war criminals who*
> *had evaded the Allied net in 1945. He had heard that its members*
> *were fanatically devoted to their task, brave people who had dedi-*
> *cated their lives to bringing some of the inhuman monsters responsi-*
> *ble for Belsen, Auschwitz, and other hellholes to justice."*
>
> Jack Higgins, *The Bormann Testament*, a novel that was originally
> published in 1962 with a different title: *The Testament of Caspar Schultz*

Sitting in his comfortable living room in his strikingly modern house
in the Afeka neighborhood of Tel Aviv in March 2014, Rafi Eitan was in a
relaxed mood as he looked back on his long service in the Mossad—and
the highlight of his career, leading the commando unit that seized Adolf
Eichmann near his home in Buenos Aires on May 11, 1960. He talked
about his good fortune to purchase the land for his house in 1950, when
he was just starting in the Mossad at age twenty-four. The property was
cheap then because there were no bridges across a nearby river that sep-
arated the area from the city just south of it, and there was no electricity

or running water. "I said I'll buy the land and one day I will be in a private house in the middle of Tel Aviv," he said, flashing a contented smile.

Today Afeka is an upscale neighborhood of chic villas and apartment buildings connected to the downtown area by pristine highways. But his house is set on a quiet street that looks like it could belong to a Mediterranean resort. The main floor is filled with flowers and plants and is flooded with light—from glass doors that open on his patio and garden, and from a large skylight. Bronze and iron wiry, minimalist sculptures of animals and people decorate the entry hall and his book-lined study. They are the product of his favorite hobby, crafted by the same powerful pair of hands that helped lift Eichmann into his team's waiting car on that fateful day more than a half century ago. A small man, Eitan had built up the strength in his arms and hands by climbing ropes in his youth.

As he began to recount the story of the most famous kidnapping of the modern era, Eitan—who is a Sabra, as Jews who were born in Palestine or later Israel are called—let slip that he visited Germany for the first time in 1953. As he stepped out of the train in Frankfurt, he recalled thinking to himself: "Just a few years ago, eight years ago, if I would be here, probably I would be executed. But now I am a representative of the Israeli government." He hastened to add that his visit had nothing to do with Nazi hunting.

One of the great myths of the postwar era was that Israeli agents were constantly scouring hideouts all over the world, relentlessly tracking down Nazi war criminals. Nothing could be further from the truth, he explained. When he showed up in Frankfurt, his mission was to meet with the Mossad agents charged with monitoring the Jews arriving from Eastern Europe and the Soviet Union and then proceeding to the new Israeli state.

The influx of immigrants from that region during the early days of the Cold War proved to be a major challenge to the Mossad. "The intelligence services of the East—Poland, Romania, Russia of course—recruited many of the immigrants," Eitan explained. The Kremlin had firmly aligned itself with the Arabs against Israel. When the KGB or their affiliates behind the

Iron Curtain received reports from their planted agents in Israel, they would promptly share that information with Israel's Arab neighbors. The new state desperately needed more settlers (Israel's population was about 1.6 million in 1953), but it also needed to identify those who were serving different masters. "We had to check everyone to understand if he was a spy or not," Eitan pointed out. "This was the first priority—not capturing Nazis."

Avraham Shalom—an Austrian-born Mossad agent who later became the head of Shin Bet, Israel's internal security service—served as Eitan's deputy for the Eichmann operation. In an interview at his home in Tel Aviv three months before he died in June 2014, he echoed Eitan's sentiments—and took them one step further. "I was never interested in Nazi hunting as such," he admitted. His attitude had been that the best solution for Jews who were upset by the thought that so many Nazi criminals were still at large "was to come and live here," he added.

In the early days of Israel's existence, there was simply not enough time, energy, or desire to hunt Nazis. That led Eitan to shrug off the controversy that surfaced later about the value of Wiesenthal's 1953 tip from the Austrian baron about the Eichmann sighting in Argentina. Even if Wiesenthal had provided more precise information about Eichmann's whereabouts, Eitan asserted, Israel was in no position to dedicate the necessary manpower and resources to track him down that early. The struggle for Israel's survival in a region filled with enemies trumped everything else.

By the late 1950s, however, Prime Minister David Ben-Gurion and other top Israeli leaders were feeling more confident about their fledgling country's prospects. The notion that they might authorize a major operation to seize a notorious Nazi war criminal no longer seemed far-fetched. That is, if such an opportunity presented itself—if, in effect, the opportunity fell into the lap of the Mossad.

Which is exactly what happened.

On September 19, 1957, Fritz Bauer, who by then was attorney general of the West German state of Hesse, arranged a meeting with Felix

Shinar, the head of Israel's reparations mission in West Germany. To make sure it was as hush-hush as possible, the two men met at an inn just off the Cologne–Frankfurt highway.

According to Isser Harel, the Mossad director who would later issue the orders that sent Eitan, Shalom, and other operatives to Argentina to kidnap Eichmann, Bauer came straight to the point. "Eichmann has been traced," he told Shinar.

When the Israeli queried whether he really meant Adolf Eichmann, Bauer responded: "Yes, Adolf Eichmann. He is in Argentina."

"And what do you intend to do?" asked Shinar.

"I'll be perfectly frank with you, I don't know if we can altogether rely on the German judiciary here, let alone on the German embassy staff in Buenos Aires," Bauer responded, leaving no doubt that he distrusted many of his country's public servants and was worried that someone would tip off Eichmann if they learned that he was in danger of arrest. "I see no other way but to talk to you," Bauer continued. "You are known to be efficient people, and nobody could be more interested than you in the capture of Eichmann." Then he threw in a word of caution: "Obviously I wish to maintain contact with you in connection with this matter, but only provided that strict secrecy is kept."

It was clear that Bauer meant that all their communications had to be kept secret from the German authorities, and Shinar happily agreed, pointing out that he would pass on the information on that basis to his higher-ups in Israel. "Thank you from the bottom of my heart for the great faith you have shown in us," he said. "Israel will never forget what you have done."

Shinar made good on his promise, filing a detailed report to the Foreign Ministry in Jerusalem. When Walter Eytan, the ministry's director general, met Harel at a café in Tel Aviv to relay the news, the Mossad chief promised that he'd investigate fully. The same evening and well into the night, he read the Eichmann file that he had instructed the agency's archivist to pull for him. "I didn't know then what sort of man Eichmann was," he wrote later, or "with what morbid zeal he pursued his murderous work." But when he got up from his desk at dawn, he knew "that in everything pertaining to the Jews he was the paramount authority and his were the hands that pulled the strings controlling manhunt and massacre."

Harel also knew that, in his words, "People were tired of atrocity stories." But he claimed that he immediately came to a critical decision: "That night I resolved that if Eichmann were alive, come hell or high water he'd be caught."

Perhaps he did, but even some members of his team would later question Harel's handling of the case, pointing out how long it took for him to act on Bauer's information because of early missteps. More than two years would elapse between Bauer's meeting with Shinar and the serious preparation for Operation Eichmann, the kidnapping of the famous fugitive. But if Harel's initial decisions were easy to second-guess later, there is no doubt that in the end he implemented a stunningly daring plan that was brilliantly executed.

Shinar, the Israeli representative in West Germany, returned to Israel for a visit shortly after Harel received the Eichmann news. That allowed the Mossad chief to question him further about his conversation with Bauer, and, most significantly, to get his personal evaluation of the man. "What Dr. Shinar told me about Fritz Bauer's personality impressed me a great deal," Harel wrote, adding that he assured Shinar that he would send a special envoy to continue the contacts with Bauer and elicit additional information.

The man he chose for that task, Shaul Darom, had gone to France in 1947 to study art and then linked up with a group there that funneled Jews to Israel. He did well both as a painter and as an intelligence agent. He had "a natural flair" for such work, Harel reported, and he moved easily around Europe as an increasingly recognized artist who spoke several languages.

Darom and Bauer met in Cologne on November 6, 1957. The meeting yielded key pieces of information. Bauer explained that his source was a half Jewish German in Argentina who had written to the German authorities after he had read in the newspapers that Eichmann had disappeared. Bauer did not reveal the man's name at that point, since he was corresponding directly with him and he wanted to protect his source. But he emphasized that the details the source provided corresponded to what he already knew about Eichmann and his family, including the ages of the sons who were born before his wife, Vera, and those boys had also left Germany, supposedly to live with a second husband. The informant provided an address for the man he presumed to be Eichmann: 4261 Chacabuco Street in Olivos, a suburb of Buenos Aires.

Bauer was open about why he had turned to the Israelis instead of going to the German authorities. "I am sure that you were the only ones who would be ready and willing to act," he told Darom. When the Israeli agent said he was worried that any extradition proceedings could tip off Eichmann and allow him to escape again, Bauer responded: "I too am worried about that and I won't reject the idea of your getting him to Israel in your own way."

Those words left little room for ambiguity. As a representative of the law in West Germany, Bauer was, in effect, urging the Israelis to come up with a practical solution that ignored normal legal procedures. The only person in Germany he had informed about what he was doing, he added, was someone he trusted completely: Georg-August Zinn, a fellow Social Democrat who was the prime minister of Hesse.

Darom was impressed by Bauer's "courage" not only in bypassing his own government and reaching out to the Israelis, but also in his willingness to offer the assurance that he was ready to accept whatever action they decided on. Harel wrote later that he viewed him as "an honest man with a warm Jewish heart." Alluding to the return of many former Nazis to public positions, he added: "I gather he is disappointed with present developments in Germany, and I have the feeling that he is not at peace with himself for having decided to resume his political activities in such a Germany."

Yet Harel's initial attempts to check out Bauer's leads resulted in apparent failure. In January 1958, he sent Yael Goren, an agent who had spent considerable time in South America, to Buenos Aires, with strict instructions not to take any actions that might attract attention. Accompanied by an Israeli who was doing research in Argentina, Goren checked out the address that Bauer had provided and the neighborhood—but they immediately concluded that something was off. It was an impoverished area, the street was unpaved, and, as Harel put it, "the wretched little house could in no way be reconciled with our picture of the life of an SS officer of Eichmann's rank." At the time, the common assumption was that prominent Nazi fugitives had managed to smuggle out vast wealth, most of it seized from their wartime victims.

The two men were also thrown off by the slovenly-looking European woman they spotted in the yard of the house. Eichmann was known as a womanizer, and they couldn't believe she could be his wife. Harel claimed that Goren's report on his mission was "a great disappointment" to him. In his account of the entire Eichmann affair that he was only able to publish in 1975, twelve years after stepping down as head of the Mossad, he declared: "The obvious conclusion was that the information passed on by Bauer was unfounded, but it was my belief that this wasn't so."

In all likelihood, Harel's "belief" was shaky at best, but he did take the logical next step: he asked Darom to meet with Bauer again, this time insisting that they had to learn the name of his source so that they could check his story further. On January 21, 1958, they met in Frankfurt and Bauer quickly relented, providing the name of Lothar Hermann and his address in Coronel Suárez, a city more than three hundred miles from Buenos Aires. Bauer also provided a letter of introduction for whoever Harel would decide to send Hermann's way.

That somebody was Efraim Hofstaetter, a top Israeli police investigator who was on his way to South America on a different case. Harel asked him to check out Hermann once he had completed his other business, supplying him with Bauer's letter of introduction. Hermann rebuffed his request that they meet in Buenos Aires, so Hofstaetter traveled on an overnight train to Coronel Suárez. When he knocked on Hermann's door, Hermann invited him in but immediately asked for assurances that he really represented the German authorities, which was the cover story that he and Harel had agreed on. "How am I to know that you are telling the truth?" Hermann asked.

Hofstaetter explained about the letter of introduction from Bauer, holding it out for Hermann. But his host ignored his extended hand. At that moment, Hermann called his wife and asked her to take the letter and read it aloud. It was only then that Hofstaetter realized that Hermann was blind. The wife read the letter and added: "The signature is without doubt Dr. Bauer's."

Hermann visibly relaxed and began telling his story. His parents had died at the hands of the Nazis, he said, and he had spent time in the concentration camps. "I have Jewish blood in my veins, but my wife is German and our daughter has been brought up according to her mother's traditions," he added. His only motivation for tracking Eichmann was "to even the score with the Nazi criminals who caused me and my family so much agony and suffering."

The Hermanns had lived in the Olivos suburb of Buenos Aires, until eighteen months earlier, where they were "accepted as German in every way." Sylvia, the daughter, began dating a young man named Nicolas Eichmann, who had no idea she was partly Jewish. He visited their house on several occasions, and once he remarked that it would have been better if the Germans had completed the extermination of the Jews. He also explained that he did not have a distinct regional accent because his father had served in many different places during the war.

Prompted by a news report about a war crimes trial where Eichmann was mentioned, Hermann concluded that Nicolas was his son. In those days, many Nazis felt so much at home in Argentina that they took only minimal precautions—and, while Adolf had been living under an assumed last name, his sons never bothered to change theirs. But Nicolas did take one precaution when he started seeing Sylvia: he made a point of never revealing his home address. When Nicolas and Sylvia wrote to each other after she moved, he instructed her to mail her letters to a friend's address. But that only strengthened Hermann's suspicions, and soon he was corresponding with Bauer.

At that point, Sylvia, "an attractive woman of about twenty," as Hofstaetter described her to Harel, entered the room. It was clear that, whatever she had once felt for Nicolas, she had decided to help her father in his quest to confirm his theory. When Bauer asked Hermann to go to Buenos Aires to investigate further, the blind man took his daughter along not just to serve as his eyes but also to exploit her ties with Nicolas. With the help of a friend, she located his house and simply knocked on the door.

When a woman opened the door, Sylvia asked if this was the home of the Eichmann family. "Her reply did not come immediately, and during the pause a middle-aged man wearing glasses came and stood beside her," she recalled. "I asked him if Nick was at home." Speaking in an "unpleasant and strident" voice, he told her that Nick was working overtime. Sylvia continued: "I asked if he was Mr. Eichmann. No reply. So I asked if he was Nick's father. He said he was, but only after long hesitation."

The family had five children, three born in Germany and two born in Argentina, Sylvia added. Although the ages of the sons born in Germany tallied with what Bauer already knew about Eichmann, Hofstaetter remained cautious. "What you say is pretty convincing but it isn't a conclusive identification," he said. He added that Vera may have remarried but allowed her first three children to keep her first husband's name. Lothar Hermann insisted that there was no doubt that the man she was living with was Adolf Eichmann.

Promising to cover his expenses, the Israeli told Hermann he needed him to get more information about the suspect—what name he was using, where he worked, any official photograph or personal document, and fingerprints. Returning to Tel Aviv, he reported to Harel that he had found Hermann to be "impetuous and overconfident," indicating he had doubts about his story. But he was favorably impressed by Sylvia, and recommended following up quickly since she was planning to travel abroad soon.

Harel approved additional funds for Hermann's expenses so he could conduct further research in Buenos Aires, but did not get the results he was hoping for. Lothar and Sylvia Hermann learned from a property registry that the owner of the house on Chacabuco Street was an Austrian named Francisco Schmidt, and that it had two apartments with separate electric meters, one for someone named Dagoto and the other for someone name Klement. Hermann concluded that Schmidt must be

Eichmann, and that he had undergone plastic surgery to change his appearance.

But when the Israeli researcher in Argentina who had worked on the case earlier followed up, he discovered that Schmidt could not be Eichmann: his family situation was different, and he did not even live in the house he owned. "These findings damaged Hermann's trustworthiness irretrievably," Harel reported. By August 1958, he added, "instructions were given to allow our contact with Hermann to lapse gradually."

That was the year when West Germany opened the Central Office for the Investigation of National Socialist Crimes in Ludwigsburg, a picturesque town just north of Stuttgart. In August 1959, Tuvia Friedman claimed to have received a letter from Erwin Schüle, the head of the Ludwigsburg office, mentioning a tip that Eichmann was possibly in Kuwait. Excited, Friedman turned to Asher Ben-Natan, his old Israeli contact from Vienna who was now serving in the Defense Ministry. He even imagined that he might be sent with a few men to Kuwait on a mission to seize Eichmann. But Ben-Natan brushed him off, and so did a senior police official he sent him to. Friedman concluded that those officials were no longer interested in hunting Eichmann, and he turned to the Israeli press to publicize the fugitive's purported presence in Kuwait.

For Bauer, the Mossad's lack of follow-up with Hermann, combined with the sudden publicity about Kuwait, was intensely frustrating; he was increasingly worried that Eichmann would learn of the efforts to track him and run again. In December 1959, Bauer went to Israel with more information. According to a new source, he reported, Eichmann had traveled to Argentina under the name of Ricardo Klement, which corresponded to the name on one of the electric meters of the house on Chacabuco Street that Hermann had been talking about all along. As Harel pointed out in his defense, Hermann had mistakenly assumed that Eichmann was the owner of the house, not one of its tenants. Realizing what had happened, the Mossad chief assigned a new man, Zvi Aharoni, to follow up. Suddenly, Hermann's lead looked promising again, but no one knew whether Eichmann was still there.

When Bauer met with Harel, Aharoni, and Israel's attorney general,

Chaim Cohen, in Jerusalem, he did not disguise his anger. "This is simply unbelievable!" he declared, pointing out that the name Klement had been mentioned much earlier by Hermann and now again by the new source. "Any second-class policeman would be able to follow such a lead. Just go and ask the nearest butcher or greengrocer and you will learn all there is to know about Klement."

Aharoni, who related that outburst, became one of the harshest critics of Harel's handling of the Eichmann investigation. "The sad truth is that Eichmann was discovered by a blind man and that Mossad needed more than two years to believe that blind man's story," he declared afterward.

Harel informed Ben-Gurion of the possible breakthrough. The prime minister told him that, if the lead panned out, he wanted Eichmann brought back for trial in Israel. As Harel related their conversation, Ben-Gurion believed such a trial "would be an achievement of tremendous moral and historical consequence."

Harel had chosen Aharoni to go to Argentina this time, checking whether now they finally could identify and locate Eichmann at the original address that Hermann had given them. The Mossad chief considered him to be "one of the best investigators" in Israel; born in Germany, he had escaped to Palestine in 1938 and later served in the British Army, interrogating German POWs.

Aharoni had to finish up another assignment first, which meant an additional delay of a couple of months that left Harel "seething with impatience." But during that time Aharoni prepared for his mission by learning the background of the case and meeting Bauer. On March 1, 1960, he finally landed in Buenos Aires, armed with an Israeli diplomatic passport under a false name; his cover was that he worked for the Foreign Ministry's accounts department.

Accompanied by a local student who had agreed to help out, Aharoni drove in a rented car to Chacabuco Street in Olivos on March 3. But when they reached the two-family house and the student walked up to it pretending to be looking for someone else, it turned out that there were no tenants in the two apartments. Instead, the student saw through the windows that they were empty, and painters were at work inside. Eichmann and his family, if they were there earlier, must have moved.

The next day Aharoni improvised a plan to learn more. Remembering from the Eichmann file that Klaus, the eldest Eichmann son, had a birthday on March 3, he instructed a local young volunteer named Juan to drive back to the empty house carrying a gift and card for him. The cover story was that a friend, who worked as a bellboy in one of the large hotels in Buenos Aires, had asked him to deliver the package, which came from a young woman; if pressed, he could maintain that he knew nothing more about its origins.

Not finding anyone at the front of the house, Juan went around to the back. There, he saw a man talking to a woman who was cleaning something near a hut.

"Excuse me please, but do you know whether Mr. Klement lives here?" he asked. Both of them immediately confirmed the name, and the man responded: "You mean the Germans?"

To avoid arousing suspicion, he claimed to have no knowledge of their nationality. The man added: "Do you mean the one with the three grown sons and the little son?"

Again, Juan pleaded ignorance, saying he was there only to deliver a small package to him. The man volunteered that the family had moved out fifteen to twenty days earlier, but he didn't know where they had gone.

This could have been devastating news, suggesting that if Aharoni had arrived just a bit earlier he would have found them at the house. But the man clearly accepted Juan's cover story and took him to one of the painters who was working in a back room. The painter was equally forthcoming, saying that the Klements had moved to San Fernando, another suburb of Buenos Aires. He didn't know the address, but suggested that they could talk to one of Klement's sons who worked in an auto repair shop nearby.

Dressed like a mechanic, the young German confirmed that he was one of Klement's sons, and Juan heard others calling him something that sounded to him like Tito or Dito. As Aharoni put it later, this was clearly Dieter, the third of the Eichmann sons. Dieter was more suspicious than the Argentine workers. He questioned Juan about his story and who had sent the package. When Juan repeated his story, Dieter said that the street where they now lived had no name or numbers. Realizing that he wouldn't learn anything more directly and to avoid further questioning, he handed the small package to Dieter, asking him to give it to his brother.

Staking out the auto repair shop, Aharoni and his small team decided to track Dieter's movements after work. The first night they never spotted him leaving; later, they saw two people on a moped, and assumed that the passenger on the back was Dieter. The moped traveled in the direction of San Fernando, and the driver dropped off the passenger near a kiosk. This turned out to be about a hundred yards from a newly built small house on Garibaldi Street, which they would soon learn was where the Eichmann family had just moved.

Aharoni was convinced that "Klement" was really Eichmann, but he kept looking for additional confirmation. He had Juan return to see Dieter at the auto repair shop and spin a story that the sender of the package had complained to him that it never was delivered. In the ensuing conversation, Dieter insisted that he had passed along the package and also revealed that it should have been addressed to Nicolas "Aitchmann," as Juan noted the name later, not "Klement." Juan believed this was bad news, indicating they had not found their man. But Aharoni, who didn't want to let him in on who they were really looking for, assured him he had done "a fantastic job."

Aharoni made repeated trips to San Fernando, initially talking to neighbors using a variety of pretexts. He confirmed that the German family had moved in recently, and an architect obtained the document showing that plot 14 on Garibaldi Street, where the new house was situated, was registered under the name of Veronica Catarina Liebl de Eichmann, listing both her maiden and married names. After repeated passes to observe the house, Aharoni caught his first glimpse of "a man of medium size and build, about fifty years old, with a high forehead and partially bald" on March 19. The man collected the wash from the clothesline and went back into the house.

Excited, Aharoni cabled his superiors that he had spotted a man at

Vera Eichmann's house "who definitely resembled Eichmann," and that there was no longer any doubt about his identity. He also recommended that he return to Israel right away to help in the planning of the operation to kidnap him. Before he did so, however, he was intent on getting a photo of their quarry.

Sitting in the back of a small truck that was covered with a tarpaulin, Aharoni had the driver park next to the kiosk and go get something to eat. In the meantime, he observed the house and pointed a camera through a hole in the tarp. He photographed the house and the surroundings. But he had to delegate the job of photographing Eichmann with a camera hidden in a briefcase to another local helper with native Spanish. Intercepting Eichmann and his son Dieter when they were outside, the helper engaged them briefly in conversation, just long enough to trigger his camera.

Aharoni left Argentina on April 9. Harel joined him on the flight from Paris to Tel Aviv. "Are you absolutely sure that he is our man?" he asked. Aharoni showed him the photo that was taken with the briefcase camera. "I have not the slightest doubt," he replied.

It wasn't just Vera Eichmann's use of her real name on the property registration that indicated the family's increasingly relaxed attitude. Wiesenthal, who kept monitoring the rest of the Eichmann family back in Austria, had spotted other telltale evidence that the purported widow was living with her infamous fugitive husband. Eichmann's stepmother had died, and a death notice in the *Oberösterreichische Nachrichten*, the Linz daily, was signed by Vera Eichmann, using her married name. "People don't lie in these notices," Wiesenthal pointed out in his memoir. She also signed a similar notice in the same newspaper when Eichmann's father died in February 1960. "The Eichmanns' family feeling evidently made them blind to danger," Wiesenthal added.

Wiesenthal reported that he hired two photographers equipped with telephoto lenses to snap pictures of the mourners at the father's funeral. They included Eichmann's brothers, and one of them, Otto, bore a striking resemblance to Adolf. Wiesenthal claimed that this explained the repeated alleged sightings of Adolf in Europe over the years. According to his account, he gave the photos to two Israeli agents who were dispatched to collect them and rushed to deliver them to their bosses. "Anyone with Otto Eichmann's photograph in his hands would be able to identify Adolf Eichmann—even if he now called himself Ricardo Klement," Wiesenthal wrote.

Harel and other critics of Wiesenthal would dismiss much of his account later, arguing that Wiesenthal was hyping his role and even making up parts of his story. The meeting with the two Israeli agents that Wiesenthal described in his memoirs "never happened," Harel insisted. Instead, Wiesenthal sent the photos to the Israeli embassy in Vienna, the Mossad chief added. No one "got excited over these photographs" since they were not that significant. But Aharoni, who afterward expressed as much admiration for Wiesenthal as contempt for Harel, credited the Nazi hunter in Austria with providing "an important piece of information."

Whatever the accuracy of those differing versions of events, there was no doubt that the growing evidence indicated that the Israelis were on the right trail and closing in on their target. But Harel and Eitan, the man he had designated to lead the operation on the ground, knew that they had to work out what they would do with Eichmann to get him out of the country before they could kidnap him. That meant arranging a safe house to hold the prisoner, and then the transport to Israel.

Harel took charge of making arrangements for the preferred option: flying Eichmann out. But El Al, the Israeli airline, had no flights to Argentina at that time, so they needed to find a pretext to send a special plane. Fortuitously, Argentina was planning to commemorate the 150th anniversary of its independence in late May, and Israel was invited to send its representatives to the celebrations. Harel suggested to the Foreign Ministry that the delegation should fly to Buenos Aires in a special plane, and he worked directly with El Al's executives to ensure that he had the airline's full cooperation. They even allowed the Mossad chief to approve the crew that would be selected for the flight.

While Harel handled the flight arrangements, Eitan looked into a backup plan: the much less desirable option of a lengthy journey by sea.

He got in touch with the chairman of Zim, the Israeli shipping lines, which had two refrigerated ships at the time. As Eitan pointed out with a laugh, they were used to transport kosher beef from Argentina to Israel. Working with the captain of one of those ships, Eitan arranged for the preparation of a special compartment that would have served as Eichmann's floating temporary prison if the flight had not worked out for any reason. In other words, he would have been smuggled out with a regular shipment of kosher beef.

After two weeks in Israel, a period when Harel prepared the team members who would soon make their way to Argentina using a variety of passports and cover stories, Aharoni landed back in Buenos Aires on April 24. He was no longer posing as an Israeli diplomat but as a German businessman, with a new passport, a new mustache, and new clothes. One of the first to follow was Avraham Shalom, Eitan's deputy for the operation. Landing in Israel after a lengthy mission in Asia, Shalom was instructed to immediately report to Harel. The Mossad chief told him he wanted him to meet up with Aharoni, check out everything about the purported sightings of Eichmann and his family on Garibaldi Street, and send a coded signal if he felt certain that they had the right man in their sights.

Shalom was an experienced agent but, for whatever reason, he nearly blew his cover a couple of times. After reaching Paris on the first leg of his journey, he picked up a German passport with new identity papers. In transit in Lisbon, he and other passengers were required to hand in their passports and then to ask for them back when they were ready to board their next flight—in his case, the flight to Buenos Aires. Shalom forgot his fake name and had to reach behind a startled airport official to point to the passport which he recognized only by its color. When he finally reached his hotel in Buenos Aires and had to register at the desk of his hotel, his mind went blank again for a long moment. Shalom claimed that he was not excited by the whole notion of Nazi hunting, but his emotions must have been churning much more than he let on.

When Aharoni took Shalom to see Garibaldi Street, Shalom was favorably impressed. It was "not a real street," he recalled. "It was a footpath for cars. It was an ideal place for an operation—no electricity, few people." The only lights came from the occasional passing car. By then, the Israelis were no longer startled by the notion that the once powerful Eichmann lived in such humble surroundings. By the time more members of the team arrived, Aharoni had confirmed that they were tracking the right man. They also observed his daily routine from a safe distance. They watched him walk to a bus stop to travel to a Mercedes factory every morning, and return by bus to the stop right at the corner of his street at the same time every evening. From there, Eichmann had a very short walk to his house.

Peter Malkin, an especially strong member of the team, was given the assignment of grabbing Eichmann first. "Never before in my career had I been even a little frightened," he recalled. "Now I was terrified of failure." But Eitan, who was one of the last to arrive, concurred with Shalom that the conditions were promising. "From the very beginning when I analyzed the situation, the area, the house, the surroundings, I was sure that there was no reason we would fail," he insisted.

Looking back at that momentous gathering of the team of agents in Buenos Aires, Eitan nonetheless admitted that there was always the possibility of something going wrong. Good cars were hard to get in Buenos Aires, and the beat-up vehicles the team had rented broke down often; there was always the possibility, too, that some slip by one of the Israelis could arouse suspicion. Harel, who also flew to Argentina but stayed in downtown Buenos Aires to monitor the action from a short distance, had given Eitan a pair of open handcuffs, keeping the key for himself. If the Argentine police should catch up with them after they seized Eichmann, he instructed Eitan, he had to be sure to handcuff his hand to Eichmann's. Then he would tell the police to bring both of them to the Israeli ambassador.

Eitan took the handcuffs. But keeping this from Harel, he and Aharoni agreed that if the operation really went wrong, they would kill Eichmann. That would not even require a weapon, he pointed out. In fact, along with the others on the mission, he would not be carrying a gun, figuring that this could only get them into deeper trouble if they were caught. "The easy way to kill someone with your hands is to break his neck," he said.

On the evening of May 10, the day before the scheduled operation, Harel gathered the whole team for a final briefing. At this point, everyone knew their assignments, and a total of seven safe houses and apartments were prepared, primarily to provide alternatives for where to hold the captive until he could be smuggled out of the country, but also for members of the team. Those who had been staying in hotels had already been told to check out and move to one of the safe houses. The Mossad chief did not want everyone checking out from hotels on the day of the kidnapping, which could tip off the police about their identities.

Since those logistics were taken care of, Harel devoted most of his briefing to the bigger picture. "I strove to impress upon the men the unique moral and historical significance of what they were doing," he recalled. "They were chosen by destiny . . . to guarantee that one of the worst criminals of all time . . . would be made to stand trial in Jerusalem."

"For the first time in history the Jews would judge their assassins," he continued, "and for the first time the world would hear, and the young generation in Israel would hear, the full story of the edict of annihilation against an entire people." He impressed upon them the importance of a successful outcome. The methods they were about to employ were regrettable, he added, "but there was no way of serving morality and justice other than through this specific operation."

Then he sounded the inevitable cautionary note. If they were caught, Harel said, they should admit that they were Israelis, but they should also assert that they undertook this action on their own initiative. They were not to admit that this was an official Israeli action.

Harel believed, and he was sure most members of his team believed, that they would succeed. But it was normal for everyone to think about the other possibility. One of the agents asked bluntly: "How long do you think we'll have to sit in prison if we're caught?"

The Mossad chief was equally blunt in his reply: "A good few years."

The team deployed two cars for the operation, which was timed to intercept Eichmann when he normally got off the bus from work, which they had established was 7:40 in the evening. Aharoni drove the first car, which also contained Eitan, an agent named Moshe Tavor, and Malkin, the designated man to seize Eichmann. Harel was particularly attentive to Malkin's role. "I'm warning you—no bodily harm," he instructed him. "Not a scratch."

Malkin, who was a master of disguises, put on a wig and wore dark clothes. He also had a pair of fur-lined gloves. Since it was winter in Argentina, this hardly looked unusual. "The gloves of course would help with the cold, but that is not the main reason I bought them," he noted. "The thought of placing my bare hand over the mouth that had ordered the death of millions, of feeling the hot breath and the saliva on my skin, filled me with an overwhelming sense of revulsion." Malkin, like so many other members of the team, had lost several family members during the Holocaust.

Shalom, Eitan's deputy, was in the second car with other agents. They were parked about thirty yards away, with the hood up as if they were doing some repairs. As soon as they spotted Eichmann, they were supposed to turn on their bright lights, blinding Eichmann so he wouldn't see the first car just up ahead.

Eichmann normally followed the same routine every day, but on that evening he did not get off the bus the Israelis were waiting for. By eight when he still hadn't arrived, Aharoni whispered to Eitan: "Do we leave or continue to wait?" Eitan replied that they should wait, but he, too, was calculating they could not do so much longer. Although it was dark, the two parked cars risked attracting attention.

Shalom had gotten out of the second car and about 8:05 he spotted Eichmann in the evening darkness. He rushed back to the car, another agent quickly slammed the hood down, and Shalom flashed the headlights. In the first car, Aharoni saw Eichmann clearly through his binoculars. Leaning out the window, he warned the waiting Malkin: "He has a hand in his pocket. Watch out for a weapon."

As Eichmann turned the corner from the bus stop and walked directly by their car, Malkin turned around and blocked his path. "Un momentito, señor," he said, using the phrase he had been practicing for weeks. Eichmann stopped abruptly, and Malkin took advantage of that instant to lunge for him. The problem was that, because of Aharoni's warning, he grabbed for his right hand instead of his throat and the two men tumbled into a ditch.

Eichmann began screaming. "This turned a well-planned and carefully exercised operation into an unholy mess," Aharoni reported later. He gunned the engine to drown out the screams, while Eitan and Tavor jumped out of the car to help. Malkin grabbed Eichmann by his legs while the two others took him by his arms, quickly pulling him into the car through the back door. They put him on the floor between the front and the back seats, where they had placed blankets both so that he would not be injured and to cover him. Eichmann's head was pressed against Eitan's knees, and Malkin sat on the other side. Their captive had no weapon.

Aharoni delivered a sharp order to Eichmann in German: "If you don't keep still, you'll be shot." Malkin still had his hand on his mouth beneath the blanket, but when Eichmann nodded, signaling he understood, he took it off. They then drove in silence. Eitan and Malkin shook hands. Eichmann, who was now outfitted in thick goggles so he could not see anything, lay completely still.

On their way to the main safe house, they stopped to switch license plates. They briefly lost the second car that was supposed to be with them, but it soon reappeared and followed them to the designated villa, where other members of the team were anxiously waiting.

The Israelis walked Eichmann to the small second-floor room prepared for him, and put him on an iron bed, shackling one of his legs to its heavy frame. They undressed him and a member of the team who was a doctor examined his mouth to make sure he did not have any poison. The prisoner protested that after all this time as a free man he was not taking such precautions, but the doctor still removed his false teeth to be sure and then inspected the rest of his body. Eitan, Shalom, Malkin, and Aharoni were all in the room, watching while the doctor checked his armpit where normally SS officers had a tattoo with their blood type. Instead, Eichmann only had a small scar, which later he admitted was the result of his efforts to burn away the tattoo with a cigarette when he had been detained by the Americans at the end of the war. His captors had failed to realize his true identity then.

Given his experience as an interrogator in the British Army, Aharoni was tasked with getting the prisoner to admit his identity this time. He had studied Eichmann's file that Fritz Bauer had shared with the Israelis, and he was ready to keep asking as many questions as needed to force a confession. His normal style was to ask them slowly and repeatedly. "He was a very boring interrogator," Shalom recalled with a smile. "You could go out of your mind until you heard his next word. He was a very smart chap. He'd ask you the same question ten times."

As it turned out, Eichmann broke down much sooner than anyone expected, making that procedure unnecessary. When Aharoni asked for his name, he replied: "Ricardo Klement." But when he asked him his height, shoe size, and clothing size, each of his answers matched those in his file. Then Aharoni asked him his Nazi Party membership number, and he provided the correct answer. The same thing happened when he asked him for his SS number. He also provided his correct date and place of birth—March 19, 1906, in Solingen, Germany.

"Under which name were you born?" Aharoni then asked.

"Adolf Eichmann," he replied.

As Aharoni put it, "We had come out of the tunnel. . . . the tensions of a long and difficult operation dissolved."

Just before midnight, Aharoni and Shalom drove to downtown Buenos Aires where Harel was waiting in a coffee shop for news. As Shalom recalled, the Mossad chief had been switching coffee shops periodically according to a schedule to avoid attracting attention. "I don't know how many teas he had," he said, laughing.

The special El Al flight, a turboprop Bristol Britannia carrying the Israeli delegation, landed in Buenos Aires just before 6 p.m. on May 19. The delegation was headed by Abba Eban, a minister without portfolio who had already served as Israel's ambassador to the United States and the United Nations; he would later become the country's highly effective foreign minister. Prime Minister Ben-Gurion had told him earlier that the flight's real mission was to bring Eichmann back to Israel, and that information was shared with only a small number of the others on board. But the presence of three unfamiliar men in El Al uniforms who did not even pretend to be carrying out any flight duties tipped off most of the crew that something was afoot.

Back at the safe house, Aharoni and Malkin kept questioning Eichmann during the wait for the plane. Offering a preview of the kind of arguments that he would make at his trial, Eichmann claimed that he was never anti-Semitic. "You must believe me, I had nothing against the Jews," he insisted. But Hitler was "infallible," and he had sworn an oath as an SS officer to him personally, which meant he had no choice but to follow orders. As Malkin summed up his message, "There was a job to do and he did it."

As a prisoner, Eichmann was more than obedient. "He behaved like a scared, submissive slave whose one aim was to please his new masters," Harel observed. Initially, the prisoner was terrified his captors would execute him or poison his food. And he seemed almost relieved to hear that the plan was to have him stand trial. He tried to convince his captors that he should stand trial in Germany, Argentina, or Austria, but when Aharoni told him this was not going to happen, he even agreed to sign a statement declaring his willingness to go to Israel to be tried there.

During this whole period, the Israeli team kept monitoring the newspapers, fearful of any indications that the Argentine authorities had learned of Eichmann's kidnapping. But as Nicolas Eichmann indicated later, the family, while suspecting the Israelis were behind the father's disappearance, were not about to make any public statements that could tip the Argentines off to his real identity.

The Israeli team's main task was to prepare to get Eichmann on board the El Al flight. Shalom had repeatedly driven to the airport to familiarize himself with the route and make himself known to the guards. When the plane was parked in the maintenance area, he could come in and out without being stopped. On May 20, the scheduled departure day, Shalom made a final inspection of the aircraft and sent a courier to Harel informing him that it was open and safe. Earlier in the day, another member of his team had told key crew members that the plane would be carrying a passenger wearing an El Al uniform who would appear to be sick. They were not told his identity, but the nature of the mission was now clear.

Back at the safe house, Eichmann was completely cooperative as he was bathed, shaved, and dressed in the airline's uniform. When the team doctor brought out an injection to sedate him, the prisoner assured him this was not necessary since he would remain quiet. The Israelis were not about to take that risk. Seeing that they were determined to stick with the plan, Eichmann once again cooperated fully. By the time the agents were ready to take him out of the house, the drug was already beginning to work. But Eichmann was still alert enough to point out that they had left off his jacket, asking them to put it on so he would look exactly like the other crew members.

Eichmann dozed as he was driven in a three-car convoy to the airport. Seeing that all the passengers of the first car were in El Al uniforms, the guard opened the gate and allowed everyone through. Once they reached the plane, the agents kept Eichmann surrounded tightly and supported him as he was maneuvered up the steps. Deposited in the first-class cabin, he was near other "crew" members who also pretended to sleep. The cover story was that they were all part of the relief crew that needed to rest up before they would take over later. Just after midnight, which meant the date was officially May 21, the plane took off. When the plane left Argentine airspace, the "crew" in the first class cabin got up to embrace each other and celebrate their success. The rest of the real crew finally learned the identity of their mystery passenger.

Harel was on board, but most of the other agents who had carried out the operation—including Eitan, Shalom, and Malkin—were not on the flight. They would have to make their way out of Argentina separately, arriving back in Israel days later. While their deed soon became public knowledge, their roles in it remained secret for years to come.

That fact contributed to the bitter skirmishes later about who really deserved credit for Eichmann's capture. The private Nazi hunters like Tuvia Friedman and Simon Wiesenthal were free to tell their versions of events—and they were more than willing to do so. Friedman quickly published a memoir where he dramatized his own efforts. According to his account, Eichmann fainted when he learned that his captors were Jews who had been after him for a long time. When he came to, Friedman continued, he reportedly asked: "Which one of you is Friedman?"

Friedman did add: "The story was given me second-hand so I will not swear to its accuracy." Eitan, the field commander of the kidnapping who had helped drag Eichmann into the car, stated flatly that nothing of the sort ever happened.

Wiesenthal also published his first account of his role in his 1961 book *Ich jagte Eichmann* (I Hunted Eichmann). The title alone suggested that he was claiming a major part of the credit, although his assertions in this and subsequent public statements and writings were often more measured. He was happy to report that Yad Vashem sent him a cable on May 23, 1960, after Ben-Gurion had announced Eichmann's capture and arrival. "HEARTY CONGRATULATIONS ON YOUR BRILLIANT ACHIEVEMENT," it read.

But speaking at a press conference in Jerusalem later, Wiesenthal chose his words carefully: "Eichmann's seizure was in no way a single person's achievement. It was a collaboration in the best sense of the word. It was a mosaic, especially during the last decisive phase, when many people, who for the most part did not even know each other, all contributed small pieces. I can only talk about my own contribution, and I do not even know if it was particularly valuable."

In his 1989 memoir, *Justice Not Vengeance,* he wrote: "I was a dogged pursuer, but I was no marksman." To his daughter, Paulinka, and her husband, Gerard Kreisberg, he never claimed all the credit. Speaking of the Israelis, he said: "I could never have done what they could. How can I compare myself to a country like Israel?"

Until his death in 1968, Bauer, Hesse's attorney general who had provided the key information that led the Israelis to Eichmann, did not seek any public recognition for his role. As soon as he had returned to Israel with Eichmann, Harel had sent a message to one of his men in Germany. The Israeli met with Bauer in a restaurant a few hours before Ben-Gurion made the announcement about Eichmann's capture. When he told him the news, Bauer embraced him and his eyes filled with tears. He was elated.

While he was circumspect about his own role, Bauer could not help but notice the media's focus on Wiesenthal as the key Eichmann hunter. "He can call himself that, even though he didn't catch him," Bauer said privately to a friend. "Hunted, yes."

But Bauer and Wiesenthal were in occasional touch with each other, and Bauer never betrayed any resentment for the fact that the other man was more in the spotlight than he was.

Harel was another story, however. Since he could not publicly claim the credit while he was still running the Mossad, he fumed from the very beginning at the growing impression that Wiesenthal had played the central role in Eichmann's capture—and at Wiesenthal's willingness to play along with that perception.

In 1975, Harel was finally free to publish *The House on Garibaldi Street*, his account of the Eichmann operation. He pointedly omitted any mention of Wiesenthal. Later, in an unpublished manuscript, "Simon Wiesenthal and the Capture of Eichmann," Harel wrote that Wiesenthal had played "no part" in Eichmann's capture and "could not countenance the truth."

The former Mossad chief did not claim that Wiesenthal "had not exerted himself over the years in the pursuit of Eichmann, nor that he had declined to lend assistance when asked." But he was incensed by what he saw as Wiesenthal's efforts to take advantage of Israel's official silence on how the operation was pulled off. "At first he proceeded with some prudence but, taking Israel's silence for consent, he became progressively bolder, to the point of arrogating to himself full credit as the brain behind the capture of Adolf Eichmann," he wrote. The choppy manuscript, which includes a collection of documents, is an emotional assault on Wiesenthal's character. Above all, it contains an implicit plea to acknowledge the author's own primary role.

Some members of Harel's team were far more inclined to give Wiesenthal credit for both keeping the hunt for Eichmann alive and providing useful leads. But the Harel-Wiesenthal feud was as much a clash of two forceful personalities as it was a debate about specific interpretations of events. Shalom, the deputy of the operational team in Buenos Aires, recognized what really was at stake. "They were competing for the prize," he said. "The prize for being famous for catching Eichmann."

In the small community of Nazi hunters, this dispute would continue unabated even after the death of both antagonists (Harel died in 2003; Wiesenthal in 2005). But for the broader public, the infighting rarely registered. Far more interesting for them was a question that Harel asked himself when he had gone to see his famed captive at the safe house in Buenos Aires.

"When I actually saw Eichmann for the first time, I was amazed at my reaction," he recalled. Instead of feeling hatred, his first thought was: "Well now, doesn't he look just like any other man!" He wasn't sure what he had expected Eichmann to look like, but he said to himself: "If I met him in the street I would see no difference between him and the thousands of other men passing by." Then he asked himself: "What makes such a creature, created in the likeness of man, into a monster?"

This would be the question on everyone's mind when Eichmann was put on trial in Jerusalem.

CHAPTER NINE

"In Cold Blood"

"That many (including me) experienced 'shame,' that is, a feeling of guilt during the imprisonment and afterward, is an ascertained fact confirmed by numerous testimonies. It may seem absurd, but it is a fact."

Auschwitz survivor Primo Levi, the Italian Jewish chemist
and writer, in *The Drowned and the Saved,* his final book
about the Holocaust. He committed suicide in 1987.

The special flight carrying Eichmann landed at Tel Aviv's Lydda Airport, which would later be named Ben Gurion Airport, on the morning of May 22, 1960. The next day Ben-Gurion told his cabinet: "Our security services have long been looking for Adolf Eichmann, and in the end they found him. He's in Israel and will stand trial here." He would announce this news to the Knesset later that day, the prime minister added, making the point that Eichmann would be tried for crimes that still carried the death penalty in Israel.

According to the top secret transcript of the cabinet meeting that was only released in 2013, Ben-Gurion was immediately peppered with questions by his astonished team. "How, in what way, where? How does one do that?" asked Transportation Minister Yitzhak Ben-Aharon. The prime minister replied: "That is why we have a security service." Others offered their congratulations, and Finance Minister Levi Eshkol suggested that Ben-Gurion express in his speech to the Knesset "special appreciation for this action, maybe with some kind of token."

"What kind of token?" the prime minister asked.

When Eshkol pointed out that Israel did not have medals to give out, Ben-Gurion responded: "The reward for a mitzvah is the mitzvah itself." In Hebrew, *mitzvah* literally means commandment, but it is generally used as shorthand for any good deed.

The cabinet members were desperately curious about where and how Eichmann had been caught, but Justice Minister Pinhas Rosen recommended that "no details" be given out.

During a brief discussion about who might serve as Eichmann's lawyer, Rosen explained that they would give him "any attorney he wants." But Foreign Minister Golda Meir interjected: "On the condition he wasn't a Nazi."

When Agriculture Minister Moshe Dayan asked what if the lawyer was an Arab, Ben-Gurion declared: "I am certain that an Arab will not agree to defend him."

Mossad chief Harel, who was also at the meeting, responded to a question about how Eichmann was behaving in prison. "He doesn't understand our behavior, he thought that we would beat him and treat him cruelly," he said. "We are treating him in keeping with the laws of the State of Israel."

There was good reason for that. As Attorney General Gideon Hausner, who would become the chief prosecutor in the upcoming trial, pointed out later, once the world learned about Eichmann's capture, "Israel itself was on trial. The whole world seemed to be watching to see how we acquitted ourselves of the task we had undertaken."

The world found out when Ben-Gurion made his brief electrifying statement to the Knesset: "I have to inform the Knesset that a short time ago one of the most notorious Nazi war criminals, Adolf Eichmann—who was responsible, together with the Nazi leaders, for what they called the 'Final Solution of the Jewish Question,' that is, the extermination of six million of the Jews of Europe—was discovered by the Israeli Security Services. Adolf Eichmann is already under arrest in Israel and will shortly be placed on trial in Israel under the terms of the law for the trial of Nazis and their helpers."

Hausner was certainly right in saying that Israel was immediately put on trial as well. As Ben-Gurion and others had expected, there was international condemnation of their country's action. While Israelis were stunned but then elated when they heard their leader's announcement, the Argentine government was shocked, embarrassed, and outraged. Its foreign minister summoned the Israeli ambassador and demanded an explanation—along with Eichmann's return.

The Israeli envoy ruled out the latter, and his government concocted a thinly disguised cover story that "Jewish volunteers, including some Israelis" had tracked down Eichmann, and then obtained his written consent to deliver him to Israel for trial. Argentina's ambassador to the United Nations pressed his country's case, winning support for a resolution in the Security Council condemning Israel for violating his country's sovereignty. But the resolution also noted that Eichmann should face a court of law.

It was not just the usual virulently anti-Israeli voices who joined in the criticism of Eichmann's abduction. An editorial in *The Washington Post* accused Israel of resorting to "jungle law" and denounced its claim that it had the right to "act in the name of some imaginary Jewish ethnic identity." Prominent Jews from abroad joined in the appeals for Israel not to hold the trial. Philosopher Isaiah Berlin wrote to Jerusalem Mayor Teddy Kollek that to do so would be "politically unwise." Much better, he argued, for Israel to hand him over to another country for trial, showing that it "refused to plunge the dagger to the hilt." Psychologist Erich Fromm called the kidnapping of Eichmann an "act of lawlessness of exactly the type of which the Nazis themselves . . . have been guilty."

The American Jewish Committee told Foreign Minister Meir that they were against holding the trial in Israel since Eichmann was guilty of "unspeakable crimes against humanity, not only against Jews." It also put together a group of judges and lawyers who recommended that Israel investigate Eichmann's crimes but then hand over the evidence to an international tribunal.

Ben-Gurion rejected all such proposals out of hand. As Hausner made clear in his opening address for the prosecution when the trial started nearly a year later on April 11, 1961, Israel's leaders truly believed that they were acting on behalf of all of the Holocaust's victims. "With me, in this place and at this hour, stand six million accusers," Hausner declared. "But they cannot rise to their feet and point an accusing finger toward the man who sits in the glass dock and cry: 'I accuse.'" He went on to say that their ashes were now scattered in Auschwitz, Treblinka, and other killing grounds "over the length and breadth of Europe."

Gabriel Bach, one of Hausner's two deputy prosecutors on the case and the only member of the team who was still alive as of this writing, pointed out another important reason why Ben-Gurion felt it was critical to hold the trial in Jerusalem. "In Israel before the trial started, teachers told me that many of the young people here didn't want to hear about the Holocaust," he said. "Why? Many of our young people were ashamed. A young Israeli can understand that you can be hurt fighting, that you can be killed fighting, that you can lose a battle, but he cannot understand how millions of people let themselves be slaughtered without an uprising. That's why they didn't want to hear about it." Some Holocaust survivors were derided as *sabonim* (soapers), a reference to the widespread belief that the Germans had made soap from their victims.

The trial would change those attitudes by showing young Israelis how the victims "were misled up to the last moment," Bach continued, and how "when it was clear to the Jews that death was waiting, like with the Warsaw Ghetto, there was an uprising, they fought to the last man in an incredibly courageous manner." But the proceedings would still be fraught with controversy, and the debates about the behavior of the Holocaust's victims were intensified by the competing narratives that began to emerge as Eichmann's accusers and an audience that spanned the globe tried to decipher the nature of the man at the heart of this drama.

• • •

The Israelis had carefully planned what they would do with Eichmann once he arrived. They put him in a large prison in Camp Iyar, a well-guarded police compound near Haifa. Eichmann occupied a cell that was ten by thirteen feet; the only furnishings were a cot, a table, and a chair. There was also an electric light that remained on at all times, and an adjoining toilet and shower room. All the remaining cells in the complex had been emptied of prisoners. The only other regulars were more than thirty police officers, and a detachment of border police whose members also served as guards. To preclude any attempt at an act of vengeance, no one was allowed to serve as a guard who had lost family members in the Holocaust.

But the same rule did not apply to the man who was chosen to be the prisoner's interrogator during the months of preparation for the trial, enabling him to spend 275 hours gathering testimony directly from Eichmann. Police Captain Avner Less had escaped Germany as a teenager after Hitler took power. His father, a Berlin businessman who had earned an Iron Cross for his service in World War I, perished in the gas chambers of Auschwitz. As Less archly noted, his father's distinguished war record had won him "the privilege of being one of the last to be deported from Berlin, and thus one of the last to be liquidated."

Eichmann's main contact with the outside world was Bach, who would become the deputy prosecutor at his trial. While Less was busy with the prisoner's testimony, Bach's role was to make sure that the investigation was running smoothly and to act as an intermediary on practical matters; for instance, he was the one who informed Eichmann that he could pick anyone as his lawyer, and the Israeli government would foot the bill. The prisoner chose Robert Servatius, a prominent Cologne attorney who had been part of the defense team in Nuremberg.

Bach lived in a hotel in Haifa during the investigation stage and had an office in the prison. On the day that he met Eichmann for the first time, the young lawyer had been reading the autobiography of Rudolf Höss, the Auschwitz commandant, who was hanged in Poland. He read the passages where Höss described the herding of mothers and children into the gas chambers, and how he always felt compelled not to betray any sign of wavering in the face of their appeals for mercy. He also read the parts where Eichmann explained the alleged necessity of this mass murder. A few minutes later, the police came and said that Eichmann wanted to see him. "I heard his steps outside [my office] and then he was sitting opposite me the way you are now," Bach recalled. "It was not so easy to keep a poker face."

Bach faced much less of a challenge than Less, who had to meet with the prisoner day after day for extensive questioning and then for careful review of the transcripts of each session, which in the end totaled 3,564 pages. All of this was later submitted as evidence for the trial.

At their first meeting on May 29, 1960, Less found himself facing a balding man wearing a khaki shirt and trousers and open sandals who "looked utterly ordinary," as he recalled. After having reviewed the files on hand about Eichmann, including those that had been provided by Tuvia Friedman, he confessed that he had a feeling of disappointment. "The very normality of his appearance gave his dispassionate testimony an even more depressing impact than I had expected after examining the documents," he wrote.

But Less also observed that Eichmann was "a bundle of nerves" during that first encounter, keeping his hands under the table to hide his trembling. "I could feel his fear, and it would have been easy to make short work of him," he reported. The Israeli realized that his prisoner was expecting the kind of treatment that he might have meted out if their roles were reversed. But after a week of unfailingly by-the-book handling by Less, Eichmann visibly relaxed. Realizing that his charge was a heavy smoker, the police captain arranged for an increased cigarette ration for him. "I did it because it made him more talkative and improved his powers of concentration," Less recalled. Jan Sehn, the Polish investigating judge, had used the same tactic with Höss.

Eichmann did everything possible to play down his role and influence during the Holocaust and to deny that he harbored any personal feelings of anti-Semitism, signaling the approach he would take throughout his trial. He explained to Less that he had a Jewish friend in elementary school, and that when he had first become involved with Jewish matters, he had worked closely with Jewish leaders in Prague. His initial goal was to find a way for Jews to emigrate elsewhere, and he "wasn't a Jew hater," he insisted.

The first times he observed the killing of Jews in makeshift gas chambers in huts or trucks where engine exhaust was piped in, Eichmann said, "I was horrified." The screams left him "shaken" and he fled after he saw the corpses dumped into a trench where a civilian began pulling out gold teeth with pliers. He claimed to have had nightmares because he could not help but be affected by violence and suffering. "Even today, if I see someone with a deep cut, I have to look away," he declared. But that did not stop him from visiting Auschwitz and other camps, inspecting the death machinery on a regular basis. He also attended the Wannsee Conference, the meeting of top Nazi security officials on the outskirts of Berlin on January 20, 1942; this was where they coordinated the implementation of the Final Solution, and Eichmann prepared the minutes of that infamous gathering. But he claimed he sat in the corner with the stenographer, which demonstrated how "insignificant" he was.

In organizing the transport of Jews to Auschwitz and other camps, he was simply following orders, Eichmann proclaimed again and again. He admitted to carrying out his duties with "unusual zeal," but argued that this did not make him responsible for murder. Others made those life-and-death decisions, he maintained. "If they had told me that my own father was a traitor and I had to kill him, I'd have done it," he said. "At that time, I obeyed my orders without thinking."

A few times Eichmann tried to demonstrate normal emotions and curiosity, trying to find a personal connection with his interrogator. He once asked Less if his parents were still alive. When the interrogator told him about his father's fate, Eichmann cried out: "But that's horrible, Herr Hauptmann [Mr. Captain]! That's horrible!"

The interrogator discovered that his best weapon for breaking through Eichmann's defenses was provided by the ghost of Höss, especially by the same autobiography of the Auschwitz commandant that Bach had been reading earlier. Because Höss's trial and execution had taken place in Poland behind the newly erected Iron Curtain, he never achieved the kind of notoriety that Eichmann would during his trial. But Less had carefully studied what Höss had written and knew how to use it.

When Less began reading from Höss's autobiography, Eichmann became visibly agitated. He made sarcastic comments about the commandant, but, as during their first encounter, his hands began to tremble. Höss had written about his many discussions with Eichmann about the Final Solution. When they were alone and "the drink had been flowing freely," Höss recalled, "he showed that he was completely obsessed with the idea of destroying every single Jew that he could lay his hands on." His message couldn't have been clearer: "Without pity and in cold blood we must complete this extermination as rapidly as possible. Any compromise, even the slightest, would have to be paid for bitterly at a later date."

When Less read him passages with a similar tone, Eichmann protested that they were completely untrue. "I had nothing to do with killing Jews," he said. "I've never killed a Jew. And I've never ordered anyone to kill a Jew." That gave him "a certain peace of mind," he added. He did admit: "I'm guilty, because I helped with the evacuation. I'm ready to pay for that." But then he promptly talked about how those who were packed into the trains he organized were going for "labor service" and he was not responsible for their fate once they reached their destinations in the East.

To undercut Eichmann's claims that he never made life-and-death decisions, Less proceeded to offer multiple examples of cases where Eichmann methodically tried to eliminate any exemptions for Jews who had initially evaded deportation. In one document he signed, Eichmann argued that the Thai ambassador in Berlin was only employing a Jewish language teacher "to shield him from difficulties." He urged the Foreign Office to pressure the envoy "to dispense with the further employment of the Jew"—which, as Less pointed out, would have meant "deportation with the next or one of the next shipments." Eichmann also instructed his representatives in The Hague to rescind an exemption for a Dutch Jewish woman who had been planning to travel to Italy, apparently at the request of Italy's fascist government, which was less than enthusiastic about helping Germany implement the Final Solution. The woman should be sent "immediately to the East for labor service," he wrote.

As Less pointed out, the practical consequence of his action was that she would be sent to Auschwitz. Confronted with such evidence, Eichmann stumbled in his reply: "That is . . . the . . . the. . . . That was our job." Once he had recovered a bit, he added the usual protestations that "these were not personal decisions." He was only following instructions, he continued, and if he had not issued such orders, anyone else occupying his position would have done the exact same thing; the real decisions were always made higher up. "I wasn't expected to make any decision at all," he concluded.

Eichmann was eager to prove that he was not a killer in thought or deed. But under persistent questioning, the prisoner could not downplay his role anywhere near to the extent that he had hoped. Less came to the conclusion that all of Eichmann's efforts were meant to conceal "the cold sophistication and cunning with which he had planned and carried out the extermination of the Jews." The trial would provide him another opportunity to offer similar rationales for his actions, and Eichmann's only hope was that the much larger audience of the courtroom and beyond would be more receptive to them than Less was.

"Thinking itself is such a dangerous enterprise," Hannah Arendt declared in what turned out to be her last television interview before her death in 1975, a conversation with French legal scholar Roger Errera. It certainly was for the German-born Jewish philosopher when she wrote her five-part series on Eichmann's trial for *The New Yorker*, and when her book, *Eichmann in Jerusalem: A Report on the Banality of Evil*, based on those articles, was published in 1963.

Arendt's description of Eichmann as "the most important conveyer belt" of Jews to the death camps, with its implication that the prisoner on trial was more a mechanical part of a killing machine than a human monster, generated both widespread acclaim and vitriolic denunciations, especially from fellow Jews—many of whom ostracized her for the rest of her life. But whatever side people chose in this debate that has continued to the present, Arendt's thesis has remained the focal point of their arguments. Every discussion about Eichmann and the nature of evil begins with Arendt's interpretation of the man and his motives.

When Arendt arrived in Jerusalem shortly before the trial opened, deputy prosecutor Bach let her know that he was willing to meet with her. "Two days later I got the message that she is not prepared to talk to anyone from the prosecution," Bach recalled. Nonetheless, he instructed the court to make all the prosecution and defense documents available to her, including the transcripts of Less's interrogation of Eichmann.

Arendt was fascinated by the voluminous transcripts, which she read carefully. She may have been there to report for *The New Yorker*, but she was also on a mission to construct her own interpretation of the man who would be seated in the glass booth during the trial. She was intent on not allowing others, especially the prosecutors, to sway her thinking. By all indications, she was also predisposed to reach the conclusions that would trigger the most controversy. A decade earlier, she had published her widely acclaimed volume *The Origins of Totalitarianism,* which signaled her preoccupations with how both Hitler's Germany and Stalin's Soviet Union used a combination of terror and propaganda to impose a system that negated all traditional Judeo-Christian values. It also dealt extensively with the origins of anti-Semitism.

Her interest in such subjects was a natural outgrowth of her personal story. Born in 1906, Arendt told one interviewer that as a child growing up in Königsberg the word "Jew" never came up. Her father died young, and her mother was not religious. It was only when other children directed anti-Semitic remarks at her that Arendt was "enlightened," as she put it. When Hitler took power in 1933, she fled Germany. "If one is attacked as a Jew, one must defend oneself as a Jew," she declared.

She landed in Paris, where she helped ferry German and Polish Jewish youngsters to Palestine. After Germany conquered France in 1940, she escaped again, this time to the United States, where she would start her new life. Despite her early involvement with the Zionist movement, she later became a harsh critic of Israel and many of its prominent figures, particularly Eastern European Jews who occupied top leadership positions. This translated into personal contempt for Hausner, the chief prosecutor, who, as she put, was "a typical Galician Jew" with a "ghetto mentality."

From the beginning, Arendt was critical of his approach to the Eichmann trial, which opened on April 11, 1961. While Hausner focused on demonstrating the heinousness of Eichmann's crimes, his personal responsibility for them, and his fervent anti-Semitism, she had a different intellectual construct in mind. "One of my main intentions was to destroy the legend of the greatness of evil, of the demonic force," she declared in her last television interview. On another occasion, she insisted: "If there was ever anyone who deprived himself of any demonic aura, it was Herr Eichmann."

In her articles and book, she portrayed Eichmann as a drab functionary with limited intellectual abilities. Pointing out that "he was genuinely incapable of uttering a single sentence that was not a cliché," she wrote: "The longer one listened to him, the more obvious it became that his inability to speak was closely connected with an inability to *think*, namely to think from the standpoint of somebody else." Then came the assertion that generated the greatest blowback: "Despite all the efforts of the prosecution, everybody could see that this man was not a 'monster', but it was difficult indeed not to suspect that he was a clown." In fact, this seemingly ordinary man exemplified "the banality of evil."

It was not ideological conviction and hatred of the Jews that were Eichmann's motivating factors, she argued, it was careerism, a desire to get ahead within the Nazi bureaucracy. "Except for an extraordinary diligence in looking out for his personal advancement, he had no motives at all," she wrote. In other words, he would have sent millions of any other group of people, regardless of their race or religion, to their deaths if they had been targeted by the Nazi regime the way the Jews were.

In the courtroom, the prosecution pursued its dramatically different narrative, intent on offering stark illustrations of what Eichmann's deep commitment to Nazi doctrine meant in practice. A procession of witnesses offered heart-wrenching testimony about life and death in the camps, all of which contributed to the broader picture that has shaped the world's understanding of the Holocaust ever since. Frequently accompanied by gasps and sobs from those in attendance, survivors shared their final memories of their loved ones. But unlike almost everyone else who was present, "Eichmann displayed no sign of being affected," Hausner pointed out. Until he testified himself, the man who had described himself to Less as "only a minor transport officer" sat through such proceedings "tense, rigid and silent in his glass cubicle."

When the prosecution prepared a film about the Holocaust, they invited Eichmann and his lawyers to the courtroom to see it first, before it would be shown as part of the trial. Since Bach had watched the film already, he closely monitored the prisoner's behavior as he saw it. Eichmann did not react at all to the footage showing gas chambers and corpses, but at one point he spoke excitedly to the prison warden. Later, Bach asked the warden why he had suddenly become so agitated. The explanation: Eichmann was incensed that he had been brought to the courtroom wearing a sweater and his gray suit; he reminded the warden that he had been promised that he would be allowed to wear his dark blue suit anytime he was to appear in court. With a sardonic laugh, Bach recalled that Eichmann had protested this alleged mistreatment, insisting that such promises had to be kept—while never saying a word about the film.

At the trial, many of the witnesses described the selection process as the bewildered, exhausted, starved victims were unloaded from the trains arriving at Auschwitz-Birkenau. More than half a century later, Bach recalled one witness who recounted how an SS officer instructed his wife and little girl to go left, while the witness, who was an engineer, was told to go right. The man asked the SS officer where his son should go, and, after briefly consulting his superior officer, he told the boy to run after his mother and sister. The witness said he was worried that the boy would not catch up with them because there were already hundreds of people in between them moving to the left—and the boy quickly disappeared into the crowd. But he could track his daughter because she was wearing a red coat, which became a red dot that grew smaller and smaller. "This is how his family disappeared from his life," Bach noted.

Steven Spielberg included a similar scene with a little girl in a red coat in his film *Schindler's List*, and Bach is convinced that the director took the idea from the Eichmann trial.

Two weeks before hearing that witness, Bach had bought his own daughter, who was only two and a half at the time, a red coat. When he heard the witness's testimony, "I couldn't get any words out," he recalled. He began fiddling with his documents until he managed to regain control of his emotions and ask a follow-up question. A widely published photo of a deeply pensive Bach during the trial was taken just after he had heard this shattering account. "To this very day, I can be in a football stadium, the street, a restaurant, and I suddenly feel my heart beating when I turn around and see a little girl or boy in a red coat," he said during our interview a half a century later.

Those kinds of personal testimonies did nothing to shake Arendt's conviction that Eichmann's role was tied to his function within the Nazi bureaucracy, not a product of his personal views. At one point in the trial, Hausner confronted the accused with something he had told his men during the final days of the war: "I will jump into my grave laughing, because the fact that I have the death of five million Jews on my conscience gives me extraordinary satisfaction." According to the prosecutor, Eichmann tried to argue that he had said "enemies of the Reich" not Jews, but later admitted to one of the judges that he had indeed meant Jews. In any case, Hausner pointed out that the accused had a look of "utter amazement and, for a moment, of panic" when he heard the quote read to him.

For Arendt, such statements only demonstrated that "bragging was the vice that was Eichmann's undoing." As he had grown increasingly comfortable in Argentina, a country that felt like such a safe haven for Nazis, Eichmann had even agreed in 1957 to be interviewed at length by Willem Sassen, a Dutch Nazi journalist. Sassen sold excerpts from the interviews to *Life* magazine, and Eichmann may have imagined that at some point the full transcripts would help him present his version of events. But his self-aggrandizing tone in them was at odds with the tack he took in Jerusalem, where he was desperate to play down his role. Eichmann insisted that the interviews were held in "a saloon atmosphere" and did not contain reliable information, even though he had reviewed and corrected some of the transcripts. As a result of his objections, the court ruled that they could not be admitted as evidence.

But, as Arendt saw it, Eichmann's willingness to take such risks proved her point. "What eventually led to his capture was his compulsion to talk big," she wrote. She saw his eagerness to adapt and say whatever he felt would help him in any given situation—without thought to future consequences—as the explanation of the role he played in the Third Reich. "He was not stupid," she wrote. "It was sheer thoughtlessness—something by no means identical with stupidity—that predisposed him to become one of the greatest criminals of the period," she concluded.

The other part of Arendt's thesis that infuriated her critics, triggering the charge that she was a self-hating Jew, was her discussion of the complicity of Jewish councils in occupied Europe. One of their main tasks was to deliver whatever number of Jews the Germans demanded for transport to the death camps, making sure they met their grim quotas. During the trial, the prosecution called witnesses who testified to the lengths that the Germans went to deceive their victims as much as possible, compelling those who went east to send postcards to their relatives about the purported good living and working conditions in their new locations. And it was common for witnesses to explain how everyone hoped against hope that they could believe the German cover story.

But Arendt was having none of it, accusing Jewish leaders of taking part in this deliberate deception in the hopes of saving themselves. "To a Jew this role of the Jewish leaders in the destruction of their own people is undoubtedly the darkest chapter of the whole dark story," she wrote. Arendt gave no indication that she understood how difficult it must have been for Jewish leaders to resist the relentless pressure of the Germans to round up more people for the trains heading east, accompanied by a combination of escalating threats and what almost always turned out to be empty promises that some Jews would be spared.

This was a particularly sensitive topic in the Jerusalem courtroom. "The tragedy of the trapped Jewish leaders in occupied Europe emerged again in all its nakedness," Hausner recalled. One of the most prominent members of this group was the Hungarian Jewish leader Rudolf Kastner, who negotiated with Eichmann as he was orchestrating the deportation of more than 400,000 Hungarian Jews to Auschwitz. In the end, as Arendt acidly put it, Kastner "saved exactly 1,684 people with approximately 476,000 victims." Those saved included Kastner and some of his family, along with other "prominent Jews," as he called them. Kastner arranged to pay the Germans a hefty ransom in return for safe passage to Switzerland. He later settled in Israel, where he became a spokesman for the Ministry of Trade and Industry.

In 1953, Malchiel Gruenwald, a Hungarian-born Israeli freelance journalist, accused Kastner of collaborating with the Nazis. Since Kastner worked for the government, the Israeli authorities sued his accuser for libel. The court initially ruled in Gruenwald's favor, with the judge asserting that Kastner had "sold his soul to the devil." The government appealed that decision. In 1957, while the legal battle was still unresolved, Kastner was assassinated in Tel Aviv. Shortly afterward, the case officially concluded with his exoneration.

But public opinion remained deeply divided on Kastner's role. To Bach, who had helped with the appeal in the defamation case, and other members of the prosecution team in the Eichmann trial, Eichmann's dealings with Kastner only underscored the nefarious methods the Nazi official employed. They were not about to condemn the desperate local Jewish leaders, and Kastner's defenders viewed him as a hero for saving as many people as he did.

Arendt, however, insisted that the local Jewish leaders and their organizations made it easier for Eichmann and others to reach their goal of rounding up just about everyone. If there had been no such Jewish leaders to help them, there still would have been "chaos and plenty of misery," she wrote, "but the total number of victims would hardly have been between four and a half and six million people."

As soon as Arendt published *Eichmann in Jerusalem* in 1963, she came under withering fire from her critics. The prosecutors, of course, had never subscribed to her thesis about Eichmann. "This idea of Hannah Arendt that he was just obeying orders is absolute rubbish," Bach declared. He added that Eichmann would not have been left in charge of Jewish affairs in the security apparatus throughout the entire period of the Holocaust if he were not seen as completely dedicated to the cause of genocide. And he noted that Eichmann had continued his drive to murder Jews long after it was evident the war was lost and his superiors were already trying to cover up the physical evidence of the Holocaust. But it was left to others to mount the counterattacks on Arendt in the media and other public forums.

One of those who took the lead was Michael Musmanno, the judge in the Nuremberg trial of the commanders of the Einsatzgruppen—the special squads that had carried out mass executions of Jews and others on the Eastern Front before the gas chambers were operational. Musmanno wrote a book after Eichmann's capture that he titled *The Eichmann Kommandos* and testified for the prosecution in his trial in Jerusalem. When questioned by defense attorney Servatius, he described his conversations with the top Nazi prisoners at Nuremberg. Göring, he asserted, "made it very clear that Eichmann was all-powerful on the question of the extermination of the Jews. . . . [He] had practically unlimited power to declare who was to be killed among the Jews." This was a direct refutation of Eichmann's repeated claims that he had no authority to decide anything on his own.

On another occasion, Musmanno—who was never hesitant to strike the dramatic note—wrote that in Nuremberg Eichmann's name "kept recurring in the testimony like the sighing of the wind through a deserted, empty house, and the rustling of tree branches against the roof suggesting supernatural visitations."

Musmanno was offered a major forum for his views when *The New*

York Times asked him to review Arendt's *Eichmann in Jerusalem,* clearly knowing what to expect. He produced a predictably scathing review, contemptuously dismissing her arguments, as he put it, "that Eichmann was not really a Nazi at heart, that he did not know Hitler's program when he joined the Nazi party, that the Gestapo were helpful to the Jews in Palestinian immigration, that Himmler (Himmler!) had a sense of pity." He added that Arendt sympathized with Eichmann when no one believed his protestations that he did not hate Jews, and that in general had fallen for Eichmann's mendacious presentation of his personal history and views.

Musmanno reserved his most caustic remarks for her willingness to believe that Eichmann never saw "the killing installations" at Auschwitz, despite the fact that he "repeatedly" visited there. "Her observation is like saying that one repeatedly sojourned at Niagara Falls but never noticed the falling water," he wrote. As for her condemnation of the Jewish councils, he echoed the sentiment of those who felt that her indignation was completely misdirected. "The fact that Eichmann with threats of death coerced occasional Quislings and Lavals in 'cooperation' only adds to the horrors of his crimes," he concluded.

The review, as much as the book, was a huge sensation, with readers picking sides in this battle of two well-known public figures. In a subsequent *Book Review* section, the *Times* published a rebuttal by Arendt, a rebuttal of the rebuttal by Musmanno, and impassioned letters from both sides of the debate. In her reply, Arendt castigated the newspaper for its "bizarre" choice of Musmanno as the reviewer, since she had earlier dismissed his views on totalitarianism and Eichmann's role as "dangerous nonsense." Yet neither the *Times* nor Musmanno bothered to inform readers of that fact, which suggested "a flagrant break with normal editorial procedure," she charged. As for the review, it was an attack on "a book which, to my knowledge, was never either written or published." In other words, Musmanno had totally misrepresented it.

Musmanno fired back that it had been his obligation to point out "Miss Arendt's many misstatements of facts in the Eichmann case," and that he was not guilty of any "misrepresentations of any kind." Pro-Arendt readers called his review "a new low in reviewing," "a gross misreading" of the book, and indicated that he was "blind to her gift of irony." Anti-Arendt readers praised Musmanno for his effort "to set the record straight" and accused Arendt of attempting "to lean over backwards" to understand Eichmann, and of "disregard for, or ignorance of, historical facts."

The battle did not end there. Jacob Robinson, who had been a consultant on Jewish affairs to Justice Robert Jackson at the Nuremberg trials, and later served as the legal advisor to the Israeli delegation to the United Nations, wrote an entire book dedicated to demolishing Arendt's arguments: *And the Crooked Shall Be Made Straight: The Eichmann Trial, the Jewish Catastrophe, and Hannah Arendt's Narrative*, published in 1965. As a lawyer and a scholar, he was intent on addressing almost every assertion, finding almost no detail too insignificant to dispute.

Robinson, of course, attacked her view that Eichmann's role in the Holocaust had been exaggerated by the prosecution. "One stands baffled before Hannah Arendt's image of Eichmann," he wrote, adding that the documents demonstrated that "the real Eichmann" was "a man of extraordinary driving power, master in the arts of cunning and deception, intelligent and competent in his field, single-minded in his mission to make Europe 'free of Jews' (*judenrein*)—in short, a man uniquely suited to be the overseer of most of the Nazi programs to exterminate the Jews."

Robinson declared himself particularly "aghast" at what he characterized as Arendt's "distortion of the historical facts" in her discussion of the role of Jewish councils in occupied Europe. He offered a lengthy explanation on the origins of these Jewish organizations that the Germans used to administer the ghettos. He pointed out the councils' "positive attempts to preserve the physical and moral existence of the communities in all circumstances," although admitting that they "took pains to offer no open defiance to the Nazi masters, deeply convinced that this approach protected the community from greater misfortune." He also tried to distance the councils from the Jewish police, which the Nazis frequently used in roundups for deportations, saying that the police reported directly to the Germans in such cases.

Arendt was not alone in finding such arguments unconvincing. Simon Wiesenthal similarly criticized the widespread reluctance to discuss the role of the Jewish councils and Jewish police, rejecting the idea that to do so risked diminishing the guilt of the Nazi overlords who were the real perpetrators. "We have done very little to condemn Jewish collaboration with the Nazis," he wrote. "No one else has a right to blame us for it—but we ourselves must face up to it sometime."

But such voices were usually in a distinct minority. As Robinson summed up the more widely accepted view: "Legally and morally, the members of the Jewish Councils can no more be judged accomplices of their Nazi rulers than can a store owner be judged accomplice of an armed robber to whom he surrenders his store at gunpoint."

Especially on the question of Eichmann and the nature of the evil that he represented, the anti-Arendt voices were often louder than those of people willing to come to her defense—at least in intellectual circles, where she was often treated like a pariah. In the 2012 feature film *Hannah Arendt*, German director Margarethe von Trotta conveyed the degree to which Arendt was deserted by former friends and colleagues, along with their increasingly poisonous sniping at each other.

But even among the Israeli agents who captured Eichmann, there was some sympathy for her view of what the man they hunted down represented. "In a way she was right," said Rafi Eitan, who led the Mossad team in Buenos Aires. "He himself never hated Jews—that was my feeling. That's the banality of evil. Tomorrow tell him to kill French people, and he would do the same."

That battle about what Eichmann really represented has continued for decades. In 2011, another German philosopher, Bettina Stangneth, published a book based on extensive additional research into Eichmann's records, including the transcripts of his interviews with Willem Sassen, the Dutch Nazi, focused on his time in Argentina. The English-language version, called *Eichmann Before Jerusalem: The Unexamined Life of a Mass Murderer*, was published in 2014. It marshaled an impressive body of evidence to buttress the case that Robinson and others had made earlier.

Eichmann was hardly a mediocre bureaucrat who happened to become a critical part of the machinery of mass murder, Stangneth argued.

Instead, he was a rabid anti-Semite who was "in thrall to totalitarian thought," far from the image of someone who simply followed whatever orders he received. "An ideology that scorns human life can be very appealing if you happen to be a member of the master race that proclaims it, and if it legitimizes behavior that would be condemned by any traditional concept of justice and morality," she wrote.

Stangneth credited Arendt with launching a much needed discussion in that early period of Holocaust studies. Her book "achieved the primary goal of philosophers since Socrates: controversy for the sake of understanding." But her conclusion was that Arendt had fallen into a trap set by her subject as he constructed a deliberately false narrative of his life. "Eichmann-in-Jerusalem was little more than a mask," Stangneth wrote. "She didn't recognize it, although she was acutely aware that she had not understood the phenomenon as well as she had hoped."

There is little doubt that Arendt, who relied primarily on the transcripts of Eichmann's interrogation along with his direct testimony in the latter part of the trial, accepted at face value some of his protestations about his purportedly subordinate role and lack of personal enmity against Jews. She was eager to prove her thesis about how totalitarian systems made effective use of mediocre individuals who lacked genuine convictions of their own. She was also undeniably arrogant, convinced that she had provided the only proper intellectual framework for understanding the man and his role in history.

But Arendt was correct in saying that her views were often distorted beyond recognition by her angry critics, and she fought back in a series of interviews for German and French television during the decade that followed the publication of *Eichmann in Jerusalem*. She was easily misunderstood, and she did not help her case by repeating the phrases that caused some of the confusion in the first place. In an early interview, she continued to insist that Eichmann was "a buffoon," adding that she "laughed out loud" when she read the transcript of his interrogation.

In subsequent interviews, she offered clearer explanations of what she meant. Speaking with the German historian Joachim Fest, she pointed out that by banal behavior she didn't mean anything positive—quite the contrary. She decried the "sham existence" of Eichmann and the earlier Nuremberg trial defendants, who claimed they weren't responsible for mass murders because they were simply obeying orders, freeing them of any responsibility for their actions. "There's something outrageously stupid about this," she added. "The whole thing is simply comical!" In her interviews, "comical" clearly doesn't mean funny.

Nonetheless, she stuck with her thesis that Eichmann was a "mere functionary" and that ideology did not play a major role in his behavior. The interpretation of many of her critics—that he was a monster, the devil incarnate—was highly dangerous because it offered Germans an alibi for their behavior, she maintained. "If you succumb to the power of the beast from the depths, you're naturally much less guilty than if you succumb to a completely average man of the caliber of an Eichmann," she declared. That was why she was so intent on rejecting the demonic explanation of him and his ilk.

While Arendt presented a highly sophisticated argument about her view of Eichmann that, at the very least, should have made some of her overwrought accusers pause, she did not back off much on her charge about Jewish collaboration. Still, she exhibited more understanding of the Jewish council leaders as "victims," pointing out that, however questionable their behavior, they can never be equated with the perpetrators. This represented an indirect concession that her original account came across as too harshly judgmental.

One overlooked passage in *Eichmann in Jerusalem* demonstrates that Arendt was not blaming the victims, as her critics so frequently maintained. As Bach pointed out, one of the goals of the Israeli leaders in holding the trial was to demonstrate to the younger generation the methods the Germans used, dangling the illusion of hope to their victims until the last moment. While Arendt mentioned the popular perception that Jews "went to their death like sheep," she wrote: "But the sad truth of the matter is that the point was ill taken, for no non-Jewish group or people had behaved any differently." In that sense, Arendt and the prosecutors were in agreement.

From the perspective of a half century later, there is a credible argument to be made that Eichmann embodied many of the traits of the competing versions of him—Arendt's version and her critics' version. He was both a careerist in a totalitarian system, willing to do anything to please his superiors, and a virulent anti-Semite who reveled in his powers to dispatch his victims to their deaths, systematically tracking down anyone who sought to elude the Nazi net. He was more consciously evil than Arendt was willing to admit, and yet he embodied her concept of the banality of evil. Those two notions are not necessarily contradictory. He committed monstrous acts in the name of a monstrous system, but labeling him a monster lets too many others off the hook and ignores how easily tyrannical regimes can enlist average citizens in their criminal behavior.

One of the immediate consequences of Arendt's writing was to stimulate new studies about the propensity of those average citizens to obey orders without thinking. Most famously, Yale University psychologist Stanley Milgram conducted experiments in the early 1960s with unsuspecting volunteers who were led to believe that they were administering powerful electric shocks to people in a separate room. Told they were participating in an educational experiment, the participants could back out at any time—yet in most cases they kept following orders to administer what they believed were increasingly painful shocks, even when they heard screams or banging on the wall. The subjects were actors and they were not receiving real shocks.

Milgram concluded that such behavior indicated "that Arendt's conception of the *banality of evil* comes closer to the truth than one might dare imagine." Nazi Germany and other societies were able to make people obey blindly, he explained, by taking advantage of "the disappearance of a sense of responsibility" in modern societies; instead, individuals are focused on narrow technical tasks, responding to orders from above. "The person who assumes full responsibility for the act has evaporated," he wrote. "Perhaps this is the most common characteristic of socially organized evil in modern society."

Milgram described his experiments in his book *Obedience to Au-*

thority, which, just like Arendt's *Eichmann in Jerusalem*, stirred new impassioned debates. His conclusions were clearly aligned with a point of view on human behavior and totalitarian systems that had begun to emerge even before the Holocaust. After witnessing the rise of Hitler in Germany, Sinclair Lewis published his novel *It Can't Happen Here* in 1935—with the exact opposite message of its title: a Nazi-like regime *could* come to power in the United States. In other words, the greatest danger facing mankind is not represented by monsters, but by those who would blindly obey their monstrous orders.

The urge to identify evil traits in particular human beings is a powerful one, especially when confronted with truly horrifying behavior. Few people want to believe that they or their neighbors could be capable of seemingly senseless violence merely because some authority figure decided such acts were necessary. Most people instinctively agreed with British Prime Minister David Cameron's characterization of the terrorists who beheaded both American and British hostages in 2014 as "monsters," just as many people were prone to categorize top Nazis as monsters earlier.

But the efforts to identify personality traits peculiar to the major Nazi war criminals, wherever they were caught and tried, produced no consensus among the psychiatrists and investigators who questioned them. There were some recurring characteristics: their zealous dedication to what they saw as their work, a complete lack of empathy for their victims, the sense that they were not responsible for their actions since there was always someone higher up to blame, and hefty doses of self-pity. Also, in many cases, there was an astonishing capacity for self-delusion. Göring, who was seen as the most intelligent and social of the defendants in Nuremberg, told the American psychiatrist Douglas Kelley that he was "determined to go down in German history as a great man." Even if he failed to convince the court, he would convince the German public, he insisted. "In fifty or sixty years there will be statues of Hermann Göring all over Germany," he said. "Little statues, maybe, but one in every German home."

Fellow American psychiatrist G. M. Gilbert concluded that someone like Auschwitz commandant Höss exhibited the traits of "a frank psychotic." But Kelley was persistently frustrated in his efforts to identify anything that would indicate that these criminals were insane in any way—or that they fundamentally differed from other human beings. In other words, they were not the products of any "monster gene."

"Insanity is no explanation for the Nazis," Kelley wrote. "They were simply creatures of their environment, as all humans are; and they were also—to a greater degree than most humans are—the makers of their environment." For someone who had hoped to find rigorous scientific answers using Rorschach tests, this vague explanation was a de facto admission of failure. But it also led Kelley to a more clear-cut and frightening conclusion: if there was no indication of outright madness among the Nazis, the argument that "it can happen here"—or anywhere, for that matter—was right.

Those kinds of debates were certainly not resolved by the Eichmann trial, or by Arendt's interpretation and early criticisms of it. In fact, her televised discussions in the decade following the trial indicated that she had revised much of her thinking about the value of the whole exercise. Despite her stinging critique of many aspects of the trial, she was increasingly appreciative of the role it played, serving "as a catalyst" for future trials in Germany itself—and for the beginning of the moral self-examination that would allow her former country to begin to regain its international standing.

Arendt was not alone in revising her view. Much of the initial skepticism about Israel's ability to conduct a fair trial, so evident in the early coverage of Eichmann's abduction, faded away once the proceedings started. About six weeks into the trial, a Gallup survey showed that 62 percent of those polled in the United States and 70 percent of those polled in Great Britain believed Eichmann was getting a fair hearing.

On December 15, 1961, Eichmann was sentenced to death by hanging, marking the first and only time that an Israeli court approved the death penalty. On May 29, 1962, the Supreme Court rejected his appeal and two days later, at 7 p.m. on May 31, he was told that Ben-Gurion had rejected his plea for clemency. But the world was only informed about this decision at 11 p.m., without any mention of how long it would be before the actual execution. Bach had suggested an interval of no more than two hours in order to prevent any Eichmann sympathizers from having a chance to seize a hostage to try to stop the hanging. "I was afraid that if there is a long period they might take a Jewish child somewhere, whether in Hawaii, Portugal, or Spain," the deputy prosecutor said.

Bach did not know exactly when Eichmann would be hanged until the announcement was made. On May 30, he had visited the prisoner for what turned out to be the final time. He was in his bath the following evening at 11, in the same apartment near the presidential residence in Jerusalem where the Bachs still live today, when his wife, Ruth, called out that she had just heard the news on the radio about the president's rejection of the clemency plea. Bach was among the small group of officials who knew this meant the execution would follow within an hour or two. "Look, I had no doubts about the matter, but I did grow pale a little bit," he recalled. "When you've met a person practically every day for two years . . ."

The designated hangman was Shalom Nagar, a twenty-three-year-old Yemenite Jew who was one of the prison guards. Eichmann's last request was for white wine and cigarettes. When he was offered a hood, he refused it. To Nagar, this indicated that he did not fear his fate.

Eichmann made a final declaration: "Long live Germany. Long live Argentina. Long live Austria . . . I had to obey the laws of war and my flag. I am ready."

Nagar, who had initially questioned why he had to carry out this assignment, pulled the lever at midnight. As he explained much later in an interview with the American Jewish magazine *Zman*, everyone present "felt the revenge; it's only human." He hastened to add: "But revenge wasn't the point. If he could have, he would have done it to all of us. I would have been on his list, too. Yemenite or not."

Nagar's next job was to prepare the body for immediate cremation. As he noted, he was completely inexperienced in such matters, and he was terrified when he looked at the corpse that seemed to be staring at him. He also had no idea that when a person is strangled air remains in his lungs. "So when I lifted him, all the air that was inside came out in

my face and the most horrifying sounds was released from his mouth—
'grrrreeerrererere . . .' It sounded like, 'Hey, you Yemenite . . .' I felt the
Angel of Death had come to take me too."

Two hours after the body was cremated, the ashes were collected in
a canister and taken to a patrol boat that was waiting in the port of Jaffa.
After the captain drove it out just beyond Israel's territorial waters, Eichmann's ashes were dumped from the canister into the sea.

As for Nagar, he had returned home and explained what he had done
to his initially disbelieving wife. He was supposed to have gone to Jaffa
for the final journey with the ashes, but he felt so shaken by the ordeal
of hanging Eichmann and then handling his body that he was relieved of
that duty. For the next year, he recalled, "I lived in terror." When his wife
asked why he was so jittery, he told her that he had the feeling that Eichmann might be chasing him.

"In truth, I don't know what I was afraid of," he admitted. "I just was
afraid. An experience like that does things to you that you don't even
realize."

CHAPTER TEN

"Little People"

> *"What should our second generation have done, what should it do with the knowledge of the horrors of the extermination of the Jews. . . . Should we only fall silent in revulsion, shame, and guilt? To what purpose?"*
>
> Bernhard Schlink, *The Reader*, a novel about Germany's postwar generation that became an international bestseller

In the immediate aftermath of World War II, most West Germans were eager to put the memory of the Third Reich quickly behind them as their new democratic leaders produced what became known as an economic miracle. But Fritz Bauer was always an exception. Ensconced in his office in Frankfurt, Hesse's attorney general was determined to use all means at his disposal to keep forcing his countrymen to confront their recent past. As far as he was concerned, it wasn't enough for them to view the Eichmann trial from afar; they needed to see perpetrators brought to trial at home.

Even before the Israelis acted on his lead and kidnapped Eichmann, Bauer was on the receiving end of a tip that would later lead to the filing of charges against twenty-four Auschwitz officials and guards, presenting exactly the kind of opportunity he had been looking for.

Thomas Gnielka, a young reporter for the *Frankfurter Rundschau* who had been investigating restitution cases and gathering evidence against former Nazis, interviewed Auschwitz survivor Emil Wulkan in early January 1959. At one point, Gnielka either asked about a stack of documents on his cupboard that was bound by a red ribbon or Wulkan simply handed them to him. "Maybe this is something that interests you as a journalist," he reportedly said.

The documents were Auschwitz records from August 1942 on the subject of the "Shooting of Fleeing Prisoners," which had been collected as part of an unspecified internal investigation. They included lists of prisoners and the names of the SS officers who shot them. Whatever the reason for the Nazi investigators' decision to examine such lists, there was little doubt that they constituted evidence of specific acts of murder. Wulkan explained to Gnielka that a friend of his had salvaged them from the burning rubble of a police court building in Breslau at the end of the war, and that he had held on to them as a "souvenir." Although Wulkan had later become a member of the Frankfurt Jewish Council, this was apparently the first time he recognized that those documents might be "of legal significance," as Gnielka put it.

When Gnielka returned home after seeing those execution lists, his wife Ingeborg recalled, "he was green in the face"—he looked sick. He had asked Wulkan for the chance to put the lists to good use, and he quickly passed them along to Bauer. This set off a chain of events that would eventually lead to West Germany's longest and most publicized postwar trial. Although Bauer allowed two young members of his team to prosecute the case and never played an official role in the courtroom, he was the driving force behind the trial and the person who was most intent on making his countrymen understand what he saw as its lessons.

There was nothing simple about those lessons or the trial itself, which lasted from December 20, 1963, to August 20, 1965. A total of 183 sessions were held in the Frankfurt courtroom, watched by more than twenty thousand visitors and covered intensely by the German and international press. The twenty-two defendants who showed up in court were not like the top Nazis who had been the "stars" of Nuremberg; nor did they play the kind of pivotal role in orchestrating the Holocaust that Eichmann did. Instead, they would become infamous because they had found themselves in the dock for their supporting roles in Auschwitz, their individual records of staggering brutality exposed by the list Gnielka had passed along to Bauer and by 211 concentration camp survivors who offered their testimony as witnesses.

For Bauer, the twenty-two defendants were "really only the chosen scapegoats" who were supposed to expose the crimes committed in the name of all the German people. "The question is what will we do with these people," he said, adding that he was not referring merely to the twenty-two defendants but to "50 million Germans, or more precisely said, for 70 million." By throwing in the latter figure, he left no doubt that he was referring to the combined population of West and East Germany, and what they should conclude from the trial. The proceedings "can and must open the eyes of the German people to what happened." The real lesson, he insisted, was "whoever operated this murder machinery is guilty of participation in murder, whatever he did, of course provided he knew the aim of the machinery."

But as Judge Hans Hofmeyer repeatedly stated, his vision of the trial was radically different: it was "an ordinary criminal trial, regardless of its background." When it pronounced its verdict, the court pointed out that it "could consider only criminal guilt—that is, guilt in the sense of the penal code. Political guilt, moral and ethical guilt, were not the subject of its concern," according to the summation by Bernd Naumann, the *Frankfurter Allgemeine Zeitung* reporter who provided the most detailed coverage of the trial. In other words, this was not a trial meant to establish a definitive account of Auschwitz or to demonstrate the principle that all the camp officers and guards were guilty; it was focused on the individual deeds of the defendants.

For all his attempts to portray the proceedings as an ordinary criminal trial that would be handled as dispassionately as any other case, even Hofmeyer could not avoid betraying an occasional flash of emotion, precisely on the subject of individual responsibility. "I have yet to meet anyone who did anything in Auschwitz," he caustically remarked as the defendants and their lawyers kept protesting their innocence.

The defendants in the dock in Frankfurt immediately created a different impression than Eichmann did when he sat alone in his glass booth in Jerusalem. According to the writer Robert Neumann, "As they all sit close together in their seats, you can't tell them apart anymore. . . . Each prosecutor is a potential defendant. . . . Each defendant your mailman, bank clerk, neighbor." Newsreel footage of that period also showed five of them walking the streets of Frankfurt during a break in the court sessions, looking indistinguishable from the other pedestrians except for the fact that a policeman saluted as one of the defendants tipped his hat to him.

The German authorities had hoped to have at least one defendant who was unquestionably a senior figure. As the prosecution pursued its lengthy investigation, it scored a major breakthrough: after launching a nationwide manhunt, the police found and arrested Richard Baer, the last commandant of Auschwitz, in December 1960. Höss, the first commandant, and Arthur Liebehenschel, his immediate successor, had been executed in Poland in 1947 and 1948. Baer had managed to disappear and, using an assumed name, found work as a forester on the estate of the great-grandson of the Prussian statesman Otto von Bismarck. When his photo ran in *Bild*, the country's largest tabloid, a co-worker recognized him and tipped off the police. But on June 17, 1963, Baer died in prison, six months before the start of the trial.

Deprived of the defendant they had expected to garner the most attention, the prosecution focused even more intently on the individual actions of the remaining defendants. That reinforced Judge Hofmeyer's contention that this was a criminal trial despite its whole backdrop, not the kind of broader educational-political exercise that Bauer envisaged. Yet, in the end, some elements of both approaches were visible in the proceedings.

What attracted the most attention of the media and the packed audiences, which included many concentration camp survivors, were the harrowing descriptions of wanton brutality. Auschwitz was not simply a mechanized killing machine that operated according to impersonal rules; it was also very much the product of the personal actions, idiosyncrasies, and sadism of those who were charged with running that machinery. As the Frankfurt proceedings demonstrated, there were many ways to die or live—and an almost infinite range of suffering that could be inflicted on anyone at any time, depending on the whims of the defendants and others like them.

As the prosecution presented its case, some of the defendants stood out from the others, precisely because of the devastating testimonies against them. SS Staff Sergeant Wilhelm Boger was one of the camp's most feared interrogators because of his frequent use of the "Boger swing." As explained by Lilly Majerczik, a former prisoner who had served as a secretary in the political department where Boger worked, "the victims were tied by their wrists to a stick on this apparatus and then worked over with a whip." In fact, the apparatus was a trestle and prisoners found themselves hanging upside down during those torture sessions. She and other prisoners who worked in the office could not see the procedure but they heard "the piercing wails of the victims. While being forced to testify loudly, the prisoners would then have their nails ripped out and have to undergo other tortures."

Another witness described how Boger shot prisoners with his pistol as they were brought into a courtyard and lined up against the "Black Wall"; on one occasion, he shot fifty to sixty of them as they were brought in two at a time. But perhaps the most chilling testimony came from survivor Dounia Wasserstrom. She described seeing a truck full of Jewish children stop in front of the political department. A four- or five-year-old boy jumped out, with an apple in his hand—and at that moment Boger came to the door. "Boger took the child by his feet and smashed his head against the wall," she recounted. Wasserstrom was ordered to wash the wall and later called in to do some translation for Boger. "He was sitting in his office eating the boy's apple," she added.

While the gas chambers consumed the largest number of victims, there were many forms of murder. Medical orderly Josef Klehr, another

SS staff sergeant, may have injected as many as twenty thousand prisoners with phenol, killing them instantly. Dr. Victor Capesius, a Romanian SS major in charge of the Auschwitz pharmacy, had supplied the deadly poison to Klehr. Then there was SS Corporal Oswald Kaduk, who tortured and killed with a fury that made him stand out in a dock filled with brutal murderers. When he drank, he often shot prisoners at random. And, like Boger, he was associated with a special type of torture: in his case, placing a cane over his victim's neck and standing on it until the prisoner died.

Such testimony underscored the prosecution's contention that there was nothing automatic about how the guards and officers behaved in Auschwitz. Dr. Ella Lingens, an Austrian physician who had helped several Jews hide or escape before she was arrested and sent to Auschwitz, was especially emphatic in her testimony about the broad range of individual behavior of the officers and guards, arguing that the accused were not forced to act the way they did. Incredulous, Judge Hofmeyer asked: "Do you wish to say that everyone could decide for himself to be either good or evil in Auschwitz?" Lingens, who along with her husband was later honored by Yad Vashem for her efforts to save Jews, both before and during her imprisonment, responded: "That is exactly what I wish to say."

This corresponded to the argument that U.S. Army Prosecutor Benjamin Ferencz had made during the Nuremberg trial of the commanders of the Einsatzgruppen. At the Frankfurt trial, Hans-Günther Seraphim, an expert witness from the University of Göttingen, referred to those earlier proceedings when he testified that SS officers who decided for whatever reason not to participate in those massacres were never punished. During ten years of research, he testified, he had "not found one case that resulted in 'damage to life and limb' when an SS officer refused to carry out an 'annihilation order.'" But he acknowledged that such officers could be sent off to fight on the Eastern Front instead, which many of those serving in the camps wished to avoid at all costs.

The defendants and their lawyers did everything possible to counter such testimony. "As a little man in Auschwitz, I did not have a voice over life and death," Klehr maintained, alluding to his murders by injection.

"I only carried out the orders of the doctors and only with deep inner reluctance." Capesius portrayed himself as just a helpful pharmacist: "In Auschwitz I did no harm to anyone. I was polite and friendly toward all and ready to help wherever I could." He added that his wife was half Jewish, and that it was only "unfortunate circumstance" that led to his assignment to the camp's pharmacy.

Then there were the purely surrealist touches inside and outside the courtroom. Interviewed by a film crew, the wife of Boger—of "Boger swing" fame—insisted that the couple had led "a very harmonious life" during their twenty-four years of marriage. This included the time she lived with him at Auschwitz. "I can't imagine him doing all the things he was supposed to have done," she said. She conceded that he was strict, "but the accusation of killing children, when he himself had children, just to come back home and be a good, loving father, that's unimaginable to me." And survivor Lingens, who had worked as a doctor, recalled that the wife of Höss, the first commandant, had once sent "a pink sweater and fond regards into this hell," apparently seeking to display her compassion for the prisoners.

The press coverage of the Auschwitz trial focused on the most horrifying charges against the defendants, portraying them as "monsters," "devils," and "barbarians," with Auschwitz itself depicted as Dante's Inferno or hell on earth. A cursory sampling of the headlines leaves no doubt about their tone: "The Torture Swing of Auschwitz," "The Devil Sits on the Defendants' Bench," "Women Thrown Alive into the Fire," and "Deathly Ill Gnawed on by Rats."

Quoting such headlines, the writer Martin Walser, a frequently controversial commentator about Germans and their struggle to deal with the Nazi past, warned of the dangers of demonizing the Auschwitz defendants. "The more horrible the Auschwitz quotations, the more pronounced our distance from Auschwitz becomes," he wrote. "We have nothing to do with these events, with these atrocities; we know this for certain. The similarities [with the defendants] aren't shared here. This trial is not about us." Like Arendt, who maintained that demonizing Eichmann allowed others who served the Third Reich to dismiss him as an aberration, Walser attempted to drive a similar point home. "Auschwitz was not Hell, but a German concentration camp," he pointed out.

This was Bauer's argument as well. Even if the defendants were justifiably singled out for especially vicious behavior, he did not want to create the impression that others who had served there—those who operated the machinery of death without any distinctive displays of sadism—were not guilty, too. This was not what most of his countrymen wanted to hear; nor did they want to read the occasional coverage in the press that suggested that the defendants were not so different from everyone else. In the *Suddeutsche Zeitung,* Ursula von Kardorff sounded like she was echoing Arendt's "banality of evil" theme when she wrote of the defendants: "Grey haired men with small mouths and average faces. Is this the way the accomplices to murder look?"

In his presentation of the court's verdict, Judge Hofmeyer continued to insist that the trial was about the criminal guilt of the individual defendants, not a broader political indictment of all those who had carried out the Nazis' murderous policies. At the same time, however, he rejected the notion that lower level functionaries could elude responsibility for criminal acts, pointing out that "it would be a mistake to say that the 'little people' are not guilty because they did not initiate things." He added: "They were just as vital to the execution of the extermination plan as those who drew up this plan at their desks."

The verdict itself satisfied almost no one. Five of the defendants left the courtroom as free men, with three of them acquitted and two released on the grounds that they already had served enough time in pretrial detention. Boger, Klehr, and Kaduk received life sentences, but the pharmacist Capesius only received nine years; most of the others were given lighter sentences, as low as three years in one case.

Bauer considered those sentences far too lenient. But, as he saw it, the greater failure of the judges in Frankfurt and other courts handling Nazi-era cases was their insistence on treating the perpetrators as ordinary criminals. As he put it, this encouraged "the residual wishful fantasy that there were only a few people with responsibility in the totalitarian state of the Nazi period and the rest were merely terrorized, violated hanger-ons or depersonalized, dehumanized characters who were compelled to do things that were completely contrary to their nature. Germany was not, as it were, a society obsessed by Nazism, but a country occupied by the enemy." Then he pointedly added: "But this had little to do with historical reality."

Bernd Naumann, the *Frankfurter Allgemeine Zeitung* reporter who published his meticulous accounts of the trial in a book shortly after the proceedings concluded, offered another sobering assessment. "The criminal facts, the guilt of Auschwitz, and the attempt at expiation are not commensurable," he wrote. "Neither the planners, the assistants, the murderers, nor the victims can hope to find ultimate justice in a regular court of a legal state."

Hannah Arendt wrote the introduction to Naumann's volume, allowing her to expand on her earlier views. In one key respect, she voiced her agreement with Bauer. "'Mass murder and complicity in mass murder' was a charge that could and should be leveled against every single SS man who had ever done duty in any of the extermination camps and against many who had never set foot into one," she wrote. As for the import of the whole proceedings that Naumann described, she concluded: "Instead of *the* truth . . . the reader will find *moments of truth*, and these moments are actually the only means of articulating this chaos of viciousness and evil."

Many Germans had no desire to follow the trial or to glimpse any moments of truth. For them, the extensive media coverage was a growing source of irritation. One reader wrote to the Frankfurt tabloid *Abendpost*: "Damn it! Give it a rest with your reporting about Auschwitz already. Do you seriously think that you can convince the world that you are interested in the truth? No, you and your dear compatriots are only interested in cheap thrills." A poll taken at the beginning of 1965 when the trial was still in full swing indicated that 57 percent of Germans had concluded that they did not want any more such trials, which represented a huge jump from the 34 percent who responded that way in a 1958 poll.

Emmi Bonhoeffer—the widow of the lawyer Klaus Bonhoeffer, who paid with his life for his staunch anti-Nazi views—was not surprised by the popular mood. "Naturally the Auschwitz Trial is unpopular," she wrote in a letter to a friend. "This makes it all the more peculiar that the press corps provides daily coverage, if not always very thoroughly. They write stories that nobody actually wants to read, certainly not those most in need of it." The theologian Helmut Gollwitzer echoed her thoughts when he explained that the trial made their countrymen uncomfortable, since it left the impression that many of them could be "in the same boat as the defendants."

All of this was true despite the barrage of news stories that portrayed the defendants as monsters, a breed apart. As University of Toronto historian Rebecca Wittmann pointed out in her insightful account of the trial, this was no accident. "In many ways, the press coverage simply reflected the legal strategy, especially since it satisfied the need for sensational headlines and lurid details," she wrote. But nothing could completely quiet the sense of gnawing unease of the millions who instinctively felt implicated, even while they protested that they had nothing to do with the crimes committed by those who had found themselves in the dock.

"It would be quite unfair to blame 'the majority of the German people' for their lack of enthusiasm for legal proceedings against Nazi criminals without mentioning the facts of life during the Adenauer era," Arendt wrote after the trial. Specifically, she pointed out that "the West German administration on all levels is shot through with former Nazis." This prompted a public perception that *"the small fish are caught, while the big fish continue their careers,"* she added, italicizing the phrase for emphasis.

No one symbolized the government's failure to make a clean break with the Nazi past more than Hans Globke. During the Third Reich, Globke had worked for the Ministry of the Interior and served as a commentator on the Nuremberg race laws that institutionalized Nazi anti-Semitic doctrine and practices, which meant explaining and justifying them. Yet he emerged as a state secretary under Adenauer, running the chancellor's office and serving as his trusted advisor from 1953 to 1963, when Adenauer stepped down.

Bauer tried to investigate Globke's role, particularly when his name came up in the Eichmann trial in 1961. He requested documents about Globke from the East German authorities. But the Adenauer government viewed all the accusations from that quarter as a smear campaign, part of the ongoing Cold War battle between the two German governments. Soon, Bauer was forced to hand over his investigation to the Bonn public prosecutor's office, which decided to drop the case.

In 1963, the East German Supreme Court proceeded to indict Globke for war crimes and crimes against humanity. The West German government spokesman dismissed it as a "show trial," arguing that Globke had been investigated already and all the charges were "found to be untrue." The spokesman added that there was evidence that Globke had helped shield some people from persecution in that period.

Of course East Germany was playing its usual propaganda game and ignoring the former Nazis in its ranks, but West Germany's record on this issue was distinctly unimpressive. So was its record of prosecuting those who had served the Nazi regime. From 1950 to 1962, the authorities investigated thirty thousand former Nazis. But of the 5,426 who were brought to trial, 4,027 were acquitted and only 155 were convicted of murder. Given the kind of tight constraints of West German law that Bauer frequently complained about, this was hardly surprising.

When the Central Office for the Investigation of National Socialist Crimes was opened in Ludwigsburg in 1958, its staffers were only given the power to conduct the preliminary investigation of cases. If they turned up enough evidence to suggest that a case should be pursued further, they then had to turn it over to regional prosecutors, who might or might not be interested in following up and seeking an indictment. To this day, this frustrates the Ludwigsburg team. "We do not have the possibility to bring [a case] to court," Deputy Director Thomas Will pointed out in 2014. "We should have had it."

But back in the 1950s, the Adenauer government wanted both to demonstrate that it was serious about investigating war crimes and to reassure its jittery citizens that such investigations would not be pushed too far. This led to the policy of deliberately limiting the powers of the investigators. One measure of the popular mood was the hostility that the staffers of the Ludwigsburg office often faced. "In the first years, this office was not welcomed here," Will explained. When staffers looked for apartments they avoided mentioning where they worked. Some even had problems getting a taxi driver to take them to the office, which is housed in a former nineteenth-century prison. All this would change over time, but very slowly. Today the office, which continues its investigations and also has accumulated an impressive historical archive about the Third Reich, is largely accepted and, to some extent, a source of local pride.

Despite the widespread dissatisfaction that the Auschwitz trial generated, both from those who were instinctively opposed to the prosecution of former Nazis and those who felt the proceedings did not go far enough, it qualified as a major breakthrough. First of all, the sheer magnitude of the coverage meant that many Germans who had routinely ignored earlier trials could not help but pay attention to the drama in the Frankfurt courtroom. And while the initial public reaction was largely negative, one indicator that some people began to reconsider their views about closing the book on the Third Reich was another poll that was conducted one year later. As compared to the 1965 poll that showed that 57 percent opposed any further trials of former Nazis, the 1966 poll showed a drop in that figure to 44 percent.

Aside from exposing the public to a wealth of new evidence about the horrors of Auschwitz, the trial also enabled a rare display of cooperation across the Cold War divide. It was no accident that the two men responsible for that particular breakthrough were Fritz Bauer and Jan Sehn, the Polish investigating judge who had orchestrated his country's earlier Auschwitz trial and the conviction of its commandant Rudolf Höss. Sehn had provided his German counterparts testimonies and other evidence he had gathered in Poland for use in their trial, and he traveled to Frankfurt to deliver such materials on more than one occasion.

Sehn was equally helpful when Frankfurt organized a special exhibition, "Auschwitz: Pictures and Documents," which opened on November 18, 1964, during the trial. It was meant to teach young people, in the words of Carl Tesch, "that something like that can never happen again." Tesch had organized the exhibit, but Bauer was both its catalyst and staunchest supporter. Sehn made sure that the Auschwitz Museum, situated in the remains of the concentration camp in Poland, provided the artifacts that the exhibition needed for its display.

During the trial, Sehn also played a critical role in arranging a visit by a West German delegation, which included a judge, prosecutors, defense attorneys, and government representatives, to Auschwitz in December 1964. This allowed them to examine the site and to check the accuracy of the testimony of witnesses based on such considerations as the actual distances within the camp. At a time when Poland still had not established diplomatic relations with West Germany as a result of lingering postwar tensions, this was a considerable feat. Sehn and Bauer worked with their respective governments to remove the barriers to the visit, with an eye to increasing cooperation beyond this particular case. "May it smooth the way for closer relations between the two peoples," Sehn declared.

The trial had an impact in other ways as well. Playwright Peter Weiss wrote *The Investigation*, which was billed as "a dramatic re-construction of the Frankfurt War Crimes trials" and an "Oratorio in 11 Cantos." It was staged simultaneously in thirteen theaters in East and West Germany on October 19, 1965, a mere two months after the conclusion of the trial. Directed by Peter Brook, the Royal Shakespeare Company also performed a reading of the work at the Aldwych Theatre in London that same evening.

The Investigation consisted of compressed extracts of the testimonies at the trial. In Weiss's version, a witness offers this account of his narrow escape from death at the hands of Boger, the camp's particularly infamous sadist:

> *When I was taken down from the swing*
> *Boger said to me*
> *Now we've made you ready*
> *for a happy trip to heaven*
> *I was brought to a cell in Block Eleven*

There I waited from hour to hour
to be shot
I don't know
how many days I spent there
My buttocks were festering
My testicles were black and blue
and swollen to gigantic size
Most of the time I lay unconscious
Then I was led
along with a large group of others
into the washroom
We had to undress
and our numbers were written
on our breasts
in blue pencil
I knew that this
was the death sentence
As we stood there naked in a row
The Liaison Chief came and asked
how many prisoners he should register
as shot
After he left we were counted
once again
It turned out there was one too many
I had learned
To always place myself last
so I received a kick
and got my clothing back
I was supposed to be taken to my cell
to wait for the next batch
but a male nurse
who was also a prisoner
took me with him to the hospital
It just happened

that one or two were supposed to live
and I was
one of them

Born in 1944, Bernhard Schlink was part of West Germany's postwar generation that eventually became known as the 68ers—the young people who began questioning their parents in the 1960s and just about all authority figures by 1968, the year when they took to the streets in protests that swept across Europe and the United States. While the protests elsewhere were sparked by the Vietnam War, the civil rights movement, and other causes, West Germany had a special factor that contributed to its unrest. "Nineteen sixty-eight cannot be understood without understanding that this was a worldwide thing, but in Germany it cannot be understood without [understanding] the Auschwitz trial," Schlink pointed out.

For Schlink, who would go on to become both a law professor and a successful writer, there is no doubt about the impact of that trial. "The Auschwitz trial left a much bigger imprint on me and my generation than the Eichmann trial," he said. "Of course the Eichmann trial was something that we registered and followed very closely. All the papers wrote about it. But the Auschwitz trial was much closer." Since the defendants were not senior figures, he added, one of the immediate questions it raised in his generation's mind was "who were the higher-ups?"

During the trial, Schlink tried to satisfy his curiosity on that point by reading the autobiography of Rudolf Höss, who had written his story at the urging of Jan Sehn before he was hanged in 1947. He still recalled "his absolute shock at the way he writes like a manager who is overwhelmed by a difficult task." There was Höss fretting about the influx of Hungarian Jews, as Schlink put it, "Oh God . . . how can we house them, how can we burn them, how can we kill them?" He recognized that the commandant was "a technocrat" who "just solved the problems that this criminal regime created. This was frightening, frightening." He found Höss's account to have "an authenticity" that all the subsequent protestations of the defendants in other trials, who desperately tried to spin their stories to seek absolution, never did.

The other question it raised for the postwar generation was what roles had their parents, relatives, and other older acquaintances played during the Third Reich, a subject that was so often passed over in silence when he was growing up. "Under the pressure of my generation, these things came out," Schlink noted—and in many cases led to the discovery of dark secrets. But while the Auschwitz trial was the trigger for such discussions for students like Schlink, the broader self-examination of German society, including by their elders, did not come till a decade later. The trigger then was the showing of the 1978 NBC miniseries *The Holocaust* that riveted German viewers with its vivid portrayal of a Jewish family and an ambitious lawyer who turns into an SS mass murderer.

The process of discovering the past had no single eureka moment. As a law student, Schlink and many of his friends greatly admired Bauer for his efforts to prod that process along. But Peter Schneider, another 68er who became a prominent writer, conceded that he only learned about Bauer and his role in the Auschwitz trial in the 1980s, when he was writing a novel about the son of Josef Mengele, the fearsome camp doctor. Nonetheless, Schneider was influenced by the Auschwitz trial in the 1960s, particularly when he read Peter Weiss's dramatic rendition of it. It proved to be a part of his education that helped propel him to the forefront of the protest movement in 1968.

Schlink did not take a similarly vocal role in the protests of the 1960s, but the era left its mark on him in other ways, planting seeds that would only blossom decades later. The best-known result: his lyrical 1995 short novel *The Reader*, which rocketed to the top of bestseller lists after it was published in English and Schlink was invited to discuss it on *The Oprah Winfrey Show*. In the early postwar era, the fifteen-year-old narrator falls in love with a tram conductor who is twice his age. After a lengthy affair, she disappears—only to reappear as a defendant in a trial of concentration camp guards that he is obliged to observe as a law student. But the story is far from as simple or as morally unambiguous as the plot outline suggests, and Schlink deftly navigates the terrain of personal guilt and betrayal.

Strictly speaking, *The Reader* is not autobiographical; Schlink did not have a similar romance as a teenager. But in his Heidelberg high school, he had a "beloved and admired English teacher" who had been in the SS. In those days, he had believed that this "great teacher" could not have been implicated in anything shameful during the war. After the teacher retired, Schlink learned otherwise—but he is still unwilling to discuss the specifics since he was given the information in confidence. Schlink soon recognized that this was a common experience for his generation: "You love someone, you admire someone, you owe someone, and then you find out." He added: "For many, it was a lot closer, the father or the uncle." This, too, was the legacy of Auschwitz and everything it stood for.

Jan Sehn had a regular routine when he was leaving his director's office in Kraków's Institute of Forensic Research to travel abroad. He would hand over the keys to most of the drawers in his desk to Maria Kozłowska, his younger colleague and neighbor, but not to the middle section, which held his private papers. Much to Kozłowska's surprise, he changed the drill as he was embarking on another trip to Frankfurt in late 1965. "The last time he was leaving, he gave me the keys to the middle section as well," she recalled. Then, as if still pondering the meaning of his action, she spelled out the obvious: "I had all the keys."

For Kozłowska, her boss's action took on particular significance in retrospect because Sehn died during that visit to Frankfurt. On December 12, 1965, as he was getting ready for bed, he sent out his official bodyguard, who was also tasked with monitoring his contacts with foreigners by the Polish communist authorities, to pick up a pack of cigarettes. When the bodyguard returned, Sehn was dead. He was only fifty-six. As his stunned colleagues in his institute in Kraków mourned him, Kozłowska said, there was speculation "that maybe someone helped him in this dying."

She and most of her colleagues dismissed that theory since there was no evidence to support it. Besides, Sehn was a chronic smoker and was known to have undergone treatment for heart problems earlier. The assumption was that he had died of a heart attack. The unanswered question, though, was whether his decision to entrust all the keys to Kozłowska signaled that he had some premonition about his fate.

Sehn had received anonymous letters threatening him on several occasions. Some consisted of cut-out printed letters to spell out the messages. Some were in German and others in Polish, but Kozłowska was under the impression that most of them were written by German speakers. Presumably, they were from people who were incensed by his efforts to bring Auschwitz personnel and other war criminals to justice.

But Sehn was a far less controversial figure—and much less of a public figure—in Poland than Bauer was in West Germany. Although Bauer had let his younger prosecutors handle the Auschwitz trial, he spoke frequently in public, including on television, about the need for those who were responsible for mass murder to be held to account. "The trial should show the world that a new Germany, a new democracy, is willing to protect the dignity of every human being," he declared at the beginning of the proceedings. At the same time, he made no secret of his exasperation with the way the defendants in the Auschwitz trial behaved. In an interview in the midst of the trial, he pointed out that the prosecution had been waiting "for one of the defendants . . . to address the witnesses who had survived and had their whole families annihilated with one humane word . . . it would have cleared the air." That never happened.

Bauer also pressed for a cleansing of the West German judges and prosecutors, whose ranks were still filled with former Nazis. Exasperated by his generation's apparent indifference to that kind of continuity between the old and the new, he spent more and more time discussing the wider implications of the efforts to bring Nazis to justice with young people with whom he had an easy rapport. He often joined them in pubs or living rooms for long sessions as he smoked cigarette after cigarette and nursed his wine. When the youth protests gained momentum in 1968, some of his detractors accused him of instigating the ensuing violence.

Many Germans were angered by Bauer's actions and words. He received far more threatening letters than Sehn did, along with threatening phone calls—although he had an unlisted number. "When I leave my office, I find myself in a hostile foreign country," Bauer remarked. During the Auschwitz trial, a swastika was painted on the wall of his apartment building; when it was wiped clean, it kept reappearing. Bauer kept a 6.35mm pistol in his apartment for his protection, and he was assigned a bodyguard. Reporting an alleged assassination plot, the *Frankfurter Rundschau* headlined its October 14, 1966, story: "The Attorney General Was Supposed to Be Murdered."

But Bauer was never intimidated. He openly talked about the need for more trials of Nazi criminals in the coming years, and about Germany's "burning anti-Semitism." In 1967, he blocked the confiscation of the *Braunbuch*, "Brown Book," at the Frankfurt Book Fair; that volume, which was published in East Germany in 1965, contained the names of about 1,800 prominent West Germans who were alleged to have held official positions in the Nazi period. The government in Bonn denounced it as propaganda, but Bauer held firm. By then, the West German chancellor was Kurt Georg Kiesinger, who had joined the Nazi Party in 1933 and worked in the propaganda department of the Foreign Ministry during the war. The contrast between Bauer's pronouncements and the general atmosphere that could allow a former Nazi to assume the country's top post could not have been greater.

Bauer always stressed that he was not criticizing his countrymen for failing to actively undermine Hitler's regime. But he still set a standard that implicated millions of them. "There is only a duty to passive resistance, only a duty to refrain from doing evil, only a duty not be an accomplice to injustice," he declared in one of his last speeches. "Our trials against the Nazi criminals are based exclusively on the assumption of such a duty to disobedience. This is the contribution of these trials to defeat the unjust state in the past, present and future."

On July 1, 1968, Bauer, who was just a couple of weeks away from his sixty-fifth birthday, was found dead in his bathtub; he had apparently died about twenty-four hours earlier. There was immediate speculation that he had been killed or committed suicide, but the coroner who examined the body ruled out both theories. Like Sehn, Bauer was a chain-smoker. He also suffered from chronic bronchitis, and, as the 2014 Frankfurt exhibition about his life pointed out, he sometimes mixed sleeping pills with alcohol. Bauer always shrugged off concern about his unhealthy habits. Asked by a reporter how many cigarettes he smoked, he replied: "How long do I need for a cigarette?" When the reporter offered a guess of five minutes, he declared: "Then divide 18 hours by 5 minutes, and you have my consumption."

But not everyone was convinced that Bauer died as a result of the toll that such habits took on his body. In her powerful documentary about him that premiered in 2010, Ilona Ziok pointed out that no autopsy was performed and featured testimony from those who raised doubts about his death. Rolf Tiefenthal, Bauer's Danish nephew, is shown admitting that there is only speculation on that score but added: "His enemies, his many enemies, could have helped him, could have forced him to take his own life or they could have murdered him. There were reasons enough for that."

In the current debates in Germany about what aspects of Bauer's life should be highlighted, there is a sharp divide about his death as well. The 2014 Fritz Bauer exhibition at Frankfurt's Jewish Museum appeared to accept the coroner's verdict. Ziok never leveled a direct accusation of foul play in her documentary and conceded that there is "no proof" of that. But asked point-blank whether she believes he was killed, she replied: "Yes."

At Bauer's funeral, Robert Kempner, the German-born Jewish member of the U.S. prosecution team at Nuremberg, spoke about his legacy. "He was the greatest ambassador that the Federal Republic ever had," he declared. "In contrast to many short-sighted men, he had a clear vision of what needed to be done to help Germany and he helped it." The weekly *Die Zeit* pointedly noted: "He won us much honor abroad, which we didn't deserve."

Until the recent revival of interest in Bauer's life, many Germans knew nothing about him. In Poland, Sehn is almost completely forgotten except by those who continue working for the institute he once headed, which was subsequently renamed the Jan Sehn Institute of Forensic Research. And what no one in either country seems to have noticed is that both of these men who once cooperated in their efforts to bring Nazis to justice died in Frankfurt, two and a half years apart in circumstances that remain murky to this day. The conspiracy theories may be entirely wrong, but those similarities are eerily disturbing.

U.S. Army Master Sergeant John C. Woods (center) was supposed to hang eleven top Nazis in Nuremberg on October 16, 1946. Hermann Göring (top left) eluded the noose by committing suicide. The other ten were (top row, after Göring) Hans Frank, Wilhelm Frick and Julius Streicher; (second row) Fritz Sauckel and Joachim von Ribbentrop; (third row) Alfred Jodl and Arthur Seyss-Inquart; (bottom row) Alfred Rosenberg, Ernst Kaltenbrunner and Wilhelm Keitel. The lingering question: did Woods deliberately botch one or two of the hangings?

No other Nazi hunter achieved as much fame— or generated as much controversy and, at times, fury—as Simon Wiesenthal. But even his critics acknowledge that he played a pivotal role in keeping up the pressure on Hitler's executioners who had evaded justice.

Like Wiesenthal, Tuvia Friedman was a Holocaust survivor who ended up in Austria, tracking war criminals. The two Nazi hunters worked together on occasion, but largely parted ways when Friedman moved to Israel.

William Denson, the U.S. Army chief prosecutor at the Dachau trials of concentration camp personnel, produced a remarkable scorecard: guilty verdicts in all 177 of his cases. But his success rate led to accusations that there had been a rush to judgment.

Dubbed "the Bitch of Buchenwald," Ilse Koch, the widow of the camp's commandant, was infamous for sexually taunting prisoners. Denson called witnesses who offered lurid testimony, including dubious stories about lampshades made of the skin of her victims.

Benjamin Ferencz was only twenty-seven when he became the chief prosecutor of what the Associated Press called "the biggest murder trial in history": the Nuremberg trial of twenty-two commanders of the Einsatzgruppen, the special mass murder units on the Eastern Front.

Otto Ohlendorf was the highly educated commander of Einsatzgruppe D, the most notorious killing squad. General Telford Taylor called him and the other defendants the leaders of "the trigger men in this gigantic program of slaughter." Ohlendorf was hanged in 1951.

Polish investigating judge Jan Sehn (right) interrogated Rudolf Höss, Auschwitz's longest serving commandant, and convinced him to write his memoirs before he was hanged in 1947. The account reflected his pride in the "improvements" he made in the camp's machinery of death, providing a chilling glimpse into the mind of a mass murderer. Subsequent Nazi hunters viewed the book as essential reading.

From left, Richard Baer, the last commandant of Auschwitz, at a retreat with Josef Mengele and Rudolf Höss (front, right of center) in July 1944, following Höss's reassignment to the Concentration Camp Inspectorate.

After receiving the tip that Eichmann was in Buenos Aires, Mossad chief Isser Harel (right) launched the investigation that eventually led to Eichmann's capture. He deployed a team of agents to Buenos Aires who mounted the elaborate operation that stunned Argentina and the world.

Rafi Eitan (above, at a shooting range in Israel in 1984) was in charge of the commando unit that kidnapped Eichmann in Buenos Aires on May 11, 1960. He emphasized that, until then, Israel had not made Nazi hunting a top priority.

12

13

From the bulletproof glass booth constructed for his trial in Jerusalem, Adolf Eichmann, a chief architect of the Holocaust, heard the court sentence him to death on December 15, 1961. After Israeli agents kidnapped Eichmann in Buenos Aires and smuggled him on a special flight to Israel, his case triggered new debates about the Holocaust and "the banality of evil." (Right) Eichmann pacing the yard of his Israeli prison cell.

A Social Democrat from a secular Jewish family, the German judge and prosecutor Fritz Bauer spent most of the Nazi era in exile. Returning to West Germany after the war, he played a critical secret role in the capture of Eichmann. In the 1960s, he orchestrated the Frankfurt Auschwitz trial that forced many Germans to confront their past.

Among the defendants in the Auschwitz trial in Frankfurt, SS Staff Sergeant Wilhelm Boger stood out because of his particularly sadistic interrogations. The descriptions of his elaborate torture devices produced mesmerizing—and repelling—testimony.

By the 1970s, bestselling novels and hit movies provided highly entertaining but misleading tales of Nazi hunters. In *The Boys from Brazil*, Gregory Peck played Josef Mengele, who is pursued by a Simon Wiesenthal–like character. In *Marathon Man*, the evil Nazi is a fugitive concentration camp dentist played by Laurence Olivier (below), who tortures Babe Levy, his young American pursuer played by Dustin Hoffman.

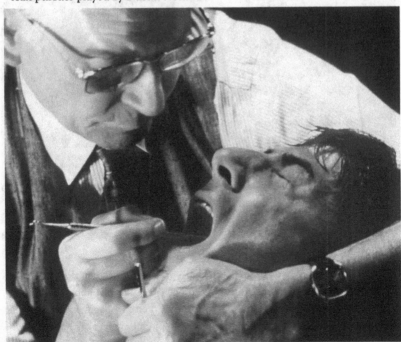

18

In May 1941, this group of foreign Jews in France was arrested and dispatched from the Austerlitz station in Paris to internment camps. Later, French Jews were also rounded up both by the German occupiers and their French collaborators, and thousands were sent to death camps.

19

Nazi hunters Beate and Serge Klarsfeld at a press conference in Bonn in 1979, presenting evidence against former SS officer Kurt Lischka about his role in the deportation of French Jews. Serge's father died in Auschwitz, giving the French-German couple a powerful motive to pursue such cases.

One of the Klarsfelds' most famous feats was to track down Klaus Barbie, the former Gestapo chief known as "the Butcher of Lyon," in Bolivia. (Left) Barbie entering the Lyon court in 1987, where he was given a life sentence.

The children's home in the French village of Izieu served as a refuge for Jews until Barbie's Gestapo arrested all forty-four children and seven guardians there on April 6, 1944. Except for one guardian, they all perished in Auschwitz.

As the longest-serving director of the U.S. Justice Department's Office of Special Investigations, Eli Rosenbaum led the government's efforts to identify and strip Nazi war criminals living in the United States of their citizenship.

In an early case, Rosenbaum targeted Arthur Rudolph, one of the German rocket scientists brought to the United States. Rudolph developed the Saturn V rocket that sent the first astronauts to the moon, but he had also worked thousands of prisoners to death while producing V-2 rockets during the war. (Left) Rudolph's wartime identification card with an added postwar British stamp on it.

24

Former UN Secretary-General Kurt Waldheim campaigning for the Austrian presidency in 1986. Eli Rosenbaum, then the general counsel of the World Jewish Congress, highlighted new evidence that Waldheim had hidden his wartime record in the Balkans, when he served on the staff of a general who was later executed as a war criminal.

Never one to shy from confrontation, Beate Klarsfeld (above) led protests against Waldheim both before and after his victory. The bitterly divisive campaign also split the Nazi hunters, with Simon Wiesenthal blaming the World Jewish Congress for the ensuing wave of anti-Semitism in Austria.

Josef Mengele, the infamous SS Auschwitz doctor known as "the Angel of Death," managed to elude the Israelis and other Nazi hunters after fleeing to South America. He drowned while swimming off a beach in Brazil in 1979, but the search continued until his remains were discovered in 1985.

Like Mengele, Aribert Heim, "Dr. Death" in the Mauthausen concentration camp, successfully eluded his pursuers. He was still the subject of wild speculation and alleged sightings long after he died in Cairo in 1992.

Until 1994, Erich Priebke lived comfortably in Argentina, despite his role in the execution of 335 men and boys, including 75 Jews, near Rome in 1944. But after ABC's Sam Donaldson confronted him with a camera rolling, Argentina extradited him to Italy. Priebke (left) was sentenced to life in prison and then kept under house arrest because of his age.

Efraim Zuroff, the director of the Simon Wiesenthal center in Jerusalem, mounted the campaign "Operation Last Chance" to track down aging Nazi criminals. Here, in 2013, he displays one of the posters he placed in German cities proclaiming "Late but not too late."

No case was as long or took as many convoluted twists and turns than the one of retired Cleveland auto worker John Demjanjuk, who did his best to look his worst in court. Initially misidentified as "Ivan the terrible," a notorious Treblinka guard, he was sent to Germany in 2009. Found guilty of serving as a guard in another death camp, he died in 2012.

CHAPTER ELEVEN

A Slap to Remember

"Because we were weak, we had to take strong actions. And the strongest action is to go on the spot where the enemy is powerful and to tell the truth there."

French Nazi hunter Serge Klarsfeld

Beate Klarsfeld was certainly not brought up to be a risk taker. Born in Berlin on February 13, 1939, just months before Nazi Germany's invasion of Poland that signaled the start of World War II, she was too young to have many memories of the conflict. But she does recall, shortly before the fighting finally ended with Germany's surrender, "reciting little poems in honor of the Führer in kindergarten."

Her father served in the Wehrmacht in France in 1940, until his unit was transferred to the Eastern Front the following year when Hitler ordered the attack on the Soviet Union. But he had the good fortune to develop a case of double pneumonia, leading to his return to Germany where he worked as a bookkeeper for the army. After a brief stint in British captivity at the end of the war, he rejoined his family in a village where they had taken refuge during the Allied bombing of Berlin. In late 1945, they returned to Berlin, where Beate enrolled in elementary school and played hide-and-seek with her friends in the bombed-out buildings and piles of rubble.

As she recalled, she was "a conscientious and well-behaved student" in elementary school. "In those days no one ever spoke of Hitler," she added. Both teachers and parents largely avoided the whole topic of what had happened in Germany under his rule. Her parents had not joined the Nazi Party, but they had voted for Hitler like so many of their countrymen. "Still, they felt no responsibility for what had happened under the Nazis," she noted. Instead, they and their neighbors bemoaned their losses in the war with "never a word of pity or understanding for other nations." Growing up, she heard no real explanation for their situation. Instead, she kept hearing people say: "We have lost a war and now we must work."

As a teenager, unlike her parents, who supported Chancellor Adenauer's Christian Democrats, she favored Willy Brandt's Social Democrats. But that had more to do with the fact that Brandt's "young open face contrasted with those of the other politicians" than with any understanding of his party's politics. She was developing a typical teenager's impatience with what she saw as "the stifling atmosphere" of her household. Her father was drinking heavily and her mother wanted her to start looking for a suitable husband. Instead, after attending a commercial high school, she took a job as a stenographer in a large pharmaceutical firm. Her ambition was to earn enough to strike out on her own.

In March 1960, at the age of twenty-one, she landed in Paris, where she studied French and worked as an au pair. She slept "in a disgusting attic and trembled in fear of the spiders," she recalled. But, not surprisingly, she quickly fell in love with the city, finding it both so much livelier and more elegant than West Berlin. She also quickly fell in love with her future husband.

On May 11, 1960, two months after her arrival in Paris, Beate was waiting at the Porte de Saint-Cloud, her usual metro station. A young man with dark hair was staring at her. "Are you English?" he asked. As Beate noted later, "Of course it was a trap." The young man, Serge Klarsfeld, later admitted that it was a familiar tactic used to engage German girls in conversation. Once they replied "no," it was difficult to cut things off. By the time Serge got off at his stop near the School of Political Science, where he was finishing up his graduate work before embarking on what he expected to be a career as a history professor, he had Beate's phone number.

In Buenos Aires on that same day, the Israeli team moved in to capture Eichmann. At the time, neither Serge nor Beate knew anything about that, of course. But sitting together in their son's Paris apartment in 2013, reviewing their life's work, they could not help but feel that this was more than mere coincidence. The couple who would later gain fame—and, as others saw it, notoriety—as new, highly confrontational Nazi hunters had first connected on the day that the Mossad had sprung into action in Argentina.

Three days later, on the couple's first date, they went to see the movie *Never on Sunday*—and then began sharing their life stories for the first time while sitting on a bench in the Bois de Boulogne. That's where Beate learned that Serge was Jewish and his father had perished in Auschwitz. For a young German who, as she admitted, was largely "ignorant of my own country's history," this came as a jolt. "I was surprised and moved, but also in a certain sense shrank back a little," she noted. "In Berlin I had heard hardly anything good about the Jews. Why was this complication befalling me now?"

But Serge would not be put off, gently educating her during their endless discussions. "We never stopped talking," Beate recalled. "He brought history, art, the whole world of ideas into my life." Most of all, he filled her in on her country's recent history, "the terrifying reality of Nazism," as she put it. And that reality was all too apparent in his life story.

Arno and Raissa, Serge's parents, were Jews from Romania who had settled in France in the 1920s; Arno was Armenian and Raissa was from an ethnic Russian area in Bessarabia. Serge was born in 1935 in Bucharest, when his parents were visiting relatives there. His father enlisted in the Foreign Legion in 1939, fought against the Germans during their swift conquest of France in 1940, escaped from a POW camp, and joined the Resistance in Nice. But the entire family was in danger not because of anything he had done, but simply because they were Jews.

In June 1943, SS Captain Alois Brunner was sent to France to oversee the roundups of Jews there; he would soon send an estimated 25,000 Jews to death camps in the East. Working closely with Eichmann, he had already performed similar tasks in his native Austria and Greece, where the number of his victims was even higher. When Brunner began rounding up Jews in Nice, Arno prepared a thin plywood partition that served as the false back of a deep closet; behind it, there was just enough space for the whole family to hide.

On the evening of September 30, 1943, German troops surrounded the area where the Klarsfelds lived and started going from apartment to apartment. When they arrived next door, the Klarsfelds heard the screams and desperate pleas of their neighbors, including their eleven-year-old daughter, who had the temerity to ask the Germans for some identification. A Gestapo officer broke her nose with his pistol, resulting in more panic. Her father shouted out the window for the French police: "Help us! Save us! We are French!"

Hearing all this from the family's hiding place in the closet, Arno made a quick decision. "If the Germans arrest us, I will survive because I am strong, but you won't," he told his wife and Serge, and Serge's sister, Tanya. Raissa tried to stop him, but he crawled out of the closet. When the Germans pounded on the door, Arno opened it without hesitation. Serge heard a German asking him in French: "Where are your wife and children?" Arno responded that they had gone to the countryside while the apartment was disinfected.

The Germans immediately began a search of the apartment, and one of them even opened the closet. But he only poked around the clothing without reaching the partition. Later, when Serge documented the roundups by Brunner and others of French Jews, he wrote: "I knew him well, and yet I have never seen him." He added that the thin plywood partition was "all that stood between him and me that night." Looking back at that moment, Klarsfeld noted that he could not be sure that Brunner was in the apartment. "He could have been there personally, but I had no proof of that," he said, pointing out that Brunner worked with a team of Austrian SS officers and Frenchmen paid by the Gestapo. But regardless of who entered the apartment, Brunner was the man orchestrating the arrests, the subsequent transport of the prisoners to the Drancy detention center, and then their one-way journey to Auschwitz.

Raissa fled with the two children to the Haute-Loire, a region in south-central France. They lived in Saint-Julien-Chapteuil, a small village that was "a very hospitable place for Jews," according to Serge. Perhaps so, but Raissa still tried to keep their Jewish identity secret. She claimed her husband was in a POW camp and she sent the children to the local Catholic school. Once she felt that Nice was no longer a target for round-ups of Jews, Raissa moved back with Serge and Tanya to their apartment there. Nonetheless, she took nothing for granted. She told the children: "If the Germans will come, you will go in the hiding place and I will open the door."

Serge's family story prompted Beate to ponder what she should conclude as a German. She did not feel responsible for Nazism as an individual, "but insofar as I was one tiny part of the German nation, I became aware of new obligations," she recalled. But when she speculated whether she should stop considering herself a German, Serge rejected the idea out of hand, saying that would be too easy. "It was exciting as well as difficult to be a German after Nazism," Beate concluded.

Serge also told her about Hans and Sophie Scholl, the German brother and sister who organized a group that staged a desperate act of resistance in Munich in 1943, distributing anti-Nazi leaflets. They were quickly arrested, condemned, and sent to the guillotine. For Beate, this served as an inspiring example of Germans who had refused to submit to Hitler's regime. "Although it seemed meaningless and sterile in 1943, the significance of their act has grown with time until it reached Serge and, through him, me," she wrote. "In them I saw myself."

None of that was immediately apparent, however. Serge and Beate were married on November 7, 1963, and started what looked like normal jobs. Serge became a deputy director of the French Radio and Television System (ORTF) and Beate began working as a bilingual secretary at the

Franco-German Alliance for Youth (OFA), a newly created organization that had the backing of both Chancellor Adenauer and French President Charles de Gaulle. The idea was to forge new ties at all levels between the formerly warring neighbors.

As Beate recalled, there was nothing yet to indicate the real trajectory that their lives would take. "We had set the scene to live a stable, orderly life like that of thousands of other young couples," she noted. In 1965, Beate gave birth to a boy. The couple decided to name him Arno, in honor of Serge's father.

It didn't take long to see the first signals that the Klarsfelds would not settle for a stable, ordinary life. Beate did not hide her increasingly leftist political views, which included not only supporting Brandt's Social Democratic Party but her defiance of the taboo against treating East Germany as a legitimate partner. As part of her OFA job, she compiled a list of Franco-German cultural associations for a handbook for German au pairs that she was preparing; one of the associations she listed was a French friendship association with East Germany. The West German publisher hastily recalled the edition to redo the listing, omitting what was seen as a deliberately provocative mention. "You must be out of your mind!" she was told.

She also publicly voiced her feminist views. In an article in the publication *Women in the Twentieth Century*, she wrote: "I have come to wonder what made me and plenty of other German women leave our homeland." While conceding that there were often prosaic reasons like studying a new language and culture, she concluded: "I think the efforts we made reveal a more powerful and often unconscious motivation—the desire to be free."

As for the role of women in her homeland, she wrote: "Since the war, women have made a real contribution to the creation of a new Germany, which has turned out to be not so new after all and in which now, as in the past, they play hardly any role in politics." She also warned that public opinion "is now in the process of taking a dangerous turn which will once again lead to a domesticated woman dedicated to providing her husband with the greatest possible comfort and to her natural reproductive function."

None of this played well with her conservative bosses, who reported to a board of directors that included at least two German Foreign Ministry officials who were former Nazis. When she went back to work after her maternity leave ended in 1966, her job in the information department was cut for "budgetary reasons." She was once again assigned to lowly secretarial work, typing and answering phones.

But it was a far more momentous event in 1966 that triggered Beate's transformation from a somewhat troublesome low-level employee with unconventional views to a crusading activist intent on atoning for her country's Nazi past. That was the year when Kurt Georg Kiesinger became chancellor, despite the fact that he had been a Nazi Party member starting in 1933 and served as the deputy director of the Foreign Ministry's radio division during the war, disseminating Nazi propaganda. In his defense, Kiesinger claimed he had become disillusioned early with Nazi doctrine and that he was even denounced for holding dissident views.

There were voices of protest as Kiesinger was preparing to take power. The philosopher Karl Jaspers declared: "What seemed impossible ten years ago is now happening almost without opposition." While conceding that it was inevitable that some former Nazis would rise to high positions, he continued, "if a former Nazi should become chief of state, it would mean from now on the fact that a man has been a Nazi would be of no importance."

For Beate, the elevation of Kiesinger felt like a personal challenge. She thought of Hans and Sophie Scholl, who had given their lives to protest Hitler's regime, and treated this as an example of how to strike back quickly, even if the chances for success were slim. "Above all, it is necessary to be brave, follow your conscience, keep your eyes open, and act," as she put it. When Kiesinger paid his first official visit to Paris in January 1967, she penned what turned into a series of articles for *Combat*, a leftist newspaper that had been started by the French Resistance during the war. "As a German I deplore Kiesinger's accession to the Chancellorship," she wrote. "Sociologist Hannah Arendt used the phrase 'the banality of evil' in speaking of Eichmann. To me Kiesinger represents the respectability of evil."

In an even more incendiary article, she wrote: "If the USSR recognized the danger Kiesinger represents to democracy in Germany in the future, and if it truly wanted to get rid of him, there is no doubt that would be morally justified in the eyes of the world."

On August 30, 1967, a month after that article appeared, Beate was fired from her job at the Franco-German Alliance for Youth. When she was leaving her office, none of her co-workers said good-bye or shook her hand; they clearly did not want their bosses to see that they had anything to do with her. She hurried to see Serge, who had switched jobs and was then working for Continental Grains, a multinational cereal firm. While he had not engaged in public protests the way Beate had, he, too, had become more aware of the import of his father's legacy. In 1965, he visited Auschwitz. "In 1965 nobody from the West was going to Auschwitz," he recalled decades later. "But I felt I had to keep that link with my father."

Serge had learned how his father had died almost immediately when he arrived at the camp. Struck by a *Kapo*, a prisoner serving the SS officers, Arno had hit back. This cost him his life. Recognizing that his father had provided him a life lesson in courage, he vowed to himself that he would always honor the memory of the Jews who died in the Holocaust, and he would always defend Israel. When war broke out on June 5, 1967, he went to Israel to volunteer to help. By the time he arrived, the Six Day War was already almost over and he did not get directly involved, but the show of solidarity was important for him.

All of which formed the backdrop of the crisis in the Klarsfeld household when Beate was fired from her job in late August. While many of their friends advised them to accept what had happened and move on with their lives, Serge rejected such a course. "How can I take your being fired without making some protest?" he told Beate. "You're the first woman in France since the war ended to tell the truth about a Nazi. That would be the worst kind of submission."

• • •

The Klarsfelds launched what became a long legal battle to fight Beate's dismissal. Since she had become a French citizen, she appealed to senior French officials to help her, finding little sympathy there. But the main focus of the Klarsfelds' efforts was both to demonstrate that she had been fully justified in so vociferously denouncing Kiesinger and his Nazi past and to step up the pressure on the German chancellor.

To that end, Serge took time off from his job to travel to East Berlin, where the East German Interior Ministry gave him access to the documents they had on Kiesinger's role during the Third Reich. When he returned to Paris, he brought a large folder containing copies of the key documents. Much of that material was used in a book they hastily assembled to publicize Kiesinger's Nazi past, particularly emphasizing his role in coordinating Nazi propaganda efforts.

This was the beginning of a relationship with the East Germans that would continue sporadically as the Klarsfelds intensified their campaign to expose former Nazis in West Germany. Their critics accused them of doing the propaganda bidding of the East German regime, which was always delighted to see the Bonn government embarrassed. Beate provided them with plenty of ammunition. For example, she wrote in *Combat* on September 2, 1968, that Germany should be reunified "into a truly socialistic, democratic, and pacifistic nation"—language that echoed East German rhetoric.

After the fall of the Berlin Wall and the opening up of the files of the Stasi, the East German secret police, and the SED, the Communist Party, there were additional accusations that the Klarsfelds had received funding from the East Germans. "Beate Klarsfeld, Armed by the Stasi and the SED," a headline in the conservative daily *Die Welt* proclaimed on April 3, 2012.

The Klarsfelds readily admit that they received East German help in gathering documents, especially in the Kiesinger case. The East Germans also published two of their books about Nazi criminals they were targeting because of the crimes they committed in France during the occupation; the Klarsfelds then sent copies of those books to West German parliamentarians and officials. Such actions both bolstered the Klarsfelds' publicity campaign and helped them in their legal battles. "We do not deny the support of East Germany," Serge said. But the Klarsfelds point out that they collected documents and received help elsewhere as well—in France and the United States, in particular. "We kept our freedom of thinking," Serge insisted.

In fact, Beate would soon discover that her protests were less appreciated when she traveled to places like Poland and Czechoslovakia in 1970 to denounce the "anti-Zionist" campaigns of the communist governments there that were nothing more than thinly disguised appeals to anti-Semitism. Her attempts at public protest in the Eastern bloc, including chaining herself to a tree in Warsaw and distributing leaflets to passersby there and in Prague, led to her arrest and expulsion from both countries.

But it was the earlier battle to discredit Kiesinger that proved pivotal to elevating the Klarsfelds' activism into an international news story, with Beate cast in the role of agent provocateur. This was no accident. While they continued to publish articles denouncing Kiesinger and Beate's arbitration hearings afforded her the opportunity to repeat their allegations against the chancellor, she was frustrated by the fact that the press did not seem particularly interested in their crusade. "I recognized that my exposures would have small impact unless I did something so sensational that the papers would want to report it," she recalled. Or, as Serge put it: "Because we were weak, we had to take strong actions."

In Kiesinger's case, this meant not just a strong action but a highly risky one. Beate reserved a ticket in the visitors' section of the West German parliament under her maiden name so as not to arouse suspicion, and traveled to Bonn for the March 30 session when she knew Kiesinger was scheduled to speak. Her plan was straight-forward: to heckle him in front of a full house of parliamentarians. But once she was actually in the parliament, she recalled, "I was afraid I would not have the courage to open my mouth."

She overcame that when the moment she had chosen came. "Kiesinger, you Nazi, resign!" she shouted as loudly as she could—and then repeated her words. Kiesinger stopped speaking and the security guards quickly jumped her, covered her mouth, and dragged her out of the hall. She was held in a nearby police station for three hours and then released. The newspapers on the following day showed her gesturing with her fists and then the scene as the guards tackled her. Back in Paris, she helped organize a demonstration in front of the West German embassy where students held up signs "Kiesinger Is a Nazi." Meanwhile, leftists in West Germany showed up at a local election rally shouting similar slogans.

Beate was pleased and encouraged, determined to do more. This was 1968 when theatrical, often violent demonstrations had become increasingly commonplace. During one demonstration in West Germany, she vowed to the audience to "publicly slap the Chancellor." Many of those in attendance sneered at what they took to be her empty, foolish rhetoric. But she was serious.

In November 1968, Kiesinger's Christian Democrats held their party convention in West Berlin, and Beate set her sights on that venue. Raissa, her mother-in-law, tried to talk her out of her mission, warning her that she could be killed. Serge went along with the plan but recognized the risks. Besides, he knew that she could not be dissuaded. Arriving in West Berlin, she mingled with the press corps and managed to get a pass from a photographer. Holding a notebook to make it look like she was a reporter, she edged her way to the front of the hall where Kiesinger and other senior officials were seated on the platform. After convincing a security guard that she was just taking a shortcut behind them to reach a friend, she walked up behind the chancellor. As he looked around, she screamed "Nazi! Nazi!" and delivered her slap.

Pandemonium broke out. As Beate was pulled away, she heard the chancellor say: "Is it that Klarsfeld woman?" Once she was in custody, Ernst Lemmer, one of Kiesinger's Christian Democratic colleagues, asked her why she had slapped the chancellor. When she answered that she did so "to let the whole world know there are some Germans who will not be put to shame," he simply shook his head. To the reporters outside, Lemmer declared: "That woman, who could be very pretty if she were not so sickly looking, is a sexually frustrated female." Later, he wrote a letter of apology to the magazine *Stern* that had quoted his statement. "When I made that remark, I did not know that Frau Klarsfeld is married and has a child, or that her father-in-law perished in Auschwitz."

Beate was given a one-year prison sentence, but was freed the same day. She appealed and eventually was given a four-month sentence, which was promptly suspended. But prison time was far from the greatest risk she had faced. Looking back at that episode, Serge pointed out that Kiesinger's bodyguards "had guns out but couldn't shoot" since too many people were there. Nonetheless, there was no guarantee that all of them would show such restraint. This was the same year that Martin Luther King and Robert Kennedy had been assassinated, so a woman slapping the chancellor could easily be mistaken for a potential assassin. "It would not have taken much for them to strike me down," Beate admitted.

The following year Kiesinger's Christian Democrats lost their parliamentary majority to the Social Democrats led by Willy Brandt, who took over as chancellor. "Once defeated, Kiesinger was immediately forgotten," Beate noted with satisfaction, adding that she had played "a modest but tangible role in this victory of the forces of progress."

Beate was elated to see Brandt, her favorite politician, in power. The new chancellor pardoned her, putting an end to the suspended sentence for the Kiesinger slap. But neither she nor Serge had any intention of letting up on their campaign to expose former Nazis. Or to avoid taking more risks while pursuing that mission. Serge, who often stayed in the background gathering evidence, would be an equal partner when it came to taking the lead in their next dangerous escapade.

For obvious reasons, the Klarsfelds were particularly intent on seeing that the senior SS and Gestapo officers who had been responsible for the arrest and deportations of Jews from France not live out the rest of their lives in peace. But because of the complex legal arrangements between France and Germany, many of them appeared to be doing just that.

The French side had initially written in a provision that they would not provide German courts with records of Germans accused of crimes in France, effectively preventing them from being tried after they returned to West Germany. In the early postwar era, the French had feared that sympathetic German judges, many of whom had served Nazi justice earlier, would let them off the hook. But this proved totally counterproductive. Since the Germans also had a provision that barred them from extraditing their nationals, the result was that convicted or suspected German war criminals who had served in France could live without fear of retribution once they returned to their homeland.

A battle ensued to change the Franco-German agreement, with the French reversing themselves and requesting that German courts be given jurisdiction over those who had committed war crimes in France. The Klarsfelds lobbied for this much overdue fix of a dysfunctional system. Along with Wiesenthal and others, they also argued for an extension of the German statute of limitations for war crimes, which—if unchanged— would allow countless war criminals to breathe easy. Both battles dragged on for years, but ultimately produced significant victories, first partial ones, and then in 1979 the complete abolition of the statute of limitations for murder, crimes against humanity, and genocide.

But none of that came easily, and a major factor in the final result was the Klarsfelds' aggressive tactics as they went after the criminals themselves. They waged a campaign to expose the crimes of several prominent former Nazis, primarily focusing at first on Kurt Lischka, Herbert Hagen, and Ernst Heinrichsohn. As Serge put it, these three SS officers bore a major portion of the responsibility for the deportation of Jews from France. "The Paris Gestapo was Lischka," noted Beate; he was in charge of the entire security apparatus in France. Hagen, who had close ties to Eichmann, was in charge of the SS's information section dealing with Jewish issues and also had been in charge of the police in the Atlantic region of France. Heinrichsohn, while of lower rank, had been particularly brutal with children.

The remarkable part of the saga of these men is that they were living in the open in West Germany, clearly not afraid that their past crimes could still come back to haunt them. Beate found out that Lischka was living in Cologne, and obtained his address and telephone number simply by calling information. As she told an Israeli television correspondent in France: "It's only in detective stories that Nazis live a hunted life, quivering in far-off Patagonia every time a door squeaks."

But if the trio and others in similar positions were not looking over their shoulders then, they soon would be. Beate prepared a new article for *Combat*, and Israeli television indicated it would welcome a film about Lischka and Hagen if they could get footage of them. Accompanied by an Israeli cameraman, the Klarsfelds parked opposite Lischka's apartment building in Cologne at 8 a.m. on February 21, 1971, figuring they would confront their quarry as he left the building. By 2 p.m. there was still no sign of him, but in the meantime Beate had phoned his apartment and Lischka's wife had answered. That was enough to prove that someone was home, and Beate hung up. After ringing several doorbells of their neighbors, the raiding party was buzzed in.

Reaching the top floor of the four-story building, they faced a blond woman who was anything but welcoming. But when Beate told her that they had arrived to interview her husband for French television, she called out: "Kurt, come and see what these people want."

Lischka, a very tall man with short cropped thinning hair, appeared right away. Beate used her maiden name as she introduced herself as the interpreter for the French journalist "Herr Klarsfeld." Lischka clearly did not recognize the Klarsfeld name, but he was wary, asking to see Serge's press identity card. The "crew" had come prepared, and Serge pulled out a press card he had obtained from *Combat*.

Serge quickly dispensed with any pretense that this was merely a fact-finding visit. He told Lischka that, in the wake of the signing of the new German-French treaty, he was making contact with Nazi criminals sentenced in absentia in France, and that Lischka was the first person on his list. "But before we start a campaign against you, we want to know whether you have anything to say in your defense," Serge concluded.

Lischka maintained his calm at first, saying he did not have to account to him or a French court. "If I eventually have to account for my actions to a German court I will do so," he added. "I have nothing to say to you."

Serge tried to press him to acknowledge his role in the persecution of French Jews, but Lischka didn't allow the cameraman to film him. The atmosphere had become extremely tense, and Beate thought that Lischka might smash the camera if they tried to use it.

The Klarsfelds had one more card to play. "Would it interest you to see orders that you yourself signed?" Serge asked, noting that those documents had survived in Paris and bore Lischka's signature. He added that this could lead to his trial and conviction.

Lischka could not resist looking at the stack of papers that Beate held out to him. With his wife reading them over his shoulder, his hand shook visibly as he looked them over. "Doubtless he was seeing his past rise up before him—a past that we had been the only ones to reconstruct from our countless hours in the archives," Beate noted.

On one level, this encounter was a failure: they had not managed to get any footage of Lischka or get him to respond to any questions. But they had made their first approach, and clearly had shaken him up.

That same day Beate phoned Herbert Hagen's house in Warstein, a town 125 miles northeast of Cologne. When Hagen's wife answered the phone, Beate asked whether her husband would agree to an interview with a French journalist. There was "no chance" of such an interview, the woman responded, adding that "my husband does not understand why you want to interview him."

The next day the Klarsfelds and their cameraman drove to Warstein and parked about a hundred yards from the house, hoping to intercept Hagen whenever he stepped out. They waited for several hours and shadowed someone who turned out to be the wrong man. But a man who was clearly Hagen finally walked out of the house to the garage and got into a large Opel. As the car emerged from the driveway, Beate jumped in front of it. "Herr Hagen is that you?" she asked.

Hagen nodded and then caught sight of the cameraman filming him. He stopped the car, got out and looked like he was about to assault him. Then, realizing that such an action could backfire, he hesitated, allowing Beate to say that Serge was a French journalist who wanted to ask him a few questions.

In excellent French, he told Serge: "Sir, you have no right to film me here in front of my house." He added that he was not in hiding. "I have gone back to France more than twenty times since the war."

"It's too bad the French police didn't notice your name," Serge responded. "You should have been arrested."

When Serge tried to ask him questions about his duties in France, Hagen, like Lischka, insisted he had nothing to say. "All I want is to live quietly," he added. But the Klarsfelds had no intention of giving up that easily on either man.

A month later, the Klarsfelds—along with Marco, one of Serge's friends from his student days, a doctor and a photographer—drove back to Cologne in a rental car. They had all agreed to participate in a scheme that, if successful, would attract major attention to the fact that someone like Lischka had paid no price for his crimes as an SS officer in France. The plan: to kidnap him. Serge brought along a pair of handcuffs and Marco brought two blackjacks. The operation would involve seizing Lischka on the street, pushing him into a car, and then switching to another car before returning to France. "We looked about as much like a commando unit as a council of bishops," Beate observed.

When Lischka got off a trolley, the "unit" surrounded him and Beate shouted "Come with us! Come with us!" He automatically took a couple of steps toward the car, then pulled back. The photographer struck him on the head with the blackjack. Lischka shouted for help, and dropped to the ground, although more out of fear than anything else. All of this attracted more and more attention as people surrounded the Klarsfeld group. A policeman pulled out his badge. At that point, Serge yelled "Into the car!" The group ran away leaving Lischka behind; they didn't stop running until they made it back to France.

Beate immediately began calling German newspapers. Using another name, she told them to check out what had happened to Lischka. Their goal, as Beate put it, "was to bring to the Germans' attention the impunity Lischka and his colleagues were enjoying"—even if that meant going to jail themselves. In Beate's case, this was exactly what happened when she returned to Cologne to share the documents about Lischka and Hagen with the German courts and press. She was locked up, but only for three weeks. As happened on several occasions with Beate, the authorities came to realize that putting her behind bars for long only attracted more attention to the Klarsfelds' cause.

When it came to Lischka, Serge had planned one more touch of high drama. On December 7, 1973, a snowy, freezing day in Cologne, he staked out Lischka's car, parked in a lot near the city's cathedral. When Lischka showed up, Serge stuck a gun between his eyes. The German was terrified, convinced he was about to be killed. But the gun was unloaded. For Serge, it was enough that his victim "looked death in the eye." Serge had written a letter to the local prosecutor saying that his group could kill Nazis, but that it had no such intention. It simply wanted them to face trial.

If Beate's act of slapping Kiesinger was her most dangerous moment, this was surely Serge's. But when asked about it four decades later, he casually denied that he had been really at risk. "I knew he had a gun," Serge admitted. But he argued that Lischka had neither the time to get it out nor, since he was wearing gloves because of the freezing weather, could he have pulled the trigger easily. "I didn't feel I was risking to be killed," he said.

For the Klarsfelds, the biggest satisfaction came when Lischka, Hagen, and others who were guilty no longer could live peacefully. As *Vorwärts*, the Social Democratic newspaper, put it: "Several middle-aged men, well-employed gentlemen have not been able to sleep well in the Federal Republic. They have shut themselves up in their apartments. . . . They are not at home to anyone."

Beate remained in and out of trouble with the law, and she was dismissed as a crazed fanatic on more than one occasion. The Klarsfelds were also at the receiving end of threats and, in two cases, bombs. In 1972, Serge was suspicious enough about a package that arrived labeled "sugar," especially when some specks of dark powder trickled out, to alert the police. The Parisian bomb squad confirmed that it was packed with dynamite and other explosives. In 1979, a bomb on a self-timer destroyed Serge's car in the middle of the night.

But slowly the case against Lischka, Hagen, and Heinrichsohn gained momentum. The three men finally stood trial in Cologne and, on February 11, 1980, the court found them guilty of complicity in the deportation of fifty thousand Jews from France to their deaths. They had "completely and fully understood" the fate that awaited their victims, the judge declared. Hagen was sentenced to twelve years in prison, Lischka to ten, and Heinrichsohn to six. It wasn't the length of the sentences that was particularly important; it was that they were tried and convicted at all. And there was no doubt that it was the Klarsfelds, with all their agitation and theatrics, who had made that happen.

In 1934, when aviation was still a novelty in many parts of the world, Latvian Air Force Captain Herbert Cukurs became a national hero overnight by flying a small biplane he had designed from his homeland to Gambia, on Africa's west coast. Acclaimed as the "Baltic Lindbergh," Cukurs received adoring coverage in the local press as he then embarked on flights to Japan and British Palestine. Returning from the latter journey, he delivered a lecture to a packed audience at the Jewish club of Riga. Historian Yoel Weinberg, who was still a student when he attended the lecture, recalled: "I remember Cukurs speaking with wonderment, amazement, even with enthusiasm, of the Zionist enterprise in Israel. . . . Cukurs' tales fired my imagination."

But Cukurs was a fervent nationalist and, in the late 1930s he joined a fascist organization called Thunder Cross. The Soviet Union annexed the Baltic states at the start of World War II, part of the division of the spoils between Hitler and Stalin under the terms of the Molotov-Ribbentrop Pact that made them de facto allies from 1939 to 1941. When Hitler's armies invaded the Soviet Union in June 1941, they swiftly moved into the Baltic states. In Latvia, Major Victor Arajs, a former Latvian police officer, led a unit called the Arajs Kommando, composed of volunteers from far-right groups who were eager to help the new occupiers. His deputy commander was Cukurs. They immediately began rounding up, beating, and killing Jews.

After the war, survivors of such actions testified before a commission on Nazi crimes in the Baltic states, and many of them vividly remembered Cukurs's role. According to Raphael Schub, he "started the annihilation of the Jews of Riga" in early July. He and his men gathered three hundred Latvian Jews in the Great Synagogue, ordering them "to open the holy ark and spread the Torah scrolls on the synagogue's floor" as they prepared to torch the building. When the Jews refused to follow that order, "Cukurs beat many of them savagely." His men then poured gasoline over the floor, positioned themselves near the exits, and threw a hand grenade inside. As the synagogue went up in flames, the Jews tried to escape, but Cukurs's men shot at anyone trying to get out. "All 300 Jews inside the building, among them many children, burned to death," Schub concluded.

Abraham Shapiro, who was sixteen at the time, was at home when Cukurs showed up, announcing to his family that he was taking over their apartment for his personal use. He forced everyone to leave and arrested the head of the household, who was quickly executed. Shapiro was sent to the Latvian police headquarters, where about a hundred tiny prison cells were jammed with Jewish prisoners. On several occasions, Shapiro saw Cukurs and his men loading hundreds of Jews on trucks. It was the job of Shapiro and others to put shovels and spades in the trucks. The trucks would return empty a few hours later. "The shovels were dirty with dust and soil, and also with blood stains," he testified.

Later the Germans rounded up about ten thousand Jews and took them to the forest where they were shot. David Fiszkin, another survivor, testified that Cukurs accompanied the Jews on the march to the forest, bringing up the rear of the column and shooting anyone who could not keep up. "When a child was crying, Cukurs snatched him from his mother's arms and shot him to death," he recalled. "With my own eyes I also saw how he shot and killed ten children and babies."

Because Cukurs was such a celebrity in Latvia before the war, survivors had no trouble identifying him, unlike in so many other cases where the murderers were often indistinguishable from one another. His unit was responsible for the deaths of about thirty thousand Jews, and he became known as "the Hangman of Riga." But after the war, he escaped from Europe and ended up in São Paulo, Brazil, where he operated a marina and continued to fly his own plane. For nearly two decades, he lived a comfortable life in the sun; he was so confident that he had put his past behind him that he never changed his name. Cukurs was aware of Eichmann's fate, of course, but by comparison he was "a low-level sadistic killer," as one Israeli writer later put it, which encouraged him to believe that he would not be a priority for any Nazi hunters.

On February 23, 1965, Cukurs arrived in Montevideo, Uruguay, to meet with Anton Kuenzle, an Austrian businessman who had recently befriended him in São Paulo. Kuenzle had been looking for new investment opportunities in South America, and he had enlisted Cukurs as a partner. The plan was to set up a temporary office in Montevideo, and Kuenzle wanted to show Cukurs the house that could serve that purpose.

Kuenzle led the way into the house, with Cukurs right behind him. As soon as Cukurs stepped into the semidarkness, Kuenzle slammed the door shut behind them. At that moment, the Latvian saw several men, dressed only in their underwear, jumping at him. He immediately realized what was happening—and, although he was nearly sixty-five, "he fought like a wild and wounded animal," Kuenzle recalled. "The fear of death gave him incredible strength." But then one of his attackers hit his head with a hammer, splattering blood everywhere. Another attacker finished him off, putting a gun to his head and firing twice.

In reality, "Kuenzle" was Yaakov Meidad, a master of disguises who had been a member of the Mossad team that had kidnapped Eichmann five years earlier; changing his appearance frequently, he had rented the safe houses and cars in Buenos Aires and purchased the necessary supplies. This time, Meidad had posed as an Austrian businessman to ingratiate himself with Cukurs and lure him into the trap he had set. His fellow Mossad agents had been dressed only in their underwear because they did not want their clothing soaked in blood when they had to make their getaway. That had proved to be a wise precaution.

The Israelis loaded Cukurs's large body into the trunk of a car that they had brought for that purpose. Before closing the trunk, they placed a sheet of paper on his chest with a message written in English:

VERDICT

Considering the gravity of the crimes of which HERBERT CUKURS is accused, notably his personal responsibility for the murder of 30,000 men, women and children, and considering the terrible cruelty shown by HERBERT CUKURS in carrying out his crimes, we condemn the said CUKURS to death.

He was executed on 23 February 1965

By "Those Who Will Never Forget"

After they left Uruguay, Meidad and his team waited for the press to report the discovery of Cukurs's body. When nothing happened for several days, they tipped off the news agencies in West Germany, even providing the address of the murder scene. The story ran in papers around the world, mentioning the fact that the mysterious group responsible called itself "Those Who Will Never Forget." As *The New York Times* pointed out, "Like the Eichmann case, the Cukurs case had its cloak and dagger aspects."

But for most of the press, this was a one-day story, with no follow-up. Outside Latvia, Cukurs was hardly the household name that Eichmann was, and of course there was no trial to make him and his crimes more widely known. Even in Israel today, many people are not aware of this Mossad operation—the only one that was triggered by an official decision to assassinate one of the perpetrators of the Holocaust.

So why was Cukurs targeted? His crimes were horrifying, but no more so than those of countless other murderers who were still enjoying quiet lives at the time. In 1997, Meidad finally published a book in Hebrew describing the Cukurs mission in detail; a British edition appeared in 2004 titled *The Execution of the Hangman of Riga: The Only Execution of a Nazi War Criminal by the Mossad.* But he still took the precaution of writing it under the name of Anton Kuenzle. Most readers only learned his true name when they read his obituary after his death on June 30, 2012.

In his book, Meidad recounted his initial conversation with the senior Mossad officer who gave him the assignment. The officer, whom he only identified by the first name Yoav, told him the government was alarmed by the possibility that West Germany's statute of limitations would allow such criminals completely off the hook, since the outcome of the debate whether to extend the statute was still uncertain. He also noted that the Eichmann kidnapping and trial four years earlier had "raised public consciousness throughout the world of the Nazi horrors, but it seems that the strong impact . . . is losing its effect."

Yoav insisted that it was the obligation of Israelis "to stop this sweeping trend." Success in the Cukurs operation, he added, would "put the fear of death into the hearts of tens of thousands of Nazi war criminals. . . . They must not have one single moment of peace and tranquility until their last dying day on earth!" Although he conceded that Israel did not have the resources to go after many such criminals, Cukurs could serve as an example for lower-level killers.

Those are all plausible explanations, but not necessarily the full explanation. Rafi Eitan, who was the leader of the team that pulled off the Eichmann kidnapping but was not involved in the Cukurs operation, pointed out during our meeting in 2013: "To kill a man, it's easier to shoot him from a distance. No need to make an operation." The fact that the Mossad decided to send its agents to kill him at close quarters, so that he would know what was happening, suggested that "personal ambition" was involved, Eitan added. By that, he meant that someone high up may have had a personal score to settle with Cukurs.

It was only after Cukurs was killed that Meidad learned that one member of his assassination team had had a large family in Riga. "They were all killed by Cukurs and his men," Meidad noted. But a low-level member of his team would not have been involved in the original decision to go after the Hangman of Riga. The lingering questions about the decision making that triggered this singular event have never been fully answered.

There is a recent postscript, however. In 2014, Latvian audiences were treated to a musical about Cukurs. While there was a brief scene at the end where he was surrounded by people shouting "killer," the production focused on his role as a celebrity aviator before the war. Because Cukurs never was put on trial, producer Juris Millers argued, he "is still innocent if we are looking at him from a court system point of view. There are a few people who testify that he was a killer and others who say that he was a hero."

The Latvian Council for Jews, Israel, Russia, and others promptly denounced the play as the whitewashing of a mass murderer. "There must be no tolerance for any attempt to turn a heinous criminal into a cultural hero," an Israeli Foreign Ministry spokesman declared. The Latvian government, which had rejected efforts by Cukurs's family to clear his name, left no doubt that it was unhappy with the production. While pointing out that the country's commitment to free speech meant it could not try to stop it, Foreign Minister Edgars Rinkēvičs said: "Being a member of the Arajs Kommando is not worth singing about. Let those who attend the performance appraise the production for themselves; however, the position of the government is that this is not in good taste."

But many Latvians enthusiastically applauded the performances, preferring to remember Cukurs as the popular aviator of the 1930s while ignoring his murderous record afterward. In that sense, Yoav, the Mossad officer who instructed Meidad on his mission, was right: when it comes to the Holocaust, memories are often short—and dangerously selective.

Nazi hunters were always aware of that. For those who refused to give up the fight, it only spurred them on.

CHAPTER TWELVE

"Model Citizens"

"To the police and the press he's a boring old nuisance with a file cabinet full of ghosts; kill him and you're liable to turn him into a neglected hero with living enemies still to be caught."

Dr. Josef Mengele, Auschwitz's "Angel of Death," speaking
about the character modeled on Simon Wiesenthal in
Ira Levin's bestselling novel *The Boys from Brazil*

Among the many myths that developed about Nazi hunters, none is more off the mark than the portrayal of Wiesenthal as an avenger who was eager to confront his prey directly, personally tracking fugitive Nazis down to the most remote hiding places in South America if necessary. As portrayed by Laurence Olivier in the 1978 film *The Boys from Brazil*, the Wiesenthal character caught up with Mengele (played by Gregory Peck) at a farm in Lancaster, Pennsylvania, leading to a life-and-death battle. When Olivier literally unleashed the dogs—the famed snarling Dobermans—to prevail, the popular image of Wiesenthal lost all touch with reality: from then on, he was seen as part-Columbo, part–James Bond.

Wiesenthal bore some of the responsibility for those misconceptions.

He had published his book *Ich jagte Eichmann* (I Hunted Eichmann) in 1961 when Mossad chief Isser Harel could not claim credit for the kidnapping or explain what leads had proved to be critical to its success. Despite Wiesenthal's protestations that he was only one part of "a mosaic" of people who made small contributions to Eichmann's capture, he was delighted to see his fame growing. That helped him recover from the closure of his Linz Documentation Center in 1954. On October 1, 1961, he launched his new Documentation Center in Vienna with the help of that city's Jewish community.

Wiesenthal was reenergized, and he would continue to demonstrate an uncanny knack for self-promotion that included cooperating on occasion with those who transformed the story of Nazis on the run and Nazi hunters into a staple of popular culture. Frederick Forsyth turned to him for help in providing background for *The Odessa File*, his 1972 bestselling novel, which was made into a hit movie two years later, telling him that he was inspired by a chapter in his 1967 memoir, *The Murderers Among Us*. Wiesenthal was happy to oblige. He even persuaded Forsyth to make his villain a real person: Eduard Roschmann, an Austrian who was the former commander of the Riga Ghetto. Like the Latvian Herbert Cukurs, he was infamous for his brutality.

After the war, Roschmann fled to Argentina, but the book and film ratcheted up the pressure for his capture and extradition. "Roschmann became the hunted man portrayed in the film," Wiesenthal noted with satisfaction. The former Nazi fled to Paraguay in 1977, dying from a heart attack two weeks after he arrived there. In the film, there was an even more cathartic ending: he was caught and killed.

Wiesenthal claimed he was offered the chance to play himself in the movie for a hefty fee, "but I didn't want to get involved to that extent with the entertainment industry." Still, the entertainment industry could not get enough of him, and in a recent rendition it came pretty close to capturing Wiesenthal's ambivalence and amusement about how he was portrayed. In the advertisements for the 2014 Off-Broadway play *Wiesenthal*, written by Tom Dugan, who also starred in the one-man show,

the Nazi hunter is described as "the Jewish James Bond." Dugan's Wiesenthal laughingly dismissed all such notions. "My weapons are per-
sistency, publicity and paperwork," he told the audience. Which was
exactly right.

But if Wiesenthal could both exploit and mock his image, he was
very serious about defending his reputation as the leading private Nazi
hunter—and dismissing or at least keeping at a distance anyone who
might have aspired to challenge him on that score. Tuvia Friedman,
who had set up the first Documentation Center in Vienna after the war
but then moved to Israel in 1952, was visibly frustrated by how he was
eclipsed by Wiesenthal, particularly in the aftermath of the Eichmann
kidnapping. "You are the great Nazi hunter, and I am the little puppy,"
Friedman wrote to him. Wiesenthal biographer Tom Segev maintained
that his subject treated Friedman "like a poor relation" who had made a
critical mistake by moving to Israel, where his activities attracted less and
less attention.

Wiesenthal remained firm in his resolve to stay put in Vienna, even
after a group that included a former German Nazi who had escaped from
prison planted a bomb at the entrance to the building where he lived on
July 11, 1982. The device exploded, damaging his building and shattering
windows in the house next door, but no one was hurt. While the Vienna
authorities placed a guard at his office and house to protect him, he continued to rebuff anyone who suggested that the incident and the hate
mail he received might be good reasons to finally move to Israel. "No, I'm
still chasing alligators and I have to live in the swamp," he told an American lawyer with his characteristic wry smile.

Serge Klarsfeld was one of the younger Nazi hunters who had admired Wiesenthal, and he made a point of visiting him for the first time
in Vienna in August 1967. The Frenchman, who was thirty-one then, was
surprised that Wiesenthal was "not shaken" by the fact that Kiesinger, a
former Nazi propagandist, was the German chancellor at the time. Wiesenthal later disapproved of Beate Klarsfeld's famous slap of the German
leader and the Klarsfelds' other dramatic protests. "We did not have the
same vision on how to act vis-à-vis the Germans, nor the same methods,"

Serge concluded. "While Simon Wiesenthal maintained good relations with the German leaders, we went to prison."

Serge maintained—and continues to maintain today—that Wiesenthal deserves great recognition for having kept up the fight to bring Nazis to justice during the 1950s and early 1960s when so many of them were freed or not hunted at all. But he and Beate found themselves quickly at odds with him. Aside from deploring their confrontational tactics—which Beate, in particular, continued to employ on trips to Latin America to demand that Nazis be brought to justice and to protest against right-wing regimes there—Wiesenthal had no sympathy for their leftist politics.

Wiesenthal was conservative both in his personal style and politics, and staunchly anticommunist, denouncing the Polish communist regime for "using anti-Semitism in exactly the same way it had been used for centuries: to divert attention from its own incompetence and its own crimes." He often charged that the Polish communists and the Kremlin were spreading malicious disinformation about him, including forged documents that accused him of everything from collaboration with the Nazis to working for the Israelis and the CIA. Beate, by contrast, was proud of the accolades she regularly received from the East German government and press and wrote articles for a pro-communist West German weekly, although she, too, protested against the use of anti-Semitic propaganda by communist regimes.

Such differences would lead to growing tensions among the Nazi hunters in the years ahead.

From the very beginning, Wiesenthal believed that his mission was as much about educating the next generation as it was about seeking a measure of justice for the millions of victims of his generation. Those two goals were intertwined, and so were the methods to achieve them. The exposure and, in the best case, capture and trial of former Nazis provided the evidence to counter the postwar efforts to, if not deny outright, at least downplay the horrors of the Third Reich. In some cases, mere exposure—in effect, the personalization of actions that were otherwise too huge and abstract to make an impact—was enough for Wiesenthal to feel that he had scored a genuine success, even when this did not lead to any legal consequences.

The most dramatic example: his quest to find the Gestapo officer who arrested Anne Frank. In October 1958, when Wiesenthal was still living in Linz, the Landestheater staged *The Diary of Anne Frank*. A friend called him one evening to tell him to come quickly to the theater to witness the open displays of anti-Semitism that were taking place. Arriving at the theater when the play had just ended, Wiesenthal learned that teenage hecklers had been shouting "Traitors! Toadies! Swindle!" They also threw leaflets in the theater claiming that the famous diarist never existed: "The Jews have invented the whole business to squeeze out more compensation. Don't believe a word of it. It's all pure invention."

All of this, as Wiesenthal saw it, was part of a broader effort by former Nazis and their sympathizers to discredit the hugely popular book that personalized the Holocaust in a way that they found immensely threatening. They were trying "to poison the minds" of the young generation, he concluded. Two days later when he and a friend were sitting in a coffeehouse discussing the incident, some high school boys were sitting at the next table. Wiesenthal's friend asked one of them what he thought of the whole controversy, and the boy echoed the claim that Anne Frank was not a real person.

"But the diary?" Wiesenthal asked. The boy replied that it could be a forgery and offered no proof that Frank had existed. Nor was he swayed by the fact that Otto Frank, Anne's father and the only survivor of the family, had testified about how the Gestapo had arrested them, which led to their deportation to Auschwitz. (Later, Anne and her older sister, Margot, were transferred to Bergen-Belsen, where they both died just as the war was ending; Anne was only fifteen at the time.)

Finally, Wiesenthal asked whether he would be convinced if he could hear what happened from the officer who had carried out the arrest. "Okay, if he admits it himself," the boy replied, clearly convinced that would never happen.

Wiesenthal took the boy's statement as a challenge. He did not make any progress for years, but an appendix to the young girl's diary mentioned a former employee of Otto Frank's company who had gone to Gestapo headquarters after the family was arrested, hoping to help them. The man recalled that he had spoken to the officer who had carried out the arrest, an SS man from Vienna whose name started with something like "Silver." Wiesenthal assumed that had to be "Silber" in German. He found several "Silbernagels" in the Vienna phone book who had been SS men, but none of them panned out.

His break came on a visit to Amsterdam in 1963. A Dutch police officer gave him a photocopy of the 1943 phone directory for the Gestapo in Holland, which listed three hundred names. On his flight back to Vienna, under a heading that read "IV B4, Joden (Jews)," he found the name "Silberbauer." Knowing that most of the officers in that department were police officers, Wiesenthal contacted an Interior Ministry official who claimed they would look into the matter. They did, but tried to hush up the discovery that Karl Silberbauer, the officer who admitted to arresting Anne Frank, was still on duty in the Vienna police. They suspended him, but *Volksstimme*, the Austrian Communist Party newspaper, picked up on the story after Silberbauer complained to a colleague that he was "having some bother because of Anne Frank." Radio Moscow trumpeted the story as well.

Wiesenthal did not succeed in getting anyone to prosecute Silberbauer. But his efforts paid off when other journalists picked up on the story. Tipped off by Wiesenthal, a Dutch reporter went to interview Silberbauer in Vienna. "Why pick on me after all these years?" the former SS officer complained. "I only did my duty." Asked if he felt sorry about what he did, he replied: "Sure I feel sorry. Sometimes I feel downright humiliated." Why? Because he had been suspended from the police force and lost his privilege of riding trams for free; he had to buy tickets like everyone else.

The reporter asked if he had read Frank's diary. "Bought the little book last week to see whether I'm in it," Silberbauer said. "But I am not." It seemingly did not occur to him that his arrest of its author meant that she no longer had the opportunity to write in it.

Silberbauer only became known because of his famous victim, but he was a minor functionary of the Third Reich. Like so many others who sent less famous people to their deaths, he never paid any real price for his actions. Wiesenthal would have liked to have seen something more than his public exposure, but the authorities were not interested in pursuing a case against him.

Nonetheless, Wiesenthal had ample reason to feel vindicated. In the decades since then, Anne Frank's diary has continued to serve as one of the most powerful personal testimonies about the Holocaust, educating successive new generations of schoolchildren. The efforts to discredit it fizzled out. Even the most ardent Nazi sympathizers could not contradict the direct testimony of a former SS officer who saw nothing wrong with what he had done.

As Wiesenthal recalled in his later memoir, *Justice Not Vengeance*, he was sitting on the terrace of the Café Royal in Tel Aviv in January 1964 when he was paged to come to the phone. Returning to his table, he found it occupied by three women. He was about to take the magazine he had left there and look for another place when one of the women got up and apologized in Polish for sitting at his table. "But when we heard your name on the loudspeaker we wanted to talk to you," she said. "All three of us were in Majdanek. So we thought we should ask you. You must know what happened to Kobyła."

In Polish, "Kobyła" means mare, but Wiesenthal did not know who or what she was talking about.

"Forgive me, we always think everybody must know who Kobyła was," she added. She explained that this was the nickname for an Austrian guard who was especially feared because of her habit of viciously kicking women prisoners and freely using the whip that she carried whenever a new transport arrived. Her real name was Hermine Braunsteiner.

The woman speaking to Wiesenthal grew more and more agitated as she described one incident. "I'll never forget that child, the child . . . a small child, you know," she started. When a prisoner carrying a rucksack on his back had walked by, Braunsteiner lashed the rucksack with her whip. A child hidden in it cried out. As Braunsteiner ordered the man to open the rucksack, the child jumped out and started running. "But Kobyla ran after it, grabbed it hard so it screamed, and fired a bullet through . . ." The woman's words gave way to sobs.

Her companions quickly joined in with other horror stories. When new transports arrived, mothers would cling to their young children as the trucks arrived to take them to the gas chambers. Braunsteiner physically tore them apart. Along with two other women guards who were equally brutal, she made a special point of terrorizing young girls. "She struck them with her whip right across their faces, preferably across their eyes," one of the women recalled. It wasn't enough to send these girls to the gas chambers; Braunsteiner and her fellow guards were intent on tormenting them first.

The Red Army reached the Polish city of Lublin and liberated Majdanek in July 1944, and in late November the SS guards and staff who were captured were put on trial, resulting in eighty convictions. After his talk with the women in Tel Aviv, Wiesenthal checked to see if Braunsteiner was among them; she wasn't. But he learned that she had been arrested in the southern Austrian state of Carinthia in 1948, and then put on trial in Vienna for her brutal treatment, including kicking and whipping, of women prisoners when she was a guard at Ravensbrück, another concentration camp. Her service at Majdanek was only briefly mentioned. She was sentenced to "a mere three years' imprisonment," Wiesenthal noted.

That meant that Braunsteiner had to have been released more than a decade earlier, and Wiesenthal was determined to see if he could find her. Her last known registered address was in Vienna in 1946, so he decided to check if her former neighbors knew anything about her current whereabouts. The first neighbor he approached slammed the door in his face when he explained who he was looking for. But another neighbor, an elderly woman who had known the family, quickly volunteered that she could not believe the charges that were leveled against Braunsteiner, who she remembered as a young girl who was always "prettily dressed" when she was walking to church on Sundays. The woman did not know where Braunsteiner had gone after she was released, but she did know the names and addresses of some of her relatives in Carinthia.

Recognizing that he was unlikely to be trusted by Braunsteiner's relatives, Wiesenthal turned for help to one of the young Austrians who had recently come to his office to volunteer his services. Richard, as he called him, freely admitted he came from an anti-Semitic family and his father had been killed in action in 1944, fighting for the Third Reich. But Richard was convinced his father would not have approved of mass murder. It was no accident that several such young people offered their help to Wiesenthal after the Eichmann trial had heightened awareness of the Holocaust. "People like Richard give people like me the assurance that there was a purpose in surviving and in remaining in Austria," Wiesenthal noted.

Richard traveled to Carinthia and, following Wiesenthal's plan, managed to ingratiate himself with Braunsteiner's relatives. He told them that an uncle of his had been unfairly convicted and sentenced to five years, which prompted the relatives to say that Braunsteiner was a similar case. He soon learned that, after she was released from prison, "Kobyła" had married an American and moved to Halifax. From an Auschwitz survivor in that Canadian city, Wiesenthal learned that Braunsteiner and her husband, a Mr. Ryan, had recently moved again, this time to Maspeth in Queens, New York.

Wiesenthal knew that up to that time the United States had not tried or extradited any Nazis who had settled there. As a result, he could safely assume that she was still there—or that she could still be tracked. At that point, he decided to pass what he had learned to Clyde A. Farnsworth, a correspondent for *The New York Times* who had recently written a profile of him headlined "The Sleuth with 6 Million Clients." Farnsworth promptly relayed the tip to his home office.

The editors on Times Square assigned the story to Joseph Lelyveld, a freshman general assignment reporter. His recollection is that the message he saw included the information that Hermine Braunsteiner, now known as Mrs. Ryan, lived in the blue-collar neighborhood of Maspeth but did not include an exact address. Wiesenthal claimed he had provided the address. In any case, Lelyveld knew he was supposed to locate "a notorious death camp guard and convicted war criminal," as he put it, following up on the tip from "the renowned Nazi hunter in Vienna."

Since he did not know the first name of Braunsteiner's husband at that point, Lelyveld wrote down all the Ryans listed in the Queens phone book with Maspeth addresses. He expected to have a long day ringing doorbells, but the first Mrs. Ryan immediately knew who he was looking for when he asked about a woman with the same last name who had come from Austria. That would be the woman with a German accent who was the wife of Russell Ryan, she informed him. The couple lived nearby, at 52-11 72nd Street, she added helpfully.

Lelyveld knocked on the door, and there she was. "Mrs. Ryan, I need to ask about your time in Poland, at the Majdanek camp during the war," the reporter told her.

"Oh my God, I knew this would happen," she replied, sobbing. It was "as if she'd expected me," Lelyveld recalled.

He stepped into a living room that was "extremely tidy in a German way, with doilies and cuckoo clocks and Alpine scenes." Sitting opposite her, he listened to her "weepy, self-pitying narrative" where she protested her innocence. It was a brief conversation but produced a dramatic story headlined: "Former Nazi Camp Guard Is Now a Housewife in Queens."

Crediting Wiesenthal for the discovery, Lelyveld noted that Braunsteiner had served a prison sentence in Austria but had denied that she had ever been convicted of a crime when she came to the United States in 1959.

In the article that ran on July 14, 1964, he offered a vivid description of their short encounter:

> A large-boned woman with a stern mouth and blond hair turning gray, she was wearing pink and white striped shorts with a matching sleeveless blouse.
>
> "All I did is what what guards do in camps now," she said in heavily accented English.

"On the radio all they talk is peace and freedom," she said. "All right. Then 15 or 16 years later why do they bother people?

"I was punished enough. I was in prison three years. Three years, can you imagine? And now they want something again from me?"

Lelyveld reached Russell Ryan later by phone. "My wife, sir, wouldn't hurt a fly," he said. "There's no more decent person on this earth. She told me this was a duty she had to perform." But he also admitted to the reporter that his wife had never told him until then that she had been a concentration camp guard and had served a prison sentence already.

Not telling her husband about her past was one thing, but lying to the Immigration and Naturalization Service was another. Lelyveld wrote in his piece that an INS official had said that this could prompt a review of her citizenship, but that "he indicated that such reviews rarely result in the withdrawal of citizenship."

It would take seven years to prove that official wrong. After long legal battles, Braunsteiner was stripped of her citizenship in 1971. Both Poland and West Germany had sought her extradition, prompting her to declare her willingness to go to West Germany because she feared she would be treated far more harshly in Poland. Sent to West Germany in 1973, she became the most famous defendant in the trial of Majdanek personnel that opened in Düsseldorf two years later; the proceedings dragged on until 1981, resulting in a life sentence. In 1996, she was released for health reasons and sent to a nursing home where her American husband, who never abandoned her, was already living. She died in 1999.

For Lelyveld, his story about her was a singular event, and he never followed up on it. On the same day that he returned from Maspeth, he learned that his father, Rabbi Arthur Lelyveld, had been beaten in Mississippi, as the Freedom Summer turned violent. The young reporter was soon busy covering the race riots that were taking place and then sent to Africa in the fall. He was on his way to becoming a star reporter, editor, and Pulitzer Prize–winning author. From 1994 to 2001, he ran the *Times* as its executive editor, the top editorial job in that storied institution.

Sitting in a coffee shop near his apartment on the Upper West Side in early 2014, Lelyveld appeared genuinely startled when I alluded to the fact that his piece on Braunsteiner, the result of a quick trip to Maspeth, precipitated the first serious stirrings of interest in the wider story of Nazis in the United States. Hadn't he known about the wider impact of his article for a long time? "Not till right now," he said.

Eli Rosenbaum despises the term "Nazi hunter," since he is convinced that a combination of popular fiction, in novels and films, and misleading or distorted information in media reports and books has imbued the term with mythological connotations. And, as in most myths, fiction usually trumps the facts that inspired the myths in the first place. But, as much as he may cringe when he is categorized as America's leading Nazi hunter, Rosenbaum fits the bill. He has dedicated most of his life to tracking down Nazis in the United States, seeking to strip them of their citizenship and get them to leave the country either by deportation or, when a deal is struck, voluntarily. Of course, "voluntarily" is not the most accurate term either, since the Nazis are always acting under duress—the intense pressure that he and others in the Justice Department have applied to make them do so.

Rosenbaum's exploits prompted Alan Elsner, a veteran Reuters correspondent, to make him the model for his hero in his 2007 suspense novel *The Nazi Hunter*. The main character channels the real Rosenbaum's feelings when he ruminates:

> To this day, I still get a kick out of those words, Nazi hunter! They summon images of fearless adventurers tracking down ruthless Gestapo torturers to fortified jungle hideouts in South America. If only it were even a little like that. The truth is much less glamorous. I'm an attorney, not an adventurer, not a secret agent, not even a private investigator. I wear dark suits and sober ties. I spend my days in archives going through microfilm, and in meetings, and occasionally in courtrooms. The Nazis I deal with—far from being dangerous warlords—usually turn out to be gray little men in their seventies or eighties leading dull, anonymous lives in the suburbs of Cleveland or Detroit.

Of course Elsner's Mark Cain, his name for the fictional version of Rosenbaum, then proceeds to have the kind of fantastic life-and-death adventures that build on the popular image of Nazi hunters that the real Rosenbaum dismisses as nonsense.

Born in 1955 of Jewish parents who fled Germany in the late 1930s, Rosenbaum grew up in the Long Island town of Westbury. While he and his classmates read *The Diary of Anne Frank* in junior high school, the Holocaust received nothing like the attention that it would as he grew older. He knew that many members of his family in Europe had not survived, but it was not a topic that his parents ever wanted to discuss. "The fact that it wasn't spoken of in my house actually told me how serious a subject it was, that it was too painful to be addressed," he recalled.

But Rosenbaum began to get glimpses of the subject that his parents would not discuss. When he was about twelve, he watched Peter Weiss's *The Investigation*, the reenactment of the Frankfurt Auschwitz trial that was performed on Broadway and then broadcast by NBC, on his black-and-white TV. "That's when I learned for the first time what happened in the concentration camps," he noted. "And I was shocked, deeply shocked." One particularly vivid memory: the testimony of a Polish Catholic woman about the grotesque medical experiments performed on her leg. "I was just stunned," he added. A couple of years later, he read Wiesenthal's *The Murderers Among Us*, which made him realize how many of the perpetrators had gone unpunished—and he was shocked again.

When he was about fourteen, an unexpected revelation from his father made all of this more personal. The two of them were driving from Long Island to upstate New York, where his father had some business meetings planned and then they were going to ski. Slowed by a blizzard on the New York Thruway, his father resumed a favorite pastime, telling his son about his Army adventures during the war. He had served initially in North Africa and then transferred to the psychological warfare branch of the 7th Army in Europe, which desperately needed German speakers. He had told Eli about how they would string loudspeakers near the front lines and exhort the German troops to surrender, assuring them that they would be well treated. He also recounted tales of boxing for his unit, and the one time he got drunk with his buddies—which seemed more to amuse than anger his commanding officer.

But on that trip upstate, his father may have run out of the familiar stories—and he abruptly told Eli something that he had never heard before. "You know, I was at Dachau the day after its liberation," he said. By then, Eli knew what Dachau was. His father was not part of the unit that liberated Dachau, but he was nearby and word had quickly spread that something terrible had happened there. Ordered with another soldier to go check out the camp and report back, he had done so. At that point in the story, Eli wanted to know the answer to the obvious question: what did his father see when he got to the camp?

The snow was coming down hard at that moment. "It was scary driving, it was a blizzard," Eli recalled. "So we're both locked on the road in front of us and I'm waiting for an answer and I don't hear anything." He looked over at his father and saw that his eyes had filled with tears, his mouth appeared to be trying to say something but no words came out. Finally, after a long pause, his father began talking about something else. "I got it," Eli said, echoing his reaction to his parents' previous avoidance of such subjects. "The fact that it was so devastating that he couldn't speak about it told me what I needed to know."

From then on, the young Rosenbaum's radar was particularly attuned to stories about Nazis—and, in the 1970s, there was a growing number of them. *New York Times* reporter Ralph Blumenthal followed up the Braunsteiner case by writing extensively about other Nazi criminals in America, and a young writer named Howard Blum produced *Wanted! The Search for Nazis in America.* The hero of that instant nonfiction best-seller was Anthony DeVito, a World War II veteran who, like Rosenbaum's father, had visited Dachau shortly after its liberation. After he returned to the United States with a German wife, DeVito worked as an investigator for the INS—which assigned him to the Braunsteiner case. From then on, he was off and running, trying to follow up on a list of fifty-nine Nazi criminals living in the United States that he obtained from a researcher at the World Jewish Congress.

DeVito was constantly battling his bosses and finally resigned from the INS in 1974, claiming that its leadership was doing everything to obstruct further investigations of Nazis living in the United States. "He was a lone figure calling for vengeance," Blum wrote. The dramatic portrait of the crusader battling a cover-up of Nazis, some of whom had worked for the CIA and other government agencies, captured the popular imagination—and the imagination of Rosenbaum, who at that point was headed to Harvard Law School. "I certainly believed it, hook, line and sinker," Rosenbaum recalled. "I bought into the whole thing."

Later, Rosenbaum would conclude that Blum had overplayed the drama, ignored earlier efforts by the United States to keep many Nazis out, and hyped DeVito's role. As for DeVito himself, Rosenbaum added, he came to believe in Blum's portrayal of him and conflated fact and fiction when it came to Nazi hunting. "His life became a thriller," Rosenbaum said. "He was one of these guys who had read too many of these novels." Still, there was no question that Blum's book contributed to a growing awareness that something had gone seriously wrong, allowing numerous Nazi criminals to find sanctuary in the United States.

Blum and DeVito were not alone in reaching that conclusion. Shortly after Elizabeth Holtzman became a member of Congress in 1973, the Brooklyn Democrat was approached by a mid-level INS official who wanted to see her unofficially. Their encounter set off a chain of events that, six years later, would culminate in the creation of the Justice Department's Office of Special Investigations, which Holtzman explained was to be "an effective Nazi-fighting unit." It could not bring the Nazis to trial for the crimes they had committed elsewhere or seek prison sentences for them. But it could expose the lies they had told about their past when they had entered the country, leading to their loss of citizenship and deportation—in the best scenario, to countries that could then put them on trial.

When Holtzman first read about the Braunsteiner case, she viewed it as an aberration. So when the INS official showed up in her office in the Longworth House Office Building to tell her that the immigration service had a list of fifty-three Nazi war criminals and was doing nothing about it, she was disbelieving at first. "This seemed impossible," she recalled. Given America's sacrifices in World War II, she added, "It made no sense for our government to allow Nazi war criminals to live here."

But the conversation left an inkling of doubt in Holtzman's mind that was reinforced by an article she subsequently read about Valerian Trifa, a former member of Romania's fascist Iron Guard who led its student group; he was accused of instigating a pogrom against Jews in Bucharest in 1941. After the war, Trifa had settled in the United States and risen through the ranks of the North American Romanian Orthodox Church, ultimately serving as its archbishop and leader. Charles Kremer, a Romanian-born Jewish dentist, had been waging a lonely campaign to bring him to justice starting in the 1950s. Trifa denied the charges, claiming that the Romanian authorities were trying to smear him because of his anticommunist activism.

A few months after her encounter with the official who had talked about Nazi war criminals, Holtzman had the chance to question INS commissioner Leonard F. Chapman, a former commandant of the Marine Corps, who was testifying before the immigration subcommittee.

"Does the Immigration and Naturalization Service have a list of alleged war criminals living in the United States?" she asked.

"Yes," Chapman replied.

Holtzman had been fully expecting him to say "no," and, as she recalled later, "I almost fell out of my seat." When she asked how many people were on that list, he answered equally clearly: "Fifty-three." But when she recovered enough to ask what the INS was doing about this list, he retreated behind "a cloud of words, a smokescreen of words" that provided no answers.

Frustrated by her inability to learn what had happened with the list, which was similar to the one that DeVito had obtained earlier, she asked to see the files. Again to her surprise, the commissioner readily agreed.

The files were in Manhattan, and on a trip home the following weekend she was ushered into an office where a neatly prepared stack of them was waiting for her. As she began opening them one by one, she encountered similar stories: there were accusations that each of the alleged Nazi war criminals was responsible for some atrocity, often the killing of Jews. But it was also clear that, if INS officials had followed up at all, it was only to locate the named persons and visit them, inquiring about their health and not much more. It had not investigated the actual charges against them, nor checked any documentary evidence or looked for possible witnesses. "The INS is doing nothing," she concluded. "This is outrageous."

From then on, Holtzman mounted a campaign to demand the creation of a special unit to investigate those and other possible cases. She had no idea how many Nazi war criminals had settled in the United States, but she was convinced that the INS was "at best a reluctant enforcer and at worst a non-enforcer." She believed that DeVito and INS attorney Victor Schiano, who had worked with him on the Braunsteiner case, had been dedicated to changing that record but failed. As far as she could see, they had been the only INS officials interested in seriously pursuing Nazi cases—and both of them had resigned by that point.

With the help of Pennsylvania Democrat Joshua Eilberg, the immigration subcommittee chairman, and other colleagues from both parties, Holtzman kept up the pressure. In 1977, the INS announced the formation of a Special Litigation Unit that was supposed to handle the Nazi cases. Attorney General Griffin Bell tapped lawyer Martin Mendelsohn—who, like Holtzman, grew up in Brooklyn—to get it up and running and serve as its director. "I don't know anything about this stuff," Bell told Mendelsohn. "But this lady from Brooklyn is driving us crazy so make her happy."

Mendelsohn knew that his new unit would face huge challenges in seeking to establish the record of what happened decades earlier. "The evidence in these cases can be viewed as pieces of a jigsaw puzzle that have been warped by time so they don't fit," he said. Alluding to the difficulty of getting reliable testimony even when surviving witnesses could be found, he pointed out: "Even good memories fail." Many survivors could not identify their tormentors. "When I was in the camp, I looked at their feet; I didn't look at their faces," one of them told him.

To have a chance to fulfill their mission, Mendelsohn needed a top-notch team. But most of the investigators and lawyers at the INS, he quickly concluded, were "less than adequate, less than competent." He even dismissed former investigator DeVito as "a total fraud" who had vastly exaggerated his accomplishments and convinced himself that "he was Simon Wiesenthal."

The Special Litigation Unit proved singularly ineffective, but Holtzman was not about to let that slow her efforts to make up for government inaction. In 1978, she won passage of a bill that she had been pushing since 1975. The Holtzman Amendment, as it became known, provided the authority for the INS to deport anyone who participated in Nazi persecutions. "This action confirms my belief that it is not too late to make our stand against war crimes clear and unequivocal," she declared in a press release at the time.

In January 1979, she took over as chair of the House immigration subcommittee and stepped up her efforts to achieve another goal of her campaign: to shift responsibility for such cases from the INS to the Justice Department, which was far better equipped to handle them. Frustrated by his own experiences in the INS, Mendelsohn was fully supportive—but they encountered initial resistance from top Justice Department officials, who made clear they had no desire to take this on.

Holtzman left them no choice. "I said you can do this voluntarily or I'll write this into law," she recalled. That same year, 1979, marked the creation of the Office of Special Investigations (OSI), operated as part of the Justice Department's Criminal Division. This was a far more ambitious unit than the one it was replacing at the INS. With an initial budget of about $2 million, OSI was able to put together a fifty-person team of lawyers, investigators, historians, researchers, and support staff.

At about the same time, Rosenbaum was driving back to Harvard Law School from the wedding of a friend in Philadelphia. Stopping to get a soda, he picked up a newspaper as well. That's where he spotted a short item about the Justice Department's plans to set up OSI. As a second-year law student, he needed to look for a summer job and he immediately decided to see if he could apply there. "More than anything else in the world that's what I want to do," he thought.

Returning to his apartment in Cambridge at about midnight, he called the Justice Department to get the number for the new office. At nine the next morning, he reached Mendelsohn, who had already transferred over from INS to help set up OSI. Mendelsohn had only one question for him: did he know Alan Dershowitz, the famed Harvard Law School professor? Rosenbaum responded that he had been in his class the previous semester. After Mendelsohn called Dershowitz, who confirmed that Rosenbaum was "a good guy," he offered Rosenbaum the summer internship on that basis alone. Referring to the elaborate vetting process for applicants now, Rosenbaum pointed out: "This could never happen today."

While Mendelsohn soon left OSI and pursued Nazi-related cases as a private lawyer, Rosenbaum had taken his first step on a journey that, after a few detours, propelled him to the very top of OSI, making him its longest-serving director and the country's leading Nazi hunter.

It was no accident that most of those involved in Nazi persecution who made it to the United States were not from Germany or Austria, but from the countries that Hitler's army conquered. In Europe's postwar chaos, many of those who had fled from the former occupied territories or survived the Holocaust ended up in displaced persons' camps in Germany, Austria, and Italy. In 1948, President Truman signed the Displaced Persons Act, allowing 200,000 DPs to come to the United States over two years. But in a period when anti-Semitism was still all too prevalent and many Americans feared an influx of Jewish refugees, the initial legislation deliberately favored other groups—those coming from countries that had been "de facto annexed by a foreign power," such as the Baltic states, which were swallowed up by the Soviet Union, agricultural workers, and even *Volksdeutsche*, the ethnic Germans who had fled from the formerly occupied territories.

The rules would change over time, with a liberalization of the provisions leading to the inclusion of about eighty thousand Jewish DPs among the nearly 400,000 admitted before the act expired in 1952. While the arrivals from the Baltic states and Ukraine were seen as victims of communism, they also included numerous Nazi collaborators. When it came to ethnic Germans who had lived in territories conquered by Hitler, the probability of collaboration was even higher. As Allan Ryan, who was the director of OSI from 1980 to 1983, pointed out: "The DP Act had cast U.S. nets into waters known to be rife with sharks, and it was inevitable that sharks would be brought in."

Ryan added that it would be wrong to imply that a majority of the new immigrants were implicated in Nazi crimes. But positing that perhaps 2.5 percent of them were guilty, he calculated that "nearly 10,000 Nazi war criminals came to America." That figure was merely a guess, and Rosenbaum, among others, believes that it is much too high. But given the fact that there was no serious vetting of the new arrivals, the guilty easily slipped in with the innocent. At that point, they usually made themselves as inconspicuous as possible. These were not the villains that were portrayed in Hollywood movies, eager to hatch new Nazi plots. As Ryan put it, "they became model citizens and quiet neighbors."

Up until 1973 when pressure began to build to go after more of the perpetrators, the government had only pushed for the deportation of nine Nazi collaborators, and failed in most of those cases. When it was formed in 1979, OSI was charged with making up for more than three decades of almost complete neglect. The idea was to send the message that, even at that late date, the United States was serious about ridding itself of the Nazi perpetrators who had lied about their personal histories to gain entry in the first place.

Looking ahead to his internship in the new unit, Rosenbaum was full of ideas about the dark conspiracies of government officials that Blum had written about in his bestseller, echoing the charges that DeVito had made when he left the INS. He would have access to the files, Rosenbaum reasoned, which meant that "this coming summer I'll get to the bottom of this cover-up." Instead, he found himself doing legal research on complex but fascinating cases, working with members of the new team, who struck him as dedicated and smart. "I did not, of course, uncover any grand conspiracy or cover-up," he added with a grin. By the end of the summer, he had a more realistic goal: to return to OSI after he graduated from law school the following year, which is what he did.

The new unit faced the kind of huge obstacles that Mendelsohn highlighted when he initially attempted to get the INS to move more aggressively. "'Nazi hunting' so many years after the war is dramatic, tedious and difficult," a 2010 Justice Department internal report on the history of OSI pointed out. There was the added complication of collecting evidence from territory that was now behind the Iron Curtain. Building on contacts that Holtzman and others had developed with Soviet officials, OSI was able to gather testimony from witnesses inside the Soviet Union, bringing along both its lawyers and defense attorneys. But American judges were wary of anything emanating from the Eastern bloc, whether in the form of testimony or documents, especially since Ukrainian and Baltic groups charged that many of those under investigation were victims of communist smear campaigns. Columnist Pat Buchanan, the future presidential candidate, joined in the denunciations of OSI as a purveyor of Kremlin misinformation.

In a few cases, OSI achieved relatively quick results—sometimes with unexpected consequences. In 1981, it identified Albert Deutscher, a sixty-one-year-old railway worker who had arrived in the United States in 1952, as a Ukrainian ethnic German who had been part of a paramilitary group that shot Jews who arrived by train in Odessa. The day after OSI filed its complaint, Deutscher committed suicide by jumping in front of a freight train in Chicago.

But most of the legal battles took years or even decades, including those that were started before the creation of OSI. Valerian Trifa, the Romanian archbishop accused of instigating pogroms against Jews, proclaimed his innocence all along. When he was shown a photo of himself in an Iron Guard uniform, he had to admit that he had been a member of that fascist organization. Still, he insisted he had done nothing wrong. OSI then took up his case. Trying to stop the legal proceedings against him, Trifa surrendered his citizenship in 1980. Two years later, with the government still pressing charges, he agreed to be deported.

But that was not the end of his story. One of OSI's most difficult tasks was to find a country that was willing to take such war criminals, particularly if it might mean subsequent pressure to prosecute them as well. OSI tried and failed to get Israel to take him. That country's leaders did not want to signal that they were ready to hold more Nazi trials; they always saw the Eichmann case as something exceptional, not a precedent. In 1984, Portugal finally admitted Trifa, where he lived openly and continued to sound defiant. "All this talk by the Jews about the Holocaust is going to backfire," he proclaimed. He died three years later.

During his final year at Harvard Law School, Rosenbaum was browsing through the Holocaust section of a used bookstore in Cambridge when he came across a volume about Dora, a concentration camp that he had never heard of. The author was Jean Michel, a former French Resistance fighter who has survived his ordeal as a prisoner there. Even for someone who was already familiar with many horror stories from that era, Michel's account of conditions in this facility where German scientists produced their famed V-2 rockets was singularly chilling.

"The missile slaves worked ceaselessly in fear for their lives, terrorized by the sadistic SS and Kapos," Michel wrote. The prisoners, who came from a variety of occupied countries, had to dig and prepare tunnels with minimal tools, often using their bare hands. "They carried rocks and machines in the most shocking conditions. The weight of the machines was so great that the men, walking skeletons at the end of their strength, were often crushed to death beneath their burden. Ammonia dust burnt their lungs. The food was even insufficient for lesser forms of life." Working eighteen-hour days and even sleeping in the tunnels, only strong prisoners survived. Of the sixty thousand who were dispatched to Dora, Michel reported, thirty thousand died.

Rosenbaum then picked up another book called *The Rocket Team*, an admiring study of Wernher von Braun and his group of fellow German rocket scientists, many of whom were brought to the United States to play a key role in the American missile and space program. Among them was Arthur Rudolph, who oversaw the development of the Saturn V rocket, which sent the first astronauts to the moon. But the book's American authors also pointed out that Rudolph was responsible for missile production at Dora. This meant he was one of the masters of the "missile slaves."

As Rosenbaum frequently notes, OSI's cases were often triggered by tips from foreign governments or the media. But in this case he was anxious to provide his own tip as soon as he returned to the Justice Department after he graduated. While von Braun had died in 1977, Rudolph was still alive. On his first day back at OSI, Rosenbaum brought the subject up in his meeting with Neal Sher, the unit's deputy director. Sher had not heard of Rudolph, but immediately asked whether he was part of Operation Paperclip, the postwar program to bring the German scientists over. Rosenbaum said he was. Sher warned him that other Paperclip investigations appeared to be going nowhere since it was hard to implicate scientists in specific crimes. But he agreed to let him look into it—"as long as you don't spend too much time on it."

Rosenbaum freely admitted he disregarded that admonition. With the help of an intern, he dug up documents from the National Archives and traveled to West Germany to examine records from the Dora-Nordhausen war crimes trial, one of the series of U.S. Army trials at Dachau in 1947. Rudolph was not a defendant, but on June 2, 1947, he was interrogated by Major Eugene Smith—and Rosenbaum came up with the incriminating transcript. Rudolph admitted to attending the execution of "six maybe twelve" prisoners. The SS hung them slowly from an electric crane that was used to move rocket components, while other prisoners were forced to watch. As Rudolph explained, the point was "to show the penalty of making a plot for sabotaging the factory."

Based on such evidence, Sher became just as convinced as Rosenbaum that they should move against Rudolph. The German scientist was by then living comfortably in retirement in San Jose, California. Confident of his good standing as an honored American scientist, he did not appear alarmed when Rosenbaum, Sher, and OSI director Ryan showed up there to meet with him in 1982. He met with them alone, without a lawyer, eager to convey the notion that he was willing to be fully cooperative, and the message that he had tried to make life easier rather than harder for the Dora prisoners. But it was a narrative that was hard to sustain, particularly in face of the evidence of the brutality and executions in the camp that the OSI lawyers had at their disposal.

By their second meeting, Rudolph came with his lawyers and asked if there was a way to end the case against him without any formal legal action. The two sides cut a deal: Rudolph would give up his U.S. citizenship voluntarily and leave the country. Since this was done without any legal action, he would be able to keep receiving his American pension. From OSI's standpoint, this was a victory. "If it had been litigated, it would have taken years," Rosenbaum pointed out. "Basically he was agreeing to lose and we were agreeing to win."

For Rudolph, this was less than a devastating loss, even if he complained bitterly about the alleged ingratitude of the Americans who had made use of his scientific expertise. As in the case of Nazis who were later employed by the CIA, Rosenbaum does not necessarily share the indignation that such compromises were made in the early days of the Cold War. Speaking of Rudolph, he said: "I don't Monday-morning-quarterback the decision to employ him." But he was convinced that, given the evidence against him, the United States should have sent him back to Germany earlier—once he was no longer useful to the rocket program.

This was Rosenbaum's biggest case during his early years at OSI. But he was not sure how long he would stay in the Nazi hunting business— or, for that matter, how long the Justice Department unit would stay in operation. His colleague Elizabeth White, a specialist in modern European history, was hired in 1983. "At the time I was told the office would last three to five years max, and every new hire was told that for the first twenty-five years of its existence," she pointed out with a laugh. The assumption was that there would be fewer and fewer Nazi criminals to investigate due to the fact that many of them were likely to die soon. She worked there for twenty-seven years, vastly expanding the Watch Lists that were maintained to flag former Nazis who might attempt to enter the United States.

Rosenbaum was an eager pursuer, and became particularly adept at surprise visits to check on potential targets of investigations. But he also felt frustrated. "So many people you knew in your gut were in it up to their ears, but you couldn't prove it," he said. "It was inherent in the task. We didn't have enough people to do all these cases right; we were having to triage all the time."

After three years at OSI, he decided to try a more conventional path, taking a job at a big Manhattan law firm. But he soon discovered that corporate litigation "didn't have any meaning for me." He had already "had the misfortune," as he put it, "of working on cases that had great meaning for me."

By 1985, Rosenbaum was once again working on those cases—not back at OSI yet, but as the general counsel for the World Jewish Congress. It was during his two years there that he found himself not only exposing the past secrets of those who had served the Third Reich but also caught up in a rapidly escalating confrontation with another Nazi hunter. It was a battle that pitted him against the man he had idolized when he first became fascinated by the hunt for war criminals: Simon Wiesenthal.

CHAPTER THIRTEEN

To La Paz and Back

"Forty-four children deported—no mere statistic, but rather forty-four tragedies which continue to cause us pain some forty years after the event."

Beate and Serge Klarsfeld

The French Nazi hunter Serge Klarsfeld readily admitted that SS Captain Klaus Barbie, who served as the Gestapo chief in Lyon, was hardly in the same league as Eichmann, Mengele, or Auschwitz Commandant Rudolf Höss. "Barbie is not a member of the board of directors of the Nazi crime, but a middle manager," he noted. Nonetheless, he argued that this in no way diminished his guilt or significance. "He is the very symbol of the Gestapo as it raged in our land. The higher-ups of the Nazi police had no contact with their victims; they acted through the Barbies. It was Barbie himself who left a palpable memory with those of his prisoners who survived. He was a particularly zealous and fanatical local operative."

Barbie was responsible for thousands of deaths during the German occupation of France, and personally tortured countless victims. Even in a world awash with wanton brutality, he quickly developed an outsized reputation—and fully earned the nickname the "Butcher of Lyon." His most prominent victim was Jean Moulin, the leader of the French Resistance. Barbie beat and tortured him mercilessly to get him to talk, but the battered Moulin never revealed anything; he died on a train to Germany.

Aside from seeking to crush the Resistance, Barbie focused on rounding up Jews—and here, too, he earned special notoriety. On April 6, 1944, acting on a tip from a French informer, the Gestapo from Lyon closed in on a school and refuge for Jewish children in the tiny village of Izieu. A local farmhand who was working nearby witnessed the scene. "The Germans were loading the children into the lorries brutally, as if they were sacks of potatoes," he recalled. The terrified children started calling to him for help, but when he moved in their direction, he was stopped by a rifle butt. One of the boys tried to jump out and escape, and he watched helplessly as the Germans "started beating him brutally with the butts of their rifles, and kicking him in the shins."

Barbie immediately sent a signed telex to Gestapo headquarters in Paris reporting the arrests and the closure of the "Jewish children's home" in Izieu. Barbie's message, Klarsfeld wrote, "has entered into history, proof of a ruthlessness that in intensity—and in absolute evil—outstripped that which was loosed against the Resistance." The forty-four children, ranging in age from three to thirteen, and their seven guardians were quickly transported to Auschwitz; only one of the adults survived. She described how one of the youngest girls was ripped from her hands so that she could be sent with the others to the gas chamber.

For Klarsfeld the fate of those children was more than just another tragedy during the war; it felt intensely personal. After all, he and his sister had been saved in a similar village when they were about the same age. A letter from one of the children of Izieu, Nina Aronowicz, written to her aunt in Paris several months before the Gestapo raid, conveyed how secure she and the others had felt in the village refuge:

I'm very happy to be here. There are beautiful mountains, and from high up you can see the Rhone flow by, and it's very pretty. Yesterday we went for a swim in the Rhone with Miss Marcelle (that's a teacher). Sunday we had a birthday party for Paulette and two other children and we put on a lot of skits and it was really great.

Klarsfeld and his wife, Beate, decided early on to do everything possible to make Barbie pay for his crimes—and to rescue his victims from anonymity. They also were determined to expose the fact that the Butcher of Lyon had worked after the war for U.S. intelligence services, and that it was the Americans who subsequently facilitated his escape via the ratline to Latin America. It would be a quest that spanned two decades, but ultimately they succeeded in all parts of their mission. In doing so, they also sparked an unprecedented effort by the U.S. government to examine its role in helping a Nazi war criminal.

A tribunal in Lyon had sentenced Barbie to death in absentia on two occasions after the war—first in 1947 and then in 1954. In 1960, the Association of German Victims of Nazism triggered an investigation in Munich of Barbie's crimes in France. But Barbie had long disappeared. In 1951, he had left his homeland and settled with his family in Bolivia. Living under the name Klaus Altmann, he prospered as a "businessman" who enjoyed close ties with right-wing politicians and military officers. By the summer of 1971, when Beate Klarsfeld first heard that the German prosecutor in Munich was abandoning the investigation of Barbie's crimes, "Altmann" had good reason to feel confident he had put his past behind him. He was on particularly good terms with Hugo Banzer, the military dictator who ruled the country for almost all of the 1970s.

But Barbie had not reckoned with the passion and determination of the Klarsfelds. They started with the most basic step: assembling every bit of evidence they could about Barbie's war record and how he had been interned by the Americans at the end of the war. They soon concluded that he must have been working for them immediately afterward. Beate, in particular, worked on publicizing their findings in the press, and mobilized former Resistance fighters and others to join her on a trip to Munich to pressure the prosecutor to keep the case open.

Serge located Raymond Greissmann, a Lyon Jewish community leader during the occupation, who provided testimony that Barbie knew exactly what would happen to the people he arrested. "Shot or deported, there's no difference," he quoted him as saying in front of him. Jean

Moulin's sister wrote a letter in support of the Klarsfelds' efforts. And in Munich, Beate held a sign over the head of Holocaust survivor Fortunée Benguigui, who had been deported to Auschwitz a year before her three boys had followed her there from Izieu, never to return. "I am on a hunger strike for as long as the investigation of Klaus Barbie, who murdered my children, remains closed," it proclaimed.

Munich public prosecutor Manfred Ludolph not only relented, reopening the case, but also provided Beate's delegation with two photos. One was of Barbie in 1943. The second photo showed a group of businessmen seated around a table, and one of them looked very much like an older version of the man the Klarsfelds had targeted. Ludolph told them the photo had been taken in La Paz, Bolivia, in 1968. "That is all that I can say at this time," he added. "Since you have demonstrated how efficient you are, why don't you help me identify the man?"

After the Klarsfelds circulated the photos, they began gathering affidavits of people who had known Barbie and could identify him in the latter one, taken in La Paz. Once the 1943 photo appeared in both the French and German press, a German living in Lima reported to the Munich prosecutor that he had met "Klaus Altmann" when he had recently visited the Peruvian capital. Ludolph passed along the contact to Beate, and soon the Klarsfelds had Barbie's address in Bolivia. Ludolph and the Klarsfelds also put together a report that all but proved Altmann was Barbie. It noted that the birth dates of Altmann's children were a perfect match with those of Barbie's children. As always, Beate was ready to take direct action. She flew to Lima and then La Paz, meeting with journalists there to tell the Barbie story. At the same time, she denounced the Banzer regime, which was protecting him. "I was helping the Bolivians make a connection between what happened under Hitler and what was going on under Banzer," she recalled. Not surprisingly, the Bolivian authorities were not grateful for that help, and she was hustled out of the country. On a stopover in Lima, two policemen kept her in an office so she would not be free to move around the city. "We are here to see to your safety," one of them told her. "You risk being killed by Nazi organizations in Lima that are furious over the campaign you have launched against them in South America."

By early 1972, the Klarsfelds' publicity campaign began to prod the French authorities into action. President Georges Pompidou wrote to Banzer, arguing that the French people would not permit the crimes of the past to be "forgotten through indifference." Beate returned to La Paz, this time with another mother of two children of Izieu who had perished in Auschwitz. Given the attention they were attracting, the Bolivian authorities allowed the women in but warned them not to speak publicly. Beate played along at first—until she could arrange a press conference. The two women followed up by chaining themselves to a bench in front of the offices of the shipping company where Barbie worked. One of the signs proclaimed in Spanish: "In the name of the millions of Nazi victims, let Barbie-Altmann be extradited!"

That visit, too, ended quickly—but they had scored another public relations coup. Barbie soon gave up the pretense that his real name was Altmann, and his case received growing coverage in the media. But the Klarsfelds also recognized that, even with more support from both the German and French authorities, the chances that the Bolivian regime would give him up were almost zero. A counselor to the Foreign Ministry in La Paz had told Beate: "Bolivia is an inviolable asylum, and all who take refuge in it are sacrosanct." He also informed her that the country had a statute of limitations for the prosecution of major crimes of only eight years, which meant that whatever Barbie did during the war was "ancient history."

Barbie knew that he was protected by the Banzer regime and could afford to be dismissive of the whole campaign the Klarsfelds were waging against him. Like so many other Nazi criminals he claimed that he had only done his duty during the war, and he had nothing to atone for. "I have forgotten," he said. "If they have not forgotten, that is their business."

That impasse left the Klarsfelds with a dilemma: should they simply continue campaigning for his extradition, hoping that some part of the equation would change eventually to make that possible, or should they consider more drastic action? In her memoir, which she published in French in 1972 and then in English in 1975, Beate asserted that some people had asked them why they had not gone ahead and simply killed Barbie. "None of the people who said that would have done it himself," she noted, seemingly dismissing such a possibility. Besides, she added, "Killing Barbie would not have proved a thing. . . . It would be merely a settling of scores." She argued that she and Serge were intent on bringing him to trial, where incontrovertible evidence of his guilt could be presented and the public would once again learn about Nazi crimes.

What she did not mention then, but she and Serge admitted later, was that they had not ruled out using force if they could not extract Barbie by legal means. "First we tried kidnapping," Serge explained during my interview with the couple in Paris in 2013. In December 1972, he flew to Chile to meet with Régis Debray, the French Marxist who had joined Che Guevara, the Argentine veteran of the Cuban Revolution, in his bid to overthrow the Bolivian regime. That effort failed: in 1967, Guevara was killed and Debray ended up in a Bolivian prison with a thirty-year sentence. Facing a major international campaign to free him, the Bolivian authorities released Debray in 1970.

The plan was to team up with some Bolivian rebels, cross the border, and snatch Barbie. Serge had brought $5,000 with him to buy a car for the operation. According to Serge, the effort failed when the car broke down. But it may have also been doomed by the rapidly deteriorating situation in Chile, where Marxist President Salvador Allende was toppled by a military coup in 1973.

For nearly ten more years, the Klarsfelds kept the Barbie case alive but appeared to be making little progress. They were also preoccupied with the cases they were pursuing against Lischka, Hagen, and Heinrichsohn, who were also former SS officers who had served in occupied France. They were much more vulnerable than Barbie since they were still living in West Germany. When those three were finally convicted in 1980 for their role in the deportation of fifty thousand Jews from France to their deaths, the Klarsfelds had real reason to celebrate.

Still, they were not giving up on Barbie—quite the contrary. Despite what Beate had written about rejecting the idea of assassinating him a decade earlier, both she and Serge now say they were ready to back such an effort by the 1980s. Banzer, Barbie's Bolivian protector, had lost power in 1977, but a new military strongman soon took over who also offered him protection. In 1982, a Bolivian who lived in France came to the Klarsfelds and told them that he was returning to his homeland and he wanted to kill Barbie. "We told him we are in favor," Serge told me, explaining that such an action could only be justified in a situation where a dictatorship was protecting a Nazi criminal, thus offering no alternative.

But when the would-be assassin arrived in Bolivia, he reported that the military regime was crumbling. The Klarsfelds abandoned the assassination plan and went back to work convincing the French government to find a way to get Barbie back to France to stand trial. This time they had a ready ally. As Serge pointed out, Debray "was then no more a terrorist but a special counselor to [French President] Mitterrand."

After a civilian government replaced the military rulers in La Paz, Barbie was arrested on January 25, 1983, ostensibly for defrauding the government in a business deal. The new Bolivian authorities left no doubt that they were eager to get rid of their problematic resident. When the West Germans balked at an offer to send him back to his homeland, the Klarsfelds' efforts with the French government paid off. The Bolivians flew Barbie to French Guiana, and a French military jet then whisked him to France.

In preparation for Barbie's trial, Serge published his book *The Children of Izieu: A Human Tragedy.* In it, he profiled each of the forty-four children who had been sent to their deaths; their names and faces were rescued from the anonymity of statistics to offer their mute but powerful testimony. Together with Beate, he wrote an introduction that stressed that one of the key reasons for bringing Nazis to justice was to document their crimes. "And it was for the children of Izieu—and for them alone—that we tracked down and unmasked Klaus Barbie," they added.

Barbie did not stand trial until 1987, and he continued to proclaim his innocence till the end. The proceedings took place in Lyon, the city where he had exercised his murderous powers as Gestapo chief. He was convicted for crimes against humanity, given a life sentence, and died at the age of seventy-seven in the Lyon prison four years later.

During the maneuvers to bring Barbie to justice, there was one significant loose end: the allegation that U.S. intelligence services had employed him after the war and then arranged for his escape to South America. Allan Ryan, who was the director of the Justice Department's Office of Special Investigations at the time of Barbie's return to France, admitted that he was caught by surprise by the story—and, in particular, by the reports that Barbie had worked for U.S. intelligence services. "I didn't know a damn thing, and I said so," he declared.

But faced with questions from Congress and the media, Ryan had every intention of finding out. On February 11, 1983, less than three weeks after Barbie was flown to France, he met with the director of Army Counter Intelligence, who had prepared a three-inch-thick file about him. The most recent document was dated March 27, 1951: it was a report by two Army intelligence agents who had provided him with false papers using the name "Altmann," escorted him to Genoa, and sent him on his way to South America. "The evidence of American complicity with Barbie was unmistakable, and if we did not put together the story, every network, newspaper, and self-styled Nazi hunter would do if for us," Ryan concluded.

In an earlier era, Washington would have hid behind denials and claims of national security. But with OSI now in the picture and the government officially committed to tracking down Nazis, it could hardly ignore such a serious allegation. Nonetheless, Attorney General William French Smith initially attempted to do so. To Ryan's astonishment, Smith decided there was no need for an official investigation, although he stopped short of announcing his decision. While the Justice Department kept ducking questions about Barbie, both the press and members of Congress demanded to know why it was not taking any action. Ryan had to sit quietly, but he was fuming.

Finally on March 14, John Martin of ABC called to say he was working on a story for that evening's newscast and checking whether there were any new developments. "The clear implication was that something was being covered up," Ryan recalled. He called Smith's press secretary to alert him. It took Smith only half an hour to reverse his decision and announce that he was authorizing an investigation. Martin was able to include that news in his report.

Ryan quickly put together a small team at OSI to unearth what they could. Although there was no longer any doubt that Barbie had worked for the Army's Counter Intelligence Corps and benefited from its protection, it was still unclear how much the American officers who dealt with him knew about his record in Lyon during the war and about the French efforts to find him. It was also unclear whether he had worked for the CIA, and whether he had continued to work for the Americans after he found refuge in Bolivia in 1951.

The result of OSI's exhaustive investigation was a detailed report that, while carefully maintaining a dispassionate tone, painted a picture of internal intelligence intrigue and deceptions worthy of a John le Carré spy novel. Although CIC headquarters had already sent information to its regional office in January 1947 identifying Barbie as the former Gestapo chief in Lyon and as a "dangerous conspirator" in a network of former SS officers, the CIC agents in the field were focused on their top priority: gathering information about suspected communist activity in occupied Germany. One of those agents, Robert S. Taylor, received a tip from a former German intelligence agent in France that Barbie could be very helpful in those efforts.

Taylor and his immediate superior decided that, instead of notifying headquarters, which was liable to seek his arrest, they would use Barbie as an informant. According to Taylor, Barbie struck him as "an honest man, both intellectually and personally, absolutely without nerves or fear. He is strongly anti-Communist and a Nazi idealist who believes that his beliefs were betrayed by the Nazis in power." Within two months, Taylor and his superior were confident enough of his value to openly appeal to headquarters that he should remain free as long as he was working for CIC.

In October 1947, an officer from headquarters ordered the arrest of Barbie so that he could be sent to the European Command Intelligence Center for "detailed interrogation." But Barbie emerged unscathed from that experience. He was seen as particularly valuable because of his knowledge of French intelligence, which the Americans believed was heavily infiltrated by communists. And, perhaps more importantly, his interrogator believed it was safer for the Army to keep him in their employ because his knowledge of "the mission of CIC, its agents, subagents, funds, etc. is too great."

The French government made repeated attempts to locate Barbie, with its ambassador in Washington and other senior officials pressing the State Department and the U.S. High Commission for Germany for their assistance. At the same time, CIC continued to employ him. In OSI's report, Ryan carefully worded his key conclusions. He argued that the CIC agents who initially employed Barbie should not be "vilified for that decision" since they were "on the whole, conscientious and patriotic men faced with a difficult assignment." Their decision to enlist Barbie in that assignment was "neither cynical nor corrupt."

The report also pointed out that at the time Barbie was not known as a major war criminal, and it gives the benefit of the doubt to the CIC officers who first worked with him. According to David Marwell, OSI's historian on the investigation, it was "unclear if they knew at the time they recruited him that he was more than a journeyman intelligence officer." But by May 1949, the evidence was certainly there that Barbie was wanted for serious war crimes, and the CIC repeatedly hid the fact that he was working for them, fending off all inquiries from the U.S. High Commission for Germany. The result was that the military brass there "did not know that Barbie's whereabouts were known to CIC officers, and had no reason to suspect that CIC was not telling the truth." This led to the High Commission's repeated denials to the French that they knew anything about Barbie's whereabouts.

The report concluded that the CIC also deliberately kept the CIA in the dark about Barbie. The two agencies were fierce rivals and deeply suspicious of one another. After Barbie arrived in South America, the report added, there was no evidence that he ever worked for the CIA or any other U.S. government agency.

All of which led Ryan to assert in the report's conclusions that "the decision to use a former Nazi, even a former Gestapo officer, is one thing; the decision to use a person wanted for war crimes is another." As for the CIC's record once it knew it had crossed that line, his judgment is even harsher. "Fear of embarrassment cannot be a valid excuse for one government agency knowingly providing false information to another," he wrote.

The report was equally blunt in spelling out the CIC's role in getting Barbie out of Europe. While the Americans had helped other former Nazis get out of Germany before, this was the first and only case, it maintained, when they had used the infamous ratline to do so. They paid Father Krunoslav Dragonović, a Croatian priest who had helped a stream of alleged war criminals from his homeland escape by the same route, to arrange for Barbie and his family to sail from Genoa on a ship to Buenos Aires. From there, they made their way to Bolivia.

In his memoirs, Ryan called the whole episode "a chronicle of dishonor." But he was proud of OSI's report and the immediate impact it had. In a formal note to the French government that accompanied the copy of the report, Secretary of State George Shultz expressed "deep regrets to the Government of France" for the U.S. role in delaying justice for so long. While the media coverage also played on that theme, there was widespread praise for Washington's willingness to deal honestly with its historical record. Ryan was especially pleased by the message that French Minister of Justice Robert Badinter dispatched to Attorney General Smith. "This particularly rigorous work reveals a concern for the investigation of the truth that honors your society," he wrote.

The Klarsfelds' long campaign to track down Barbie had produced a ripple effect that was larger than they had ever imagined.

CHAPTER FOURTEEN

Wartime Lies

"There is a history in all men's lives."

—William Shakespeare, *Henry IV*

If the handling of the Barbie case represented an unmistakable win for justice and a laudable effort to set the historical record straight, the Kurt Waldheim affair could not have been more different. When the former secretary-general of the United Nations emerged as the leading candidate in Austria's 1986 presidential election, a series of revelations about his wartime past not only ignited a fiery debate on the campaign trail but also led to angry recriminations among rival Nazi hunters, and between the Jewish community in Austria and the New York–based World Jewish Congress. No one emerged a clear winner, and many reputations were tarred in the process.

On January 29, 1986, Eli Rosenbaum was attending the WJC's Global Plenary Assembly in Jerusalem when Israel Singer, the organization's secretary general, abruptly informed him that he was dispatching him to Vienna. There was something that needed checking out there. "It has to do with Kurt Waldheim," he explained. "Believe it or not, it looks like our Dr. Waldheim may have been a Nazi. A *real* one."

Rosenbaum, who had only recently ended his brief stint at a Manhattan law firm to take the job of general counsel at the WJC, was skeptical. It was no secret that Waldheim had served in the Wehrmacht and that he had been wounded on the Eastern Front, but that was no indication that he was either a member of the Nazi Party or had done anything beyond his duty as a soldier. Rosenbaum's earlier job at the Justice Department's Office of Special Investigations had made him acutely aware of how difficult it was to pin personal responsibility for specific crimes on those who had served the Third Reich. "Too frustrating," he told Singer, trying to fend off the assignment. He was only thirty at the time, but he already felt weary just thinking about the possibility of returning to his old line of work.

Singer, whose parents had fled Austria, was not about to be put off so easily. He took Rosenbaum over to meet another participant in the conference. Leon Zelman was a Polish-born survivor of Auschwitz and Mauthausen who ran the Jewish Welcome Service in Vienna, situated in a small office just opposite St. Stephen's Cathedral. In that capacity, he had worked hard to encourage Jews to visit Austria and to combat manifestations of that country's deep-seated anti-Semitism. A recent troubling development, he immediately told Rosenbaum, had raised new questions about Waldheim's past.

Zelman pulled out an article from the Viennese weekly *Profil* about a controversy triggered by the decision of an Austrian military academy to install a plaque honoring General Alexander Löhr, the commander of the country's air force before the Anschluss with Germany. As a Luftwaffe commander in World War II, Löhr supervised the surprise bombing of Belgrade on April 6, 1941, obliterating much of the Yugoslav capital and killing thousands of civilians. In 1947, he was tried in Yugoslavia, sentenced to death, and hanged as a war criminal.

In 1942, Löhr had been transferred to the Wehrmacht to serve as the commander of Army Group E, which was responsible for Yugoslavia and Greece. At the very end of the article, the writer mentioned "a rumor" that Waldheim had served on Löhr's staff during his tenure there. It emphasized that he was only a junior officer, but Zelman saw this as potentially explosive information.

Given the scrutiny Waldheim had undergone during the time he was the head of the United Nations, Rosenbaum was still skeptical. If he had indeed served on the staff of a convicted war criminal, why had that fact not surfaced before? And since Löhr was hanged for crimes he committed before he switched over to the Wehrmacht, thus before any possible involvement on Waldheim's part, Rosenbaum reasoned that this was "not grounds for condemnation" even if the "rumor" could be confirmed.

Before Rosenbaum could express those doubts, Zelman pointed out the "missing ingredient" in the *Profil* report. In his autobiography, official biographies, and correspondence, Waldheim had omitted any mention of wartime service in the Balkans. After he was wounded on the Eastern Front in 1941, he returned to Austria—and his accounts had always indicated that this had ended his military career. In a 1980 letter to U.S. Congressman Stephen Solarz, for example, he offered his standard explanation of what happened next: "Being incapacitated for further service on the front, [I] resumed my law studies at Vienna University where I graduated in 1944."

"But then something is very wrong, you see," Zelman continued. "If he left [active service] in 1941, how could he ever have served with Löhr in the army? Löhr did not even arrive from the Luftwaffe into the Army *until* 1942. There must be a deception."

Zelman offered to accompany Rosenbaum to Vienna once the conference ended, urging him to make "discreet" inquiries there. Although the American remained doubtful that there was anything new to discover about Waldheim and had been looking forward to returning to New York, he felt he had no choice but to agree. At least Zelman would be there to help provide him with the leads he would need to check out the questions raised by the *Profil* article.

But on his first day in Vienna, Zelman apologetically disabused him of that notion. When Rosenbaum asked him for suggestions on how to start inquiring about Waldheim's past, his whole demeanor changed. He turned pale and he suddenly looked older and fearful. "You know my situation in Austria is already a difficult one, my dear Eli," he said. "I love this city, really, but also I know what is underneath the surface."

The message was clear: as a Jew living in Vienna, he did not want to be linked to anything that Rosenbaum might uncover. When the American asked if he could at least keep him posted about his progress, Zelman was emphatic: "Please, no. No, I don't think so. You please must keep me out of this."

He added that he would like to hear the final result, and that Rosenbaum could turn to him if he got into any sort of trouble. But beyond that he was clearly ending his involvement.

"Evidently, it was one thing to be a fearless old Jew in Jerusalem; it was quite another matter in Vienna," Rosenbaum concluded.

It was not a simple matter of courage or fear, as Rosenbaum initially assumed. Zelman knew that any probe of Waldheim's wartime record during the presidential race would trigger a backlash from his supporters, which could be easily directed both against Jews and his Socialist opponents. Waldheim was a candidate of the conservative People's Party, while the Socialists had put up Kurt Steyrer, who was the underdog in the race. The front-runner was playing up his U.N. leadership role to impress his countrymen with his international credentials. "Dr. Kurt Waldheim: An Austrian the World Trusts," his campaign posters proclaimed. As Rosenbaum sardonically observed, Waldheim was "the best-known Austrian since Hitler."

Thanks to other contacts that Singer had provided, Rosenbaum started connecting with people who had been digging into Waldheim's past. As he noted, most of them were linked to the ruling Socialist Party; they were the ones who had leaked the initial story to *Profil* but were disappointed that it seemingly had no impact. Rosenbaum's arrival in Vienna gave them another shot at it—and, in the meantime, they had made more discoveries about Waldheim. The American visitor arranged a meeting with "Karl Schuller," the pseudonym he gave to the man who swore him to secrecy about his identity. Schuller and some associates had launched the informal investigation, hoping to nail Waldheim.

They had checked in at the U.S.-run Berlin Document Center, which held captured Nazi records, but found nothing on him. They had much better luck tapping into the Austrian State Archives. Waldheim's military service record was in a sealed file there, but Schuller said "a friend of mine who works in the government" had managed to make a copy of a few pages. Although Waldheim had presented his family background as anti-Nazi and he in fact had campaigned against Austria's incorporation into Germany, those records indicated he had quickly adapted to the new regime once the Anschluss took place in 1938. He was soon listed as a member of the Nazi student organization and, more tellingly, of a riding unit of the SA, the Nazi paramilitary arm known as the Storm Troopers.

As if all that were not explosive enough, Schuller produced a photo taken on May 22, 1943, bearing an official military stamp, showing four officers on an airstrip. As the caption indicated, they included an Italian officer, an SS major general, and First Lieutenant Kurt Waldheim. The location of the photo was listed as Podgorica, placing him in Montenegro's capital at a time when he had consistently implied he was only studying law in Vienna. This served as additional confirmation that he had served in the Balkans, where Löhr was in charge.

As Rosenbaum realized, the information Schuller and his team had pulled together on Waldheim's war years was far from exhaustive, but his initial skepticism gave way to the growing conviction that it could fuel major media coverage. Still, he wanted to see what else they had done to verify their findings. He asked what he thought was the obvious question: "Have you shown the photographs and documents to Simon Wiesenthal? I could call him and—"

Schuller cut him off. "Oh, God, no!" he said, and immediately asked if Wiesenthal knew that Rosenbaum was in Vienna.

When Rosenbaum said he had not told him yet, Schuller was relieved. "Good. He must not find out what you are doing," he said. He explained that Wiesenthal despised the Socialists and, as a result, favored the People's Party. If the Nazi hunter was looped in, he "would go straight to Waldheim," Schuller maintained.

According to Rosenbaum's account of their conversation, he tried to argue that it would be a mistake to keep Wiesenthal in the dark. "We are in Vienna," he said. "It's right under Wiesenthal's nose. If we don't involve him from the start, it'll be very difficult to ask him for help later."

But Schuller wouldn't budge. He told the American he would cut off all cooperation with him if he contacted Wiesenthal.

Rosenbaum chose to obey. The consequences would prove far more serious than even he had predicted.

Rosenbaum returned to New York to brief his bosses about his findings. WJC President Edgar M. Bronfman, the billionaire chairman of Seagrams, initially questioned whether their group should go public with what it had learned to date. "We're not in the Nazi-hunting business," he said. Everyone knew that this would be seen as "political mudslinging" aimed at stopping Waldheim's election, Rosenbaum recalled. But they also knew that if they kept quiet until after the voting, they could be accused of trying to protect Waldheim. Singer, armed with a memo from Rosenbaum, urged Bronfman to approve immediate action. After pondering their arguments, Bronfman sent back Rosenbaum's memo with the handwritten message: "Do it—EMB."

Rosenbaum reached out to *The New York Times*, and John Tagliabue, one of its most talented correspondents, took the lead on the reporting. *Profil* continued its investigation as well, and broke the news of Waldheim's membership in the Nazi student organization and the SA in its issue that was published on March 2.

Tagliabue had interviewed Waldheim a day earlier to confront him with the information unearthed to date and the *Times* ran his article on March 3. The story immediately turned into an international sensation. "Files Show Kurt Waldheim Served Under War Criminal," the headline proclaimed. Tagliabue explained that Waldheim had been attached to General Löhr's command that brutally suppressed partisan units in Yugoslavia and deported Greek Jews from Salonika to Auschwitz and other camps. It also pointed out that he was assigned to the army command in Salonika in March 1942, and had served as an interpreter for German and Italian officers in Yugoslavia.

Covering the story for *Newsweek*, I soon caught up with Waldheim in the mountain resort town of Semmering, where he was spending the night after a long day of campaigning. He was hardly eager to field more questions about the revelations in *Profil* and the *Times*, but he agreed to an interview at his hotel, clearly figuring that he could engage in damage control. He was in a testy mood, yet he still managed to keep his emotions sufficiently in check to convey the impression that somehow the sudden uproar was all the result of a "misunderstanding" that he could easily clear up.

When it came to discussing the SA and the Nazi student organization, Waldheim used precisely that word. He had never joined the SA or any Nazi organization, he insisted. As a student at the Consular Academy in Vienna, he participated "in a few sporting exercises" of a student riding group, he said. Only later and unbeknownst to him, he insisted, the lists of participants of such groups were incorporated into the SA. Similarly, he had attended "a few meetings and nothing more" of a student discussion group. "I was not a member of either of the organizations. There seems to be a misunderstanding."

Unlike the SS, the SA was never declared a criminal organization by the victorious Allies, and its members did not carry a similar stigma. Besides, once young men like Waldheim joined the army, they could not maintain their SA membership. Thus, the issue was more one of Waldheim's credibility: had he been lying about his past all those years when he was rising to the top of the world's largest international organization? Had he deliberately covered up his service in the Balkans under Löhr? If so, what else might he be hiding?

In contrast to his protestations that he was not a member of the SA or the Nazi student group, he did not deny that he had been assigned to the Balkans. "My service in the German Army is no secret whatsoever," he said. But up till then he had only been open about the first part of his military career. The documents left no doubt that he had returned to active service after he recovered from the leg wound he suffered in Russia, and that he had been dispatched to the army command in Salonika, while at the same time he intermittently worked on his law degree.

I asked why he always had omitted that part of his history, including in his recently published autobiography. "I did not enter into all these details, which in my opinion were not very important," he replied. It was hardly a convincing explanation, but he seemed to believe he could slide by with that.

He became far more animated when I pressed him about his claim during his *Times* interview that he had known nothing about the deportation of Jews from Salonika. In 1943 while he was based there, thousands of Jews were loaded onto the trains that kept departing for the death camps. Yet he insisted his Balkan duties were largely that of a translator, which explained his photo with the Italian and German generals. In Salonika, he said, he was also focused on analyzing reports from the field about enemy troop movements. "Of course I deeply regret this," he said, referring to the deportations. "This is part of that terrible Holocaust experience, but I can only tell you I had no knowledge whatsoever . . . for the first time [now] I heard that there were such deportations."

As we talked, he grew more and more insistent. "Whether you believe it or not, that is the truth and I really just want to finish with this thing because there's not a word of truth that I knew about this. Nothing. I was never involved in such things. I had no knowledge of this. This is a well-organized campaign against me."

But "this thing" was hardly about to disappear; it was only just beginning.

Simon Wiesenthal was caught by surprise when the Waldheim story broke. As he noted bitterly in his memoir, he found out only then that Rosenbaum had been to Vienna "without visiting me or even telephoning me." Wiesenthal had dealt with WJC officials before, and, as Rosenbaum had predicted, he felt particularly offended that they would launch such an investigation and subsequent publicity campaign on his home turf without consulting him.

Besides, this was not the first time that there had been rumors about Waldheim's wartime record. In 1979, the Israelis had asked Wiesenthal to check whether he had a Nazi past that might explain his pro-Arab stance at the U.N. Wiesenthal reported that he contacted Axel Springer, the famed West German publisher, who agreed to examine the records at the Berlin Documentation Center for him since he had easy access to them. That inquiry produced no indication that Waldheim had belonged to any Nazi organizations. It did show that he had served in the Balkans, but at the time Waldheim's efforts to omit all mentions of that service were less evident and not seen as especially significant.

When the Waldheim affair erupted in 1986, Wiesenthal was not troubled by the revelation that Waldheim was in a Nazi student organization. Wiesenthal quoted his close friend Peter Michael Lingens, a prominent Austrian journalist, who had pointed out that such membership was sometimes necessary "even to obtain a room in a students' hostel." He wasn't terribly upset by the news that Waldheim's riding group was part of the SA, either. But despite his anger at the WJC, he was quick to denounce Waldheim not for what he had done—after all, no evidence had been produced that he was directly involved in war crimes—but for what he claimed he did not know. Wiesenthal viewed his claims that he knew nothing about the deportation of Jews from Salonika as simply unbelievable. "He is reacting as if he is in a panic," he told me. "I don't understand why he is lying."

Waldheim called Wiesenthal after he made that accusation. The candidate reiterated that he had been unaware of what was happening to the Jews in Salonika while he was there. "It is impossible that you didn't notice anything," Wiesenthal replied. "The deportations went on for six weeks. Some two thousand Jews were deported every other day; the military trains which brought down equipment for the Wehrmacht, that is for your people, took away the Jews on their return run."

Waldheim continued to insist he knew nothing. Wiesenthal pointed out that the Jews made up almost a third of the population of Salonika, and surely he must have noticed something—Jewish shops locked up, Jews escorted through the streets and other telltale signs. When he met with the same response, he told Waldheim: "I cannot believe you."

Wiesenthal was equally skeptical about Waldheim's claims that he did not know about the atrocities committed by German troops in Yugoslavia, even though they were part of his army group. His position as an intelligence officer, not just an interpreter as he initially tried to empha-size, meant that he was "one of the best-informed officers," Wiesenthal concluded.

None of this meant, however, that Wiesenthal was ready to applaud the World Jewish Congress for its offensive against Waldheim—quite the contrary. Despite its name, that organization was "no more than a small Jewish organization of inferior importance," he declared. While he was convinced that Waldheim was both a liar and an opportunist, "he had been neither a Nazi nor a war criminal," he maintained. But the WJC, Wiesenthal added, had immediately "proclaimed Waldheim a hard-line Nazi and well-nigh convicted war criminal."

Waldheim's defenders made the same charge and roundly denounced what they saw as a Jewish plot to stop their candidate. Rosenbaum cor-rectly noted that the *Times*'s story, which reflected the WJC findings, did not accuse Waldheim of war crimes, and that the issue at first was one of Waldheim's lies. Still, as he admitted in his own account of the affair later, he and other WJC officials were stunned by the ferocity of the backlash, including in much of the Austrian press, and unable to parry questions effectively about what their goals were. Asked if they were trying to in-fluence the election, they claimed they had only been interested in how Waldheim was elected twice as U.N. secretary-general in the 1970s given all the questions about his past. "But it was so obviously disingenuous that it convinced no one," Rosenbaum conceded. "We very much wanted Waldheim to quit—or to be forced from—the race."

Both the WJC and a growing army of reporters set out to see if there was more damning information that had not come to light yet. The WJC called in historian Robert Edwin Herzstein of the University of South Carolina to dig through the records. The ensuing stories raised new questions about what role Waldheim had played in the Wehrmacht's Bal-kan campaign, how he had ended up on the Allies' list of suspected war criminals in 1948, and why no government had sought his extradition—especially Yugoslavia, which had not pursued its own war crimes charges against him. Waldheim was far from a mere interpreter: his duties as an intelligence officer included handling reports about the capture of British commandos who subsequently disappeared, and prisoner interrogations. As he had earlier conceded, they also included reporting on partisan activity in Yugoslavia.

Mounting a public relations counteroffensive, Waldheim sent his son Gerhard to Washington to present the Justice Department with a thirteen-page memo defending his military record and denying any role in war crimes. This included a rebuttal to accusations that he may have had a role in the massacres that took place in three villages in Yugoslavia in October 1944. This was a time when German troops were retreating nearly everywhere, and Löhr was pulling his troops out of the southern Balkans, pushing north through Macedonia. To do so, they needed to control a key stretch of road between the towns of Stip and Kocani. On October 12, as the documents unearthed by the WJC indicated, Waldheim signed a report about "strengthened bandit [partisan] activity along the Stip-Kocani road."

There was no doubt that German troops had quickly unleashed their fury against the three villages on that road, but the critical question was how quickly and whether the bloodletting was triggered by Waldheim's report. In the memo his son carried to Washington, Waldheim maintained that the German troops arrived in the villages on about October 20, which meant more than a week after his report about partisan activity there. If that was accurate, it would be much harder to link his report to what had happened next.

Along with a Yugoslav journalist, I traveled to Macedonia to see if I could discover anything in the three villages at the center of the dispute. What I learned there stood in stark contrast to Waldheim's bland assertions on the campaign trail that implied that German troops in the Balkans were engaged in ordinary warfare, however violent, not in war crimes. "There were victims on both sides," he said. The survivors offered a very different view, and they all recalled that the massacres took place on October 14, not October 20 as Waldheim had maintained.

Petar Kocev described how he was coming home to his village of Krupiste after working in the fields that day. German officers rounded up all the men of the village and arranged them in rows of ten. Kocev was in the first row—but he was the eleventh man, so the officers pushed him out of the row at the last moment. "All ten were shot immediately," he recalled. The Germans then opened fire on everyone else. Kozev ran to a river a mile away and hid out in the hills for a month. "When I returned, I found only the walls of our house. Everything had been burned."

Risto Ognjanov pointed to a small monument commemorating the village's forty-nine victims. When the Germans showed up, he said, they ordered him and several other villagers to crouch on all fours on that spot. "I just dropped when the shots started," he recalled. "Two dead bodies fell on top of me. After the shooting, the Germans began to check who was alive by shooting bullets into the feet." The bodies covering Ognjanov protected him. When the Germans left, he and two other survivors crawled out from under the bloody pile. "For me, October 14 is my second birthday," he said, breaking into tears. "It was the beginning of my second life." There were similar stories in the other villages.

None of this proved that Waldheim was directly responsible for the massacres. But it established that his report on "bandit activity" in the area was filed only two days before they took place, making it much more likely that it was part of the chain of events leading to them.

At that point, I had never talked to Rosenbaum, since a colleague in New York was handling the interviews with him and other WJC officials. But after my article ran in the magazine, Rosenbaum called me to check that all the survivors I had talked to were certain of the date of the massacres. They were absolutely certain, I told him.

The impact of the cascade of stories was that, in the eyes of much of the world, Waldheim was increasingly suspect, but in the eyes of many of his countrymen he was the victim of a slander campaign. The latter, of course, was the message that Waldheim and his backers kept peddling at campaign rallies. After he fell just short of winning an outright 50 percent of the vote in the first round of the presidential elections in May, necessitating a run-off in early June, they redoubled their efforts to play up attacks from people like WJC's Singer and Israel's Foreign Minister Yitzhak Shamir. At a rally I attended, Waldheim focused on the "circles from abroad" who he charged were running a smear campaign. "Neither a Herr Singer in New York nor a Herr Shamir in Israel . . . has the right to meddle in the affairs of another state," he declared.

It was language that hardly needed to be decoded: its message was that the Jews needed to be taught a lesson. "Ladies and gentlemen, enough of the past!" he added. "We have more important problems to solve."

Concentrating all his fire in that direction, Waldheim refused to debate his Socialist opponent and announced that he would not take more questions from the foreign press. When I approached him at the beginning of the rally to see if he would make an exception, he let loose with his anger. "I tell you frankly that the reporting of your magazine was so bad and so negative and so against good faith that I do not intend to give any interview. You accept always the negative arguments and never accept the positive as far as I am concerned." As for the accusations against him, "it's all not true, it's all an invention," he said. Then, pointing to the tape recorder I had been holding up to him, he added: "It's not an official statement."

All of which encapsulated the widespread bitterness as the campaign entered its final days. Vienna psychiatrist Erwin Ringel pointed out "the absurdity" of Waldheim's campaign that had started by playing up his stature abroad and ended the way it did. "At first, it was 'Elect Waldheim because the world loves him,'" he said. "Now it's 'Elect Waldheim because the world hates him.'"

In electoral terms, those tactics worked: Waldheim won the run-off decisively. In the wake of that victory, he could not resist taunting the group that he held responsible for the "slander campaign" that he had been subjected to. "Even if the World Jewish Congress rummages around in archives until the end of time, it will not find anything to incriminate me," he declared.

In the end, the WJC could claim a partial victory when, in April 1987, the Justice Department's Office of Special Investigations, Rosenbaum's former employer, issued its own report on Waldheim, arguing that an examination of his duties in the Balkans "reveal him to have assisted in the smooth operation of a Nazi military organization that committed numerous and direct acts of persecution against Allied nationals and civilians." It specifically mentioned, among other events, "the Kocane-Stip massacres, and the deportation of Greek Jews." On that basis he was placed on the U.S. Watch List, which meant he was not permitted entry to the United States ever again, even to speak at the United Nations, the organization he once headed. He served out one term in office and then did not seek reelection in 1992.

Herzstein, the World War II historian the WJC dispatched to investigate Waldheim's record, produced a book summing up his conclusions. While agreeing with the Justice Department decision to put Waldheim on the Watch List, he noted that Waldheim was "a man who was not evil but merely ambitious and clever. . . . He was a man, like many of his generation, who had tried to dispose of the awkward baggage of his past by forgetting about it." He concluded: "Given what we know now, it is fair to say that while Waldheim assisted many individuals who fell into the war-criminal category, he was not a war criminal himself. Rather he was a bureaucratic accessory to both the criminal and the legitimate military activities [of his unit]. . . . Waldheim was a facilitator. The Western Allies did not generally prosecute such individuals after the war."

That was a far more nuanced view than the WJC leaders and their supporters had offered during the campaign. "In a perfect world he would stand trial," WJC executive director Elan Steinberg declared, ignoring the fact that no smoking gun was ever produced that could have led to a conviction. Beate Klarsfeld showed up at Waldheim rallies to harass him, joining small groups of protesters who released balloons saying "Happy is he who forgets" and holding up posters denouncing the candidate as a liar and a war criminal. Waldheim supporters angrily tore the posters from their hands.

"I came here to show that it's a danger for Austria to elect a man like Waldheim," Klarsfeld told me in between her protests in Vienna. "The Austrians have to open their eyes to this." But such warnings only seemed to help Waldheim. When Klarsfeld attempted to interrupt the candidate as he spoke at another rally, she was blocked from taking the microphone. "Sit down, Mrs. Klarsfeld," said Vienna Mayor Erhard Busek, who was chairing the session. "You are a guest here. This is not a Klarsfeld rally." Members of the audience shouted "Get out, Mrs. Klarsfeld."

Singer, the WJC secretary general, did not help matters by appearing to make a direct threat in a widely quoted interview in *Profil.* "It should be clear to the Austrian public that if Waldheim is elected, the next few years won't be easy for the Austrians," he said. He added that the accusations the organization had leveled would "haunt and follow" not just Waldheim but also the Austrian nation, and tourism and trade would suffer.

Even Rosenbaum conceded later that his boss had spoken "intemperately," but the top leaders had few second thoughts. WJC President Bronfman dismissed those who flinched at their tactics. "Many Jewish leaders believed this 'attack' would create bad will, and worse," he wrote in his memoirs. "I believed it was a moral imperative, and everywhere I went, the audiences I spoke to were 100 percent behind me." He added that the campaign was "terrific publicity for the WJC, and put us front and center."

But many members of Austria's small Jewish community were appalled by the blowback from that publicity. Wiesenthal was the most vociferous among them, directly blaming the WJC for the resurgence of open anti-Semitism. "We had created many friends of Israel within the young population," he said, referring to the Jewish community's efforts to promote dialogue and understanding. "Now this whole building effort has been destroyed."

Other leaders of the Austrian Jews shared Wiesenthal's frustration with the WJC for failing to consider their perspective or to consult with them. Paul Grosz called the organization's performance "very apt as far as publicity in the Western media was concerned [but] very amateurish as far as the whole case was handled, especially as regards the repercussions within Austria. A lot of damage has been done." At a meeting of European Jewish members of the WJC where he represented the Austrians, Grosz won support for his recommendation that in the future local Jewish communities had to be consulted before actions were taken that could affect them.

Still keeping quiet about how he had tipped the WJC to the initial Waldheim news, Zelman said it was the WJC's obligation to raise the issue "but they were speaking from the perspective of American Jews, which is not understood here." He was deeply troubled by what he called the return of a "we and you" mentality when Austrians dealt with Jews. "The worst thing they [the WJC] did was to identify Waldheim with everyone here over 65," he added. "That was terrible." Wiesenthal argued that their mistake was even greater. "They threatened the whole Austrian nation, seven and a half million people, and among them are five million who were born after the war or were small children at the end of the war."

It was not only a question of the nature of the accusations but also how they were delivered. "They first accused and then looked for the documents," Wiesenthal charged. That was an oversimplification, since the WJC already had significant evidence in hand when they began their publicity campaign. But by their own admission, it was far from complete—which meant they had to keep scrambling to search for more evidence afterward. According to Grosz, this dramatically weakened the impact of their findings. "The fact that the evidence against Waldheim was put forth piecemeal had the effect of immunization," he said. "Like when you get a drop of poison every few days until you are able to drink a full glass."

There was a critical reason why so many Austrians felt defensive to begin with. During the early postwar period they had successfully presented themselves as the first victims of the Third Reich, rather than the enthusiastic supporters that so many of them were. For many Austrians, including demobilized Wehrmacht soldiers, the moment of truth never came. "Nobody told these men after they came home that those were lost years and that this had been an unjust war," said Erika Weinzierl, the director of the Institute of Contemporary History in Vienna.

By comparison, Germans had been forced to confront such truths on an almost daily basis, including their responsibility for the horrors of the Holocaust and other mass killings. I was based in Bonn when the Waldheim affair was propelled into the headlines, and many Germans I knew made no effort to hide their Schadenfreude. They loved seeing the debunking of the myth that the Austrians were victims not perpetrators. "The Austrians have convinced the world that Beethoven was an Austrian and Hitler was a German," they joked. A Bonn official who had served in the Wehrmacht at the end of the war told me: "I'm one of those Germans who say the Austrians are finally getting the justice they deserve."

A positive result of the Waldheim affair was that at least some Austrians, particularly younger teachers, began pushing to offer a more honest accounting of their country's recent history. And in the wake of Waldheim's victory, Foreign Minister Peter Jankowitsch argued that "a new kind of sensitivity" had emerged that was producing a period of "soul searching." Lectures and conferences on topics like anti-Semitism proliferated, and Austrian diplomats stepped up their efforts to convince foreign audiences that the country was no bastion of neo-Nazi thinking. This may have been mostly a public relations exercise at first, but it allowed the discussion of issues that had largely been ignored before.

Nonetheless, emotions were still extremely raw on all sides. And in the conflict between Wiesenthal and the World Jewish Congress, those emotions escalated even further after Waldheim's victory.

As Rosenbaum repeatedly pointed out, he had considered Wiesenthal his hero when he was growing up. But during and after the 1986 campaign, he and the leaders of the WJC were furious that, as they saw it, he undercut their assault on Waldheim at every turn. Wiesenthal questioned much of the evidence, arguing that none of it constituted proof that Waldheim was involved in war crimes. But what infuriated his accusers even more were his assertions that the WJC was to blame for the anti-Semitism that had become all too visible in the People's Party campaign.

Venting to Singer about Wiesenthal, Rosenbaum declared: "I hate to say it, but that's the anti-Semites' line: 'The Jews are getting what they deserve.'" Singer was equally enraged. "What's *wrong* with Wiesenthal?" he demanded as he reviewed the Nazi hunter's latest statements. "Somebody oughta remind him: Jews don't cause anti-Semitism; *anti-Semites* cause anti-Semitism." It was a short leap from that to charging that Wiesenthal was, in Singer's words, "in bed with those People's Party pigs"—in effect, defending their candidate.

By the time Waldheim emerged battered but victorious, Rosenbaum wanted to go public with all his pent-up frustrations and accusations. He drafted a response for Singer to an article by Wiesenthal in Vienna's Jewish newspaper *Der Ausweg* where he once again attacked the WJC. "There can be little doubt that it was Mr. Wiesenthal who ensured the electoral victory of Dr. Waldheim," he wrote, adding that whenever more evidence was produced about the candidate "the world's most famous Nazi hunter was there with one or another unlikely 'explanation.'"

Rosenbaum also pointed out that Wiesenthal had rejected the WJC's belated offer to him, after the Waldheim story broke, to examine their documentation. "His whitewashing of Kurt Waldheim will long be a stain on his reputation," he concluded. "He has humiliated himself and embarrassed the Jewish world. For Simon Wiesenthal, we have only pity." Although a colleague toned down his draft before sending it off to *Der Ausweg*, it was never published.

In his subsequent book about the Waldheim affair, Rosenbaum developed an even more elaborate theory, which was spelled out in its title: *Betrayal: The Untold Story of the Kurt Waldheim Investigation and Cover-Up*. He argued that both Waldheim and Wiesenthal were guilty of a cover-up—"each had a secret, and their secrets would have to share the same destiny," he wrote. Wiesenthal's secret, he maintained, was that he had previously absolved Waldheim when he was asked by the Israelis to check him out in 1979. "If one can be guilty of malpractice in the field of Nazi-hunting, this was surely it," he wrote. Which was why he was desperate to discredit the WJC's accusations; otherwise it would be clear that "he had failed so horribly."

Having arrived at that conclusion, Rosenbaum turned much of his book about the Waldheim affair into a scathing denunciation of Wiesenthal's entire career. Picking up on the charges of Mossad chief Isser Harel that Wiesenthal had built his early reputation on false claims of credit for Eichmann's capture, he painted a portrait of a man who "played loosely with the facts of his background" in his autobiographies, inflating both the drama of his wartime experiences and his accomplishments in the postwar period. "Those of us who had actually prosecuted Nazi criminals knew that the myth of the man was far larger than his life," he wrote. Many people, he added, knew that he was "pathetically ineffective" as a Nazi hunter. "But who was daring—or foolish—enough to stand up and say so?"

Rosenbaum had clearly decided to become that someone from then on. He does acknowledge Wiesenthal's critical role in keeping the issue of "unprosecuted, unpursued Nazis" alive during the early days of the Cold War. "Without in particular Simon Wiesenthal's work and Tuvia Friedman's as well, I think the pursuit of justice would have ended sometime in the late 1960s," he told me in 2013. But ever since the Waldheim affair, he has fumed whenever Wiesenthal is characterized as an accomplished Nazi hunter with a legitimate claim to that designation. His anger has never abated.

A variety of factors fed into the Rosenbaum-Wiesenthal conflict, some intensely personal. After he left government service, Martin Mendelsohn, the lawyer who first hired Rosenbaum as an intern at OSI, frequently cooperated with Wiesenthal and the Simon Wiesenthal Center in Los Angeles as he handled other Nazi cases. He ascribed Rosenbaum's anger at Wiesenthal to his disillusionment with his former hero. "He started out idolizing Simon, and when he found out the man had clay feet and was actually a human being not a god, he turned on him," he said. Another former OSI colleague suggested that Rosenbaum felt like a spurned son when Wiesenthal contemptuously dismissed his efforts to build a case against Waldheim. "I think Eli was personally offended the way Wiesenthal treated him like a little kid," he said.

Their clash was also a product of the broader tensions between American and European Jews. In private and in public, Wiesenthal regularly complained about what he saw as the propensity of the WJC and other U.S.-based Jewish organizations to "think they can speak in the name of all Jews." The Americans, he argued, all too often dismiss the concerns of European Jews as insignificant, not understanding how different their situation is from theirs. He attributed the often combative mode of American Jewish activists to "the fact that many American Jews have something akin to a sense of guilt in their subconscious anyway, for not having done enough for the persecuted Jews of Europe during the war." The Waldheim case, he added, "offered them an opportunity to take a demonstrative stance."

Such tensions were at times even visible in the relationship between Wiesenthal and the Simon Wiesenthal Center. Founded in Los Angeles in 1977, it is an independent organization that compensated him for the use of his name, which was critical to its fundraising efforts. Wiesenthal and the center often worked together, but they also had their differences. Rabbi Marvin Hier, the center's founder and dean, recalled more than one phone conversation when Wiesenthal shouted at him: "How can you do that?"

During the Waldheim crisis, Hier was much more publicly critical of the Austrian presidential candidate than Wiesenthal was. It was no accident that, during the fight between Wiesenthal and the WJC, Singer fired off a blunt message to Hier: "TELL WIESENTHAL TO SHUT UP; ENOUGH IS ENOUGH." Hier did argue with Wiesenthal—up to a point. He recalled telling him: "Simon, if we can't lock him up, we should do something to him. He should be embarrassed, he shouldn't be allowed again on a plane." His center came out in support of the decision to put Waldheim on the U.S. Watch List, which Wiesenthal opposed—all of which prompted some real strains in their relationship.

But Hier also pointed out that Wiesenthal was proven right that there was no evidence to pin any specific war crimes on Waldheim. And contrary to Singer's exhortations, he was not about to try to dictate to Wiesenthal, who would not listen anyway, or risk a full break with him. He stressed that Wiesenthal was proud of the center, and the center was proud to be affiliated with a man who had dedicated his life to bringing Nazi criminals to justice. "He was the iconic figure," Hier maintained. The Waldheim affair did not change his view on that score.

One of the ironies of Rosenbaum's and the WJC's insistence that Wiesenthal was an apologist for the new Austrian president was that the Nazi hunter had a long track record of exposing the role of Austrians in the Third Reich. He frequently asserted that Austrians, while constituting less than 10 percent of the population of Nazi Germany, were responsible for about 50 percent of its war crimes; about three-quarters of the commanders of death camps were Austrian, he added.

Most famously, Wiesenthal had repeatedly clashed with Bruno Kreisky, the Socialist leader who served as chancellor from 1970 to 1983, over his lax attitude toward former Nazis. They also disagreed violently about Israel and the Middle East.

Although Kreisky was from a secular Austrian Jewish family, he took on the mantle of a champion of Third World causes, including harsh denunciations of Israel on a regular basis. Kreisky also dismissed the whole idea of the existence of a "Jewish people." As Wiesenthal acidly noted, Kreisky considered himself especially superior to Eastern European Jews like himself. "He does not wish to have anything in common with us," he declared. "It is bad enough for him to be connected with the Jewish people at all—but to be connected with us is intolerable." He speculated that growing up in anti-Semitic Austria, Kreisky chose to try "to prove to those around him that he is not really different from them. . . . A Jew [in Austria] striving for total assimilation must adopt that anti-Jewish attitude."

The biggest clash between Wiesenthal and Kreisky was triggered by the Socialist chancellor's political appointments and alliances. When Kreisky took office in 1970, Wiesenthal denounced him for including four former Nazis as ministers in his government. Later, he also berated him for his ties to Friedrich Peter, the head of the Liberal Party, which was notorious for attracting former Nazis. When Kreisky was leaning toward elevating Peter to the post of vice chancellor, Wiesenthal broke the story that the Liberal leader had served in an SS Einsatzgruppen unit that massacred Jews. Forced to admit that he was part of that unit, Peter denied he had participated in the killings.

Kreisky furiously called Wiesenthal a "Jewish fascist" and a "mafioso," adding that he was "a reactionary and they do exist among Jews, just as there are among us Jews [who are] murderers and whores." In an eerie echo of Wiesenthal's attacks on the WJC a decade later, Kreisky charged that the Nazi hunter was making a living by "telling the world that Austria is anti-Semitic." He also reportedly threatened to close down Wiesenthal's Documentation Center in Vienna. As a final touch, the chancellor resurrected the allegations circulated by the Polish communist government that Wiesenthal had collaborated with the Nazis. Later, he would have to back off that charge in order to get Wiesenthal to drop a libel suit against him.

There was no doubt that Wiesenthal's profound hatred of Kreisky and the Socialists prompted him to favor the People's Party, although he always denied that he was in its camp. But Rosenbaum and others, like Beate Klarsfeld, considered him a staunch supporter. When the Waldheim controversy broke, it wasn't just Beate who sided with the WJC in its attacks on the candidate. As Wiesenthal noted, "on French television Serge Klarsfeld had a real go at me."

But even among those who believed that the WJC was right in marshaling the evidence against Waldheim, there was skepticism about Rosenbaum's charge that Wiesenthal had something to cover up about his role in 1979 when the Israelis asked him to check the U.N. secretary-general's wartime history. Herzstein, the historian the WJC commissioned to conduct his own inquiry into Waldheim's past, noted that the U.S.-controlled Berlin Document Center provided Wiesenthal's contact with a report that indicated Waldheim was never listed as a member of the SS or the Nazi Party. "After carefully studying the reports, Wiesenthal accurately informed the Israelis that there was nothing incriminating in Waldheim's BDC record," he wrote.

Herzstein added that "what Wiesenthal could not know" was that Waldheim had been a member of the SA Cavalry Corps and the Nazi student group. The reason was that those organizations were not included in the checklist of Nazi-related organizations on the Berlin Document Center's report form. Those records were not stored there, as those who had dug into Waldheim's past seven years later discovered. They, too, had struck out at the Berlin Document Center.

Peter Black, who was a historian at OSI at the time and is now the senior historian of the Holocaust Memorial Museum in Washington, praised Rosenbaum's "very credible job" in investigating Waldheim. But he, too, rejected the notion that Wiesenthal attempted a cover-up. "I don't see him in a conspiracy," he said. "I think Wiesenthal's motives were not evil." Black added that Wiesenthal may not have looked "too carefully" at Waldheim's record and "he just thought that Waldheim was like any other number of military officers who were there and sort of stayed out of it." Pointing out that it was only in the late 1980s and 1990s that scholars began examining in more detail "how deeply mired the Wehrmacht was in Nazi crimes" in occupied lands like Greece, Yugoslavia, and the Soviet Union, Black argued that Wiesenthal initially had no reason to view Waldheim's military service as a red flag.

But Rosenbaum has never retreated from his impassioned attacks on Wiesenthal and *his* record. The wounds that were inflicted by the WJC-Wiesenthal firefight during the Waldheim affair have still not healed. In the end, the entire Waldheim affair was as much a battle among the Nazi hunters as it was between them and those who had served the Third Reich.

CHAPTER FIFTEEN

Chasing Ghosts

"At this way station, the innocent people wait, and then when their savager comes, they get to exact a little portion of revenge. God says revenge is good for the soul."

"Babe" Levy, the hero of William Goldman's 1974 bestselling
novel *Marathon Man*, talking to the fictional Auschwitz
SS dentist Christian Szell right before he kills him

If you believed everything you read, Nazi hunters exacted much more than a little portion of revenge. In 2007, for example, Danny Baz, a retired Israeli Air Force colonel, published a purported memoir in French called *Ni oubli ni pardon: Au cœur de la traque du dernier Nazi* (Not Forgiven, Not Forgotten: On the Trail of the Last Nazi); it was followed by the English version called *The Secret Executioners: The Amazing True Story of the Death Squad That Tracked Down and Killed Nazi War Criminals.*

At the time, there was still an ongoing search for Aribert Heim, who was one of the most prominent fugitive Nazis after the war. The Austrian-born doctor had served in Mauthausen, fully earning his nickname "Dr. Death." He killed Jews by injecting gasoline and other poisonous substances into their hearts; he also carried out particularly sadistic medical experiments, including cutting open healthy prisoners and removing their organs, leaving them to die on the operating table. As a result, he was sought by everyone from the German government to the Simon Wiesenthal Center, which had put him at the top of its most wanted list. But Baz made a startling claim: they had been chasing a ghost for a quarter of a century.

According to Baz's account, he had been part of a secret all-Jewish death squad that executed Heim in 1982. Dubbed "the Owl," the group was started by wealthy Holocaust survivors and made up of highly trained former U.S. and Israeli members of a variety of security services. "The names of my companions in arms have been disguised, in order not to break the confidentiality of our organization, which benefitted from a limitless budget, worthy of the largest secret services," he wrote. "This book recounts facts that are rigorously true."

From there, he spun a dramatic tale. The Owl was responsible for capturing and killing dozens of Nazi war criminals, Baz claimed, but their biggest challenge was to find Heim and capture him alive. After that, he would be made to face a tribunal of Holocaust survivors before he would be executed. "We want the rats to face their victims before they die," one longtime member of the Owl explained to Baz. It turned out that Heim was hiding in the United States, not anywhere more exotic as was frequently reported, and the avengers tracked him in upstate New York, then to Canada, kidnapping him from a hospital in Montreal; finally, they delivered him to other members of the Owl in California, who conducted the tribunal and carried out the execution.

And this was far from the only story about a prominent Nazi war criminal who supposedly was killed in complete secrecy. Martin Bormann, Hitler's powerful personal secretary and the head of the Nazi Party Chancellery, had disappeared from Hitler's Berlin bunker after the Führer committed suicide. The International Military Tribunal in Nuremberg sentenced twelve top Nazis to death; Bormann was the only one who was sentenced in absentia. His apparent vanishing act triggered contradictory reports about whether he had survived. There were claims that he had either been killed or ended his life by biting into a cyanide capsule shortly after he emerged from the bunker. As in Heim's case, there were also numerous reported sightings of Bormann in northern Italy, Chile, Argentina, and Brazil, among other locations. But in 1970, the sensationalist *News of the World* serialized an account by Ronald Gray, a former British Army intelligence agent, which was subsequently published as a book with the title *I Killed Martin Bormann!*

"Bormann is dead, his body riddled by a burst from a Sten gun," he wrote. "And it was my finger that pulled the trigger." Gray described how he was stationed in northern Germany after the war, close to the Danish border. When he was approached by a mysterious German contact to smuggle someone across the border for 50,000 kroner (then $8,400) in March 1946, he agreed, figuring that he would unmask part of the network that was providing safe passage to Nazi war criminals out of the country. Once he was in his military van, he realized that his passenger was Bormann. It was late evening, but there was enough moonlight to confirm the identification when he got him to his destination on the Danish side of the border and they came to a stop opposite two men waiting for them. Suddenly, Bormann started running to his greeting party—and Gray immediately realized he had been set up for an ambush. He opened fire and watched Bormann go down. The two men who had been waiting let loose with a volley of shots in his direction.

Gray dropped to the ground, pretending to be dead. From that position, he caught sight of the men as they dragged Bormann's lifeless body away. Shadowing them, he watched them take the body out on a fjord in a small rowboat; about forty yards offshore they dropped it into the water. "From the size of the splash, I guessed that Bormann's two compatriots had weighted his body with something, perhaps chains," he wrote. "It struck me that the boat—and the chains—might have been meant for me."

Gray's account did not put an end to other versions of the Bormann story. In 1974, the military historian and bestselling author Ladislas Farago published *Aftermath: Martin Bormann and the Fourth Reich*. He claimed to have tracked down Bormann to a hospital in southwestern Bolivia after dispensing numerous bribes to various contacts and guards on the Peruvian-Bolivian border. All of this effort resulted in a brief sighting of the man, he insisted. "When I was taken into his room for what we agreed would be a five-minute visit . . . I saw a little old man in a big bed with freshly laundered sheets, his head propped up by three big downy pillows, looking at me with vacant eyes, mumbling words to himself," he wrote. Bormann's only purported words to his visitor: "Dammit, don't you see I'm an old man? So why don't you let me die in peace?"

Such accounts provided plenty of fodder for the tabloids and sometimes even serious newspapers, but there was just one problem: they were all products of their authors' fervid imaginations, instead of the "true stories" they were always billed as. In Heim's case, *The New York Times* and the German television station ZDF produced convincing evidence that Dr. Death had lived in Cairo after the war, converted to Islam, and taken the name of Tarek Hussein Farid. The evidence consisted of a briefcaseful of his correspondence, medical and financial records, and an article about the search for him. Both names—Heim and Farid—appeared on these documents, and the birthday listed was June 28, 1914, matching Heim's. A death certificate showed that Farid died in 1992, a decade after he was supposedly executed by Baz's group of avengers.

In an interview with the *Times*, Rüdiger Heim, Aribert's son, not only confirmed his father's identity ("Tarek Hussein Farid is the name my father took when he converted to Islam," he said), but revealed that he was visiting him in Cairo when he died of rectal cancer. The two *Times* reporters on the story, Nicholas Kulish and Souad Mekhennet, subsequently wrote a book providing a detailed account of Heim's postwar existence in Germany, where he continued to work as a doctor in the spa town of Baden-Baden until 1962, and then his flight to Egypt when it looked like the authorities were finally about to arrest him. The authors benefited from the cooperation of his son, other relatives, and the Egyptians who knew him by his new name.

Among Heim's writings, they found repeated references to Wiesenthal, whom the fugitive saw as the orchestrator of the Zionist plot to track him down. The Nazi hunter failed in that quest, but as far as Heim was concerned, he was the "absolute dominator of all German agencies." If nothing else, this demonstrated that Heim—and, more than likely, other fugitive war criminals—feared Wiesenthal and believed in his popular image as an almost all-powerful avenger. This was certainly an exaggeration, but it illustrated one of Wiesenthal's key strengths: he was able to fulfill part of his mission, instilling fear in the hunted, by playing on such inflated views of his role.

As for Bormann, Gray's tale of shooting him and Farago's claim that he had visited him in Bolivia were also fully discredited. The purported remains of Bormann had been found at a Berlin construction site in 1972, but it was only in 1998 that DNA testing provided a clear match with a relative of the once powerful Nazi. The conclusion was that he had died on May 2, 1945, shortly after leaving Hitler's bunker as Red Army troops were taking the city. In the intervening years, there had been even more claims of Bormann sightings, usually in South America.

Baz had been right that in some cases the Nazi hunters had been chasing ghosts, but that was usually the result of a lack of reliable information combined with guesswork. At least they had not concocted tall tales of vengeance killings. But in terms of the popular culture, such tales left their mark, contributing to the popular misconception that the script for every Nazi hunting adventure could have been written in Hollywood.

Normally, the hunt for Nazi war criminals—whether it was by government or private investigators—proceeded according to much slower-paced scripts, especially when seemingly interminable legal battles were involved. And they certainly did not feature the kind of dramatic shootouts or other violent confrontations that were the staple of the fabricated "true stories." But there were the rare exceptions. In those cases, life appeared to imitate fiction, with avengers striking from the shadows.

One of the villains in Howard Blum's 1977 groundbreaking book *Wanted! The Search for Nazis in America* was Tscherim Soobzokov, who had grown up as part of the Circassian minority in the Soviet Union's North Caucasus. At first glance, "Tom" Soobzokov, as he was known in his hometown of Paterson, New Jersey, was a typical American success story. According to an article in the *The Paterson News*, when the Germans captured the Caucasus in 1942, he was shipped "as a semi-forced laborer to Rumania." At the end of the war, he joined other Circassian exiles in Jordan, before coming to the United States in 1955. Settling in Paterson, he started working at a car wash, but quickly graduated to organizing for the Teamsters Union and then the local Democratic Party, and landing a job as Passaic County's chief purchasing inspector. He was the go-to guy to get things done, especially among his fellow immigrants from the Caucasus. He was smooth, well connected, and increasingly prosperous.

But some of his fellow Circassian immigrants were not buying either his life story or his claims to represent them. His name had appeared on the list of Nazi war criminals in the United States that ended up in the hands of Immigration and Naturalization Service investigator Anthony DeVito in the early 1970s, and his neighbors in Paterson were eager to explain why. Kassim Chuako, one of the Circassians quoted by Blum, said that Soobzokov had immediately offered his services to the German troops when they arrived in their part of the Caucasus. "We saw him going into the villages with the Germans and rounding up people—Communists and Jews," he declared. "I saw him with the SS troops that took people away." Others added that they saw him wearing an SS uniform in Romania, where he tried to recruit refugees for an SS-sponsored Caucasian military unit.

Although he served in the Waffen SS, the fighting arm of the SS, as late as 1945, Soobzokov had no problem presenting himself as a normal war refugee once the conflict ended. In 1947, he was part of a group of Circassians who emigrated from Italy to Jordan, where he worked as an agricultural engineer. Soon, he had a new employer: the CIA. The agency was eager to use him to identify fellow Circassians who could be sent undercover into the Soviet Union, and he was happy to oblige.

Soobzokov's new bosses were under few illusions about his background. "Subject has consistent and pronounced reactions to all questions regarding war crimes, and is, no doubt, hiding a number of activities from us at this point," one CIA official reported in 1953. Still, it was clear that the agency's priority was to make the best use of his services, whatever he was hiding. After Soobzokov arrived in the United States in 1955, he kept doing part-time jobs for the CIA. But his wildly inconsistent stories led another CIA official to conclude that he was "an incorrigible fabricator," and he was dropped by the agency in 1960.

Nonetheless, when the INS began investigating his background in the 1970s, a senior CIA official claimed that, while there were "unresolved doubts" about him, he had performed "useful service" for the United States, and the agency had never found any concrete evidence that he was involved in war crimes. This led the INS to drop the investigation. When the Justice Department's newly formed Office of Special Investigations tried to take up his case in 1980, its investigators discovered that Soobzokov had listed some of his Nazi affiliations when he applied for a U.S. visa. Since OSI's strategy was to seek denaturalization of alleged war criminals by demonstrating that they had lied to gain admission to the country, they reluctantly backed off. His admissions, however incomplete, were enough to undercut any effort to argue that he had covered up his past.

Despite all the controversy surrounding him, it looked like Soobzokov had emerged battered but victorious. He even pursued a libel suit against Howard Blum for what he had written about him in *Wanted!*, and the author felt compelled to settle out of court—although he did not retract anything he had written.

On August 15, 1985, a pipe bomb exploded outside Soobzokov's house in Paterson. The man who had been at the center of so much controversy was severely injured and died of his wounds on September 6. The FBI later claimed that the Jewish Defense League may have been responsible, but the case was never solved.

Eight years later, there was another killing that could have been ripped from the pages of a thriller. This time the setting was a Parisian apartment in the chic 16th arrondissement, and the victim was René Bousquet, the eighty-four-year-old former police chief who had orchestrated the deportation of Jews from occupied France, including thousands of children. Although Bousquet had been tried after the war, he only received a suspended sentence, which was justified on the grounds that he had supposedly helped the Resistance. He went on to a successful career in business, and his enthusiastic participation in the Holocaust appeared to be largely forgotten. Even after his past was dug up again as part of France's efforts to confront its legacy of collaboration and there were efforts to bring new charges against him, he remained unapologetic and seemingly confident that he had nothing to fear. He continued to walk his dog twice a day in the Bois de Boulogne.

On June 8, 1993, a man called Christian Didier arrived at Bousquet's apartment, claiming that he was about to serve him court documents. When the former police chief opened the door, as Didier told French TV crews later, he "pulled out the revolver and fired at point-blank range." Although he hit his target, Bousquet ran toward him. "The guy had incredible energy," he continued. "I fired a second time and he kept coming at me. I fired a third time and he started to stagger. The fourth time I got him in the head or the neck and he fell with blood falling out of him."

Didier escaped and then convened the TV crews to make his confession. But he was anything but apologetic. Bousquet "incarnated evil" and his act was "like killing a serpent," he declared; he added that he "incarnated good." In reality, the self-described frustrated author appeared to be motivated by the desire to achieve fame at any price. He had tried earlier to kill Klaus Barbie, broken into the gardens of the French presidential palace, and sought to force his way into TV studios. He had spent time in a psychiatric hospital, and, after killing Bousquet was sentenced to ten years in prison. When he was released after serving half of that sentence, he expressed regret for his deed, but added: "If I had killed him fifty years ago, I would have received a medal." He also altered his explanation of his motive, offering a new twisted logic. "I thought that by killing Bousquet, I would kill the evil in me," he said.

For Serge Klarsfeld and others who had hoped to make Bousquet face a new trial, the assassination was a major setback. "Jews wanted justice not vengeance," he said. Although Klarsfeld had once considered killing Barbie, his preference was always to bring him to trial and convict him, which was exactly what happened. This served the cause of justice, and helped educate the public further about the Holocaust. A trial of Bousquet would have had the added benefit of offering an object lesson on how French collaborators had actively participated in the crimes of the Germans. All of which meant that, unlike in Hollywood movies, when the gunslinger shot the bad guy no one applauded. In this case, justice had been denied.

In 1985, the on-again, off-again hunt for Josef Mengele, the Auschwitz SS doctor known as "the Angel of Death" who had been implanted firmly in the popular imagination as the embodiment of evil by the bestselling novel and hit movie *The Boys from Brazil*, suddenly revived with new urgency. The fugitive had become a Paraguayan citizen a quarter of a century earlier, but his exact whereabouts were a source of constant speculation amid reported sightings in several Latin American and European countries, including West Germany. Under mounting international pressure, Paraguay had stripped Mengele of his citizenship in 1979, and President Alfredo Stroessner, the country's right-wing dictator, claimed that his regime did not know anything more about him. But none of Mengele's pursuers believed him—and they shared one key assumption. When I filed my first report about his case from Bonn to my editors in New York on April 16, 1985, I wrote: "That Mengele is still alive is not disputed by anyone."

Wiesenthal was constantly reporting new alleged leads and near misses at tracking him down. While he was sometimes accused of indiscriminately spreading rumors, he was hardly alone in his eagerness to keep Mengele in the news—or to see the clues as presenting clear evidence to justify an intensified search. In May, Fritz Steinacker, a lawyer in Frankfurt, went beyond his usual "no comment" to declare: "Yes, I have represented Mengele and I still do represent him." Despite the denials of Mengele's son Rolf and other relatives in his Bavarian hometown of Günzburg where the family farm machinery business still prospered, Wiesenthal was convinced they were fully aware "all the time where he was, even today," as he told me. Pointing out that the family continued to say "no comment" to all the reports about Mengele, he insisted that this meant that he was still alive and on the run. "When they can say the man is dead, the embarrassment will be finished," he said.

Serge and Beate Klarsfeld were similarly convinced, and Beate traveled to Paraguay to protest the government's role there. "Mengele is in Paraguay under the protection of President Stroessner," Serge flatly asserted. Wiesenthal, the Simon Wiesenthal Center in Los Angeles, the Klarsfelds, the West German and Israeli governments, and others offered numerous rewards for the Auschwitz doctor's capture that totaled more than $3.4 million by May 1985. Hans-Eberhard Klein, the Frankfurt prosecutor who was in charge of West Germany's search for Mengele, explained that "we have folders and folders of tips" from people who claimed to have seen him, but "none of them have produced success." That was why West Germany and others were upping the rewards they were offering, he explained. Also in May, Klein and members of his team met with U.S. and Israeli officials in Frankfurt to coordinate the efforts of their three countries.

But as everyone involved in the chase would learn a month later, at that point they, too, had all been chasing a ghost for six years: Mengele had drowned while swimming off a beach in Bertioga, Brazil, in 1979, probably after suffering a stroke. His remains had been found in a grave near São Paulo, and a forensic team had made what was widely accepted as conclusive identification. Rolf Mengele finally admitted what Wiesenthal and others had suspected all along: the family had not only been in touch with his father, he had visited him in Brazil in 1977. He also said he returned to Brazil two years later "to confirm the circumstances of his death." In 1992, DNA testing offered final confirmation. Mengele, who was sixty-seven at the time he drowned, had managed to elude justice and deceive his pursuers even in death.

While solving the riddle of his fate, the discovery still left unanswered the question how the most hunted man since Eichmann had succeeded in doing so. His name had surfaced during the International Military Tribunal's case against the top Nazis at Nuremberg. Testifying as a witness, Auschwitz commandant Rudolf Höss specifically mentioned "experiments on twins by SS medical officer Dr. Mengele."

Auschwitz survivors later offered detailed accounts of his outsized role in the death and torment of the prisoners in the camp. Eagerly meeting the incoming trains, he participated regularly in the selection process, sending thousands to their deaths in the gas chambers immediately upon arrival. He often spared twins at first, so that he could obsessively conduct experiments on them. He injected dyes into the eyes of babies and children to change their color, and performed multiple blood transfusions and spinal cord taps. He tested the endurance of other prisoners by, in the case of Polish nuns, exposing them to massive X-ray doses that burned them. He also operated on sexual organs, transferred typhus and other diseases to healthy prisoners, and extracted bone marrow. In a report, a superior officer praised him for his "valuable contribution in the field of anthropology by using the scientific materials at his disposal." Mengele personally executed numerous prisoners who managed to survive his experiments, thus disposing of the leftover "scientific materials."

According to Robert Kempner, the German Jewish lawyer who left his homeland in 1935 and returned as a member of the U.S. prosecution team at Nuremberg, Mengele's name came up in relation to the "Doctors Trial" in 1947, the first of the follow-on trials after the International Military Tribunal. "We started the search for Mengele in Nuremberg," he told me in 1985. "They tried to get him but they couldn't find him in Germany. He was already underground somewhere." He added that Mengele had, in fact, been in U.S. custody immediately after the war, but his jailers did not know who he was. The prisoner, who was incredibly vain, had managed to convince the SS that he did not need the standard SS tattoo since he did not want to mar his appearance; as a result, the Americans did not spot him for what he was.

Although Mengele was already on war criminal lists, Kempner was not surprised that someone who had been part of the huge roundups by U.S. troops quickly slipped free during that chaotic period. "These fellows just disappeared," he said. "It was not too difficult. The real criminals were just smarter than our boys." Kempner was convinced that, unlike Klaus Barbie, Mengele cut no deals with the Americans to do so. "He was an independent fellow," he said. "In contrast to many others, he was a man of means."

Because of the Barbie case, the U.S. Justice Department was particularly eager to examine the record on that score once Mengele's remains were found. The Office of Special Investigations conducted another exhaustive study, which was finally published in 1992. While it noted that Mengele had lived under an alias as a farmhand in the U.S. occupation zone until he made his way to South America in 1949, it concluded: "Mengele fled Europe without U.S. assistance or knowledge. There is no evidence that he ever had a relationship with U.S. intelligence."

Mengele initially lived in Buenos Aires, at one point in Olivos, the same suburb where Eichmann resided. When the Israelis began their operation to kidnap Eichmann, Isser Harel, the Mossad chief, had heard that Mengele might be there, although he stressed that the information was unconfirmed. His feelings about the Auschwitz doctor were clear. "Of all the evil figures who played principal parts in the macabre attempt to wipe out the Jewish people, he was conspicuous for his abominable enjoyment of his role as death's messenger," he noted. When a question came up about the cost of the Eichmann operation, he told one member of his team: "To make the investment more worthwhile, we'll try to bring Mengele with us as well."

While Harel was eager to find Mengele, he did not want to do anything "that might endanger our primary objective, Operation Eichmann," as he put it. His team in Buenos Aires was fully occupied shadowing their quarry, arranging safe houses and transportation, and planning both the kidnapping and its aftermath. They were aware that Mengele could become a target as well, but they agreed with the decision to focus on their main target first. "None of us showed any enthusiasm for the Mengele operation," recalled Zvi Aharoni, a key member of the Eichmann team who was slated to be his interrogator after the kidnapping. "This certainly had nothing to do with a lack of courage. We only feared that such a questionable double-Rambo action would endanger the success of 'Operation Eichmann.'" According to him, Harel was the most anxious to get Mengele, and it was Rafi Eitan, the field leader of the operation, who initially talked him out of taking any steps in that direction, invoking the Hebrew saying: "Try to catch a lot—and you will catch nothing."

As soon as the Israelis had seized Eichmann, though, Harel pressed Aharoni to question him about Mengele. At first, the captive refused to reveal anything, but then he admitted that he had met Mengele once in a restaurant in Buenos Aires, claiming it was a chance encounter. He did not know Mengele's address, he said, but indicated that he had mentioned a guesthouse in Olivos owned by a German woman. Aharoni believed him, but, as he recalled, Harel did not. "He is lying to you!" Harel said. "He knows where Mengele is!" As Aharoni saw it, the Mossad chief "seemed possessed."

In fact, Mengele had left Argentina for Paraguay the previous year after West Germany issued a warrant for his arrest. If he had any doubts that he should retreat to a country that was even more likely to offer protection to Nazi war criminals than Argentina, Eichmann's kidnapping would have dispelled them completely. But Paraguay did not feel safe either. After the successful kidnapping of Eichmann, Harel dispatched Aharoni and other agents to look for him in several Latin American countries. With the help of other former Nazis who had settled in the area, Mengele had moved to a farm near São Paulo, working as a farmhand again but feeling mawkishly sorry for himself—especially when he learned that West German newspapers were reminding readers of his ghoulish record at Auschwitz.

"As you can see, my present mood is pretty bad, especially since I have had to deal these last weeks with this nonsense about attempting to strip bodies in B [Auschwitz-Birkenau]," he wrote in his diary. "In this mood one finds no joy in a radiant sunny sky. One is reduced to being a miserable creature without love for life or substance."

Aharoni claimed that in 1962, thanks to payoffs to one of Mengele's contacts in South America, he was pointed in the direction of Wolfgang Gerhard, a Nazi living near São Paulo who had provided shelter for Mengele. "We did not know at the time how close we already were to our target," he wrote. He began scouting the area, and in retrospect believed he may have caught a glimpse of Mengele with two other men on a jungle path. But to the surprise of Aharoni and the other agents assigned to the case, Harel abruptly recalled them to deal with a new high-priority project: to search for an eight-year-old boy who had been smuggled out of Israel by religious extremists in defiance of a court order. The agents found the boy in New York and brought him back to his mother. Afterward, they were not sent back to South America.

A shift in leadership of the Mossad accounted for the dwindling interest in the search for Mengele. When Harel stepped down in March 1963, he was replaced by Meir Amit. The new chief was soon preoccupied with preparations for the next looming conflict with Israel's Arab neighbors, the 1967 Six Day War. "We gave little weight to finding Mengele so we didn't find Mengele," explained Eitan, who had led the Eichmann operation and continued to work for the Mossad after the change at the top. Once again, Nazi hunting was no longer a priority.

When Mengele's body was discovered in 1985, his son Rolf offered an explanation for why his father was never caught. "His house was small and extremely poor . . . so small that no one suspected him," he told the West German magazine *Bunte*. Because he came from a wealthy family, the people on his trail "were looking for a man who lived in a white villa by the sea, with a Mercedes, protected by bodyguards and Alsatian dogs," he added. The implication: it was almost as if they imagined they would encounter the Mengele portrayed by Gregory Peck in *The Boys from Brazil*.

Rolf offered no apology for his long silence, even after he knew his father had died. "I have remained silent until now out of consideration for the people who were in contact with my father for 30 years," he declared. His father had been equally unrepentant about his crimes. In a letter to Rolf, he wrote: "I do not have the slightest reason to try to justify or excuse whatever decisions, actions or behavior of mine."

The fact that, as Rolf finally admitted, the family and so many others had helped Mengele elude justice for all those years also raised questions about the West German investigation led by Frankfurt prosecutor Klein. No search warrants had been issued for the homes or businesses of Mengele family members, and there appeared to have been little effort to question them. According to Dieter Mengele, a nephew of the fugitive, he was never approached by the prosecutor. Klein asserted that the family had been "only" partly placed under surveillance, whatever that meant.

When the Justice Department's Office of Special Investigations issued its report on Mengele in 1992, it conceded the obvious. "That Ausch-witz's 'Angel of Death' was allowed to perpetrate his crimes and to die an old man's death in Brazil is evidence of failure," it concluded. But it also pointed out that West Germany, Israel, and the United States belatedly had mounted "an unprecedented worldwide search," indicating that they were not content with that failure. More significantly, "the many years he consequently spent hiding in near squalor in Brazil, tortured by his fear that Israeli agents were on the verge of capturing him, arguably provided a kind of rough, albeit inadequate, 'justice.'" He paid the price, the report added, in the sense that he was "transformed into a prisoner of his own nightmare of capture."

Mengele had escaped the Nazi hunters, but he had not escaped their lengthening shadows.

CHAPTER SIXTEEN

Full Circle

"Survival is a privilege that entails obligations. I am forever asking myself what I can do for those who have not survived."

Simon Wiesenthal

In April 1994, an ABC News camera crew carefully staked out their man. They had located Erich Priebke in San Carlos de Bariloche, an Argentine resort city in the foothills of the Andes where nineteenth-century German immigrants had constructed Alpine houses. Like many Nazis implicated in mass killings, the former SS captain had fled Europe after the war and led a seemingly normal existence ever since. He ran a delicatessen and even traveled back to Europe on occasion, never bothering to change his name. His past looked to be well behind him—until the day he was confronted by ABC's pugnacious reporter Sam Donaldson as the camera rolled.

Priebke's claim to infamy was his role in organizing the execution of 335 men and boys, including seventy-five Jews, in the Ardeatine Caves on the outskirts of Rome on March 24, 1944. Italian partisans had killed thirty-three Germans earlier, and Herbert Kappler, the Rome Gestapo chief, ordered the massacre on the principle that ten Italians should die for every dead German. Unlike Priebke, Kappler did not get out of Italy in time, and he was given a life sentence; but in 1977 he was sprung from a military hospital and lived as a free man for a year before his death. There were also reports that Priebke had participated in the deportation of Italian Jews to Auschwitz.

"Mr. Priebke, Sam Donaldson of American television," the reporter called out, approaching Priebke on the street as he was about to get into his car. "You were in the Gestapo in Rome in 1944, were you not?"

Priebke did not appear unduly rattled at first—and he made no effort to pretend he was not involved in the executions. "Yes, in Rome, yes," he said, speaking accented but good English. "You know the communists blew up a group of our German soldiers. For every German soldier ten Italians had to die."

Wearing a polo shirt, windbreaker, and a Bavarian hat, Priebke looked like just another German who had decided to make his home in the picturesque town.

"Civilians?" Donaldson asked.

Maintaining his level tone but beginning to show some discomfort, Priebke responded that they were "mostly terrorists."

"But children were killed," the reporter pressed on.

"No," Priebke insisted. When Donaldson pointed out that fourteen-year-old boys were killed, he shook his head and repeated, "No."

"But why did you shoot them? They had done nothing."

"You know that was our order. You know that in the war that kind of thing happens." By this time, Priebke looked eager to cut things off.

"You were just following orders?"

"Yes, of course, but I didn't shoot anybody."

Donaldson said again that he had killed civilians in the cave, and again Priebke protested: "No, no, no."

After another round on the issue of orders, Donaldson declared: "But orders are not an excuse."

Priebke was visibly indignant at the American reporter's seeming inability to understand how things worked. He had had to carry out orders, he reiterated. "At that time an order was an order."

"And civilians died," Donaldson followed up.

"And civilians died," Priebke conceded. "Many civilians died on all parts of the world [*sic*] and still they are dying." With a nervous smile and flicking his head back and forth, he added: "You live in this time, but we lived in 1933," referring to the year Hitler took power. "Can you understand that? Whole Germany was . . . Nazi. We didn't commit a crime. We did what they ordered us. That was not a crime."

Donaldson just kept coming at him, asking if he had deported Jews to concentration camps.

Priebke shook his head: "Jews, no, nobody . . . I was never against Jews. I was from Berlin. We lived together in Berlin with many Jews. No, I didn't."

With that, he got into his car and slammed the door. His final words to his pursuer were delivered through his open window: "You are not a gentleman."

It was the reporter's turn to laugh sardonically as Priebke drove off. "*I* am not a gentleman," he repeated.

Born in 1934, Donaldson was much too young to have fought in World War II, but he was always fascinated by that conflict, and how Hitler managed to mesmerize the German people. At ABC, he repeatedly watched Leni Riefenstahl's *Triumph of the Will* with interns to study what he considered to be "the first real propaganda film."

By the time that his producer Harry Phillips had tracked Priebke down and run surveillance on him for about two weeks before setting up the camera ambush, Donaldson was convinced that public interest in Nazis and their crimes was waning. But Donaldson and Phillips's story reverberated around the globe, and led to the first serious push to bring Priebke to justice. Argentina extradited him to Italy in 1995, and a major legal battle followed. At first a military tribunal ruled that he should be freed on what amounted to a technicality, but he was rearrested, tried again, and sentenced to life in 1998. Because of his advanced years, he was kept under house arrest in Rome, where he died at age one hundred in 2013.

The Catholic Church refused to hold a public funeral for him in Rome, and neither Argentina nor Germany was ready to provide that service either. It was left to the Society of St. Pius X, a splinter Catholic group that opposes the reforms in the Church in recent decades and has voiced doubts about the Holocaust, to organize the funeral in a church in Albano Laziale, a tiny hilltop town south of the capital. As the hearse moved through the streets, riot police did their best to restrain angry protesters who pounded the vehicle.

Priebke had remained defiant till the end, sticking with the line that he had only done his duty. Except in one respect: instead of killing 330 Italians as the 10:1 ratio required, he admitted they had rounded up 335 people, which meant that five more were killed than required. Apparently Priebke had added the five extra names when he was compiling the execution lists. "It went wrong," he told a reporter for the German newspaper *Süddeutsche Zeitung*. But it was clear that he considered that a minor glitch—basically an accounting error that could not be reversed—in an otherwise smooth operation, which reportedly involved leading the victims, their hands tied behind them, to the caves. They were then forced to kneel and shot in the back of the neck.

Looking back at his long career in television, Donaldson said he was particularly proud of the Priebke story. "When people have asked me over the years what was *the* one interview, expecting me to say Reagan or Sadat or something like that, I would tell them about Priebke," he said, calling it "the most important and interesting piece I did."

While journalists were not Nazi hunters per se, the credo of the hunters had clearly rubbed off on Donaldson, as it did on some of his colleagues who pursued similar stories. These were stories that they felt mattered not just because of the headlines they generated. As Donaldson put it, "I believe in the old idea that if you don't keep the memory of these things alive for future generations, Santayana's dictum proves correct: if you do not remember history, you're doomed to repeat it."

In most cases, journalists covered whatever the Nazi hunters discovered or followed up on their tips, including the subsequent legal repercussions. In Priebke's case, Donaldson's dramatic on-the-street interview was the result of journalistic sleuthing rather than any breakthroughs by the Nazi hunters themselves. When the interview aired, it sealed the former SS captain's fate, ending his comfortable life in Argentina and leading to his extradition and sentencing.

The year 2015 marked the seventieth anniversary of the liberation of Auschwitz and other concentration camps, and of the end of the war that produced the most astronomical body count in history. It was hardly surprising that there were fewer and fewer Nazi war criminals to be pursued and tried. The senior officers were probably all gone. A concentration camp guard who had been twenty in 1945 would have been ninety by then, which meant that inevitably the last cases involved junior personnel. This prompted disputes even among the Nazi hunters about the value of those remaining cases, at a time that the saga of those hunters was drawing to a close.

Ironically, one of the oldest cases of just such a lowly concentration camp guard took some startling new twists in the early part of this century, revising the rules of the game for whatever perpetrators still remained. It played out over several decades in the United States, Israel, and Germany, sparking controversy every step of the way. And even when the ninety-one-year-old retired autoworker from Cleveland at the center of the case, John Demjanjuk, died in a nursing home in Germany in 2012, it left unanswered questions about the broader issues triggered by the successive proceedings against him.

Only the earliest part of Demjanjuk's story is beyond dispute. Like so many others caught in the upheavals of the twentieth century, he had the misfortune of growing up in a region that would quickly feel the brunt of the murderous policies of both Stalin and Hitler. Born in a tiny village near Kiev in 1920, Iwan Demjanjuk (he changed his first name to John when he became a U.S. citizen) only had four years of schooling before he found himself working on a collective farm. When Stalin unleashed his campaign to destroy all Ukrainian opposition to forced collectivization in the early 1930s, the Soviet leader triggered a famine that cost millions of lives. Demjanjuk and his family barely survived. When Hitler's armies invaded the Soviet Union, he was drafted into the Red Army, seriously wounded, and, after a long recovery, returned to the fighting. In 1942, he was captured by the Germans, joining the ranks of Soviet POWs, many of whom quickly succumbed to brutal treatment, starvation, and disease.

As Stalin saw it, all the soldiers who were captured by the Germans were "traitors who had fled abroad"; they were to be punished immediately upon their return, and, in the meantime, their families were to be punished as well. Given those circumstances and the harsh conditions they had endured before the war under Soviet rule, it was hardly surprising that some POWs decided that they were better off casting their lot with their captors to survive. They responded to calls for "volunteers" to serve as camp guards or later as soldiers in the Russian Liberation Army, commanded by General Andrei Vlasov, an early Soviet hero of the war who switched sides after his capture. Vlasov claimed his goal was to topple Stalin, not serve Hitler, but his action meant that he was ready to fight alongside the German invaders.

According to Demjanjuk, he served first in an all-Ukrainian unit of the Waffen SS, which meant getting a tattoo of his blood type on his upper arm, and then in Vlasov's Russian Liberation Army. But he said he never saw action at the end of the war, and managed to keep his background secret during his time in a displaced persons camp in Germany afterward. He thus avoided the forced repatriation of Vlasov's men to their homeland, where their leader and many of his followers were promptly executed. He married a fellow Ukrainian in the DP camp, and found work as a driver for the U.S. Army.

Applying for refugee status, he invented a story about working as a farmer for much of the war in Sobibor, a Polish village that became infamous because of the death camp the Germans set up there. Demjanjuk insisted that he only picked this particular village because many Ukrainians lived there. In 1952, he settled in the United States with his wife and daughter. He had two more children, and fit in well with the Ukrainian exile community in Cleveland, where he was seen as a staunchly anticommunist Christian dedicated to freeing his native land from Soviet oppression.

But in 1975 Michael Hanusiak, a former member of the U.S. Communist Party who was the editor of the *Ukrainian Daily News*, put together a list of seventy alleged Ukrainian war criminals in the United States. One of them was Demjanjuk, who was identified as an SS guard in Sobibor. Both the FBI and the Ukrainian community viewed Hanusiak's paper as a highly suspect source that channeled Soviet disinformation. But the INS, which was already under pressure from Congresswoman Elizabeth Holtzman for failing to do anything about most of the Nazi war criminals living in the United States, began making inquiries. Its investigator sent photos of Demjanjuk and several other suspected war criminals to Israel, all taken when they were young. The idea was to see if those who had survived the camps remembered any of the faces in the photo spreads presented to them.

Miriam Radiwker, a Ukrainian-born police investigator who had worked in the Soviet Union and Poland before immigrating to Israel, showed the photos to camp survivors. When she brought in Treblinka survivors to see if they could identify another suspect in the spread, one of them pointed to Demjanjuk's picture and exclaimed: "Iwan, Iwan from Treblinka, Iwan Grozny." The latter term meant "Ivan the Terrible," the designation for a guard who operated the gas chambers and reveled in beating, whipping, and shooting prisoners. Since the information the Americans had sent indicated that Demjanjuk was a guard at Sobibor not Treblinka, Radiwker was both startled and skeptical.

But then two other Treblinka survivors picked out Demjanjuk's picture and identified him as Ivan the Terrible, one with certainty and the other with a cautionary note that he could not be completely sure since the photo was not from the same period as Demjanjuk's alleged service in the camp. While their physical descriptions of Ivan the Terrible suggested a close match with Demjanjuk, they were not perfect, especially when it came to memories of his height.

Radiwker reported her findings to the Americans, who were left to sort them out. In 1977, the U.S. attorney's office in Cleveland formally charged Demjanjuk, claiming that he was the Treblinka guard known as Ivan the Terrible. The Justice Department's Office of Special Investigations, which was launched in 1979, was quick to take up the case. Since Treblinka's records were destroyed by the Germans, one of its investigators began searching for documents from Trawniki, the training camp for Soviet POWs who were destined to become SS guards. On the assumption that the records were in Soviet hands, he made an inquiry through the U.S. embassy in Moscow. In early 1980, the Soviet embassy in Washington sent over an envelope to OSI containing a copy of an SS identity card in the name of Iwan Demjanjuk. The birth date and his father's name were correct. The card was also featured in some Ukrainian newspapers.

Allan Ryan, who had joined OSI as deputy director, and his team compared the photo on the card to Demjanjuk's 1951 photo on his U.S. visa application. "There was no doubt that the two photos were of the same man," he concluded. Although the card indicated that Demjanjuk had been posted to Sobibor and made no mention of Treblinka, Ryan concluded they had their man. "You son of a bitch," he recalled thinking. "We've got you."

But not everyone was convinced the government was making the right case. The *Ukrainian Daily News* had reported earlier that a former Ukrainian SS guard, who had served a long prison sentence in the Soviet Union and then remained in Siberia, claimed he had served with Demjanjuk in Sobibor, not Treblinka. George Parker, a Justice Department attorney who had worked on the Demjanjuk case from the beginning, was troubled enough by the inconsistencies to write a memo to OSI Director Walter Rockler and Ryan warning that they consider other options such as at least adding service at Sobibor to the charges—and possibly dropping the Treblinka charge altogether. But Ryan, who replaced Rockler in the top job, decided to stick with the accusation that Demjanjuk was Treblinka's Ivan the Terrible.

During the subsequent courtroom battles, the government won its case and Demjanjuk was stripped of his citizenship. The American Ukrainian community vociferously protested that OSI had railroaded an innocent man based on fabricated evidence from Moscow, but that did not stop Israel from requesting his extradition. On January 27, 1986,

Demjanjuk was hustled onto an El Al flight for Tel Aviv. For the first time since Eichmann, Israel had decided to put an alleged Nazi war criminal on trial.

While Foreign Minister Yitzhak Shamir proclaimed that Israel was doing so in the name of "historic justice," the decision was highly controversial. Avraham Shalom, who had been the deputy commander of the Eichmann operation in Buenos Aires, was by then the director of Shin Bet, the internal security agency. Before Israel requested Demjanjuk's extradition, Prime Minister Shimon Peres asked Shalom for his view. "I told him don't do that because there's only one Eichmann," Shalom recalled, alluding to the fact that Demjanjuk was a minor figure by comparison. "If we diminish the prize, it would diminish the effect."

In emotional testimony at Demjanjuk's trial in Jerusalem, Treblinka survivors swore that he was Ivan the Terrible. "He's sitting here," Pinchas Epstein shouted, pointing to the defendant. "I dream about him every single night. . . . He is etched in me. In my memory." Spectators applauded, and at other times screamed curses at both Demjanjuk and Yoram Sheftel, his Israeli defense lawyer. "You're a liar. You murdered my father," a Polish Jew shouted at Demjanjuk. They denounced Sheftel as a "Kapo," "Nazi," and "shameless bastard." In April 1988, the court found Demjanjuk guilty and sentenced him to death.

But by the time his defense team appealed the decision to the Israeli Supreme Court, new evidence had surfaced that the real Ivan the Terrible was a guard named Ivan Marchenko. CBS's *60 Minutes* broke the story that a Polish prostitute whom Marchenko had visited frequently had agreed to talk; earlier, her husband had both confirmed what she said and added that Marchenko, who bought vodka in his shop, talked openly about operating the gas chambers. Combined with other information that undercut the case against Demjanjuk, this signaled disaster for the prosecution.

The Israeli Supreme Court acquitted Demjanjuk in July 1993, and the U.S. Sixth Circuit Court ruled that he could return to the United States. To make matters worse, it also restored his citizenship and declared that OSI was guilty of prosecutorial misconduct. Demjanjuk's defendants had charged all along that OSI was withholding evidence that cast doubt on its case, and they even had sifted through the dumpster outside its offices to dig up incriminating documents. "The allegations that were trumped up about improprieties in the investigation still rankles," former OSI Director Ryan told me in 2015. But Eli Rosenbaum, who held the same post starting in 1995, admitted: "We got a huge black eye on that case, and I would say we deserved a black eye."

That did not mean that Rosenbaum was swayed by Demjanjuk's protestations of his innocence. "It was clear that Demjanjuk was lying, that he was a death camp guard, at a minimum at Sobibor," he said. In other words, just as his SS identification card had indicated. Under Rosenbaum's direction, OSI launched a new investigation and painstakingly rebuilt its case, relying mostly on the identity card and new documents from the German and Soviet archives rather than on purported eyewitnesses.

Among the findings: Demjanjuk was never a soldier in Vlasov's Russian Liberation Army as he had maintained. Like his U.S. visa application claim that he had been a farmer in Sobibor, this was another cover story. In 2002, the Sixth Circuit Court stripped Demjanjuk of his citizenship for a second time. The subsequent deportation battles finally ended in 2009, when Demjanjuk was once again sent out of the country to be tried—this time in Germany.

Demjanjuk had been pleading that he was too old and ill to travel or face a new trial, and he boarded the flight to Munich on a stretcher. In court, he was wheeled in on a gurney, and he looked almost lifeless. He was eighty-nine at that point and far from healthy, but his opponents were convinced that he was putting on an act every time he appeared in public. Shortly before he was flown to Munich, the Simon Wiesenthal Center had posted a video on YouTube showing him walking down a street in his neighborhood and getting in a car without any problems or assistance.

In May 2011, the court ruled against Demjanjuk, finding the evidence that he had served as a guard in Sobibor convincing. Unlike in previous German cases, it ruled that this was sufficient grounds to convict him of being an accessory to the murder of 29,060 people, the total number of people who died in the camp during his time there. He was sentenced to five years in prison, although he was given credit for the two years he had already spent in pretrial detention. While his lawyers appealed the verdict, he was allowed to live in a nursing home. He died there on March 17, 2012, with the appeal still pending.

That allowed his son to claim that, in practical terms, the court's verdict was no longer valid. He also voiced the conviction of many in the Ukrainian American community that Germany had used his father "as a scapegoat to blame helpless Ukrainian POW's for the deeds of Nazi Germans." Columnist Pat Buchanan had waged a furious campaign against OSI's prosecution of "this American Dreyfus," as he labeled Demjanjuk. "How many men in the history of this country have been so relentlessly pursued and remorselessly prosecuted?" he asked.

Demjanjuk's defenders can always point to the early misidentification of him as Ivan the Terrible and his initial death sentence in Israel as proof that both prosecutors and judges are capable of grievous errors. But after nearly three decades of legal battles, his guilt was finally established, and his cover stories were exposed for what they were. More significantly, the Munich verdict set a new precedent for how Germany could handle the prosecution of the dwindling number of alleged war criminals who were still alive. The rules of the game had suddenly changed.

Until the Demjanjuk case, German prosecutors had been faced with the challenge of proving alleged Nazi criminals guilty for specific acts of murder and other crimes. The result was a very low conviction rate. Finding witnesses and corroborating evidence that pointed to mass murder was not difficult; finding documents and witnesses who could pin responsibility for specific murders on specific individuals was a huge challenge. According to the Institute of Contemporary History in Munich, West Germany conducted investigations against 172,294 people from 1945 to 2005. This produced 6,656 convictions, but only 1,147 of those guilty verdicts were for homicide. Considering the enormous tally of the Third

Reich's victims, this meant that only a tiny fraction of the murderers were held accountable for their deeds.

What was different about the Demjanjuk case was that, instead of demanding that the prosecution prove him guilty of specific acts of murder, the Munich court accepted the formulation that he was an accessory to mass murder. In other words, those who served in the death camps were guilty by virtue of the positions they held. Kurt Schrimm, the head of the Central Office for the Investigation of National Socialist Crimes in Ludwigsburg, soon made it clear that he would apply that new standard. In September 2013, he announced that his operation was about to send information on thirty former Auschwitz-Birkenau guards to state prosecutors to investigate whether they, too, were accessories to murder. "We take the view that this job [in Auschwitz-Birkenau], regardless of what they can be individually accused of, makes them guilty of complicity in murder," he declared. The thirty former guards ranged in age from eighty-six to ninety-seven, and many of them would be effectively let off the hook because of death, illness, or other factors. As of early 2015, thirteen of those cases were still under investigation, and only one had led to an indictment.

When Oskar Gröning, the ninety-three-year-old SS "bookkeeper of Auschwitz" who was accused of complicity in the deaths of 300,000 prisoners, went on trial in the German town of Lüneburg in April 2015, he admitted he served as a guard and tallied the money seized from prisoners on the way to the gas chambers. But like so many other defendants in earlier trials, he claimed he was only a small cog in the huge killing machine. "I ask for forgiveness," he said. "I share morally in the guilt but whether I am guilty under criminal law, you will have to decide." This was more of an admission than most Nazi defendants ever made, but still implied that he should not be held legally accountable.

On July 15, 2015, the court found Gröning guilty, sentencing him to four years in prison—a more severe sentence than the three and a half years that the state prosecutors had asked for. Judge Franz Kompisch pointed out that he had joined the SS and taken "a safe desk job" at

Auschwitz of his own free will, and that made him complicit in mass murder. Addressing Gröning, he declared that his decision "was perhaps affected by your era, but it was not because you were unfree."

Schrimm had explained that the goal was not so much to punish the former guards as to show that there was still an effort to achieve a measure of justice. "My personal opinion is that in view of the monstrosity of these crimes one owes it to the survivors and the victims not to simply say 'a certain time has passed, it should be swept under the carpet,'" he added.

The irony was that the Munich court that convicted Demjanjuk had finally accepted the arguments made decades earlier about what constituted adequate evidence of guilt for those who served in the Nazi machinery of death. William Denson, the U.S. Army's chief prosecutor in the Dachau trial that opened in late 1945, had based his case on the theory of "common design." Instead of having to prove individual crimes, it was enough, he had argued, that "each one of these accused constituted a cog in this machine of extermination." Fritz Bauer, the German prosecutor who spearheaded the efforts to hold his countrymen accountable for their actions during the Third Reich, had similarly argued during the Frankfurt Auschwitz trial in the 1960s that "whoever operated this machinery is guilty of participation in murder, whatever he did, of course provided he knew the aim of the machinery."

There was a still bigger irony. If the German courts had accepted that approach starting in the 1950s or 1960s, there would have been a huge surge in trials and convictions. As Piotr Cywiński, the current director of the Auschwitz-Birkenau State Museum, put it, "This often happens: you have an accounting for the crimes only when there's almost no one left who can still be held accountable." The whole earlier rationale of the German courts was flawed, Cywiński maintained. "If you have the mafia shooting at people, no one will care whether someone was shooting or standing guard to make sure that no one is coming. He is participating in the crime. It was shocking that the Germans decided differently."

The German newsmagazine *Der Spiegel* offered another explanation in its August 25, 2014, cover story entitled "The Auschwitz Files: Why the

Last SS Guards Will Go Unpunished." Klaus Wiegrefe, the author of the lengthy report, concluded that Germany's poor record on convictions was the result of more than just the rigid legal requirements. "The punishment of crimes committed at Auschwitz did not fail because a few politicians or judges tried to thwart such efforts," he wrote. "It failed because too few people were interested in decisively convicting and punishing the perpetrators. Many Germans were indifferent to the mass murder at Auschwitz after 1945—and thereafter."

Nonetheless, Cywiński and many other foreign critics were encouraged by the Demjanjuk decision—and by the determination of Schrimm of the Ludwigsburg office to act on it. "We are in the area not only of law but also of morality," Cywiński said. "Those who say you shouldn't convict people in their nineties claim this is some kind of moral wrong. The bigger moral failure would be to avoid passing judgment. That would be a triumph of injustice."

As their handling of Demjanjuk and other cases showed, U.S. officials needed no convincing on that score. On July 23, 2014, Eastern Pennsylvania District Court Magistrate Judge Timothy R. Rice ordered Johann Breyer, an eighty-nine-year-old former SS Auschwitz guard and retired toolmaker living in Philadelphia, extradited to Germany to face trial. In its extradition request, Germany had offered the kind of justification that reflected the reasoning in the Demjanjuk case. Breyer was "part of an organization which purposefully executed the orders to carry out the murders within the chain of command," it declared, referring to his "Death's Head" SS guard unit. Breyer did not deny he served in Auschwitz, but he claimed he was not involved in the killings.

In his ruling, the American judge departed from dry legal language to convey the reasoning behind his decision. "As outlined by Germany, a death camp guard such as Breyer could not have served at Auschwitz during the peak of the Nazi reign of terror in 1944 without knowing that hundreds of thousands of human beings were being brutally slaughtered in gas chambers and then burned on site," he wrote. "A daily parade of freight trains delivered hundreds of thousands of men, women, and children, most of whom simply vanished overnight. Yet, the screams, the smells, and the pall of death permeated the air. The allegations establish that Breyer can no longer deceive himself and others of his complicity in such horror." He also pointed out "no statute of limitations offers a safe haven for murder."

But on the same day that Rice announced his decision, the former SS guard died. This was not the first time that Nazi war crime suspects had died before they could be deported from the United States to face charges elsewhere. The legal process was often a tortuous one, if it was started at all. For those who worked for years to win their cases against alleged Nazi war criminals like Breyer, this was an important victory, but his death was also frustrating. It felt like another opportunity lost, not so much to punish the culprit, but to offer a new lesson in a German court about accountability and history—a lesson that individuals are responsible for their actions in such a situation, no matter what orders they may have received.

Breyer's death right before he could be extradited also raised the question why such cases came to fruition so late—and how much had really been accomplished. Since its creation in 1978 to 2015, the U.S. Office of Special Investigations won 108 cases against participants in Nazi crimes, according to its director Eli Rosenbaum. It stripped eighty-six people of their citizenship, and deported, extradited, or otherwise expelled sixty-seven such persons.

Former Congresswoman Elizabeth Holtzman, whose intense lobbying led to the creation of OSI, believes that this is an impressive record—especially given the difficulties of trying to prosecute people for crimes committed so long ago. "I'm very proud of the people who led these efforts," she said. "We got the unit to function in a professional manner, to seek evidence worldwide. They succeeded against all odds. No country in the world had done anything more than we have in this period of time."

Rosenbaum, who returned to OSI in 1988, taking over as director in 1995, certainly agrees with that assessment. He readily concedes that Cold War politics was responsible for a long period when the U.S. lost interest in pursuing Nazi perpetrators, and, in some cases, enlisted them in the new battle against the Soviet Union. But he points out that even in the late 1940s and through much of the 1950s, the United States kept files on Nazi perpetrators and tried to keep many of them from entering the country. The decision to work with others has to be seen in the context of the times, when the superpower struggle felt like a life-or-death contest, he maintains. "In law enforcement, we use bad people all the time," he noted.

Were the subsequent efforts by OSI to go after alleged war criminals, like the recent cases pursued by German prosecutors, a matter of doing too little, too late? In some ways, yes. But they have already had a significant impact, signaling that the United States no longer is willing to turn a blind eye to the remaining perpetrators who can still be identified and targeted for denaturalization and deportation.

OSI was merged with the Justice Department's Domestic Security Section to create a new unit called the Human Rights and Special Prosecutions Section in 2010, but Rosenbaum and his team continued to press ahead on the remaining Nazi cases. Those efforts, Holtzman noted, "create a historical record and show that the United States is not going to become a sanctuary for mass murderers." They also should serve as "a signal for future generations," educating them about genocide and how to handle such cases. In the most optimistic scenario, they might also have a deterrent effect—although she conceded that the record of genocide in countries like Cambodia and Rwanda indicates failure on that score.

"There is a natural tension between law enforcement and government officials and people like us who have no mandate whatsoever," Efraim Zuroff, the director of the Israel office of the Simon Wiesenthal Center, explained during an interview in Jerusalem. "Our mandate is based on the support of the public. It's not from the ballot box; it's more in the checkbooks [of donors]."

Born in 1948, Zuroff was raised in Brooklyn before moving to Israel in 1970. From 1980 to 1986, he worked as a researcher for OSI there. He founded the Israel office of the Simon Wiesenthal Center in 1986, and in recent years he has been frequently described as the last Nazi hunter—

a designation he happily accepts. He never worked for Wiesenthal, who always operated independently, although outsiders often assume that those ties existed. Zuroff described the work of a Nazi hunter as "one-third detective, one-third historian, one-third lobbyist." He added that Nazi hunters don't prosecute anyone, but help make prosecutions possible.

As controversial as Wiesenthal could be, Zuroff is even more so—often accused of stirring up publicity merely for publicity's sake, and antagonizing not just opponents but also putative allies in the process. In the Baltic states, which he frequently attacks for covering up their wartime record of collaboration with the Nazis and rewriting history to downplay the Holocaust, some local Jewish leaders have been alarmed by his tactics. "These communities are very vulnerable," he conceded. "They don't have the resources and courage to fight these battles alone." His efforts, he argued, are meant to give them that support. But like Vienna's Jewish community during the Waldheim affair, the Baltic Jews often felt that such actions were rekindling deep-seated local anti-Semitism.

Zuroff also made highly publicized journeys to look for Nazi war criminals—most notably, for the Mauthausen doctor Aribert Heim. As late as the summer of 2008, he traveled to Chile and Argentina "tracking Aribert Heim," as he put it. When the story broke soon afterward that Heim had died in Cairo in 1992, he confessed that it was "shocking information"—and, at first, maintained that the case was still open pending adequate proof of that fact.

More recently, Zuroff has mounted a new campaign under the rubric "Operation Last Chance." In 2013, he arranged for posters to go up in major German cities that featured a photo of the Auschwitz-Birkenau camp and giant lettering proclaiming "Late, but not too late." They appealed for people to provide information on anyone who might have participated in Nazi crimes and was still alive. Zuroff said that the posters generated a flood of tips that included 111 names. Of those, he reported, he passed along four to German prosecutors, who looked into two of them. One concerned a Dachau guard, who it turned out had developed Alzheimer's; the other, a person who not only collected Nazi memorabilia but also guns and ammunition, had already died.

It's not just the questionable results of the campaign that generated skepticism about its value. "It's true that there are former Nazis who have been able to live peaceful lives at a time when the survivors have led tormented lives," noted Deidre Berger, the director of the Berlin office of the American Jewish Committee. "The injustice is striking and infuriating. The problem is that when a society feels that it is targeted, as a campaign like this tends to do, there is a counter-reaction in many quarters." At the same time, though, she believes that it makes sense to pursue the final cases that can be brought to court. "Whatever happens in terms of sentencing is less important than the few remaining survivors having a feeling of moral justice, of finally being able to testify," she said.

But even some Nazi hunters argued against targeting the last aging concentration camp guards. Serge Klarsfeld called the post-Demjanjuk notion that someone can be guilty simply by virtue of his or her position "quite Soviet." He and Beate are skeptical not just of Zuroff's campaign but also of the recent push by the German investigators. The Ludwigsburg officials "want to keep their offices," he said, suggesting this was a gambit to extend their mandate.

Even as the number of Nazi cases has dwindled, the infighting among the Nazi hunters has not. OSI's Rosenbaum, for instance, has continued to nurse his grievances against Wiesenthal, his nemesis from the Waldheim affair, and other freelancers who he is convinced hyped their own roles. Although he does not speak publicly about Zuroff, he undoubtedly places him in that category. "It seems that, in connection with the postwar fate of Nazi war criminals, the world is prepared to accept only that these perpetrators have been tracked down by self-styled 'Nazi-hunters' and that U.S. intelligence acted principally to obstruct efforts to pursue justice," he told a symposium about the Eichmann case at the Loyola Law School of Los Angeles in 2011. "As it happens, both premises are patently false."

Zuroff shrugs off all such criticism. "I've never met a single Nazi hunter who is willing to say a good word about another Nazi hunter," he said. "It's jealousy, it's competition, it's all these things." He claimed to be "not that sort of person" who makes such disputes personal, but then complained about the Klarsfelds. "They made a nasty comment about me as if I hunt Nazis from my living room," he recalled. He added: "I think what the Klarsfelds did in the cases with France is terrific—no question. They did wonderful things in terms of documentation. But they stopped Nazi hunting."

In Ludwigsburg, the office for investigating Nazi crimes opened an archive in 2000, and that part of the operation is expected to expand as the number of people who can be investigated continues to dwindle. Already, it is attracting regular visitors, particularly school groups, as part of their education about the Third Reich and the Holocaust. But no one is likely to announce an end to Ludwigsburg's active operations anytime soon. "We still have material to look at and we still have people who can be indicted," said Deputy Director Thomas Will.

Zuroff is even more emphatic about his intentions. "You will never have a press conference in which I will say we're throwing in the towel, that's enough, I've had it, I'm going to Tahiti to sit under a coconut tree," he said. "They [the Nazi criminals] may be all dead, but I'm not going to announce it."

"We are not placing people on trial as a symbolic gesture, or to serve some larger purpose of conscience," Allan Ryan, the head of the OSI in the early 1980s, wrote. "We are putting them on trial because they broke the law. That is the only reason people should be put on trial." As someone who headed OSI in its early days, Ryan felt obliged to say that. But he was wrong, at least on the second part: the Nazi hunters were pursuing "some larger purpose of conscience." They targeted those who, whatever the laws of the time were, violated basic concepts of humanity and civilized behavior.

The small band of men and women who were known as Nazi hunters also understood that they could not hope to make all those who violated those concepts pay for what they had done. As Fritz Bauer, Hesse's attorney general who orchestrated Germany's Auschwitz trial in the 1960s, pointed out, the defendants were "really only the chosen scapegoats." The idea was to punish some of those who had committed monstrous crimes, but also to educate a society about what had happened, even while countless others who were at least as guilty remained free.

The process of education was not an easy one, but no country has done more to acknowledge the horrors it unleashed than Germany has. In no small part, this was the result of the activities of Bauer and other Nazi hunters, including Poland's Jan Sehn, who was in charge of the first Auschwitz trial shortly after the war. They were the ones pushing for some measure of reckoning with the past.

The son of a senior diplomat of the Third Reich, Richard von Weizsäcker served in the German army that invaded Poland in 1939, burying his brother, who was killed fighting alongside him. Yet when he rose to the presidency of West Germany and then of a reunified Germany, he constantly reminded his countrymen about how much it had to atone for. "Hardly any country has in its history always remained free from blame for war or violence," he declared in his famous speech to parliament in 1985 on the fortieth anniversary of Germany's surrender at the end of World War II. "The genocide of the Jews, however, is unparalleled in history."

Weizsäcker also made a point of telling his countrymen about his feelings when he learned the war had ended. "This was a day of liberation," he said. In an interview after leaving office, he readily acknowledged to me that many of his countrymen did not feel that way at the time, especially given the widespread suffering of the period. "But there is no longer any serious debate: this date was one of liberation," he insisted. This is far from the normal language used by defeated powers. It is language that Bauer would certainly have approved of—if he had lived long enough to hear it.

Some Germans have bristled at the constant reminders of the horrors their country inflicted on others. Martin Walser, the famed writer whose novels and essays have explored the ways that Germans have rebuilt their lives after the Third Reich, has often stirred controversy by questioning what he called "a ritualized way of speaking about the German past"— implicitly questioning the kind of language that Weizsäcker and other senior public figures used. Specifically, he warned that Auschwitz should not be exploited for political purposes. "My experience has been that Auschwitz is often used as an argument to cut someone else off," he told me during the uproar over one of his speeches. "If I use Auschwitz as an argument, there's nothing left for them to say."

When I asked Walser whether he was suggesting that there was enough of talk about the Holocaust, he replied: "This chapter can never be closed; it'd be crazy to think so. But you cannot prescribe how Germans should deal with this country's shame." In other words, the underlying shame was not in dispute.

Each successive trial anywhere—whether in Nuremberg, Kraków, Jerusalem, Lyon, or Munich—helped shape the understanding of that shame. Even many of the hunts that failed contributed to that understanding, too, since they reminded the public why people like Mengele had to remain in hiding until the end of their lives.

Similarly, each of the Klarsfelds' efforts to expose and bring to trial those Germans who were responsible for crimes such as the deportation of Jews from occupied France offered opportunities to set the historical record straight, including the myth that "only the Germans" had persecuted the Jews, as Serge put it. Klarsfeld gathered much of the documentation that made it possible to convict the former Vichy regime police official Maurice Papon in 1998 for deporting Jews from southwestern France to the death camps. The Klarsfelds' son Arno, who was named after his grandfather who died in Auschwitz, was one of the attorneys for the plaintiffs in the case.

Serge Klarsfeld's meticulous documentation of the wartime record has served as a resource for any number of efforts to get France to face up to the history that it had tried to largely ignore in the immediate postwar era. Kurt Werner Schaechter, an Austrian-born French Jew, combed through many of Klarsfeld's findings for a lawsuit he filed against France's SNCF, the national railroad company, for sending his parents to their deaths. A Paris court ruled against him in 2003, but since then SNCF has taken steps to acknowledge its recent history.

In 2010, the company expressed "profound sorrow and regret" for its wartime role, and in December 2014 France and the United States announced a $60 million compensation package for French Holocaust victims who were sent to their deaths on SNCF trains, with the French government footing the bill. At the same time, a Paris exhibition entitled "Collaboration: 1940–1945" featured a 1942 telegram from Vichy police chief René Bousquet urging local officials working for the collaborationist regime "to take personal control of the measures taken with regard to the foreign Jews." Those measures, of course, were the dispatching of Jews to the deportation camps, from where they were sent to death camps.

Despite the fact that so many Nazi criminals never were held accountable for their crimes, I found the Klarsfelds to be in a reflective mood now that most of their intense, often risky personal battles are over. "I am satisfied completely with history and justice," Serge said. "Justice, in its essence, is not effective: it cannot resuscitate people who were killed. So it's always symbolic. We believe justice was done for the first time in the history of humanity."

In Germany, Beate is still a highly controversial figure. In 2012, *Die Linke* (The Left) nominated her for the post of president. Since this was a parliamentary vote and all the other major parties were backing Joachim Gauck, the former East German dissident Lutheran pastor, she was overwhelmingly defeated. But the fact that she was the opposition candidate at all, Serge pointed out, was significant. "That means that German society improved quite a lot; we were part of that improvement," he said. "When Beate slapped [Chancellor] Kiesinger, I told her: 'When you will be old you will have the gratitude of the German people.'"

Even if many Germans still disapproved of her earlier confrontational tactics, there was already something highly symbolic when the current chancellor, Angela Merkel, shook Beate's hand as parliament convened for the vote. And on July 20, 2015, Susanne Wasum-Rainer, Germany's ambassador to France, presented both Beate and Serge the Medal of Merit, her country's highest honor, expressing her thanks to them for "rehabilitating the image of Germany." For Beate, who had once slapped a West German chancellor, it was hard to imagine a more poignant moment.

At the end of his life, Wiesenthal declared that one of his greatest satisfactions was to outlive most of the perpetrators who had put him and millions of others into concentration camps. "I've tried to make sure that people don't forget what happened," he told me during our last conversation. Since his death in 2005, Austria—his postwar home and the country he so often denounced for not facing up to its Nazi past—has increasingly acknowledged his contributions. The people who bought the Wiesenthals' semidetached house in Vienna's 19th district asked his daughter, Paulinka, if they could put up a plaque in his honor—and if she could provide the wording. It reads: "Here lived Simon Wiesenthal who dedicated his life to justice and his wife who made this possible."

The story of the Nazi hunters is almost at its end, at least the part that involves trying to track down surviving war criminals. But their legacy endures.

Acknowledgments

I am tremendously grateful to all the people I interviewed in the course of my research, most of whom are listed at the end of the bibliography. But that list only tells part of the story. I am also grateful to all the people who helped me identify and connect with those and other sources once I told them about my project, whether or not they are mentioned here. As I learned while working on my previous books, I found that spreading the word about what I was doing almost guaranteed that new, invaluable leads kept materializing. As a result, I benefited from a rich body of written and oral testimonies that made it possible to construct a narrative that spans the entire postwar era.

As in the past when he worked at the Hoover Institution Archives, Brad Bauer, now the chief archivist at the United States Holocaust Memorial Museum, provided invaluable advice and contacts. Thanks to him, I connected with Benjamin Ferencz, the chief prosecutor in the Nuremberg Einsatzgruppen trial, and Gerald Schwab, a U.S. civilian interpreter in Nuremberg. Brad also put me in touch with many of the top-notch experts like Peter Black and Henry Mayer who work at the Museum, along with Alina Skibinska, its representative in Warsaw.

In Kraków, Maria Kała, the director of the Institute of Forensic Research, introduced me to the surviving co-workers of Jan Sehn when he led the institute right after the war. Arthur Sehn, his grandnephew, who divides his time between Stockholm and Kraków, helped me trace the family history that sheds special light on Jan's role as the interrogator of Auschwitz commandant Rudolf Höss. I also want to make special mention of Marcin Sehn, a young member of the clan who facilitated my

Skype interview with Jan's nephew Józef Sehn and his wife, Franciszka. Justyna Majewska provided additional assistance from Warsaw.

I owe special thanks to Gary Smith, then the director of the American Academy in Berlin, along with his colleagues Ulrike Graalfs and Jessica Biehle, for hosting me as a visiting scholar while I was conducting my research in Germany. Linda Eggert, my former student at the Bard Globalization and International Affairs Program in New York, helped me wade through the German sources. Filmmaker Ilona Ziok not only sent me her groundbreaking documentary on Fritz Bauer but also provided numerous background materials. Monika Boll, the curator of the Fritz Bauer exhibition at the Jewish Museum of Frankfurt, showed me around when the exhibit opened and patiently fielded numerous follow-up questions. In Ludwigsburg, Thomas Will was similarly forthcoming about the history and current operations of the Central Office for the Investigation of National Socialist Crimes.

In Israel, my former *Newsweek* colleague Dan Ephron provided me with several contacts who helped me reach key players in the Adolf Eichmann story. In particular, I would like to mention Dror Moreh, the director of the powerful documentary *The Gatekeepers* about Israel's internal security forces. Eli Rosenbaum, aside from discussing his own work in the U.S. Justice Department's Office of Special Investigations, provided me with an introduction to Gabriel Bach, the last surviving member of the prosecution team in the Eichmann trial—along with leads and information on a wide variety of other topics.

At the archives of the Hoover Institution, Carol Leadenham and Irena Czernichowska were, as in the past, immensely helpful. David Marwell, who was the director of the Museum of Jewish Heritage in New York and a former OSI historian, generously shared his extensive knowledge of the subjects I was exploring. My former *Newsweek* colleagues Joyce Barnathan and Steve Strasser triggered my quest to reconstruct the hangings at Nuremberg by putting me in touch with Herman Obermayer, who had worked with the hangman who would later dispatch the condemned top Nazis. Michael Hoth, a longtime friend from Berlin, introduced me to Peter Sichel, who had headed the first CIA operation in that city. My cousin Tom Nagorski, who had worked at ABC, reminded me how his former colleagues there had tracked down Erich Priebke.

Three of the people I interviewed—Avraham Shalom, the number two man in the Eichmann kidnapping team, the Nuremberg interpreter Gerald Schwab, and Józef Sehn—died before the publication of this book. Of course Simon Wiesenthal died more than a decade ago, but I was fortunate enough to have met and interviewed him frequently during my earlier reporting assignments for *Newsweek*. When I visited Israel, Wiesenthal's daughter, Paulinka, and her husband, Gerard Kreisberg, were particularly hospitable.

During the early research on this book, I was also working at the EastWest Institute. I want to thank my wonderful team—Sarah Stern, Dragan Stojanovski, Alex Schulman, and intern Leslie Dewees—for their friendship and support.

When it comes to Alice Mayhew, my extraordinary editor at Simon & Schuster, anything I can say will sound like an understatement. As usual, she provided skillful guidance from start to finish, with just the right touches of enthusiasm and gentle prodding to keep me on track. I also want to thank Stuart Roberts, Jackie Seow, Joy O'Meara, Maureen Cole, Stephen Bedford, Nicole McArdle, and the rest of the Simon & Schuster team that worked their normal magic, along with copy editor Fred Chase. My agent, Robert Gottlieb, as always, threw his full support behind this project, making it happen. At his Trident Media Group, I also want to thank his colleagues Claire Roberts and Erica Silverman.

I have been blessed with a wide circle of friends. I want to express my appreciation to David Satter, Ardith and Steve Hodes, Francine Shane and Robert Morea, Alexandra and Anthony Juliano, Eva and Bart Kaminski, Monika and Frank Ward, Linda Orrill, Ryszard Horowitz and Ania Bogusz, Renilde and Bill Drozdiak, Linda and Michael Mewshew, Anna Berkovits, Victor and Monika Markowicz, Sandra and Bob Goldman, Elaine and Marc Prager, Lucy and Scott Lichtenberg, Jeff Bartholet, Fred Guterl, Arlene Getz, and Leslie and Tom Freudenheim. My apologies for this very incomplete list.

Finally, there is my family. Now that my father, Zygmunt, is no longer with us, my mother, Marie, continued the tradition of following my research and writing progress, encouraging me every step of the way. I also want to thank my sisters, Maria and Terry, along with their spouses, Roberto and Diane.

I wish to pay special tribute to Eva Kowalski, as generous a soul as can be found anywhere. Her late husband Waldek was not just my brother-in-law; he was also a treasured friend.

I am the very proud father of four grown children—Eva, Sonia, Adam, and Alex. I hope they realize how much their love and support means to me on a daily basis. Along with their spouses, Eran and Sara, they have built their own families now, and I can boast seven wonderful grandchildren: Stella, Caye, Sydney, Charles, Maia, Kaia, and Christina.

As for Krysia, the woman who captured my heart when I first met her as an exchange student at the Jagiellonian University in Kraków, she has always served as my first sounding board about absolutely everything, including every line in these pages. I cannot imagine doing any of this without her.

Notes

Introduction

2 *"I have no"*: Harry Patterson, *The Valhalla Exchange*, 166.

2 *"Anyone who seeks"*: David Marwell interview with the author.

5 *I interviewed Niklas Frank*: Niklas Frank interview with the author; excerpts from this interview: "Horror at Auschwitz," *Newsweek*, March 15, 1999; and Andrew Nagorski, "Farewell to Berlin," *Newsweek.com*, January 7, 2000.

Chapter One: The Hangman's Handiwork

9 *"My husband was"*: Abby Mann, *Judgment at Nuremberg*, 62.

9 *On October 16, 1946:* The details of the executions are largely drawn from Kingsbury Smith, who was the pool reporter at the event. His full report: http://law2.umkc.edu/faculty/projects/ftrials/nuremberg/NurembergNews10_16_46.html.

Additional information was drawn from Whitney R. Harris, a lawyer who was part of the American staff at Nuremberg, and designated by Justice Robert H. Jackson to represent him in the Palace of Justice on the night of October 15–16. His account is in his book, *Tyranny on Trial: The Evidence at Nuremberg*, 485–88.

10 *"There is nothing"*: Telford Taylor, *The Anatomy of the Nuremberg Trials: A Personal Memoir*, 588.

10 *"his face pale"* and *"His hands"*: G. M. Gilbert, *Nuremberg Diary*, 431.

10 *"The one thing"*: Harold Burson interview with the author.

10 *"Death by hanging"*: Telford Taylor, 600.

10 *"a death which is"* and *"to commute"*: Ibid., 602.

10 *"his application"*: Ibid., 623.

11 *Herman Obermayer:* All quotes from Obermayer are from two sources: Herman Obermayer interview with the author, and his article, "Clean, Painless and Traditional," in the December 1946 issue of the *Dartmouth Jack-O-Lantern*, the college's literary magazine.

11 *347 people:* Ann Tusa and John Tusa, *The Nuremberg Trial*, 487. Others question that tally. See for example: http://thefifthfield.com/biographical-sketches/john-c-woods/.

13 *Kaltenbrunner still insisted:* Gilbert, 255.

13 *"I deserved it"*: Ibid., 432.

15 *"Everyone in the chamber"*: Stanley Tilles with Jeffrey Denhart, *By the Neck Until Dead: The Gallows of Nuremberg*, 136.

15 *"That's quick work"*: Werner Maser, *Nuremberg: A Nation on Trial*, 255.

16 *In an interview*: Ibid., 254.

16 *"died of slow strangulation"*: Telford Taylor, 611. This passage also includes Taylor's mention of the photos of the hanged Nazis.

16 *"indications of clumsiness"*: Albert Pierrepoint, *Executioner: Pierrepoint*, 158.

16 *German historian Werner Maser:* Maser, 255.

17 *He tried to deflect:* Tusa and Tusa, 487.

17 *"a more-or-less drunken moment"*: Herman Obermayer, "Clean, Painless and Traditional," *Dartmouth Jack-O-Lantern*, December 1946.

17 *"I operated"* and *"Capital punishment"*: Pierrepoint, 8.

Chapter Two: "An Eye for an Eye"

19 *"If this Jewish business"*: Christopher R. Browning, *Ordinary Men: Reserve Battalion 101 and the Final Solution in Poland*, 58.

20 *"Now we know"*: Richard Overy, *Russia's War*, 163–64.

20 *"sent back to"* and *"If I had my way"*: Michael Beschloss, *The Conquerors: Roosevelt, Truman and the Destruction of Hitler's Germany, 1941–1945*, 21.

20 *"At least fifty thousand,"* *"I will not be,"* and Roosevelt's intervention: Ibid., 26.

21 *According to his entries* and rest of account from Liddell diaries: Ian Cobain, "Britain Favoured Execution over Nuremberg Trials for Nazi Leaders," *The Guardian*, October 25, 2012.

22 *more than 450,000:* Richard Bessel, *Germany 1945: From War to Peace*, 11.

22 *"Flying Courts Martial"*: Ibid., 18.

22 *"Woe to the land"*: Norman H. Naimark, *The Russians in Germany: A History of the Soviet Zone of Occupation, 1945–1949*, 72.

22 *"Terrible things"*: David Stafford, *Endgame, 1945: The Missing Final Chapter of World War II*, 315.

23 *1.9 million:* Frederick Taylor, *Exorcising Hitler: The Occupation and Denazification of Germany*, 54.

23 *"Men were beaten"*: Naimark, 74.

23 *"came at night"*: Douglas Botting, *From the Ruins of the Reich: Germany, 1945–1949*, 23.

24 *"in a humane"*: Frederick Taylor, 70.

24 *"In one town"*: Ibid., 73.

24 *12 million* and estimate of deaths: Bessel, 68–69.

24 *On April 29, 1945:* Information on the Rainbow Division and liberation of Dachau is drawn from Sam Dann, ed., *Dachau 29 April 1945: The Rainbow Liberation Memoirs*.

25 *Designed as the first:* United States Holocaust Memorial Museum, "Dachau," www .ushmm.org.

25 *"Along the railroad":* Dann, ed., 14.

25 *"The cars were loaded"* and rest of Lieutenant Cowling's account: Ibid., 22–24.

26 *"The SS tried":* Ibid., 32.

26 *"The ones that":* Ibid., 77.

26 *"There was complete silence"* and rest of Jackson's account: Ibid., 91–92.

27 *"I will never":* Ibid., 24.

27 *"More and more"* and rest of Friedman's account and quotes: Tuvia Friedman, *The Hunter,* 50–102.

27 *The largest and most effective resistance movement:* Norman Davies, *Heart of Europe: A Short History of Poland,* 72.

28 *"diversionary activities":* Frederick Taylor, 226.

31 *"This was real soup"* and rest of Wiesenthal's account of his liberation: Joseph Wechsberg, ed., *The Murderers Among Us: The Wiesenthal Memoirs,* 45–49.

31 *Wiesenthal's father* and other autobiographical details: Tom Segev, *Simon Wiesenthal: The Life and Legends,* 35–41; and Wechsberg, ed., 23–44.

32 *"As a young person"* and *"A half hour later":* Andrew Nagorski, "Wiesenthal: A Summing Up," *Newsweek International,* April 27, 1998.

33 *"Enough!":* Wechsberg, ed., 28.

33 *"As a man":* Segev, 27.

33 *"I did have a strong desire":* Wechsberg, ed., 8.

33 *"He emerged from":* Friedman, 146.

34 *"The sight of"* and rest of Wiesenthal's Mauthausen account: Wechsberg, ed., 47–49.

Chapter Three: Common Design

36 *"We're a very obedient people":* Frederick Forsyth, *The Odessa File,* 92.

36 *"If all the Jews":* Wechsberg, ed., 11.

37 *she was "forced":* Saul K. Padover papers, 1944–45, The New York Public Library Manuscript and Archives Division.

37 *Peter Heidenberger:* Peter Heidenberger interview with the author. Unless otherwise indicated, his quotes are from that interview.

38 *"to make it impossible":* Beschloss, 275.

38 *The Alabama native* and other biographical details: Joshua M. Greene, *Justice at Dachau: The Trials of an American Prosecutor,* 17–20.

39 *"I thought here were"* and *"related substantially":* Michael T. Kaufman, "William Denson Dies at 85; Helped in Convicting Nazis," *New York Times,* December 16, 1998.

39 *When General George S. Patton* and *"See what":* Greene, 13.

39 *But Denson and his colleagues:* Ibid., 19.

39 *"I finally reached"*: Ibid., 24.

39 *Denson's main interrogator* along with Guth's background: Ibid., 26.

40 *But when Guth* and *"The Germans could hardly"*: Ibid., 36.

40 *When the trial opened* and rest of first day of trial: Ibid., 39–44, 53–54; and Peter Heidenberger interview with the author.

40 *"The German spectators, unfamiliar"*: Peter Heidenberger, *From Munich to Washington: A German-American Memoir,* 53.

41 *"common design"*: Ibid., 57.

41 *"May it please"*: Greene, 44.

42 *As Ali Kuci:* Ibid., 64.

42 *"I wish to"*: Ibid., 101.

42 *"failing to refuse"* and *"These accused"*: Ibid., 103–4.

42 *"Each one of these"*: Lord Russell of Liverpool, *Scourge of the Swastika: A Short History of Nazi War Crimes,* 251.

43 *But on December 13, 1945:* "Nazi War Crime Trials: The Dachau Trials," jewishvirtual library.org.

43 *"Nailed to a pole"*: Lord Russell of Liverpool, 252.

43 *Denson personally prosecuted* and total hanged: Greene, 2, 349.

43 *"Colonel Denson has been"*: "Chief Prosecutor Returns Home," *New York Times,* October 24, 1947; Greene, 316.

44 *His weight had dropped:* Flint Whitlock, *The Beasts of Buchenwald: Karl and Ilse Koch, Human-Skin Lampshades, and the War-Crimes Trial of the Century,* 196.

44 *"They said I looked"* and *In January, 1947:* Greene, 226–27.

44 *"that she was gaining"*: Ibid., 128.

44 *A genuine countess* and Huschi's other biographical details: Ibid., 80–85, 345.

44 *"We surrender"*: Ibid., 127.

44 *"the highlight of"*: Ibid., 348.

45 *"a chapter of"*: Whitlock, 199.

45 *"She was wearing"*: Greene, 266.

45 *"It was common knowledge"*: Ibid., 263.

45 *"I've got it"*: Heidenberger, 61.

45 *It didn't help* and story of shrunken head: Greene, 263–64.

46 *"I can't stand it"*: Ibid., 273.

46 *"In spite of"*: Heidenberger, 58.

Chapter Four: The Penguin Rule

48 *"His voice was excellently"*: Michael A. Musmanno, *The Eichmann Kommandos,* 70.

49 *"the biggest murder trial"*: Cited by Eli M. Rosenbaum in his introduction of Ferencz at

the 102nd Annual Meeting, American Society for International Law (ASIL), Washington D.C., April 10, 2008.

49 *Born in Transylvania* and other biographical details and quotes: Benjamin Ferencz interview with the author; and www.benferencz.org ("Benny Stories").

49 *"The only authority"* and other Ferencz quotes in this section, unless otherwise indicated: www.benferencz.org ("Benny Stories").

51 *"Help yourself"* and rest of story about woman who accused Ferenz of theft: Benjamin Ferencz interview with the author; and www.benferencz.org ("Benny Stories").

52 *"When I passed":* www.benferencz.org ("Benny Stories").

53 *The trial ran:* United States Holocaust Memorial Museum, "Subsequent Nuremberg Proceedings, Case #9, The Eisatzgruppen Case," *Holocaust Encyclopedia.*

53 *"I suppose that":* www.benferencz.org ("Benny Stories").

53 *"I didn't call":* Heikelina Verrijn Stuart and Marlise Simons, *The Prosecutor and the Judge: Benjamin Ferencz and Antonio Cassese, Interviews and Writings,* 18.

53 *"the deliberate slaughter":* Trials of War Criminals Before the Nuernberg Military Tribunals Under Control Council Law No. 10, Vol. IV, 30.

53 *"averaged some 1,350 murders":* Ibid., 39.

54 *It was coined:* Donna-Lee Frieze, ed., *Totally Unofficial: The Autobiography of Raphael Lemkin,* 22.

54 *"the somewhat lost":* www.benferencz.com ("Benny Stories").

54 *"the extermination":* Trials of War Criminals Before the Nuernberg Military Tribunals Under Control Council Law No. 10, Vol. IV, 30.

54 *"If these men":* Ibid., 53.

54 *"had not been engaging":* Musmanno, *The Eichmann Kommandos,* 65.

54 *"David taking":* Ibid., 126.

54 *The son of* and other biographical details for Musmanno: Len Barcousky, "Eyewitness 1937: Pittsburgh Papers Relished 'Musmanntics,'" *Pittsburgh Post-Gazette,* March 7, 2010.

55 *"If the law recognizes":* Associated Press, "Decrees Santa Claus Is Living Reality," as published in *The New York Times,* December 23, 1936.

55 *"remote hearsay"* and *"up to and including":* www.benferencz.com ("Benny Stories").

55 *"The soldier who"* and rest of Musmanno-Ohlendorf exchange: Musmanno, *The Eichmann Kommandos,* 78–79.

56 *"Germany was threatened":* www.benferencz.org, ("Benny Stories").

56 *"It is to be doubted":* Musmanno, *The Eichmann Kommandos,* 148.

56 *"the trigger men":* Trials of War Criminals Before the Nuernberg Military Tribunals Under Control Council Law No. 10, Vol. IV, 369–70.

56 *"I could never figure":* Stuart and Simons, 20.

56 *"Musmanno was"* and rest of Ferencz's reflections on Musmanno: www.benferencz.org, ("Benny Stories").

57 *"I had three thousand"* and rest of Ferencz reflections: Benjamin Ferencz interview with the author; and www.benferencz.org ("Benny Stories").

58 *"You never knew"*: Harold Burson interview with the author.

58 *"In postwar Germany"*: Richard W. Sonnenfeldt, *Witness to Nuremberg: The Chief American Interpreter at the War Crimes Trials,* 13.

58 *"There are no Nazis"*: Mann, 48.

58 *"will provide"*: Lord Russell of Liverpool, xi.

58 *"The spectators"* and all other quotes from Burson radio scripts: http://haroldburson.com /nuremberg.html.

59 *"vengeance will not"* and Agee commentary on Dachau footage: Greene, 14.

59 *"About this whole judgment"*: John F. Kennedy, *Profiles in Courage,* 199.

60 *"Punishing the German"*: Frieze, ed., 118.

60 *"The historical value"*: www.benferencz.com ("Benny Stories").

60 *Herman Obermayer:* Herman Obermayer interview with the author.

60 *"I thought it was"* and background of Gerald Schwab: Gerald Schwab interview with the author.

61 *"No, they were not"*: Stuart and Simons, 23.

61 *"That four great nations"*: Harris, 35.

61 *"Never have"*: Ibid., xxix.

61 *"The trials completed"*: Ibid., xiv.

62 *"Without them"*: Mann, 13

62 *"The great problem"*: Musmanno, *The Eichmann Kommandos,* 175–76.

Chapter Five: My Brother's Keeper

63 *"A German will think"*: William L. Shirer, *Berlin Diary: The Journal of a Foreign Correspondent, 1934–1941,* 284.

64 *He also wrote:* Dr. Jan Sehn, *Obóz Koncentracyjny Oswięcim-Brzezinka.*

64 *His writings* and Sehn's affiliations and cases: Władyslaw Mącior, "Professor Jan Sehn (1909–1965)," *Gazeta Wyborcza,* Kraków, October 12, 2005.

65 *Arthur Sehn* and other information he provided about Jan Sehn's family history: Arthur Sehn interview with the author.

65 *"passion for criminal science"*: Jan Markiewicz, Maria Kozłowska, "10 rocznica smierci Prof. J. Sehna," Wspomnienie na U.J., XII, 1975, Jan Sehn Archives.

66 *"The children were"* and other quotes from Józef Sehn and his wife, Franciszka Sehn: Józef and Franciszka Sehn interview with the author.

66 *"he looked for"* and other quotes and information from Maria Kozłowska: Maria Kozłowska interview with the author.

67 *He was fully dedicated* and population losses: Davies, 64.

67 *A former army barracks* and rest of early history of camp, along with quotes from my interviews with Polish political prisoners: Andrew Nagorski, "A Tortured Legacy," *Newsweek*, January 16, 1995.

69 *He was so successful* and Aktion Höss: Thomas Harding, *Hanns and Rudolf: The True Story of the German Jew Who Tracked Down and Caught the Kommandant of Auschwitz*, 165.

69 *"With the Führer gone"*: Rudolf Hoess, *Commandant of Auschwitz: The Autobiography of Rudolf Hoess*, 172.

69 *Taking the name:* Ibid., 173; and Harding, 201–2.

69 *When British forces:* Harding, 201–2. Harding's book provides a detailed account of Höss's initial escape and then capture, which I draw on here.

69 *In March 1946, Lieutenant Hanns Alexander* and the sequence of events that led to Höss's capture, including Alexander's methods of breaking Hedwig and then Rudolf Höss after he was captured, the "undamaged" quote, bar celebration, and Höss walking naked in the snow: Ibid., 234–45.

70 *Wrapped in a blanket:* Robert Gellately, ed., *The Nuremberg Interviews: Conducted by Leon Goldensohn*, 295.

71 *"He sat with"*: Ibid.

71 *"quiet, unprepossessing"*: Harris, 334.

71 *"that at least"* and other quotes from Höss's confession: Ibid., 336–37.

71 *Höss later told Goldensohn:* Gellately, ed., 304–5.

71 *In fact, those numbers:* Yisrael Gutman and Michael Berenbaum, *Anatomy of the Auschwitz Death Camp*, 70–72. They cite a top figure of 1.5 million, which was the estimate at the time.

71 *"That was the low"*: Gilbert, 266.

72 *"The 'final solution'"* and other quotes from Höss's confession: Harris, 336–37.

72 *"an extraordinary decision"*: Telford Taylor, 362.

73 *"the greatest killer"* and *"devoid of"*: Harris, 335.

73 *"quiet, apathetic"* and other quotes from Gilbert about Höss: Gilbert, 249–51, 258–60.

73 *"I thought I was"*: Gellately, ed., 315.

74 *Jan Sehn, who had helped:* Testimonial of Jan Markiewicz about Jan Sehn, Jan Sehn Archives.

74 *Later in his career* and other information about Sehn's behavior and habits, including his treatment of Höss: Author interviews with Zofia Chłobowska, Maria Kozłowska, and Maria Kała.

75 *"testified willingly"* and*"he wrote"*: Dr. Jan Sehn, ed., *Wspomnienia Rudolfa Hoessa, Komendanta Obozu Oświęcimskiego*, 14.

76 *"I must admit"*: Hoess, 176.

76 *"Such employment"* and remaining quotes in this paragraph: Ibid., 77.

76 *"In the following pages"* and subsequent autobiographical details and quotes pertaining to his early years and up through his work in Dachau and Sachsenhausen: Ibid., 29–106.

78 *In Auschwitz, he began* and rest of account of Höss's affair with the prisoner Eleanor Hodys: Harding, 142–46.

81 *"The ideal commandants":* Dr. Jan Sehn, ed., introduction to the second Polish edition of Höss's memoirs, 32.

81 *In his writings for Sehn* and other quotes and information from Höss's account of his time at Auschwitz: Hoess, *Commandant of Auschwitz*, 107–68.

83 *"All of his depictions":* Sehn, *Obóz Koncentracyjny Oświęcim-Brzezinka*, 32.

84 *"It's filled with evil":* Hoess, *Commandant of Auschwitz*, 19.

84 *Most members* and *Sonderkommando* testimonies: Gutman and Berenbaum, 64.

84 *That became* and Sehn's book: Sehn, *Obóz Koncentracyjny Oświęcim-Brzezinka*, 10.

85 *Among those who* and "a Soviet dupe": Joe Belling, "Judge Jan Sehn," http://www.cwporter .com/jansehn.htm.

85 *"I wouldn't assume":* Piotr Cywiński interview with the author.

85 *He was finally:* Franciszek Piper, *Ilu Ludzi Zginęło w KL Auschwitz.*

85 *"to minimize the crime":* Gutman and Berenbaum, 67.

85 *"anyone who":* Franciszek Piper interview with author.

86 *"the illegitimate child"* and other Sehn details: Maria Kozłowska and Zofia Chłobowska interviews with author; and Jan Markiewicz and Maria Kozłowska recollections in Jan Sehn Archives.

Chapter Six: See Less Evil

89 *"In our view":* Copy of telegram courtesy of Eli Rosenbaum.

90 *"Not our concern":* Saul K. Padover papers, The New York Public Library Manuscript and Archives Division.

90 *"What we are doing":* Frederick Taylor, 273.

90 *Peter Sichel was twelve* and rest of Sichel's story and quotes: Peter Sichel interview with the author.

92 *"All members":* Perry Biddiscombe, *The Denazification of Germany: A History, 1945–1950,* 37.

92 *Eight and a half million Germans* and story of Munich paper mill manager: Frederick Taylor, 247–50.

92 *"Democracy in Germany":* Noel Annan, *Changing Enemies: The Defeat and Regeneration of Germany,* 212.

93 *The Americans were* and figures on questionnaires that were reviewed and the resulting dismissals: Frederick Taylor, 268.

93 *"We couldn't have":* Jean Edward Smith, *Lucius D. Clay: An American Life,* 302.

93 *"to be done":* Ibid., 271.

93 *"major offenders"* and other categories: Sandra Schulberg, *Filmmakers for the Prosecution, The Making of Nuremberg: Its Lessons for Today,* iii.

93 *Many former Nazis:* Biddiscombe, 183.

93 *Persilschein:* Frederick Taylor, 285.

93 *in 1946* and both poll numbers: Biddiscombe, 191.

93 *In some cases:* Ibid., 199.

93 *"But I don't know":* Smith, 240.

94 *"They may not have":* Lucius D. Clay, *Decision in Germany,* 262.

94 *In June 1946* and Volkswagen dismissals and reinstatements: Annan, 205.

94 *The French* and teacher hirings and reinstatements: Frederick Taylor, 321.

94 *during a mere two and a half months* and verdicts: Patricia Heberer and Jürgen Matthäus, eds., *Atrocities on Trial: Historical Perspectives on the Politics of Prosecuting War Crimes,* 175.

95 *Already in 1946:* Henry Leide, *NS-Verbrecher und Staatssicherheit: Die geheime Vergangenheitspolitik der DDR,* 45–46.

95 *"joining the SED":* Clay, 145.

95 *"Along with the many innocent people":* Leide, 414.

95 *The Western Allies* and Berlin Airlift figures: www.trumanlibrary.org (http://www.truman library.org/teacher/berlin.htm).

96 *"no fresh trials":* Copy of telegram courtesy of Eli Rosenbaum.

96 *The U.S. Army set up:* Greene, 321.

96 *The Dachau trials* and Clay quotes: Clay, 253–54.

97 *"a sordid, disreputable":* Ibid., 254.

97 *The stories* and lamp shades: Smith, 301.

97 *"mockery":* Greene, 323.

97 *"I did not feel"* and rest of Denson's testimony at Senate subcommittee: Ibid., 328–29.

97 *"From what I know":* Ibid., 336.

98 *"Every act":* Ibid., 340.

98 *"which unanimously":* Clay, 254.

98 *"In view of":* Norbert Frei, *Adenauer's Germany and the Nazi Past: The Politics of Amnesty and Integration,* 6–7.

98 *But after Koch:* Whitlock, 258.

98 *"a small town secretary":* Peter Heidenberger interview with the author.

98 *In 1963* and fate of Koch: Greene, 347; and Whitlock, 259–61.

99 *"I cannot do":* Whitlock, 260.

99 *"utterly contemptible":* Stuart and Simmons, 17.

99 *"There is something":* Greene, 351–52.

100 *"majors and colonels":* Benjamin Ferencz interview with the author.

100 *"lesser Nazis"*: Smith, 297.

100 *Despite growing pressure*: Hilary Earl, *The Nuremberg SS-Einsatzgruppen Trial, 1945– 1958: Atrocity, Law, and History*, 276.

100 *But then John J. McCloy* and McCloy's handling of Einsatzgruppen cases: Ibid., 277–86.

101 *"the embodiment"*: Ibid., 286.

101 *"To sign"*: Stuart and Simmons, 24.

101 *"If I had"*: Earl, 286.

101 *"to impress"* and rest of account about property claims and other early organizations and their funding: Stuart and Simons, 31–32; and www.benferencz.org ("Benny Stories").

102 *"It never happened"*: Benjamin Ferencz interview with the author.

102 *On August 25, 2011:* www.benferencz.org ("Benny Stories").

102 *"Forget it"*: Benjamin Ferencz interview with the author.

102 *To make sure* and story of the Nuremberg documentary, from which most of my account is drawn: Sandra Schulberg, *Filmmakers for the Prosecution*. That booklet is included in Schulberg's restored Blu-ray version of the documentary. *See* www.nurembergfilm.org.

103 *"The Cold War"*: Sandra Schulberg interview with the author.

104 *"They still had"*: Sandra Schulberg, 6.

105 *"Claim Internal"*: Ibid., 37.

105 *"unexpectedly good"* and other Stuart Schulberg quotes here: Ibid., 42–45.

105 *"if he cut out"* and other quotes from Jackson-Royall correspondence: Photo scans courtesy of Professor John Q. Barrett. Copies from Robert H. Jackson Papers, Library of Congress, Box 115, Folder 3.

106 *"too gruesome"*: Sandra Schulberg, 46–47.

106 *"Could there be"*: Ibid., 47.

106 *"that there are those"*: Ibid., 50.

106 *William Shirer* and "scandal": Ibid., 49.

107 *In 2004* and Sandra Schulberg's film restoration story: Sandra Schulberg interview and correspondence with the author.

Chapter Seven: "Like-Minded Fools"

108 *"Nothing belongs"*: From clip in documentary *Death by Installments*.

109 *That organization's top officer* and quotes from his note: Hella Pick, *Simon Wiesenthal: A Life in Search of Justice*, 98.

109 *He also began working* and other details of his early Linz activities: Segev, 68–70.

109 *Never afraid of controversy* and *"this made me"*: Pick, 102.

109 *At the newly created* and *"I didn't believe"*: Wechsberg, ed., 51.

110 *"You'll see"*: Wiesenthal, 40.

110 *"The Americans"*: Ibid., 56.

110 *"best secret weapon"*: Wechsberg, ed., 58.

111 *In 1946:* Segev, 79, 423.

111 *By the following year:* Pick, 95.

111 *Wiesenthal had convinced:* Segev, 78–80.

111 *"Austrians accounted for":* Wiesenthal, 273.

111 *Wiesenthal's activities and calls* and pistol permit: Segev, 85, 82.

111 *threatening letters:* Pick, 103.

111 *But he always:* Ibid., 105. For a detailed account of Brichah's smuggling efforts, see Yehuda Bauer, *Flight and Rescue: Brichah.*

112 *Wiesenthal demanded:* Andrew Nagorski, "Wiesenthal: A Summing Up," *Newsweek International,* April 27, 1998.

112 *"It seems to me":* Wiesenthal, 55.

112 *"didn't seem to care"* and *"than about":* Wechsberg, ed., 65.

112 *"In 1949, my parents":* Paulinka (Wiesenthal) Kreisberg, interview with the author.

113 *In 1947,* account of Wiesenthal's writings about Haj Amin el-Husseini, and *"there is no reliable evidence":* Segev, 86–88; and www.jewishvirtuallibrary.org.

113 *In 1936:* www.jewishvirtuallibrary.org/jsource/History/muftihit.html.

113 *On his first visit, "as a recruit,"* and *"a partner,"* along with rest of account of Wiesenthal's involvement and interactions with Israeli intelligence: Segev, 90–95.

114 *He and his colleagues* and *"Our office":* Friedman, 180.

114 *On one occasion* and details and quotes from Mattner case: Ibid., 180–82.

115 *During the immediate* and numbers of cases and convictions: Heberer and Matthäus, eds., 235.

115 *"The situation grew":* Friedman, 191.

116 *"This is Austria":* Ibid., 193.

116 *From 1956:* Heberer and Matthäus, eds., 235.

116 *Like Wiesenthal* and *"Put your whole heart"* and Haganah contacts and activities: Friedman, 188–90.

116 *In 1949* and *"An odd feeling":* Ibid., 199.

117 *"My files":* Ibid., 210–11.

117 *"That was the file":* Ibid., 211.

117 *"We agreed to":* Ibid., 146.

117 *Wiesenthal claimed* and *"high official":* Wechsberg, ed., 100.

118 *According to both* and quote from landlady: Ibid., 100–101; and Wiesenthal, 67–69.

118 *This was the beginning* and questioning of Veronika Liebl: Wechsberg, ed., 101–2.

118 *"Eichmann Wiesenthal"* and *"swamped":* Wiesenthal, 69.

119 *In some cases:* See Guy Walters, *Hunting Evil: The Nazi War Criminals Who Escaped and the Quest to Bring Them to Justice,* 80.

119 *"the greatest murderer"* and *"Friedman, you must":* Friedman, 122.

119 *"Do you have":* Robert M. W. Kempner, *Ankläger Einer Epoche: Lebenserrinrungen,* 445.

119 *In 1947*, death appeal sequence, and *"This unspectacular"*: Wiesenthal, 70.

119 *According to Friedman* and *"Arthur permitted"*: Friedman, 203. Eichmann's postwar movements are recounted in Neal Bascomb's *Hunting Eichmann: How a Band of Survivors and a Young Spy Agency Chased Down the World's Most Notorious Nazi*.

120 *"The truth was"*: Friedman, 204.

120 *"keep reminding"* and *"Think of it"*: Ibid., 215.

120 *For Wiesenthal* and quotes from Wiesenthal about the Austrian baron and his meeting with him: Wiesenthal, 76.

120 *The baron's name*: Segev, 102.

120 *"Imagine whom"* and *"How do you"*: Wechsberg, ed., 123.

121 *"As an adversary"* and report to WJC and Israeli consulate: Wiesenthal, 76–77; and Weschsberg, ed., 124.

121 *"American Jews"* and *"I honestly"*: Wiesenthal, 77.

121 *"post-war phase"*: Pick, 133.

121 *He, too, packed up*: Segev, 117.

122 *By the middle*: Heberer and Matthäus, eds., 191.

122 *"I think we"*: Deborah Lipstadt, *The Eichmann Trial*, 27.

123 *"At a time"*: Irmtrud Wojak, *Fritz Bauer 1903–1968: Eine Biographie*, 15.

124 *"contributed significantly"*: Ibid., 13.

124 *"Jewish pig"* and *"Have you"*: Ronen Steinke, *Fritz Bauer: Oder Auschwitz vor Gericht*, 26, 29.

124 Death by Installments: Original German title is *Fritz Bauer: Tod auf Raten*, CV Films, 2010.

124 *"the historical figure"* and other quotes: Ilona Ziok interview with the author.

125 *"Fritz Bauer's family"* and other quotes from exhibition: Texts courtesy of exhibition curator Monika Boll. Many of the documents and write-ups are also included in the exhibition's catalogue: Fritz Backhaus, Monika Boll, Raphael Gross. *Fritz Bauer. Der Staatsanwalt. NS-Verbrechen vor Gericht*.

125 *"there were many"* and rest of Bauer's remarks to students: Wojak, 62.

125 *"the rowdy crowds"*: Ibid., 97–98.

126 *"A Jewish District Judge"* and rest of NS-Kurier case: Steinke, 83–85.

126 *"We unconditionally"* and *"incredible belief"*: Ibid., 97–98.

127 *"The Danes"*: Fritz Bauer exhibition at the Jewish Museum of Frankfurt.

127 *"It is playing"*: Irmtrud Wojak interview with the author.

128 *In 1943* and other details: Fritz Bauer exhibition at the Jewish Museum of Frankfurt; and Steinke, 106–8.

128 *"smart like"*: Steinke, 109.

128 *"Germany is"*: Wojak, 183.

129 *He also published:* Ibid., 179.

129 *From Denmark, he wrote* and *"they don't want":* Ibid., 221.

130 *He had been wounded* and Remer-Goebbels encounter: William Shirer, *The Rise and Fall of the Third Reich: A History of Nazi Germany,* 1061–63.

130 *"39 years old"* and *"recipients of"* and *"These conspirators"* and number of journalists at the trial: Alaric Searle, *Wehrmacht Generals, West German Society, and the Debate on Rearmament, 1949–1959,* 238–39.

131 *"Didn't everyone"* and *"An unjust state":* Wojak, 273–74.

131 *"The anti-Nazi sentiment":* Letter to the Austrian communist Karl B. Frank, March 2, 1945, quoted in Fritz Bauer exhibition at the Jewish Museum of Frankfurt.

131 *"It's the task":* Steinke, 144.

132 *"saw it as their task"* and *"deeply moved":* Wojak, 275.

132 *The court found* and how Remer never served his sentence: Searle, 244.

132 *"worked for":* Frei, 268.

132 *A poll taken:* Steinke, 137.

Chapter Eight: "Un Momentito, Señor"

134 *"It was well known":* Jack Higgins, *The Bormann Testament,* 49–50.

135 *"I said I'll buy":* Rafi Eitan interview with the author.

136 *Israel's population:* "Vital Statistics: Population in Israel," www. Jewishvirtuallibrary.org.

136 *"I was never":* Avraham Shalom interview with the author.

137 *According to Isser Harel* and account of Shinar-Bauer meeting, with quotes: Isser Harel, *The House on Garibaldi Street,* 4.

137 *When Walter Eytan* and *"I didn't know"* and rest of Harel's initial actions, and *"That night I resolved":* Ibid., 2–3.

138 *"What Dr. Shinar"* and details and quotes from Darom-Bauer meeting, including Harel's assessment of Bauer: Ibid., 4–9.

139 *In January 1958* and *"the wretched little house"* and rest of Goren's mission, including Harel's reaction to his report: Ibid., 10–12.

140 *That somebody was* and Hofstaetter's journey to Argentina, including encounter with Hermann, his wife, and daughter: Ibid., 12–22.

142 *Lothar and Sylvia Hermann:* Bascomb, 111–12.

143 *"These findings":* Harel, *The House on Garibaldi Street,* 27.

143 *In August 1959, Tuvia Friedman* and his actions to publicize the Eichmann-in-Kuwait claim: Friedman, 246–49.

143 *In December 1959:* Harel, *The House on Garibaldi Street,* 32–35.

144 *"This is simply"* and rest of account of Bauer's meeting in Jerusalem: Zvi Aharoni and Wilhelm Dietl, *Operation Eichmann: The Truth About the Pursuit, Capture and Trial,* 85.

144 *"The sad truth"*: Ibid., 84.

144 *Harel informed Ben-Gurion* and *"would be an achievement"*: Harel, *The House on Garibaldi Street*, 36–37.

144 *"one of the best"* and *Aharoni background*: Ibid., 35; and Bascomb, 130–31.

144 *"seething with"*: Harel, *The House on Garibaldi Street*, 36.

144 *On March 1, 1960*: Aharoni and Dietl, 88.

144 *Accompanied by* and rest of Aharoni search for Eichmann, including visits to first and second addresses, including quotes: Ibid., 90–100. In his account, Harel offers some minor variations on this story, claiming that the Israelis used an actual hotel bellboy for the reconnaissance operation.

146 *Staking out* and subsequent actions along with quotes and efforts to photograph Eichmann: Ibid., 102–25.

147 *"People don't lie"* and *"The Eichmanns' family"* and rest of story about death notice of Eichmann's stepmother and then father: Wiesenthal, 77.

147 *Wiesenthal reported* and photos at funeral: Ibid., 77–78.

148 *"never happened"* and *"got excited"*: Isser Harel, "Simon Wiesenthal and the Capture of Eichmann" (unpublished manuscript, courtesy of Eli Rosenbaum), 230.

148 *But Aharoni* and *"an important piece"*: Aharoni and Dietl, 86–87.

148 *Harel took charge*: Harel, *The House on Garibaldi Street*, 85–87.

148 *While Harel handled* and Eitan's arrangements for sea transport: Rafi Eitan interview with the author.

149 *He was no longer*: Aharoni and Dietl, 126.

149 *One of the first to follow* and Shalom's mishaps on his journey: Avraham Shalom interview with the author.

150 *"Never before"*: Peter Z. Malkin and Harry Stein, *Eichmann in My Hands*, 127.

150 *"From the very beginning"* and rest of Eitan's account: Rafi Eitan interview with the author.

151 *On the evening of May 10*, safe houses, and Harel's final briefing to the team: Harel, *The House on Garibaldi Street*, 150–52.

152 *"I'm warning you"* and *"The gloves"*: Malkin and Stein, 142, 183.

152 *They were parked* and rest of kidnapping operation: Harel, *The House on Garibaldi Street*, 162–69; author interviews with Rafi Eitan and Avraham Shalom; Aharoni and Dietl, 137–44 (Aharoni quotes).

153 "Un momentito, señor" and rest of Malkin's seizing of Eichmann: Malkin and Stein, 186–87.

154 *The special El Al flight*: Bascomb, 262–63.

155 *"You must believe me"* and *"infallible"*: Malkin and Stein, 204–5.

155 *"There was"*: Ibid., 216.

155 *"He behaved like"* and Eichmann's fears: Harel, *The House on Garibaldi Street*, 182.

155 *He tried to convince*: Aharoni and Dietl, 152–53.

155　*But as Nicolas Eichmann:* Harel, *The House on Garibaldi Street,* 179–80.

155　*Shalom had repeatedly driven:* Avraham Shalom interview with the author.

156　*On May 20,* Shalom inspection, and informing the crew: Harel, *The House on Garibaldi Street,* 249, 237.

156　*Back at the safe house* and trip to plane and getting Eichmann on board: Ibid., 252–56.

156　*When the plane left:* Bascomb, 290.

157　*"Which one of you"* and *"The story":* Friedman, 266.

157　*"HEARTY CONGRATULATIONS":* Segev, 148.

157　*"Eichmann's seizure":* Pick, 147.

157　*"I was a dogged pursuer":* Wiesenthal, 70.

157　*"I could never":* Paulinka and Gerard Kreisberg interview with the author.

157　*"As soon as":* Harel, *The House on Garibaldi Street,* 275.

158　*"He can call":* Steinke, 23.

158　*"no part"* and *"could not":* Harel, "Simon Wiesenthal and the Capture of Eichmann," 3, 23.

158　*"had not exerted"* and *"At first":* Ibid., 3, 5.

159　*"They were competing":* Avraham Shalom interview with the author.

159　*"When I actually saw":* Harel, *The House on Garibaldi Street,* 196–97.

Chapter Nine: "In Cold Blood"

160　*"That many":* Primo Levi, *The Drowned and the Saved,* 73.

160　*"Our security services"* and other quotes from transcript of cabinet meeting: "Ben-Gurion's Bombshell: We've Caught Eichmann," *The Times of Israel,* April 8, 2013.

161　*"Israel itself":* Gideon Hausner, *Justice in Jerusalem,* 288.

161　*"I have to inform":* Bascomb, 298–99.

162　*Its foreign minister* and *"Jewish volunteers"* and U.N. resolution: Ibid., 304–5.

162　*An editorial:* Adam Bernstein, "Israeli Judge Moshe Landau, Who Presided over Nazi Officer's Trial, Dies at 99," *Washington Post,* May 3, 2011; and Lipstadt, 34.

162　*Philosopher Isaiah Berlin wrote:* Ofer Aderet, "The Jewish Philosopher Who Tried to Convince Israel Not to Try Eichmann," *Haaretz,* December 28, 2013.

162　*"act of lawlessness":* Lipstadt, 31.

162　*The American Jewish Committee* and *"unspeakable crimes":* Ibid., 34.

163　*"With me":* Hausner, 323.

163　*"In Israel"* and all subsequent Bach quotes: Gabriel Bach interview with the author.

163　*Some Holocaust survivors:* "Snatching Eichmann," *Zman,* May 2012, 130.

164　*Eichmann occupied a cell:* Jochen von Lang and Claus Sybill, eds., *Eichmann Interrogated: Transcripts from the Archives of the Israeli Police,* xix.

164　*But the same rule* and *275 hours* and subsequent mention of *3,564 pages:* Ibid., xvii.

164　*Police Captain Avner Less* and *"the privilege":* Ibid., 4.

165　*At their first meeting* and Less quotes: Ibid., v–vi.

165 *He explained to Less* and *"wasn't a Jew-hater"*: Ibid., 57.

166 *"I was horrified"* and *"shaken"* and *"Even today"*: Ibid., 76–77.

166 *"insignificant"*: Ibid., 90.

166 *"unusual zeal"*: Ibid., 156.

166 *"If they had"*: Ibid., 157, vi.

166 *"But that's horrible"*: Ibid., ix.

167 *When Less began:* Ibid., xxi.

167 *"the drink had been"*: Hoess, 155.

167 *"I had nothing"*: Lang and Sybill, 101–2.

167 *To undercut Eichmann's claims* and subsequent examples and quotes: Ibid., 142–44.

168 *"the cold sophistication"*: Ibid., vi.

168 *"Thinking itself"*: Hannah Arendt, *The Last Interview and Other Conversations*, 128.

168 *"the most important"*: Hannah Arendt, *Eichmann in Jerusalem: A Report on the Banality of Evil*, 153.

169 *"Jew"* and *"enlightened"* and *"If one is attacked"*: Arendt, *The Last Interview and Other Conversations*, 11–12, 20.

170 *"a typical Galician Jew"* and *"ghetto mentality"*: Lipstadt, 152.

170 *"One of my main"*: Arendt, *The Last Interview and Other Conversations*, 130.

170 *"If there was"*: Ibid., 46.

170 *"he was genuinely incapable"*: Arendt, *Eichmann in Jerusalem*, 48–49.

170 *"Despite all"*: Ibid., 54.

170 *"Except for"*: Ibid., 287.

171 *"Eichmann displayed,"* *"only a minor transport officer,"* and *"tense, rigid"*: Hausner, 332, 325.

171 *When the prosecution:* Gabriel Bach interview with the author.

172 *"I will jump"* and Hausner's account: Arendt, *Eichmann in Jerusalem*, 46; Hausner, 359–60.

172 *"bragging was"*: Arendt, *Eichmann in Jerusalem*, 46.

173 *"a saloon atmosphere"* and court ruling on Sassen tapes: Hausner, 348–49.

173 *"What eventually"*: Arendt, *Eichmann in Jerusalem*, 47.

173 *"He was not"*: Ibid., 287–88.

173 *"To a Jew"*: Ibid., 117.

174 *"The tragedy"*: Hausner, 341.

174 *"saved exactly"*: Arendt, *Eichmann in Jerusalem*, 118.

174 *"sold his soul"*: Jonah Lowenfeld, "Rudolf Kastner Gets a New Trial," *Yom HaShoah*, April 26, 2011.

174 *"chaos and plenty of misery"*: Arendt, *Eichmann in Jerusalem*, 125.

175 *"made it very clear"*: Musmanno, *The Eichmann Kommandos*, 16.

175 *"kept recurring"*: Albert Averbach and Charles Price, eds., *The Verdicts Were Just: Eight Famous Lawyers Present Their Most Memorable Cases*, 98.

176 *"that Eichmann"*: Michael A. Musmanno, "No Ordinary Criminal," *New York Times*, May 19, 1963.

176 *In her reply* and rest of Arendt's remarks and letters from readers: "Letters to the Editor: 'Eichmann in Jerusalem,'" *New York Times*, June 23, 1963.

177 *"One stands baffled"*: Jacob Robinson, *And the Crooked Shall Be Made Straight: The Eichmann Trial, the Jewish Catastrophe, and Hannah Arendt's Narrative*, 58–59.

177 *"aghast"* and *"took pains"*: Ibid., 147, 160–62.

178 *"We have done"*: Wiesenthal, 231.

178 *"Legally and morally"*: Robinson, 159.

178 *"In a way"*: Rafi Eitan interview with the author.

178 *In 2011:* The German title of the book is *Eichmann vor Jerusalem: Das unbehelligte Leben eines Massenmörders.*

179 *"in thrall to"* and *"An ideology"*: Bettina Stangneth, *Eichmann Before Jerusalem: The Unexamined Life of a Mass Murderer*, 222.

179 *"achieved the primary goal"* and *"Eichmann in Jerusalem"*: Ibid., xxiii.

179 *In an early interview:* Arendt, *The Last Interview and Other Conversations*, 26–27.

180 *"sham existence"* and *"There's something"*: Ibid., 50–51.

180 *"mere functionary"* and *"If you succumb"*: Ibid., 44–45.

180 *"victims"*: Ibid., 42.

180 *"went to their death"* and *"But the sad truth"*: Arendt, *Eichmann in Jerusalem*, 10–11.

181 *"that Arendt's conception"* and *"the disappearance"*: Stanley Milgram, *Obedience to Authority: An Experimental View*, 6, 8.

181 *"The person who"*: Ibid., 11.

182 *"monsters"*: "British PM on New ISIS Beheading," ABC News, September 14, 2014.

182 *"determined to go down"*: Douglas M. Kelley, *22 Cells in Nuremberg: A Psychiatrist Examines the Nazi Criminals*, 71.

182 *"a frank psychotic"*: Gilbert, 260.

183 *"Insanity is no"*: Kelley, 3.

183 *But it also led:* Jack El-Hai, *The Nazi and the Psychiatrist: Hermann Göring, Dr. Douglas M. Kelley, and a Fatal Meeting of the Minds at the End of WWII*, 218–20.

183 *"as a catalyst"*: Arendt, *The Last Interview and Other Conversations*, 41.

183 *About six weeks* and poll numbers: Hausner, 464.

183 *On December 15, 1961* and rest of timing on appeals and hanging: Bascomb, 316–18.

184 *The designated hangman* and Nagar's account and quotes: "Snatching Eichmann," *Zman*, May 2012.

184 *"Long live Germany"*: Bascomb, 319.

Chapter Ten: "Little People"

186 *"What should"*: Bernhard Schlink, *The Reader,* 104.

187 *Thomas Gnielka* and his interview with Emil Wulkan, dealings with Bauer, and history of the incriminating documents: Devin O. Pendas, *The Frankfurt Auschwitz Trial, 1963–1965: Genocide, History, and the Limits of the Law,* 46–47; and Rebecca Wittmann, *Beyond Justice: The Auschwitz Trial,* 62–63.

187 *"Maybe this is"*: Claudia Michels, "Auf dem Büfett lagen die Erschiessungslisten," *Frankfurter Rundschau,* March 27, 2004.

187 *"souvenir"* and *"of legal significance"*: Wittmann, 62.

187 *"he was green in the face"*: Claudia Michels, "Auf dem Büfett lagen die Erschiessungslisten," *Frankfurter Rundschau,* March 27, 2004.

187 *A total of 183:* Pendas, 2.

187 *twenty thousand visitors:* Wittmann, 175.

188 *211 concentration camp survivors:* Fritz Bauer exhibition, Jewish Museum of Frankfurt.

188 *"really only"* and *"The question is"* and *"can and must"*: Steinke, 157, 156, 155.

188 *"whoever operated"*: Wittmann, 256.

188 *"an ordinary criminal trial"*: Ibid., 215.

188 *"could consider only"*: Bernd Naumann, *Auschwitz: A Report on the Proceedings Against Robert Karl Ludwig Mulka and Others Before the Court at Frankfurt,* 415, xiv.

188 *"I have yet"*: Ibid., Hannah Arendt, Introduction, xiv.

189 *"As they all"*: As quoted in Steinke, 180.

189 *Newsreel footage: Verdict on Auschwitz: The Auschwitz Trial, 1963–1965,* 1993 German television documentary.

189 *As the prosecution* and account of Baer's arrest and death: Pendas, 48–49.

190 *"the victims were"*: Wittmann, 139.

190 *Another witness:* Pendas, 117–18.

190 *But perhaps the most chilling* and Wasserstrom's testimony: Wittmann, 88.

190 *Medical orderly Josef Klehr:* Ibid., 75.

191 *Dr. Victor Capesius:* Ibid., 197.

191 *Then there was* and rest of Kaduk atrocities: Ibid., 140.

191 *Dr. Ella Lingens* and her background: www. yadvashem.org.

191 *"Do you wish"*: Pendas, 158.

191 *Hans-Günther Seraphim* and *"not found"*: Wittmann, 80–81.

191 *"As a little man"* and *"In Auschwitz"*: Naumann, 410, 409.

192 *Then there were* and Frau Boger and Lingens quotes: *Verdict on Auschwitz: The Auschwitz Trial, 1963–1965,* 1993 German television documentary.

192 *The press coverage* and *"monsters"*: Pendas, 262.

192 *"The Torture Swing"* and other headlines cited by Martin Walser: Wittmann, 176–77.

192 *"The more horrible"* and *"Auschwitz was not"*: Ibid., 177, 180.

193 *In the* Suddeutsche Zeitung: Pendas, 263.

193 *"it would be a mistake"*: Naumann, 415.

193 *The verdict itself* and sentences: Ibid., 412–13.

193 *"the residual wishful fantasy"*: Wittmann, 255.

194 *"The criminal facts"*: Naumann, viii.

194 *"'Mass murder'"* and *"Instead of"*: Ibid., xxii, xxix.

194 *"Damn it!"*: Pendas, 256.

194 *A poll taken* and both poll results: Ibid., 253.

195 *"Naturally the Auschwitz Trial"* and *"in the same boat"*: Ibid., 256–57.

195 *"In many ways"*: Wittmann, 190.

195 *"It would be quite"*: Naumann, xvii.

195 *During the Third Reich* and allegations: Perry Biddiscombe, *The Denazification of Germany: A History 1945-1950*, 212–13; and, for instance, "Eichmann to Testify on Dr. Globke's Role in Deportation of Greek Jews," *JTA*, January 31, 1961.

196 *He requested documents* and subsequent fate of Bauer's investigation into Globke: Fritz Bauer exhibition, Jewish Museum of Frankfurt.

196 *In 1963:* "Bonn Denounces Globke Trial in East Germany as Communist Maneuver," *JTA*, July 10, 1963.

196 *From 1950 to 1962* and statistics on investigations, trials, acquittals, and murder convictions: Wittmann, 15.

196 *"We do not have"* and Ludwigsburg's history: Thomas Will interview with the author.

197 *the 1966 poll:* Pendas, 253.

198 *"that something like that"* and exhibition: Ibid., 182–83.

198 *"May it smooth"* and visit of West German delegation to Poland: Ibid., 179–80.

198 *Playwright Peter Weiss:* Peter Weiss, *The Investigation: Oratorio in 11 Cantos.*

198 *"When I was taken down"*: Ibid., 73–74.

200 *"Nineteen Sixty-eight cannot be"* and other Schlink quotes: Bernhard Schlink interview with the author.

201 *But Peter Schneider:* Peter Schneider interview with the author.

202 *Jan Sehn had a regular routine* and Kozłowska account, including anonymous letters: Maria Kozłowska interview with the author.

203 *"The trial should show"*: Steinke, 218.

203 *In an interview: Death by Installments* documentary.

203 *When the youth protests:* Steinke, 263.

203 *Many Germans were angered* and threats, swastika, pistol, and bodyguard: *Death by Installments* documentary; and Steinke, 221.

204 *"When I leave"*: Steinke, 257.

204 *"The Attorney General"*: Wojak, 443.

204 *"burning anti-Semitism"*: Ibid., 445.

204 *In 1967* and *"Brown Book"*: Fritz Bauer exhibition, Frankfurt Jewish Museum.

204 *"There is only a duty"*: Wojak, 453.

205 *"How long"*: Steinke, 272.

205 *"no proof"* and *"Yes"*: Ilona Ziok interview with the author.

205 *"He was the greatest"*: *Death by Installments* documentary.

205 *"He won us"*: Wojak, 455.

Chapter Eleven: A Slap to Remember

207 *"Because we were weak"*: Serge Klarsfeld interview with the author.

207 *"reciting little poems"* and *"a conscientious"*: Beate Klarsfeld, *Wherever They May Be!*, 4.

207 *Her father served* and all early biographical details and quotes: Ibid., 3–23; Serge Klarsfeld with Anne Vidalie, *La Traque des criminels Nazis*, 11–13, 31–32; and Beate and Serge Klarsfeld interview with the author.

210 *In June 1943:* "Alois Brunner," jewishvirtuallibrary.org.

210 *"I knew him well"*: Jeremy Josephs, *Swastika Over Paris: The Fate of the French Jews*, Serge Klarsfeld, Introduction, 17.

213 *That was the year:* Frei, 395, n46; and "Kurt Kiesinger, 60's Bonn Leader and Former Nazi, Is Dead at 83," *New York Times*, March 10, 1988.

213 *"What seemed impossible"*: Beate Klarsfeld, 18.

213 *For Beate* and her account and quotes about their campaign against Kiesinger: Ibid., 19–63.

214 *Serge had learned* and *Recognizing that:* Serge Klarsfeld with Vidalie, 13, 76; Serge Klarsfeld interview with the author.

214 *"How can I"*: Beate Klarsfeld, 22.

215 *"into a truly"*: Ibid., 48.

216 *"We kept our"*: Serge Klarsfeld interview with the author.

216 *In fact, Beate* and Warsaw and Prague experiences: Beate Klarsfeld, 112–40.

218 *She appealed and eventually was given*; *"had guns out"*; Brandt pardon: Beate Klarsfeld, 87.

218 *But because of* and status of Germans who had served in France: Serge Klarsfeld with Vidalie, 40–41; Beate Klarsfeld, 160–64.

219 *Both battles dragged on* and rest of statute of limitations changes: Heberer and Matthäus, eds., 242, n22.

219 *As Serge put it:* Serge Klarsfeld with Vidalie, 43–44.

219 *"The Paris Gestapo"*: Beate Klarsfeld, 153. Other details on the three: John Vinocur, "3 Ex-Nazis Get Jail Terms for War Crimes," *New York Times*, February 12, 1980.

220 *"It's only in"*: Beate Klarsfeld, 166.

220 *Beate prepared* and rest of account of actions aimed at Lischka and Hagen: Ibid., 167–203; and Serge Klarsfeld with Vidalie, 43–52.

224 *The three men* and *"completely and fully understood"*: John Vinocur, "3 Ex-Nazis Get Jail Terms for War Crimes," *New York Times*, February 12, 1980.

224 *In 1934, "Baltic Lindbergh,"* and *"I remember Cukurs"*: Anton Kuenzle and Gad Shimron, *The Execution of the Hangman of Riga: The Only Execution of a Nazi War Criminal by the Mossad*, 29–31.

224 *But Cukurs was* and his war record: Ibid., 32–34.

224 *After the war* and testimonies of survivors about Cukurs: Ibid., 35–43.

226 *"a low-level"*: Ibid., xx.

226 *On February 23, 1965* and rest of killing of Cukurs, including "VERDICT": Ibid., 125–27.

227 *"Like the Eichmann case"*: "Reports from Abroad," *New York Times*, March 14, 1965.

227 *Most readers* and obituaries: See, for example, "Zvi Aharoni and Yaakov Meidad," *Telegraph*, August 16, 2012.

228 *"raised public consciousness"* and rest of Yoav's conversation with Meidad: Kuenzle and Shimron, 8–9.

228 *"To kill a man"*: Rafi Eitan interview with the author.

228 *"They were all"*: Kuenzle and Shimron, 102.

228 *"killer"* and *"is still innocent"* and *"Being a member"*: Associated Press, "Latvian Musical on Nazi Collaborator Stirs Anger," October 30, 2014.

229 *"There must be no"*: "Israel Condemns Latvia's 'Butcher of Riga' Musical," israelinternationalnews.com, October 23, 2014.

Chapter Twelve: "Model Citizens"

230 *"To the police"*: Ira Levin, *The Boys from Brazil*, 12.

231 *That helped him* and launch of Documentation Center in Vienna: Pick, 152.

231 *Frederick Forsyth* and Roschmann story, including *"Roschmann became"* and *"but I didn't want"*: Wiesenthal, 96–103.

232 *"You are"* and *"like a poor relation"*: Segev, 326.

232 *Wiesenthal remained firm*: Wiesenthal, 344.

232 *"No, I'm still"*: Martin Mendelsohn interview with the author.

232 *"not shaken"* and *"We did not have"*: Serge Klarsfeld with Vidalie, 39; Serge Klarsfeld interview with the author.

233 *"using anti-Semitism"*: Wiesenthal, 209.

233 *He often charged*: Ibid., 7; and Simon Wiesenthal interviews with the author.

234 *In October 1958* and reaction and quotes at the Anne Frank play, along with Wiesenthal's conversations and subsequent actions: Wiesenthal, 335–40; and Wechsberg, ed., 172–83.

236 *As Wiesenthal recalled* and rest of Wiesenthal's account and quotes about Braunsteiner: Wiesenthal, 139–57.

238 *"The Sleuth with 6 Million Clients"*: Clyde A. Farnsworth, *New York Times*, February 2, 1964.

238 *His recollection* and rest of Lelyveld's account: Joseph Lelyveld interview with the author; Joseph Lelyveld, *Omaha Blues: A Memory Loop*, 175–82.

239 *"Former Nazi Camp Guard"*: Joseph Lelyveld, *New York Times*, July 14, 1964.

240 *After long legal battles:* Douglas Martin, "A Nazi Past, a Queens Home Life, an Overlooked Death," *New York Times*, December 2, 2005.

241 *"To this day"*: Alan Elsner, *The Nazi Hunter*, 2.

242 *"The fact that"* and rest of Rosenbaum's account, unless indicated otherwise: Eli Rosenbaum interviews with the author.

243 *From then on:* Howard Blum: *Wanted! The Search for Nazis in America*, 19–22. Blum identified the source as Oscar Karbach, whom he described as the president of the World Jewish Congress. Rochelle G. Saidel in her book *The Outraged Conscience: Seekers of Justice for Nazi War Criminals in America* pointed out that Karbach was a staff researcher for the WJC, not its president (page 98).

244 *"He was a lone"*: Blum, 25.

244 *"an effective"* and *"This seemed impossible"* and rest of Holtzman's account: Elizabeth Holtzman with Cynthia L. Cooper, *Who Said It Would Be Easy? One Woman's Life in the Political Arena*, 90–96; and Elizabeth Holtzman interview with the author.

245 *After the war* and Trifa story: Saidel, 31–45.

246 *"I don't know"* and other Mendelsohn quotes: Martin Mendelsohn interview with the author.

247 *"This action"*: Saidel, 119.

247 *With an initial budget:* Ibid., 127, and Allan A. Ryan, Jr., *Quiet Neighbors: Prosecuting Nazi War Criminals in America*, 249.

248 *In 1948* and history of Displaced Persons Act: Ryan, 15–28; and The United States Holocaust Memorial Museum, "Displaced Persons."

249 *"The DP Act,"* *"nearly 10,000,"* and *"they became model citizens"*: Ryan, 22, 26, 268.

249 *Up until 1973:* Ibid., 42.

250 *"'Nazi hunting'"*: A redacted version of the report can be found online: http://www2.gwu.edu/~nsarchiv/NSAEBB/NSAEBB331/DOJ_OSI_Nazi_redacted.pdf. The full report has not been officially released as of this writing, although it has been cited by Eric Lichtblau in his reporting for *The New York Times* and his book *The Nazis Next Door: How America Became a Safe Haven for Hitler's Men*.

250 *In 1981:* Ryan, 268.

251 *"All this talk"* and Trifa story: Ari L. Goldman, "Valerian Trifa, an Archbishop with a Fascist Past, Dies at 72," *New York Times*, January 29, 1987; and Saidel, 43–45.

251 *"The missile slaves"* and death rate: Jean Michel, *Dora*, 62, 65.

251 *But the book's:* Frederick I. Ordway III and Mitchell R. Sharpe, *The Rocket Team*, 79–85.

252 *"as long as you"* and rest of Rosenbaum-Sher conversation: Eli Rosenbaum interview with the author.

252 *Rudolph was not* and *"to show"*: Transcript from National Archives (copy courtesy of Eli Rosenbaum).

253 *"At the time"*: Elizabeth White interview with the author.

Chapter Thirteen: To La Paz and Back

255 *"Forty-four children"*: Serge Klarsfeld, *The Children of Izieu: A Human Tragedy*. 7.

255 *"Barbie is not"*: Ibid., 15.

256 *"The Germans were"*: Tom Bower, *Klaus Barbie: Butcher of Lyons*, 112–13.

256 *"has entered"*: Serge Klarsfeld, *The Children of Izieu*, 15.

256 *"I'm very happy"*: Ibid., 45.

257 *American Special Services*: Ibid., 15.

257 *A tribunal in Lyon* and Beate Klarsfeld's account of Barbie case: Beate Klarsfeld, 215–77.

257 *"Shot or deported"* and identity of person who said this: Ibid., 234, 240.

258 *"I am on"*: Ibid., 239.

258 *"That is all"*: Ibid., 242.

258 *"I was helping"* and *"We are here"*: Ibid., 255–56.

259 *"forgotten through indifference,"* *"Bolivia is an inviolable,"* and rest of visit to La Paz: Ibid., 263–73.

259 *"I have forgotten"*: Ryan, 279.

260 *"None of the"*: Beate Klarsfeld, 247–48.

260 *In December 1972*: Bower, 18–19; Serge Klarsfeld with Vidalie, 55; and Beate and Serge Klarsfeld interview with the author.

261 *When the West Germans balked*: Ryan, 277–79.

261 *"And it was"*: Serge Klarsfeld, *The Children of Izieu*, 7.

262 *"I didn't know"* and rest of Ryan's account of Barbie investigation: Ryan, 280–323.

262 *"The evidence"*: Ibid., 282.

263 *"The clear implication"*: Ibid., 285. Although Ryan did not name the network correspondent involved in his book, he identified him in an interview with the author. In a separate interview with the author, John Martin confirmed his account.

263 *"dangerous conspirator"*: Ibid., 288.

263 *"an honest man"*: Ibid., 289.

264 *"detailed interrogation"*: Ibid., 290.

264 *"the mission of CIC"*: Ibid., 291.

264 *"vilified for"* and other quotes from the OSI report: U.S. Department of Justice, *Klaus Barbie and the United States Government: A Report to the Attorney General of the United States*, August 1983.

264 *"unclear if"*: David Marwell interview with the author.

265 *"a chronicle"*: Ryan, 321.

265 *"deep regrets"*: Ibid., 322.

265 *"This particularly"*: Ibid., 323.

Chapter Fourteen: Wartime Lies

266 *"It has to do"* and other Rosenbaum quotes, including his conversations with Zelman: Eli M. Rosenbaum with William Hoffer, *Betrayal: The Untold Story of the Kurt Waldheim Investigation and Cover-up*, 1–13.

268 *In a 1980 letter:* Ibid., 15.

269 *"the best-known"*: Ibid., 12.

270 *"A friend of mine"* and rest of Schuler-Rosenbaum exchange: Ibid., 22–33.

270 *"Have you shown"* and rest of Schuler-Rosenbaum conversation about Wiesenthal: Ibid., 46–49.

271 *"We're not"* and rest of WJC discussion, along with Bronfman's role: Ibid., 57–58.

271 *Tagliabue explained:* "Files Show Kurt Waldheim Served Under War Criminal," *New York Times*, March 3, 1986.

271 *Covering the story* and my account of Waldheim and Wiesenthal interviews, "Waldheim: A Nazi Past?," *Newsweek*, March 17, 1986, and lengthier file I sent to my editors on March 7, 1986.

273 *"without visiting"* and *In 1979:* Wiesenthal, 311.

274 *"even to obtain"*: Ibid., 313.

274 *"I don't understand"*: Wiesenthal later claimed, in a letter to the editor in *Newsweek's* April 7, 1986, issue, that he had not said explicitly to me that Waldheim was a liar. But he did not back off his assertion that he did not believe Waldheim's claim that he knew nothing about the deportations of Jews from Salonika.

274 *Waldheim called,* Wiesenthal's conversation with Waldheim, and *"one of the best-informed officers"*: Wiesenthal, 318–19.

275 *"no more than"* and *"he had been"* and *"proclaimed Waldheim"*: Ibid., 315, 313.

275 *Rosenbaum correctly* and *"But it was"*: Rosenbaum with Hoffer, 90–91.

276 *Mounting a public relations* and my report on villages, along with larger context: "Waldheim on the 'A' List," *Newsweek*, April 21, 1986; my file to *Newsweek* on April 11, 1986; and Robert Edwin Herzstein, *Waldheim: The Missing Years*, 128–29.

277 *At a rally:* "Waldheim Under Siege," *Newsweek*, June 9, 1986; and my longer file to *Newsweek*.

278 *"the absurdity"*: "Waldheim Under Siege," *Newsweek*, June 9, 1986.

278 *"slander campaign"* and *"Even if"*: "Waldheim: Home Free?," *Newsweek*, June 16, 1986.

278 *"reveal him to"*: Office of Special Investigations, *In the Matter of Kurt Waldheim*, April 9, 1987, 200–201.

279 *"a man who"* and *"Given what"*: Herzstein, 23, 254.

279 *"In a perfect world":* "Waldheim Under Siege," *Newsweek,* June 9, 1986.

279 *Beate Klarsfeld showed up:* Ibid.; and James M. Markham, "In Austrian Campaign, Even Bitterness Is Muted," *New York Times,* June 6, 1986.

279 *"I came here":* Beate Klarsfeld interview with the author. Account of her exchange with Mayor Busek at Waldheim rally: My file to *Newsweek,* May 30, 1986.

280 *"It should be"* and *"haunt and follow"* and *"intemperately":* Andrew Nagorski, "Clumsy Acts, Bad Blood," *Newsweek,* May 12, 1986; and Rosenbaum with Hoffer, 142.

280 *"Many Jewish leaders":* Edgar M. Bronfman, *The Making of a Jew,* 115.

280 *"We had created":* Andrew Nagorski, "Clumsy Acts, Bad Blood," *Newsweek,* May 12, 1986.

280 *"very apt"* and other quotes from Austrian Jews about the WJC's actions: My file to *Newsweek,* June 5, 1986.

282 *"I'm one of those":* Andrew Nagorski, "Clumsy Acts, Bad Blood," *Newsweek,* May 12, 1986.

282 *"I hate to," "What's wrong,"* and *"in bed with":* Rosenbaum with Hoffer, 165.

283 *"There can be":* Ibid., 300–301.

283 *"each had a secret":* Ibid., 461.

283 *"If one can be":* Ibid., 463.

283 *"he had failed":* Ibid., 461.

283 *"played loosely"* and *"Those of us":* Ibid., 304.

284 *"pathetically ineffective":* Ibid., 472.

284 *"But who was daring":* Ibid., 304.

284 *"unprosecuted, unpursued":* Eli Rosenbaum interview with the author.

284 *"He started out":* Martin Mendelsohn interview with the author.

284 *"I think Eli":* Former OSI official who did not want his name used in any discussion of Rosenbaum.

284 *"think they can":* Andrew Nagorski, "Wiesenthal: A Summing Up," *Newsweek International,* April 27, 1998.

285 *"the fact that":* Wiesenthal, 321.

285 *"How can you"* and other quotes from Hier: Rabbi Marvin Hier interview with the author.

285 *"TELL WIESENTHAL":* Rosenbaum with Hoffer, 149.

286 *He frequently asserted:* Simon Wiesenthal interview with the author, reported in my file to *Newsweek,* May 21, 1986.

286 *"He does not wish"* and *He speculated:* Wiesenthal, 301.

286 *"Jewish fascist"* and *"mafioso":* Herzstein, 250.

286 *"a reactionary"* and *"telling the world":* Joshua Muravchik, "The Jew Who Turned the Left Against Israel," *The Tablet,* July 29, 2014.

287 *Later, he would:* Segev, 292–93.

287 "on French television": Wiesenthal, 320.

287 "After carefully studying": Herzstein, 229.

288 "very credible job" and "I don't see": Peter Black interview with the author.

Chapter Fifteen: Chasing Ghosts

289 "At this way station": William Goldman, *Marathon Man*, 262.

289 *The Austrian-born doctor* and biographical details: Nicholas Kulish and Souad Mekhen-
     net, *The Eternal Nazi: From Mauthausen to Cairo, the Relentless Pursuit of SS Doctor
     Aribert Heim*; Souad Mekhennet and Nicholas Kulish, "Uncovering Lost Path of the Most
     Wanted Nazi," *New York Times*, February 4, 2009.

290 "The names of": Danny Baz, *The Secret Executioners: The Amazing True Story of the Death
     Squad That Tracked Down and Killed Nazi War Criminals*, xiii.

290 "We want": Ibid., 10.

291 "Bormann is dead": Ronald Gray, *I Killed Martin Bormann!*, 5; serialization of book, as
     noted in Reuters dispatch, "Most Wanted Nazi Shot, Claims Ex-British Agent," published
     in *The Montreal Gazette*, August 8, 1970.

291 "From the size": Gray, *I Killed Martin Bormann*, 73.

291 "When I was": Ladislas Farago, *Aftermath: Martin Bormann and the Fourth Reich*, 428.

292 *In Heim's case*: Souad Mekhennet and Nicholas Kulish, "Uncovering Lost Path of the
     Most Wanted Nazi," *New York Times*, February 5, 2009.

292 "absolute dominator": Kulish and Mekhennet, 173.

293 *The purported remains* and DNA identification of Bormann: "New Genetic Tests Said to
     Confirm: It's Martin Bormann," *New York Times*, May 4, 1998.

293 *According to an article* and Soobzokov's biography: Blum, 47–48, 42–61; Richard Rashke,
     *Useful Enemies: John Demjanjuk and America's Open-Door Policy for Nazi War Crimi-
     nals*, 48–50.

294 "We saw him": Blum, 57.

294 *Although he served* and rest of postwar history of Soobzokov, including "Subject has,"
     "an incorrigible fabricator," and "unresolved doubts": Richard Breitman, "Tscherim Soob-
     zokov," American University (https://www.fas.org/sgp/eprint/breitman.pdf).

295 *He even pursued*: Blum, 258–63.

295 *The FBI later*: Ibid., 263.

295 *Eight years later* and rest of Bousquet's story and killing, including his quotes: Richard J.
     Goslan, "Memory and Justice Abused: the 1949 Trial of René Bousquet," *Studies in 20th
     Century Literature*, Vol. 23, 1-1-1999; Paul Webster, "The Collaborator's Pitiless End," *The
     Guardian*, June 8, 1993; and Douglas Johnson, "Obituary: René Bousquet," *The Indepen-
     dent*, June 9, 1993.

296 "If I had killed" and "I thought that": Sorj Chalandon, "L'assassinat de René Bousquet:
     larmes du Crime," *Libération*, April 4, 2000.

296 *"Jews wanted"*: Serge Klarsfeld interview with the author.

297 *In 1985* and search for Mengele: "Hunting the Angel of Death," *Newsweek*, May 20, 1985; my longer file to *Newsweek*, April 16, 1985; and subsequent files sent through June 1985, along with my reporters' notebooks from that period (personal files).

298 *Mengele had drowned*: "Reaching a Verdict on the Mengele Case," *Newsweek*, July 1, 1985; "Who Helped Mengele," *Newsweek*, June 24, 1985; and my files to *Newsweek*.

298 *"experiments on"*: Gerald L. Posner and John Ware, *Mengele: The Complete Story*, 76.

299 *According to Robert Kempner*: Robert Kempner interview with the author.

299 *The prisoner, who was*: Posner and Ware, 63.

300 *"Mengele fled"*: Office of Special Investigations, *In the Matter of Josef Mengele*, October 1992, 193.

300 *"Of all the evil," "To make,"* and *"that might endanger"*: Harel, 210–11.

300 *"None of us," "Try to catch,"* and *"He is lying"*: Aharoni and Dietl, 149–50.

301 *"As you can see"*: Posner and Ware, 163.

301 *"We did not know"*: Aharoni and Dietl, 151.

302 *"We gave little"*: Rafi Eitan interview with the author.

302 *"His house was"*: "Mengele: The Search Ends," *Newsweek*, July 1, 1985.

302 *"I have remained silent"*: "Who Helped Mengele?," *Newsweek*, June 24, 1985.

302 *"I do not have"* and failures of the West German investigation: Ibid., "Reaching a Verdict in the Mengele Case," *Newsweek*, July 1, 1985.

303 *"That Auschwitz's"*: Office of Special Investigations, *In the Matter of Josef Mengele*, October 1992, 196–97.

Chapter Sixteen: Full Circle

304 *"Survival is"*: Wiesenthal, 351.

304 *Priebke's claim to* and rest of Priebke's story in Italy, Argentina, and then extradition: Alison Smale, "Erich Priebke, Nazi Who Carried Out Massacre of 335 Italians, Dies at 100," *New York Times*, October 11, 2013; "Erich Priebke: 'Just Following Orders,'" *The Economist*, October 26, 2013; "Erich Priebke," jewishvirtuallibrary.org.

305 *"Mr. Priebke"* and rest of Donaldson-Priebke exchange: YouTube video.

306 *Born in 1934* and Donaldson background and quotes: Sam Donaldson interview with the author.

306 *By the time* and role of Harry Phillips: Harry Phillips interview with the author; and Robert Lissit, "Out of Sight," *American Journalism Review*, December 1994.

306 *The Catholic Church* and funeral: Elisabetta Povoledo, "Funeral for Ex-Nazi in Italy Is Halted as Protesters Clash," *New York Times*, October 16, 2013.

308 *Born in* and Demjanjuk's early biographical details: Rashke, x–xiii, 548–49; Robert D. McFadden, "John Demjanjuk, 91, Dogged by Charges of Atrocities as Nazi Camp Guard, Dies," *New York Times*, March 17, 2012.

309 *"traitors who"*: Andrew Nagorski, *The Greatest Battle: Stalin, Hitler, and the Desperate Struggle for Moscow That Changed the Course of World War II*, 70.

309 *But in 1975* and preliminary investigation in the United States and Israel, and *"Iwan, Iwan"*: Rashke, 108–16.

310 *The Justice Department's, "There was no doubt,"* and *"You son of a bitch"*: Ryan, 106–7.

311 *But not everyone* and Parker memo: Rashke, 149–54.

311 *On January 27, 1986:* Ibid., 313.

312 *"historic justice"*: Ibid., 348.

312 *"I told him"*: Avraham Shalom interview with the author.

312 *In emotional testimony* and reaction of the gallery: Rashke, 361–69.

312 *CBS's* 60 Minutes: Ibid., 466–68.

313 *"We got"*: Eli Rosenbaum interview with the author.

313 *Among the findings:* Rashke, 502.

313 *Demjanjuk had been pleading* and claims of illness: Ibid., 513–15.

314 *"as a scapegoat"*: Robert D. McFadden, "John Demjanjuk, 91, Dogged by Charges of Atrocities as Nazi Camp Guard, Dies," *New York Times*, March 17, 2012.

314 *"this American Dreyfus"*: Patrick J. Buchanan, "The True Haters," http://buchanan.org /blog/pjb-the-true-haters-1495, April 14, 2009.

314 *According to:* The Central Office for the Investigation of National Socialist Crimes, Information Sheet, December 2012. The statistics span the period that includes the unification of Germany, but they reflect the records of the West German judiciary.

315 *In September 2013* and *"We take the view"*: Melissa Eddy, "Germany Sends 30 Death Camp Cases to Local Prosecutors, *New York Times*, September 3, 2013.

315 *As of early 2015:* Statistics provided by Thomas Will, deputy director, the Central Office for the Investigation of National Socialist Crimes.

315 *"I ask for"*: "Auschwitz Trial: Oskar Groening Recalls 'Queue of Trains,'" BBC News, April 22, 2015.

315 *On July 15, 2015:* Alison Smale, "Oskar Gröning, Ex-SS Soldier at Auschwitz, Gets Four-Year Sentence," *New York Times*, July 15, 2015.

316 *"My personal opinion"*: David Crossland, "Late Push on War Crimes: Prosecutors to Probe 50 Auschwitz Guards," *Spiegel Online International*, April 8, 2013.

316 *"each one"*: Greene, 44.

316 *"whoever operated"*: Wittmann, 256.

316 *"This often happens"*: Piotr Cywiński interview with the author.

316 *"The Auschwitz Files"*: Der Spiegel, August 25, 2014; the English version was posted on *Spiegel Online International* on August 28, 2014.

317 *"part of an organization"* and *"As outlined"*: United States District Court for the Eastern District of Pennsylvania, "In the Matter of the Extradition of Johann (John) Breyer," Misc. No. 14-607-M (courtesy of Eli Rosenbaum).

318 *Since its creation* and OSI statistics: Email from Eli Rosenbaum, February 4, 2015. Those statistics span the period of OSI's existence until 2010 and then the first five years of its operations as part of a newly merged unit called the Human Rights and Special Prosecutions Section.

318 *"I'm very proud"*: Elizabeth Holtzman interview with the author.

319 *"There is"*: Efraim Zuroff interview with the author.

320 *"tracking Aribert Heim"* and *"shocking information"*: Efraim Zuroff, *Operation Last Chance: One Man's Quest to Bring Nazi Criminals to Justice*, 199, 206.

320 *Zuroff said*: Efraim Zuroff interview with the author; and follow-up email correspondence, February 11, 2015.

320 *"It's true that"*: Deidre Berger interview with the author.

321 *"quite Soviet"*: Serge Klarsfeld interview with the author.

321 *"It seems that"*: Eli M. Rosenbaum, "The Eichmann Case and the Distortion of History," *Loyola of Los Angeles International & Comparative Law Review*, Spring 2012.

322 *"We still have"*: Thomas Will interview with the author.

322 *"We are not"*: Ryan, 335.

323 *"Hardly any country"*: Wolfgang Saxon, "Richard von Weizsäcker, 94, Dies: First President of Reunited Germany," *New York Times*, January 31, 2015.

323 *"This was"* and *"But there is"*: Richard von Weizsäcker interview with the author. The interview was included in "Voices of the Century," *Newsweek*, March 15, 1999.

323 *"a ritualized way"*: Martin Walser interview with the author ("Hitler Boosts Ratings," *Newsweek*, December 21, 1998).

324 *"only the Germans"*: Serge Klarsfeld with Vidalie, 57.

324 *The Klarsfelds' son Arno*: Pascale Nivelle, "Maurice Papon Devant Ses Juges," *Libération*, February 10, 1998.

324 *Kurt Werner Schaechter*: Alan Riding, "Suit Accusing French Railways of Holocaust Role Is Thrown Out," *New York Times*, May 15, 2003. Schaechter's gathering of Klarsfeld materials: Kurt Werner Schaechter collection, The Hoover Archives.

324 *In 2010*: "France Agrees Holocaust SNCF Rail Payout with US," BBC Europe, December 5, 2014.

325 *At the same time*: Maïa de la Baume, "France Confronts an Ignoble Chapter," *New York Times*, December 16, 2014.

325 *"I am satisfied"*: Serge and Beate Klarsfeld interview with the author.

325 *And on July 20, 2015*: "Nazi-Hunting Couple Honored by Germany," *The Forward*, July 21, 2015.

Bibliography

Archival Sources

Hoover Institution Archives, Stanford, California
Jan Sehn Archives, Institute of Forensic Research, Kraków, Poland
Manuscript and Archives Division, The New York Public Library, New York, New York
National Archives, College Park, Maryland
United States Holocaust Museum Archives, Washington, D.C.

Books

Aharoni, Zvi, and Wilhelm Dietl. *Operation Eichmann: The Truth About the Pursuit, Capture and Trial.* New York: John Wiley & Sons, 1997.

Annan, Noel. *Changing Enemies: The Defeat and Regeneration of Germany.* New York: W. W. Norton, 1996.

Arendt, Hannah. *Eichmann in Jerusalem: A Report on the Banality of Evil.* New York: Penguin, 1977.

——. *The Last Interview and Other Conversations.* Brooklyn: Melville House, 2013.

——. *The Origins of Totalitarianism.* San Diego: Harcourt Brace Jovanovich, 1979.

Averbach, Albert, and Charles Price, eds. *The Verdicts Were Just: Eight Famous Lawyers Present Their Most Memorable Cases.* Rochester: The Lawyers Co-operative Publishing Company, 1966.

Backhaus, Fritz, Monika Boll, and Raphael Gross. *Fritz Bauer. Der Staatsanwalt: NS-Verbrechen vor Gericht.* Frankfurt: Campus, 2014

(Catalogue for the Fritz Bauer exhibition at the Jewish Museum of Frankfurt).

Bascomb, Neal. *Hunting Eichmann: How a Band of Survivors and a Young Spy Agency Chased Down the World's Most Notorious Nazi.* Boston: Houghton Mifflin Harcourt, 2009.

Bauer, Yehuda. *Flight and Rescue: Brichah.* New York: Random House, 1970.

Baz, Danny. *The Secret Executioners: The Amazing True Story of the Death Squad That Tracked Down and Killed Nazi War Criminals.* London: John Blake, 2010.

Beevor, Antony, and Luba Vinogradova, eds. *A Writer at War: Vasily Grossman with the Red Army, 1941–1945.* New York: Pantheon, 2005.

Beschloss, Michael. *The Conquerors: Roosevelt, Truman and the Destruction of Hitler's Germany, 1941–1945.* New York: Simon & Schuster, 2002.

Bessel, Richard. *Germany 1945: From War to Peace.* London: Pocket Books, 2010.

Biddiscombe, Perry. *The Denazification of German: A History, 1945–1950.* Stroud, Gloucestershire, 2007.

Blum, Howard. *Wanted! The Search for Nazis in America.* New York: Touchstone, 1989.

Botting, Douglas. *From the Ruins of the Reich: Germany, 1945–1949.* New York: Crown, 1985.

Bower, Tom. *Klaus Barbie: Butcher of Lyons.* London: Corgi, 1985.

Bronfman, Edgar M. *The Making of a Jew.* New York: G. P. Putnam's Sons, 1996.

Browning, Christopher R. *Ordinary Men: Reserve Battalion 101 and the Final Solution in Poland.* New York: Harper Perennial, 1993.

Clay, Lucius D. *Decision in Germany.* New York: Doubleday, 1950.

Dann, Sam, ed. *Dachau 29 April 1945: The Rainbow Liberation Memoirs.* Lubbock: Texas Tech University Press, 1998.

Davies, Norman. *Heart of Europe: A Short History of Poland.* Oxford: Clarendon Press, 1984.

Earl, Hilary. *The Nuremberg SS-Einsatzgruppen Trial, 1945–1958: Atrocity, Law, and History.* Cambridge: Cambridge University Press, 2010.

El-Hai, Jack. *The Nazi and the Psychiatrist: Hermann Göring, Dr. Douglas M. Kelley, and a Fatal Meeting of the Minds at the End of WWII.* New York: PublicAffairs, 2013.

Elsner, Alan. *The Nazi Hunter.* New York: Arcade, 2011.

Farago, Ladislas. *Aftermath: Martin Bormann and the Fourth Reich.* New York: Simon & Schuster, 1974.

Ferencz, Benjamin B. *Less Than Slaves: Jewish Forced Labor and the Quest for Compensation.* Bloomington: Indiana University Press, 2002.

Forsyth, Frederick. *The Odessa File.* New York: Viking, 1972.

Frei, Norbert. *Adenauer's Germany and the Nazi Past: The Politics of Amnesty and Integration.* New York: Columbia University Press, 2002.

Friedman, Tuvia. *The Hunter.* London: Anthony Gibbs & Phillips, 1961.

Frieze, Donna-Lee, ed. *Totally Unofficial: The Autobiography of Raphael Lemkin.* New Haven: Yale University Press, 2013.

Gellately, Robert, ed. *The Nuremberg Interviews: Conducted by Leon Goldensohn.* New York: Alfred A. Knopf, 2004.

Gilbert, G. M. *Nuremberg Diary.* Boston: Da Capo, 1995.

Goldman, William. *Marathon Man.* New York: Dell, 1988.

Gray, Ronald. *I Killed Martin Bormann!* New York: Lancer, 1972.

Greene, Joshua M. *Justice at Dachau: The Trials of an American Prosecutor.* New York: Broadway, 2003.

Gutman, Yisrael, and Michael Berenbaum, eds. *Anatomy of the Auschwitz Death Camp.* Bloomington: Indiana University Press, 1994.

Harding, Thomas. *Hanns and Rudolf: The True Story of the German Jew Who Tracked Down and Caught the Kommandant of Auschwitz.* New York: Simon & Schuster, 2013.

Harel, Isser. *The House on Garibaldi Street.* London: Frank Cass, 2004.

———. "Simon Wiesenthal and the Capture of Eichmann." Unpublished manuscript.

Harris, Whitney R. *Tyranny on Trial: The Evidence at Nuremberg.* Dallas:

Southern Methodist University Press, 1954/Barnes & Noble Books, 1995.

Hausner, Gideon. *Justice in Jerusalem.* New York: Harper & Row, 1966.

Heberer, Patricia, and Jürgens Matthäus, eds. *Atrocities on Trial: Historical Perspectives on the Politics of Prosecuting War Crimes.* Lincoln: University of Nebraska Press, 2008.

Heidenberger, Peter. *From Munich to Washington: A German-American Memoir.* Xlibris, 2004.

Helms, Richard, with William Hood. *A Look Over My Shoulder: A Life in the Central Intelligence Agency.* New York: Random House, 2003.

Herzstein, Robert Edwin. *Waldheim: The Missing Years.* New York: Arbor House/William Morrow, 1988.

Higgins, Jack (pseudonym of Harry Patterson). *The Bormann Testament.* New York: Berkley, 2006.

Hoess, Rudolf. *Commandant of Auschwitz: The Autobiography of Rudolf Hoess.* London: Phoenix, 2000.

Holtzman, Elizabeth, with Cynthia L. Cooper. *Who Said It Would Be Easy? One Woman's Life in the Political Arena.* New York: Arcade, 1996.

Höss, Rudolf, Perry Broad, and Johann Paul Kremer. *KL Auschwitz Seen by the SS.* Warsaw: Interpress, 1991.

Josephs, Jeremy. *Swastika Over Paris: The Fate of the French Jews.* London: Bloomsbury, 1990.

Kelley, Douglas M. *22 Cells in Nuremberg: A Psychiatrist Examines the Nazi Criminals.* New York: Greenberg, 1947.

Kempner, Robert M. W. *Ankläger einer Epoche: Lebenserrinerungen.* Frankfurt: Ullstein Zeitgeschichte, 1986.

Kennedy, John F. *Profiles in Courage.* New York: Harper Perennial, 2006.

Kershaw, Ian. *Hitler 1889–1936: Hubris.* London: Penguin, 1998.

———. *Hitler 1936–45: Nemesis.* New York: W. W. Norton, 2000.

Klarsfeld, Beate. *Wherever They May Be!* New York: Vanguard, 1972.

Klarsfeld, Serge. *The Children of Izieu: A Human Tragedy.* New York: Harry N. Abrams, 1985.

Klarsfeld, Serge, with Anne Vidalie. *La Traque des criminels nazis.* Paris: Tallandier/L'Express, 2013.

Kuenzle, Anton, and Gad Shimron. *The Execution of the Hangman of Riga: The Only Execution of a Nazi War Criminal by the Mossad.* London: Valentine Mitchell, 2004.

Kulish, Nicholas, and Souad Mekhennet. *The Eternal Nazi: From Mauthausen to Cairo, the Relentless Pursuit of SS Doctor Aribert Heim.* New York: Doubleday, 2014.

Lang, Jochen von, and Claus Sibyll, eds. *Eichmann Interrogated: Transcripts from the Archives of the Israeli Police.* New York: Vintage, 1984.

Leide, Henry. *NS-Verbrecher und Staatssicherheit: Die geheime Vergangensheitspolitik der DDR.* Göttingen: Vandenhoeck & Ruprecht, 2007.

Lelyveld, Joseph. *Omaha Blues: A Memory Loop.* New York: Picador, 2006.

Levi, Primo. *The Drowned and the Saved.* New York: Vintage, 1989.

Levin, Ira. *The Boys from Brazil.* New York: Random House, 1976.

Lewis, Sinclair. *It Can't Happen Here.* New York: New American Library, 2005.

Lichtblau, Eric. *The Nazis Next Door: How America Became a Safe Haven for Hitler's Men.* Boston: Houghton Mifflin Harcourt, 2014.

Lingeman, Richard. *Sinclair Lewis: Rebel from Main Street.* New York: Random House, 2002.

Lipstadt, Deborah E. *The Eichmann Trial.* New York: Schocken, 2011.

Malkin, Peter Z., and Harry Stein. *Eichmann in My Hands.* New York: Warner, 1990.

Mann, Abby. *Judgment at Nuremberg.* New York: Samuel French, 2001.

Maser, Werner. *Nuremberg: A Nation on Trial.* New York: Charles Scribner's Sons, 1979.

Miale, Florence R., and Michael Selzer. *The Nuremberg Mind: The Psychology of the Nazi Leaders.* New York: Quadrangle, 1975.

Michel, Jean. *Dora.* New York: Holt, Rinehart & Winston, 1980.

Milgram, Stanley. *Obedience to Authority: An Experimental View.* New York: Harper Colophon, 1975.

Mowrer, Edgar Ansel. *Germany Puts the Clock Back.* Paulton and London: Penguin, 1938.

———. *Triumph and Turmoil: A Personal History of Our Times.* New York: Weybright & Talley, 1968.

Musmanno, Michael A. *The Eichmann Kommandos.* New York: Macfadden, 1962.

———. *Ten Days to Die.* New York: Macfadden, 1962.

Nagorski, Andrew. *The Greatest Battle: Stalin, Hitler, and the Desperate Struggle for Moscow That Changed the Course of World War II.* New York: Simon & Schuster, 2007.

———. *Hitlerland: American Eyewitnesses to the Nazi Rise to Power.* New York: Simon & Schuster, 2012.

Naimark, Norman M. *The Russians in Germany: A History of the Soviet Zone of Occupation, 1945–1949.* Cambridge: Belknap Press of Harvard University Press, 1995.

Naumann, Bernd. *Auschwitz: A Report on the Proceedings Against Robert Karl Ludwig Mulka and Others Before the Court at Frankfurt.* New York: Frederick A. Praeger, 1966.

Obermayer, Herman J. *Soldiering for Freedom: A GI's Account of World War II.* College Station: Texas A&M University Press, 2005.

Ordway, Frederick I. III, and Mitchell R. Sharpe. *The Rocket Team.* New York: Thomas Y. Crowell, 1979.

Overy, Richard. *Russia's War.* New York: Penguin, 1998.

Patterson, Harry. *The Valhalla Exchange.* New York: Stein & Day, 1976.

Pendas, Devin O. *The Frankfurt Auschwitz Trail, 1963–1965: Genocide, History, and the Limits of the Law.* Cambridge: Cambridge University Press, 2011.

Pick, Hella. *Simon Wiesenthal: A Life in Search of Justice.* Boston: Northeastern University Press, 1996.

Pierrepoint, Albert. *Executioner: Pierrepoint.* Cranbrook, Kent: George G. Harrap, 1974.

Piper, Franciszek. *Ile Ludzi Zginęło w KL Auschwitz: Liczba Ofiar w Świetle Żródeł i Badań 1945–1990.* Oświęcim: Wydawnictwo Państwowego Museum w Oświęcimiu, 1992.

Posner, Gerald L., and John Ware. *Mengele: The Complete Story.* New York: McGraw-Hill, 1986.

Powers, Thomas. *The Man Who Kept the Secrets: Richard Helms and the CIA.* New York: Pocket Books, 1981.

Rabinowitz, Dorothy. *New Lives: Survivors of the Holocaust Living in America.* New York: Alfred A. Knopf, 1976.

Rashke, Richard. *Useful Enemies: John Demjanjuk and America's Open-Door Policy for Nazi War Criminals.* Harrison, NY: Delphinium, 2013.

Robinson, Jacob. *And the Crooked Shall Be Made Straight: The Eichmann Trial, the Jewish Catastrophe, and Hannah Arendt's Narrative.* New York: Macmillan, 1965.

Rosenbaum, Eli, with William Hoffer. *Betrayal: The Untold Story of the Kurt Waldheim Investigation and Cover-Up.* New York: St. Martin's, 1993.

Rückerl, Adalbert. *The Investigation of Nazi War Crimes, 1945–1978: A Documentation.* Heidelberg: C. F. Müller, 1979.

Lord Russell of Liverpool. *The Scourge of the Swastika: A Short History of Nazi War Crimes.* London: Greenhill, 2002.

Ryan, Allan A., Jr. *Quiet Neighbors: Prosecuting Nazi War Criminals in America.* San Diego: Harcourt Brace Jovanovich, 1984.

Saidel, Rochelle G. *The Outraged Conscience: Seekers of Justice for Nazi War Criminals in America.* Albany: State University of New York Press, 1984.

Salomon, Ernst von. *Der Fragebogen.* Reinbek bei Hamburg: Rowohlt, 2011.

Schlink, Bernhard. *The Reader.* New York: Vintage, 1998.

Schulberg, Sandra. *Filmmakers for the Prosecution, The Making of Nuremberg: Its Lesson for Today.* New York: Schulberg Productions, 2014.

Searle, Alaric. *Wehrmacht Generals, West German Society, and the Debate on Rearmament, 1949–1959.* Westport, CT: Praeger, 2003.

Segev, Tom. *Simon Wiesenthal: The Life and Legends.* New York: Doubleday, 2010.

Sehn, Dr. Jan. *Obóz Koncentracyjny Oświęcim-Brzezinka.* Warsaw: Wydawnictwo Prawnicze, 1960.

————. *Wspomnienia Rudolfa Hoessa, Komendanta Obozu Oswięcim-skiego.* Warsaw: Wydawnictwo Prawnicze, 1961.

Shirer, William L. *Berlin Diary: The Journal of a Foreign Correspondent, 1934–1941.* New York: Galahad Books, 1995.

————. *The Rise and Fall of the Third Reich: A History of Nazi Germany.* Greenwich, CT: Fawcett, 1965.

Smith, Jean Edward. *Lucius D. Clay: An American Life.* New York: Henry Holt, 1990.

Sonnenfeldt, Richard W. *Witness to Nuremberg: The Chief American Interpreter at the War Crimes Trials.* New York: Arcade, 2006.

Stafford, David. *Endgame, 1945: The Missing Final Chapter of World War II.* New York: Back Bay, 2007.

Stangneth, Bettina. *Eichmann Before Jerusalem: The Unexamined Life of a Mass Murderer.* New York: Alfred A. Knopf, 2014.

Steinke, Ronen. *Fritz Bauer: Oder Auschwitz vor Gericht.* Munich: Piper, 2013.

Stuart, Heikelina Verrijn, and Marlise Simons. *The Prosecutor and the Judge: Benjamin Ferencz and Antonio Cassese, Interviews and Writings.* Amsterdam: Amsterdam University Press, 2009.

Taylor, Frederick. *Exorcising Hitler: The Occupation and Denazification of Germany.* New York: Bloomsbury, 2011.

Taylor, Telford. *The Anatomy of the Nuremberg Trials: A Personal Memoir.* New York: Alfred A. Knopf, 1992.

Tilles, Stanley, with Jeffrey Denhart. *By the Neck Until Dead: The Gallows of Nuremberg.* Bedford, IN: JoNa Books, 1999.

Townsend, Tim. *Mission at Nuremberg: An American Army Chaplain and the Trial of the Nazis.* New York: William Morrow, 2014.

Tusa, Ann, and John Tusa. *The Nuremberg Trial.* New York: Atheneum, 1984.

Walters, Guy. *Hunting Evil: The Nazi War Criminals Who Escaped and the Quest to Bring Them to Justice.* New York: Broadway, 2009.

Wechsberg, Joseph, ed. *The Murderers Among Us: The Wiesenthal Memoirs.* New York: McGraw-Hill, 1967.

Weiss, Peter. *The Investigation: Oratorio in 11 Cantos.* London: Martin Boyars, 2010.

Whitlock, Flint. *The Beasts of Buchenwald: Karl and Ilse Koch, Human-Skin Lampshades, and the War-Crimes Trial of the Century.* Brule, WI: Cable, 2011.

Wiesenthal, Simon. *Justice Not Vengeance.* New York: Grove Weidenfeld, 1989.

Wittmann, Rebecca. *Beyond Justice: The Auschwitz Trial.* Cambridge: Harvard University Press, 2012.

Wojak, Irmtrud. *Fritz Bauer, 1903–1968: Eine Biographie.* Munich: C. H. Beck, 2011.

Zuroff, Efraim. *Occupation: Nazi Hunter.* Hoboken, NJ: KTAV, 1994.

———. *Operation Last Chance: One Man's Quest to Bring Nazi Criminals to Justice.* New York: Palgrave MacMillan, 2009.

Interviews

Gabriel Bach (2014)

John Q. Barrett (2014)

Deidre Berger (2014)

Peter Black (2013)

Monika Boll (2014)

Harold Burson (2014)

Zofia Chłobowska (2014)

Piotr Cywiński (2015)

Sam Donaldson (2014)

Rafi Eitan (2014)

Benjamin Ferencz (2013)

Alice Heidenberger (2014)

Peter Heidenberger (2014)

Rabbi Marvin Hier (2015)

Elizabeth Holtzman (2014)

Maria Kała (2014)

Beate Klarsfeld (2013)

Serge Klarsfeld (2013)

Maria Kozłowska (2014)

Gerard Kreisberg (2014)

Paulinka (Wiesenthal) Kreisberg (2014)

Joseph Lelyveld (2014)

John Martin (2015)

David Marwell (2013–2014)

Jürgen Matthäus (2013)

Henry Mayer (2013)

Martin Mendelsohn (2014)

Herman Obermayer (2013)

Krzysztof Persak (2014)

Harry Phillips (2015)

Eli Rosenbaum (2013–2014)

Allan Ryan (2015)

Bernhard Schlink (2014)

Peter Schneider (2014)

Sandra Schulberg (2013)

Gerald Schwab (2013)

Arthur Sehn (2013–2014)

Franciszka Sehn (2014)

Józef Sehn (2014)

Avraham Shalom (2014)

Peter Sichel (2013)

Elizabeth White (2013)

Thomas Will (2014)

Irmtrud Wojak (2014)

Ilona Ziok (2014)

Efraim Zuroff (2014)

Selected Earlier Interviews

Niklas Frank (1998)

Zygmunt Gaudasiński (1994)

Robert Kempner (1985)

Beate Klarsfeld (1986)
Peter Kocev (1986)
Abby Mann (2001)
Risto Ognjanov (1986)
Franciszek Piper (1994)
Kurt Waldheim (1986)
Martin Walser (1998)
Richard von Weizsäcker (1998)
Simon Wiesenthal (1985–1998)
Mieczysław Zawadzki (1994)
Leon Zelman (1986)

Illustration Credits

1. AP Photo
2. AP Photo/Ronald Zak
3. AP Photo/Max Nash
4. United States Holocaust Memorial Museum
5. AP Photo/Hanns Jaeger
6. United States Holocaust Memorial Museum
7. United States Holocaust Memorial Museum
8. United States Holocaust Memorial Museum
9. United States Holocaust Memorial Museum
10. Israel Government Press Office
11. Copyright Yossi Roth
12. Israel Government Press Office
13. Israel Government Press Office
14. AP Photo
15. Bettmann/Corbis / AP Images
16. AF archive/Alamy
17. Pictorial Press Ltd/Alamy
18. United States Holocaust Memorial Museum
19. AP Photo/Fritz Reiss
20. AP Photo/Lionel Cironneau
21. United States Holocaust Memorial Museum
22. U.S.Holocaust Memorial Museum courtesy of Miriam Lomaskin
23. Copyright Eli Rosenbaum
24. AP Photo/W.Vollman
25. AP Photo/Martha Hermann
26. The State Museum Auschwitz–Birkenau in Oswiecim
27. DB/picture–alliance/dpa/AP Images
28. AP Photo/Gregorio Borgia
29. AP Photo/Kerstin Joensson
30. AP Photo/Oliver Lang, Pool

Index

About the Author

Andrew Nagorski, an award-winning journalist, was born in Scotland to Polish parents, moved to the United States as an infant, and has rarely stopped moving since. During a long career at *Newsweek*, he served as the magazine's bureau chief in Hong Kong, Moscow, Rome, Bonn, Warsaw, and Berlin. He is the author of five previous books and has written for countless publications. He lives in St. Augustine, Florida.

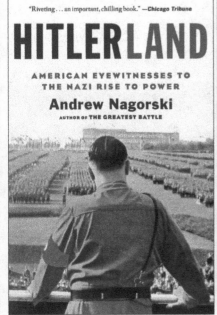
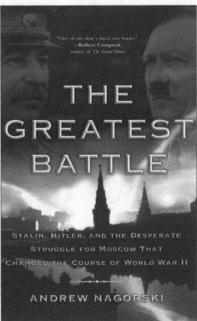